HEAVENS BELOW

STUDIES IN SOCIAL HISTORY

edited by

HAROLD PERKIN

Lecturer in Social History, University of Manchester

‹›

HEAVENS BELOW

Utopian Experiments
in England
1560–1960

by

W. H. G. Armytage

Professor of Education, University of Sheffield

University of Toronto Press

TORONTO, 1961

Contents

v

CONTENTS

Preface

The hot breath of the charismatic behind one's back is disconcerting. It always has been. For in trying to direct us from behind he uses the language of apocalypse. Desultory reading, many years ago, sharpened my interest, not so much in the language, as the programme of action it presaged. So what began as a diversion, alas, has become a book.

The excuse for the book was provided by one of the characters in it. 'It would be so useful', he wrote 'to have records of the failure of sincere and earnest movements', and asked 'Why are they so scarce?' As he saw it, 'people prefer to tell of days full of hope than days full of dejection'. 'The causes of failure', he went on 'are obscured by petty, personal conflicts . . . for the *odium theologicum* is not confined to the great churches. As the highwayman demands your money or your life, so the religious zealot in every new movement demands your acceptance of his "principles" or he proceeds to wound your character by imputation of mean motives'.[1]

The zealots of the new movements in this book were by no means so uncharitable. Indeed, Father Ronald Knox, who began over thirty years ago to examine what he thought was a 'rogue's gallery' to provide 'an awful warning against "illuminism"', found to his surprise that 'the more you got to know the men, the more human did they become, for better or worse; you were more concerned to find out why they thought as they did than to prove they were wrong'.[2]

This book does not attempt to prove them right, though the epilogue might make readers think so. Instead, it tells a number of plain tales of those who tried to save the English behind their collective backs. Help in the telling was generously provided by the correspondents and libraries mentioned in the footnotes.

[1] Aylmer Maude, *The Life of Tolstoy: Later Years* (London, 1911), 547–8.
[2] R. A. Knox, *Enthusiasm* (Oxford, 1950), vi.

vii

PHASE I

Sect to Socialism 1560–1800

1

◇◇

Filaments of Light

◇◇

(1)

UTOPIA takes its name from a book of that name published abroad in 1517 by Sir Thomas More. It was not translated into English until 1551 and then as *A Fruiteful and pleasunt worke of the beste State of a public weale, and of the new yle, called Utopia.* Not till long after were the full implications of its twenty-four garden cities, based on handicrafts, really grasped. For the medieval cast of his thought needed penetrating. It became a primer, subject, like all primers, to gloss and commentary, but important for that very reason.

More had spent some four years in the Charterhouse, and when he wrote *Utopia* the monastic ideal was before his eyes. There are many signs of this—the undyed wool dress of the Utopians, the readings and controlled conversations during meals, the apportioning of crafts, the manual trades. The book has been called 'an imaginative diagram of the contemplative life which all rational men should prefer to an active life which was yearly replacing it as an ideal'. Carthusian and Benedictine rules emerge in the details of the ideal state and in the style of presentation.

Yet medieval as More is, he exhibits two new ideals. The first is that the apprehension of Nature's secrets would alleviate men's lot on earth. For, speaking of natural science, he described the Utopians as counting :–

3

the knowledge of yt amonge the goodlieste, and mooste profytable partes of Philosophie. For whyles they by the helpe of thys Philosophie search owte the secrete mysteryes of nature, they thynke that they not onlye receaue thereby wonderfull greate pleasur, but also obteyn great thankes and fauour of the auctore and maker thereof.

The second is the overt plea for continuity with the primitive teaching of the early Church, for inwardness as opposed to outward pomp and magnificence. Utopia condemned the social abuses of Christianity in Christendom. Hythlodaye and his companions were told by the Utopians that 'it was no small healpe and furtherance in the matter that they harde us saye that Christ instytuted amonge hys all thynges commen: and that the same communitee dothe yet remayne amongest the rightest Christian companies'.

More's Utopians were pragmatists: the world of nature and man was a universal laboratory where operations had been going on throughout history to find out what was in harmony or in conflict with Nature. Thus those who could study past and contemporary history could assess the 'experiments' in living which had already been carried out during the 1760 years said to have been required to construct the Utopian commonwealth. For More's Utopians regarded science as linked to ethics and religion.[1]

At the same time as *Utopia* was translated there appeared *The Vision of Pierce Plowman*: Robert Crowley's refurbishing of Langland's vision of a holy commune on high before Lucifer fell. 'Say the holy writt that in the begynyng of holy church', wrote Henry Parker, a Carmelite friar in *Dives and Pauper*, a book much printed between 1493 and 1536, 'al thinges were comon to the multitude of al cristen people nat only to the apostylys; but to all cristen people . . . And therefore sayth the law: that common lyf is nedeful to al men, and namely to them that wyl folowe the lif of cristes desiples'.

To More's generation and the two that followed, however, the 6,000 years of the world's span were considered as coming to an end. George Gascoigne in the *Drum of Doomsday* (1576)

---

[1] *Utopia*, ed. Lupton (1895), 217–18; Paul Coles, 'The Interpretation of More's *Utopia*', *Hibbert Journal*, LVI (1958), 365–70; P. A. Duhamel, 'The Medievalism of More's *Utopia*', *Studies in Philology* (1955), 57, 99–126; R. W. Chambers, *Sir Thomas More* (London, 1935), 256–67; H. A. Mason, *Humanism and Poetry in the Early Tudor Period* (1959), 126–7.

lamented the corruption and decay of mankind. Others contrasted the golden age with the corruption of the present and Francis Shakelton in *A Blazing Starre* (1580) envisaged 'the final dissolution of the Engine of this worlde'. Phillip Stubbes in *The Anatomie of Abuses* (1587) declared 'The day of the Lord cannot be farre off'. Joseph Hall, Bishop of Exeter and Norwich, in *Virgi demiarium* (1597) compared life in its golden age with the present 'thriving in ill as it in age decays'. Samuel Purchas, writing of the explorations of his age in *Purchas, His Pilgrimage* (1613), remarked 'All Arts are but the supply of Nature's defects, to patch up her ragged and worne rents, to cover rather than cure or recover man's Fall'. God had cursed the earth and Donne in his *Anatomie of the World* shows that 'The New Philosophy' by calling 'all in doubt' had been partly responsible :–

> Freely men confesse that this world's spent,
> When in the Planets and the Firmament
> They seek so many new, they see that this
> Is crumbled out againe to his Atomies.
> 'Tis all in pieces, all coherence gone;
> All just supply, and all Relation.[1]

Such pessimism reached its climax in Godfrey Goodman's *The Fall of Man* (1616), recently described as : 'the classical expression in England of the prevailing doctrine, which was derived from the fusion between the Christian belief that man was fallen, and the pagan notion of decline from a golden age'.[2]

Goodman's thesis was attacked by Archdeacon George Hakewill in *An Apologie or the Power and Providence of God* (1627). Goodman's reply, and Hakewill's answers were published as an appendix to the third edition in 1635. Pepys, who read Hakewill's book thirty-two years later found that it 'did satisfy myself mighty fair in the truth of the saying that the world do not grow old at all'.[3] Hakewill asserted his belief in man's progress in social morality. His significance lay in this demolition of 'current theories of degeneration, which stood in the way of all possible theories of progress'.[4]

[1] Victor Harris, *All Coherence Gone* (Chicago, 1949), 87–172.
[2] G. I. Soden, *Godfrey Goodman, Bishop of Gloucester* (London, 1953), 87.
[3] *Diary*, 3 February 1667.
[4] J. B. Bury, *The Idea of Progress* (1920), 91.

Another rebel against man's acceptance of his human limitations was Francis Bacon who wrote that:—

> by far the greatest obstacle to the progress of science and to the undertaking of new tasks and provinces therein, is found in this— that men dispair and think things impossible. For wise and serious men are wont in these matters to be altogether distrustful; considering with themselves the obscurity of nature, the shortness of life, the deceitfulness of the senses, the weakness of the judgement, the difficulty of experiment and the like.[1]

His optimism was based on a theory of continuous fulfilment: 'There are still,' he wrote, 'laid up in the womb of nature many secrets of excellent use, having no affinity or parallelism with anything that is now known, but lying entirely out of the beat of the imagination which have not yet been found.'[2] And again: 'For man by the Fall fell at the same time from his state of innocency and from his dominion over nature. Both of these losses, however, can even in this life be in some part repaired; the former by religion and faith, the latter by the arts and sciences.'[3]

Describing another island Utopia—Bensalem—in his *New Atlantis*, Bacon envisages science as leading men to God. The miraculous ark bearing the Christian Scriptures could not be approached except by a pious scientist. Science, in Bensalem, has for its end the 'enlarging of the Bounds of Human Empire, to the effecting of all things possible'. Bacon had no doubts that science would provide the key to an earthly paradise; for, as he said in the *Novum Organum*, 'only let man regain his right over Nature, which belongs to him by the gift of God; let there be given to him the power; right reason and sound religion will teach him how to apply it'.[4]

(2)

Science and right religion were the especial interest of continental thinkers who sketched the dimensions of the ideal city of good men. In 1551 (the same year as More's *Utopia* was

[1] *Novum Organum* (in *Works* ed. Ellis, Spedding and Heath), vol. 1, p. xcii.
[2] ibid., vol. 1, p. cxix.
[3] ibid., vol. 11, p. lii: quoted by M. E. Prior, 'Bacon's Man of Science', *Journal of the History of Ideas* (1954), XV, 348–70.
[4] R. P. Adams, 'The Social Responsibilities of Science in Utopia, the New Atlantis and After', op. cit. (1949), X, 374–98.

translated into English), *La Citta Felice* was published by Franciscus Patrique. The dimensions became clearer with J. V. Andreae's *Reipublicae Christianopolitanae Descriptio* (1619) and Campanella's *Civitas Solis* (1623): both testaments to the value of communities or groups. Campanella was a member of the Accademia Delia in Padua, Andreae the 'founder' of the Rosicrucians.

Andreae, in fact, had said in his *Fama Fraternitatis* (circulated in manuscript) that the only way in which a truly Christian society could be produced was by the co-operative activity of a group. This advice was in a mock-serious vein; Christian Rosenkreuz, the 'hero' of his parable, was a mythical character who was supposed to have founded an order. The rules for this order were elaborated by Andreae four years later in his *Confessio Fraternitatis R.C. ad eruditos Europae*, together with its plan for reform. These plans envisaged the redemption of man by two means: science and the philosopher's stone (to produce wealth) and religious freedom (to kindle his spiritual life). Andreae's genuine interest in science was elaborated in *Chymische Hochzeit Christiani Rosenkreutz* (a satire on the get-rich-quick attitudes of alchemists) and his concern for the kindling of religious life in his *Invitatio Fraternitatis Christi ad amoris candidates* (1617) (an appeal to Christians to form a society to effect this purpose). This society Andreae outlined in *Reipublicae Christianopolitanae Descriptio* (1619); it was, incidentally, a powerful exposition of what the 'inner light' can effect in this direction.

Andreae exercised a considerable influence in England. One group gathered round Robert Fludd, a builder of ingenious machines like a wooden bull that bellowed, an automatic dragon and a performing harp. This group used language of natural philosophy to explain supernature (or the mystic), revelling in hidden meanings and ambiguities. They actually believed Christian Rosenkreuz had brought much wisdom from the East in 1422. As a rustic rhymer from Scotland put in his *Muses' Threnode* in 1638, just after Fludd's death:–

> For what we do presage is riot in grosse,
> For we are brethren of the Rosie Crosse;
> We have the Mason word and second sight,
> Things for to come we can fortell aright.

7

Fludd held that all things were 'ideally in God' before they were made. This he developed to show how God was immanent in all things. He taught that those filled with the spirit of Christ might rise before his 'second coming', and his voluminous writings— at least fifteen of them are listed in the catalogue of the British Museum—made considerable impact abroad, a 'key' to them being published at Frankfort in 1633.[1] The Rosicrucians probably stemmed from the Militia Crucifera Evangelica, a secret society in Nuremburg, founded by the Lutheran alchemist Simon Studion.

A second group did not take easily to the mysteries and alchemy of Christian Rosenkreuz but responded to Andreae's call for a rescue team of devoted men to 'fan the holy flame of faith, of love and of knowledge and in their endeavour to be ever strengthened by the consciousness of a great and united striving towards these nobel ends'. This rescue team, a *civitas solis*, a *societas Christiana* or a *unio Christiana* was taken up by, amongst others, Samuel Hartlib,[2] who in the 1620's was anxious to form a society called Antilia.

To Hartlib, Antilia was a practical proposition. After he came to London, he corresponded with Rôhmer about the possibility of founding it in Virginia. Another of his correspondents, Fridwald, suggested an experiment on an island near Liffland. But one after another of the members of the group seem to have died, and a suitable patron was not forthcoming. Antilia changed its name. It became *Collegium Charitatis* (1628), *Illustre Collegium* (1632) and *Societas Reformatorum et Correspondency* (1634). Ultimately it became *Macaria*, a Utopian kingdom which Hartlib outlined in a pamphlet, *A description of the Famous Kingdom of Macaria* (1641).[3]

One of Hartlib's friends was Robert Boyle, the chemist, who had 'great longings to peruse' his *Imago Societatis* and *Dextra Amoris* in March 1647. A month later, having done so, he presented it 'to a person of quality to whom if it takes suitably . . . may thence have no obscure influence on the public good

---

[1] J. B. Craven, *Dr Robert Fludd* (1902).

[2] G. H. Turnbull, *Dury, Hartlib and Comenius* (Liverpool, 1947), 13 n. 4 comments of Andreae 'his writings may very well have inspired Hartlib in these letters, as in other directions' and (74) 'It is very probable that Andreae's writings provided the stimulus for the efforts to found the Antilia.'

[3] See G. H. Turnbull in *Zeitschrift für deutsche Philologie*, Band 73, Heft 4, and Band 74, Heft 2.

. . . Campanella's Civitatis Solis and that same Republica Christianopolitana . . . will both of them deserve to be taught in our language'. By May of that year, Boyle was writing: 'you interest yourself so much in the invisible college, and that whole society is so highly concerned in all the accidents of your life, that you can send me no intelligence of your affairs that does not assume the nature of Utopian'.[1]

Utopia, Macaria, Antilia: Hartlib worked hard to establish it. One of his continental correspondents, Joachim Poleman, who loved Hartlib 'as his own soul', was interested in founding a similar society in Germany. Asking Hartlib's opinion of his society he wrote 'what do you think of the delineation . . . under the title Dextra amoris Christiano porrecta or Imago Societatis'.[2] 'The chief end of Commonwealth', Hartlib wrote in 1648 in *A Further Discovery of the Office of Public Address for Accommodation*, 'is Society, the End of Society is mutual Help, and the End and Use of Help is to enjoy from one another Comfort; that is, every Thing lawfully desirable or wanting to our Contentation.'[3] This society was Hartlib's main concern during the period of the Commonwealth. By 1661 he was forced to confess 'of the Antilian Society the smoke is over, but the fire is not altogether extinct. It may be it will flame in due time, though not in Europe.' Hartlib's 'Fire of Industry' and 'the Alembick' of his 'curious and rational Head' energized other Utopian writers. John Dury, his coadjutor, published *The Commonwealth of Israel* in 1650 and John Sadler *Olbia* in 1660. Peter Cornelis Plockhoy of Zierikzee had a scheme for founding a colony in Bermuda for persecuted ministers, also to be called Macaria.[4]

[1] Birch, *Life of Boyle*, 74–75.
[2] Boyle's *Works*, V (1744), 296.
[3] *Harleian Miscellany* (1765), vi. 13.
[4] J. K. Fuz, *Welfare Economics in English Utopias* (The Hague, 1952), 55–62. Plockhoy was of Mennonite parentage and associated with a group known as the Collegiants, a community which split up and a separate group crystallized out under the name 'Plockhoyisten'. Troubles with the Church authorities led him to come to England in 1658, where he was received several times by Cromwell. He organized a colony of Mennonites which settled in Delaware in 1663, but was plundered 'to a very naile' by the English in the following year. See John Downie, *Peter Cornelius Plockboy* [sic], Manchester, n.d. Whilst in England he wrote *A Way Propounded to Make the Poor in These and Other Nations happy . . . Wherein every one may keep his propriety, and be employed in some work or other, as he shall be fit, without being oppressed.*

Pilot projects for the salvation of society inspired Beale, another of his correspondents, who confessed 'I do extremely indulge the design of beginning the Building of Christian Society and that curious offer of the *right hand of the Christian love* hath taken no deeper footing in England.'

(3)

'The right hand of Christian love' was more disturbing than the industrious penmanship of the Utopists. Tyndale gave it something to grasp when he translated the Bible into English in 1526. A generation later, John Foxe remarked that:–

> The fervent zeal of those Christian days seemed much superior to these our days and times, as manifestly may appear by their sitting up all night in reading and hearing . . . some gave a load of hay for a few chapters of St. James or of St. Paul in English . . . To see their earnest seekings, their burning zeal, their readings, their watchings, their sweet assemblies . . . may make us now in these days of free profession to blush for shame.

The Sermon on the Mount especially was to initiate a long series of social experiments. Christian principles were at variance either with a national Church, or conventional society. Many Christians rejected not only the 'grace' dispensed by the Church but the Church as a repository of sacramental powers too. And often they rejected the social order. 'Graceless' groups, irradiated with Christian community love, were no new thing.[1] Those that began in sixteenth-century England owed much to Tyndale's efforts to make the meaning of the Bible as clear to a peasant as it had never been to a divine. To Tyndale 'priest', 'Church' and 'charity' meant 'elder', 'congregation' and 'love'. Such insistence on the Bible's literal truth, and its availability, made the fall of Jerusalem, the Pentecostal Revelations, St. Matthew's account of Christ's second advent (c. 24) and St. Paul's apocalyptic prophecies (2 Thessalonians 9) heady matter.[2] Not without reason was Tyndale forced to flee to Germany and Holland, chased, betrayed, arrested, strangled and

---

[1] J. Isaccs, 'Sixteenth Century Versions' in H. W. Robinson (ed.) *The Bible* (Oxford, 1954).

Ernst Troeltsh, *The Social Teaching of the Christian Churches* (trans. O. Wyon), (1931) ii. 695.

[2] N. Cohn, *The Pursuit of the Millennium* (1957).

finally, in that most pitiless of deaths, burnt. He suffered because the readers of vernacular translations were taking matters into their own hands to capture the glories of an earthly Kingdom of Heaven.

Whilst Tyndale was on the run, a group in Munster, rejecting the regenerative therapy of baptism, formed themselves into a community of mature Christians (or Anabaptists), each directly accountable to God. Some, encouraged by Acts II, 44, became communists. Like Tyndale, they met violent deaths. A year before Tyndale died, nineteen men and six women were accused at St. Paul's Church, London of anabaptism and community of goods. Fourteen of them were sent to the stake. Four years afterwards the Protestant leaders in Germany wrote to Henry VIII warning him of the spread of the sect and telling him that they believed its principles were making great progress in England. Further burnings followed and in 1551 a commission was issued to Archbishop Cranmer and others to try Anabaptists. Three searches for all 'that have conceived any manner of such heretical opinions as the Anabaptists do hold, and meaneth not by charitable teaching to be reconciled' were ordered between the years 1560 and 1568, and those found were ordered 'to depart out of the realm within twenty days' after the proclamation. Inquiries into the habits of new arrivals were equally ineffective in checking recruitment. Indeed, by 1575 the Archbishop of Canterbury was lamenting to the Secretary of State: 'This great number of Anabaptists taken on Easter Day, may move us to some contemplation.'

(4)

Consistent persecution of the Anabaptists produced a new mutation: the Family of Love. David Joris reconciled some of the violent radicals with others of the passive wing to form a mystical group animated by brotherly love. A community without worship or sacraments grew up about him as 'The Third David' or the mouthpiece of a third dispensation.

Joris influenced Henry Niclaes, a merchant, formerly a Roman Catholic, to believe that he too was the prophet of a third dispensation. Niclaes did not bind a community round himself as Joris did, but tried, like the Anabaptists, to establish the Kingdom of Christ on earth. First found in Kent (in 1552) and

Cambridgeshire (in 1574), his teaching spread: the Bible was an allegory, Moses a prophet of hope and Christ a prophet of faith, whilst Henry Niclaes was a prophet of love. Hence their name. With Vitel, a joiner, another Dutchman, Niclaes organized groups in Essex and London. They, too were discovered, and on 12 June 1575 five Familists (as his followers were called) were frightened into a public recantation at St. Paul's Cross and 'confessed themselves utterly to detest as well the author of that sect H.N., as all his damnable errors and heresies'.

By 1578 the Familists were numerous enough for the Privy Council to 'think fit to endeavour their suppression'. They were teaching 'that the Bible is not the Word of God, but a significa-tion thereof, and the Bible is but ink and paper, but the Word of God is spirit and life'. These ideas circulated amongst 'simple unlearned people', who were impressed with the missionaries' 'monstrous new kind of speech'. Through these missionaries, often vagrant tradesmen merely, Familist teaching spread to Devon in 1580, and the Privy Council was employing a special agent, Newstubbs, to smell them out. Familist principles even penetrated the Yeomen of the Guard, five of whom were sus-pected. One of them uttered 'lewde and irreverent speeches of the Councell' because of the punishment meted out to the Familists.

Familists were accused of believing that 'perfection could be attained in this life'. When attained, their leaders were accused of saying 'We the elders of the holy understanding shall reign upon earth in righteousnesse and under the obedience of loue, judge the world with equitie'. They denied the resurrection of the body. As a contemporary indignantly wrote:–

> They will have this blasphemer H.N. to be the sonne of God, Christ, which was to come in the end of the world; and say, that the day of judgement is already come; and that H.N. judgeth the world now by his doctrine . . . He maketh over one of his Family of Love to be Christ, yea and God, and himself God and Christ in a more excellent manner, saying, that he is Godded with God, and codefied with him, and that God is homified with him.

Stephen Renison called them 'White Wolfes' in a tract of that name published in 1627. Their doctrines were still being preached at Bishopsgate in 1645 by one Randall 'and many people were flocking after him'. Niclaes' spiritualization of the world was to bear rich literary fruit for John Bunyan immortalized his journey in the *Pilgrim's Progress*.[1]

(5)

Reinforcing the teaching of Henry Niclaes was that of Jacob Boehme, a self-taught shoemaker of Gorlitz, which had an extraordinary vogue in seventeenth century England. It was manifest in 1644—twenty years after his death—when a brief seven-page biography of him was published, describing his knowledge of 'Natural and Divine things' as 'the most wonderful deep knowledge' that 'any hath been known to do since the Apostles' times'. 'A Christian has', wrote Jacob Boehme, 'no sect; he may live among sects, and also attend their divine services, but yet not belong to any sect; he has only one science—Christ in him.' Boehme envisaged a seventh state in the history of the world when contention between human beings would cease, 'the branches would no longer believe they were themselves trees, but rejoice in their common root'. He looked forward, not so much to a millenium on earth, but to the restoration of this seventh state by the 'principle of light' becoming paramount and dissipating the external world. This paramountcy demanded decision on the part of man; if he set his mind to it, he would adhere to it when the last judgement is made, and become an angel. But if he set his mind against it, he would become a devil, for ever and ever.

John Sparrow, a lawyer, and his kinsman, John Ellistone, undertook the complete translation of his works during the years 1647 to 1662. It was during this period that the Behmenist ground swell grew. It was strong enough to elicit from John Anderson in 1662 *One Blow at Babel in those of the Pepol called Behmenites, whose foundation is not upon that of the Prophets and Apostles, which shall stand sure and firm for ever; but upon their own Carnal Conceptions, begotten in their Imaginations upon Jacob Behmen's writings*. It also inspired John Milton, pupil of the millenarian Mede and friend of the Andrean Hartlib, in *Paradise Lost* and *Paradise Regained*. An American, Dr. Bailey, has argued

[1] S. H. Atkins 'The Family of Love', *Notes and Queries*, CLXXV (1938), 362–4; G. Huehns, *Antinomianism in English History* (1951), calls them 'the first appreciable sect in England' (62).

that these bear striking affinities to Behmenist thought. *Paradise Regained*, as she sees it, is the story of the heaven within men: it is not so much the place where dreams come true as a state in which man is the measure of all things in heaven and earth. *Paradise Lost* in a certain sense pictures Utopia; not the ideal society to which man is progressing, it is true, but the ideal state from which he came and which he has the power to revive within himself if he but will. 'The belief of Milton's time in the expected millennium', she wrote, 'had kept the idea of paradise ever before men's minds, until regaining paradise was the most natural thought in the world to them.'

(6)

Other persecuted minorities found inspiring analogies between their own lot and that of the Israelites. Each fresh translation of the Bible (and the Authorized Version was being prepared in the early seventeenth century), gave fresh texts to sustain the hope that the Lord would gather in the elect to himself in Jerusalem.

Such a call for the establishment of Jerusalem in England was made in 1621 by William Goudge, rector of St. Anne's, Blackfriars. With Sir Henry Finch, an M.P., he issued *The World's Great Restauration, or Calling of the Jews* (1621). Finch's part in this daring prophecy was at first kept secret (for he was one of the codifiers of statute law), but King James discovered his complicity and imprisoned him. The preface was addressed 'To all the Seed of Jacob, farre and wide dispersed', and it closed with the words, 'thou shalt sit as a Lady in the Mount of comelinesse, that hill of beauty, the true Tsion, the heavenly Jerusalem, to worlde's admiration. And for myself, I shall think, I reape aboundant fruit of these my travails . . . when . . . I have layd one stone, (say it be but a peble stone) toward that spiritual building.' Finch was released having expressly repudiated all sentiments which might reflect on the Majesty of James.

Joseph Mede, the best informed Cambridge don of his day, was much impressed by the book. 'God forgive me,' he wrote, 'if it be a sin, but I have thought so many a day', and the result was that six years later he published his *Clavis Apocalyptica* in 1627. In this Mede saw the redemptive process of God working itself out in his life: the signs being "the pouring out of the seven

14

vials'. The first four were the Albigensians, Luther, Elizabeth and the Thirty Years War; the fifth was to be the destruction of Rome, the sixth the conversion of the Israelites, and the last, the final judgement, was to coincide with the millennium itself.[1]

(7)

Still more elaborate and serious attempts were made to calculate the arithmetic of the apocalypse. 'Keys' to the apocalypse preoccupied men whose other activities mark them out as curiously modern. Samuel Hartlib published two such works. The first, in 1651, was *Clavis Apocalyptica: or a Prophetical Key: By which the great Mysteries in the Revelation of St John and the Prophet Daniel are opened; it being made apparent that the Prophetical Numbers come to an end with the year of our Lord 1655.* The second was in 1655: *Mysteries made Manifest. Or The Obscure Places in the Revelations of St. John and the Prophet Daniel opened. Wherein is made manifest the great and undeniable Error of the Astrologers in their computation of years since the Creation. And that the true Date of the Prophetical Numbers expire in the yeare of our Lord 1655.*

One such attempt arose at Walton, in Surrey. Six soldiers entered the Parish Church there, one carrying a lantern. They led the congregation out into the churchyard and the lantern-bearer told them

That he had a vision and received a command from God to deliver his will unto them; which he was to deliver and they to receive upon pain of damnation. It consisted of five lights:

1. That the Sabbath was abolished as unnecessary, Jewish and merely ceremonial. And here (quoth he) I should put out my first light, but the wind is so high I cannot light it.

2. Tythes are abolished as Jewish and ceremonial, a great burden to the Saints of God, and a discouragement of industry and tillage. And here I should put out my second light, etc., as aforesaid, which was the burden of his song.

3. Ministers are abolished as anti-Christian, and of no longer use now Christ himself descends into the hearts of his Saints, and his Spirit enlighteneth them with revelations, and inspirations. And here I should have put out my third light, etc.

[1] J. Bass Mullinger, *The University of Cambridge from the election of Buckingham to the decline of the Platonist Movement* (1911), 21.

4. Magistrates are abolished as useless, now that Christ himself is in purity of spirit come amongst us, and hath erected the kingdom of the Saints upon earth; and beside they are tyrants and oppressors of the Liberty of the Saints, and tie them to laws and ordinances, mere human inventions. And here I should have put out, etc.

5. Then putting his hand into his pocket, and pulling out a little Bible, he showed it open to the people, saying, 'here is a book you have in great veneration, consisting of two parts, the Old and the New Testament; I must tell you, it is abolished: It containeth beggarly rudiments, milk for Babes. But now Christ is in Glory amongst us, and imparts a fuller measure of his Spirit to his Saints, than this can afford; and therefore I am commanded to burn it before your faces.' So, taking the Candle out of his lantern, he set fire to the leaves. And then putting out the candle, cried, 'And here my fifth light is extinguished'.[1]

Episodes of this kind show that the seventeenth-century volcano was at white heat.

The dark arithmetic of speculation added up in figures of fire. The suffering Saints were to rule Zion and the Holy Community begin. Christ was to rule in person through them. Proletarian Bible readers had no further need of Biblical warrants—life in the Kingdom of Christ would come.

Excessive immersion in the Bible turned several heads, notably that of John Robins, who planned to lead 144,000 persons to the Holy Land, sustained on a diet of dry bread, raw vegetables and water. Joan Robins, his wife, was to mother a Messiah. Robins claimed to have appeared on earth before as Adam and as Melchizedek. His little community in Ling Alley, Moorfields, was raided by the authorities on 24 May 1651, and the ten people found there were locked up in Clerkenwell prison.

His spiritual successor was Thomas Tany, a goldsmith who claimed on 23 November 1649 that he was a Jew of the tribe of Reuben, and that he must change his name from Thomas to Thereau John. On 25 April 1650 he proclaimed that the Jews would return to the Holy Land to build the temple under himself as High Priest. On 30 December he claimed to be the Earl of Essex and heir to the throne. The English version of Boehme's writings made an impression on him, and he moved to Eltham where he made tents for his expedition, with the figure of each

---

[1] Clement Walker, *Anarchia Anglicana* (London, 1649), ii. 152–3.

tribe on the tents. The expedition was diverted by Tany claiming the Crown of France and, late in December 1654, he made a great bonfire in Lambeth and burnt his tent, pistols and Bible. He tried to secure the adoption of a petition by Parliament and was last heard of sailing to Holland.

The missions of Robins and Tany were inherited by John Reeve and his cousin Ludowick Muggleton. They solemnly cursed both their predecessors and forced one of them to admit his 'crimes'. Reeve announced :–

> there are three Dispensations, or Commissions of the Lord, unto the Elect World, and but three. The *First* of *Moses* and the Prophets. The *Second* of Jesus and his Apostles. The *Third* and last are the two *Witnesses* in the Eleventh of the Revelations : who are the true Ministers of the Holy Spirit, revealing or declaring the Mind of God, the Man Jesus, unto all the Elect World.

So, in *A General Treatise of the Three Records, or Dispensations*, John Reeve 'the Holy Spirit's true Minister of the third and last Dispensation' announced his commission 'received by Voice of the Lord Jesus from Heaven'.

Reeve was at first the 'Messenger' and Muggleton the 'Mouth'; later they identified themselves with the two witnesses (Revelation XI, 3), and defined a new system of faith. Muggleton was the more robust of the two, and on Reeve's death in 1658 had the movement to himself for another forty years. He was arrested in 1663 at Chesterfield, and in 1677 in London. His followers maintained for many years after his death a reading room at Bishopsgate in London.

(8)

To the New and the Old Testament was added a third ingredient: the Jewish Cabbala. Ostensibly Christianized in the fifteenth century, it was thought useful as a missionary tool through which the Jews could be converted. But the *Zohar* (or Book of Splendour) tended to convert those who hoped to use it in this way. Its poetic and diffuse speculations as to the structure of the Halls of Heaven encouraged many scholars of seventeenth century to experience, by prayer and fasting 'the heavenly chariot ride', passing through the seven 'heavenly halls', in much the same way as Mr. Aldous Huxley passed through the 'doors of perception' by taking mescalin. Thanks to the labours of a sixteenth-century French Cabbalist, Postel, who placed the dawn of a new age in 1556 when the earthly paradise would be restored, subsequent readers of the *Zohar* preferred to deal with it analogically. Sometimes, like Postel, they tried to comprehend it as Mede, Potter and Hartlib had tried to comprehend the book of *Revelation*. But whichever way it was interpreted, the mysterious doctrine of emanations remained. This taught that from God there emanated a lesser splendour which gave rise to the rational soul. This rational soul in turn gave rise to lesser splendour that produced the vegetable soul, and so on. Between God and the universe were ten intermediaries, the sephiroth, which explained, to the initiated, the activities of a transcendent God.[1]

[1] R. J. Zwi Werblowsky, 'Milton and the Conjectura Cabbalistica', *Journal of the Warburg and Courtauld Institutes*, XVIII (1955), 90–113, illustrates his influence on Blake too. W. J. Bousma, 'Postel and the Significance of Renaissance Cabalism', *Journal of the History of Ideas*, XV (1954), 218 ff.

2

$\diamond$

Diggers

$\diamond$

(1)

'WHY may we not have our Heaven here (that is, a comfortable livelihood in the Earth) and Heaven hereafter too?'[1] Gerrard Winstanley's question, posed in 1649, marks the emergence of the real Utopian. On 1 April, a date traditionally associated with the fatuous, half a dozen poor men began to dig common land at St. George's Hill, Weybridge, under his leadership. They wanted to prepare it for seeds, but their actions set a new tradition. Winstanley, a bankrupt cloth merchant turned a cattle herdsman, had conceived a vision of universal redemption. God, he saw, was reason immanent in every man, not living apart in glory, but working in all creation.

In *The New Law of Righteousness* (1649), Winstanley proclaimed that he had received a divine injunction that people should 'work together; eat bread together'. 'When the Lord doth show me the place and manner, how he will have us that are called the common people, to manure and work the common land,' said Winstanley, he would act. Now, on 1 April, he did so.

(2)

His half dozen helpers,[2] tripled in less than a week, were soon arrested and locked up in a church at Walton. Released, they

[1] G. H. Sabine, *The Works of Gerrard Winstanley* (Cornell, N.Y., 1941), 409.
[2] op. cit., 105.

were carried off to Kingston, locked up again, and released again. A hostile neighbour reported to the Council of State on 16 April that:—

> They invite all to come in and help them, and promise them meat, drink, and clothes. They do threaten to pull down and level all park pales, and lay open, and intend to plant there very shortly. They give out they will be four or five thousand within ten days, and threaten the neighbouring people there, that they will make them all come up to the hills and work; and forewarn them suffering their cattle to come near the plantation; if they do, they will cut their legs off. It is feared they have some design in hand.

The Council of State sent an officer to investigate. He found a small group of about twenty under Winstanley and William Everard. The latter he regarded as 'no other than a mad man'. The troop commander promised

> to go with two or three men to St. George's Hill this day, and persuade these people to leave this employment if I can, and if then I see no more danger than now I do I shall march back again to London tomorrow. . . . Indeed the business is not worth the writing nor yet taking notice of: I wonder the Council of State should be so abused with information . . .

Winstanley and Everard appeared before Lord Fairfax at Whitehall. Winstanley said 'he was of the race of the Jews', and argued that 'the liberties of the people were lost by coming in of William the Conquerer, and that ever since the people of God had lived under tyranny and oppression worse than that of our forefathers under the Egyptians'. Everard then went on to claim that 'the time of deliverance was at hand, and God would bring his people out of this slavery, and restore them to their freedom in enjoying the fruits and benefits of the Earth.

'And that there had lately appeared to him a vision, which bad him arise and dig and plough the earth, and receive the fruits thereof.

'That their intent is to restore the Creation to its former condition. That as God had promised to make the barren land fruitful, so now what they did was to restore the ancient community of enjoying the fruits of the Earth, and to distribute the benefits thereof to the poor and needy, and to feed the hungry and to clothe the naked.' They stood before Fairfax with their hats on, and when asked why, replied 'Because he was but their fellow creature'.

Fairfax was so impressed that in the following month he called in to see the Diggers' work for himself.

Meanwhile, fifteen of the Diggers issued a manifesto: *The True Levellers Standard Advanced or The State of Community Opened and Presented to the Sons of Men.*

'For it is showed us, that so long as we, or any other do own the Earth to be the peculiar Interest of Lords and Land Lords, and not common to others as well as to them, we own the Curse, and hold the Creation under Bondage.' They insisted that this adherence to the principle of property was a sin against 'the light that is given into us'.

When the Diggers tried to cut and sell the wood on the common land, their horses were hurt and killed by the landowners. So they issued a manifesto, *A Declaration from the Poor Oppressed People of England*, this time signed by forty-five of them, declaring they would prevent the landlords from cutting the wood. When soldiers in the district joined with some civilians to raid them Winstanley decided to make a second visit to Lord General Fairfax.

He carried a letter, desiring 'all of you seriously in love and humility to consider of this business of Public Community, which I am carried forth in the Power of Love and clear light of Universal Righteousness to advance as much as I can; and I can do no other, the Law of Love in my heart does so constrain me'.

The local inhabitants of Walton could not wait for the Council of State to act. A number of them accompanied by 'divers men in women's apparele on foot, with every one a staffe or club' attacked the Diggers. 'Like bruit beasts that have no understanding, they fell furiously upon them, beating and striking those four naked men, beating them to the ground, breaking their heads, and sore bruising their bodies, whereof one is so sore bruised, that it is feared he will not escape with life.'

Clubs and cudgels failing to dislodge the Diggers, the landlords now took to the courts. Suits were initiated by Lord Wenman, Sir Ralph Verney and Richard Winwood on 23 June, in the Court of Record at Kingston. Winstanley, characteristically, offered a pamphlet to the court as evidence. (Later included in his *A Watchword to the City of London, and the Army*.) 'Seeing you would not suffer us to speak, one of us brought this following writing into your Court.' The Court, since Winstanley desired to plead his own cause, marked him in default for non-appearance: It ordered the arrest of his two associates. Bailiffs confiscated his cows but sympathizers recovered them.

(3)

Winstanley and Everard now moved their community from St. George's Hill to Cobham Manor. This was owned by the rector of West Horsley, and here they built four houses and prepared the land to receive a crop of winter grain. But the long arm of the Council of State stretched out, and troops were sent on 10 October and on 28 November to disperse assemblies. On the second occasion these 'Turkish Bashaws' as Winstanley called them pulled down the houses.

Deprived of houses, the Diggers built themselves 'some few little hutches like calf-cribs', and there they lay by night, after planting 'divers acres of Wheat and Rye' unmindful of the slanders spread abroad about them, 'counting it a great happinesse to be persecuted for righteousnesse sake, by the Priests and Professors'. 'They have told you,' wrote Winstanley in *A New-Yeres Gift for Parliament and the Armie* (1650) 'that the Diggers do steal and rob from others. This likewise is a slander: we have things stollen from us; but if any can prove that any of us do steal any mans proper goods, as Sheep, Geese, Pigs, as they say, let such be made a spectacle to all the world: For my part, I own no such doing, neither do I know any such thing by any of the Diggers. Likewise they report, that we Diggers hold women to be common, and live in that bestialnesse: For my part, I declare against it; I own this to be a truth, That the earth ought to be a common Treasury to all; but as for women, Let every man have his own wife, and every woman her own husband; and I know none of the Diggers that act in such an unrational excesse of female comunitie: If any should, I professe to have nothing to do with such people, but leave them to their own Master, who will pay them with torment of minde, and diseases in their bodies.'

In these calf-cribs the Diggers spent the long winter tending their crops and building fresh houses. By April 1650 they had eleven acres of corn and had built seven houses.

As Easter approached, the hostility of the vicar of Horsley was resurrected, and he sent a group of men to demolish a house at Cobham Common, so maltreating the occupant's wife that she had a miscarriage. Winstanley promptly waited upon the vicar and argued with him. The vicar said that if Winstanley in argument 'could make it good by Scriptures, he would never trouble us more, but let us build and plant: Nay he said, he would cast in all his estate and become one with the diggers'. So on Easter Day Winstanley provided this necessary scriptural proof (later reprinted as *An Humble Request*). The vicar 'seemed to consent to many things, and was very moderate, and promised . . . to read it over, and to give me an answer . . . moreover (continued Winstanley) he promised that if the Diggers would not cut the wood upon the Common, he would not pull down their houses: And the diggers resolved for peace sake, to let the wood alone till people did understand their freedom a little more.'

Alas, for the surety of promises, Winstanley got his answer. On the Friday in Easter week yet another punitive expedition of fifty men came to demolish the Diggers' houses. 'At the Command of this Parson Plat,' wrote Winstanley,

they set fire to six houses, and burned them down, and burned likewise some of their housholdstuffe, and wearing Clothes, throwing their beds, stooles and housholdstuffe, up and down the Common, not pitying the cries of many little Children, and their frightened Mothers, which are Parishioners borne in the Parish.

The poor diggers being thus suddenly cast out of their houses by fire, both they, their wives and Children were forced to lie upon the open Common all night: yet the rage of Parson Plat and his company rested not here, but in the night time, some of them came again upon the Commons, while the diggers were quiet, and some of them in bed, and said, we have Authority from our Master, that is Mr. Plat, to kill you, and burn the rest of your goods, if you will not be gone: thereupon Sir Anthony Vincents Servant, called Davy, struck at one, and cut some of their Chares and other Goods to peeces, frighting the women and Children again. And some of the Diggers asked them, why they would do thus cruelly by them, they answered, because you do not know God, nor will not come to Church.

Nay farther, if this satisfies not Mr. Plat, but he & Tho: Sutton, of Cobham, have hired three men, to attend both night and day, to beat the Diggers, and to pull down their tents or houses, if they make any more; and if they make Caves in the earth, they threaten to murther them there, so that they will not suffer the poor Diggers to live, neither above nor below ground: if they beg they whip them by their Law for vagrants, if they steal they hang them; and if they set themselves to plant the Common for a livlihood, that they may neither beg nor steale, and whereby England is inriched, yet they will not suffer them to do this neither: And so hereby these Gentlemen take away both creation-right, and Common-wealths right from the poor Diggers; for they command the poor enslaved Tenants and Neighbors likewise, nor to suffer any of the Diggers to have any lodging in their houses, not to sell them any meat for their money.

And now they cry out the Diggers are routed, and they rang bells for joy; but stay Gentlemen, your selves are routed, and you have lost your Crown, and the poor Diggers have won the Crown of glory.

(4)

Meanwhile at Wellingborough in Northampton a similar disturbance took place; there were over a thousand inhabitants receiving alms and public relief had to be organized. Nine enterprising men, led by Richard Smith began 'to bestow their righteous labour upon the common land at Bareshanke'. To this, they argued, the Law of the Land, Reason and Scriptures entitled them. They resolved not to dig up any man's property 'until they freely give us it'. And to their comfort and surprise there were not wanting those who did.

So pleased were they by their success that they desired that 'some that approve this work of Righteousnesse, would but spread this our Declaration before the great Council of the Law, so that they may be pleased to give us more encouragement to go on'. To secure this, they published *A Declaration of the Grounds and Reasons Why We the Poor Inhabitants of the Town of Wellingborough, in the County of Northampton, have begun and give consent to Dig up, Manure and Sow Corn upon the Common, and Waste Ground, called Bareshanke.* As a publisher, they secured John Calvert, who had not only published Winstanley's works, but those of other apostles of the 'inner light' too.

321.07 An 55

C. 1

(5)

These experiments were not so much important at the time, as for their place in the tradition of community experiments. As Winstanley said in *The True Leveller's Standard Advanced*, they were prepared to wait 'till the spirit in you make you cast up your land and goods'. The earth was the focus of the struggle and the desire to own it the cause of all laws. It was, he asserted, the Normans who brought tyranny into England and in *The New Law of Righteousness* he stated succinctly his creed: 'Reason requires that every man should live upon the increase of the earth comfortably.'

Having made his protest, Winstanley now sharpened his thought to put forward his plan for a complete revolution of society, outlined in *The Law of Freedom in a Platform* (1652). When Reason (which he saw as God's immanence in man) pervaded all social institutions, private property would, with wage labour, be abolished, money would disappear and communal storehouses would be set up. Elective councils, embodying reason, would govern villages, towns, counties and the nations. Officers responsible to them would supervise trade, agriculture and distribution. A complete educational system would emerge enabling men to discover the 'secrets of Nature and Creation within which all true knowledge is wrapped up'. Hanging, whipping and imprisonment would pass away. No one would work beyond the age of forty. It was a Utopia based on household production. As a manifesto it has been aptly summed up by a recent writer as consummating 'the transition between two classic types of Utopian outlook: from the blazing chiliastic expectancy of the religious radical who daily looks for Jesus' second coming to inaugurate a reign of righteousness, to the rationalistic communism, abounding in plans and projects, which appears as an aspect of the thought of enlightenment.'[1]

---

[1] Perez Zagorin, *A History of Political Thought in the English Revolution* (London, 1954), 57.

3

∽◇∽◇∽◇∽◇∽◇∽◇∽◇∽◇∽◇∽◇∽◇∽◇∽◇∽◇∽◇∽◇∽◇∽◇∽◇∽

Quakers

∽◇∽◇∽◇∽◇∽◇∽◇∽◇∽◇∽◇∽◇∽◇∽◇∽◇∽◇∽◇∽◇∽◇∽◇∽◇∽

(1)

GERRARD WINSTANLEY subsequently joined a group led by George Fox, and his book *The Saints' Paradise* showed how far he had come within their orbit. Indeed, Comber, the Dean of Durham, in his book *Christianity No Enthusiasm* (1678) contended that Winstanley and his Diggers were the real founders of Fox's group, for like the Philadelphians, they were irradiated with Behmenist thought. Richard Baxter, the shrewd recorder of those days, regarded them as 'proper Fanatics, looking too much to Revelation within, instead of the Holy Scripture'.[1] 'All along through most ages these Hereticks have sped, even down to the David-Georgians, Weigellans, Familists, and the like of late.'

Thomas Underhill in *Hell broke loose: An History of the Quakers* (1660) also saw in them affiliations to Behmenists, as did the Cambridge Platonists, Henry More, and the prophet Ludowick Muggleton. Perhaps the best example of their affiliations with the Behmenists was George Fox himself, who in 1651 actually appeared before Justice Hotham, a relation of the earliest translators of Boehme who, as Fox says, 'tooke me

---

[1] *Reliquiae Baxterianiae*, II, 387, 285. For the minor sects see C. E. Whiting, *Studies in English Puritanism from the Restoration to the Revolution 1660–1688* (1931), 233–322.

26

into his closett, and saide hee had knowne yt principle (i.e. the "inner light") this 10 yeare: and hee was glad yt ye Lord did now publish it abroad to people'.[1]

A year before Winstanley had embarked on his Digger experiment George Fox felt 'experimentally' that 'all Christians are believers and are born of God'. As he graphically put it, he 'came into the state that Adam was in before his fall'. The whole earth 'had a new smell' for him and he 'came up through the flaming sword into the paradise of God'. God, as he felt, was Truth and Love, his grace intended for all men. This apprehension changed his life. From now until his death, forty-four years later, many of the sects regrouped around him, and from this regrouping emerged 'The Children of Light' or 'Friends in the Truth', best known as the Society of Friends.[2]

On evangelistic tours Fox fostered the formation of little Quaker societies. Baptists and Familists helped to swell these societies and Fox began to organize them. Exhaling an optimistic gospel, they stressed the personal experience of the Inner Light, a personal experience greater than any theological notion. God, immanent in all, was recognizable by all, and could be inwardly known by all.[3]

This social mysticism was cultivated by pooling experience in a meeting. Any member with a truth, experience or exhortation, could share it. The business of each meeting was conducted in the spirit of worship, the meeting ascertaining the will of God in a common judgement. Any impulse that was anti-social was not of God.[4]

Sometimes a naïve interpretation was put upon Fox's conviction that Christ was within the believer. For one enjoying an outstanding manifestation of Christ became thereby an object of worship. Before the 'Children of Light' were ten years old, such a situation actually developed, showing how close to the surface lay the chiliastic aspirations of that troubled age. James Naylor entered Bristol on the 24 October 1656 as a messiah. His horse was led by two women who grasped the bridle, ploughing knee-deep through the mud, and singing continuously. One

[1] M. L. Bailey, *Milton and Jacob Boehme* (Oxford, 1914), 100–1.
[2] W. C. Braithwaite, *The Beginnings of Quakerism* (2nd ed., 1955), 38.
[3] Evelyn Underhill, *Worship* (London, 1936), 307.
[4] R. M. Jones, *The Later Periods of Quakerism* (1921).

intoned 'Holy, Holy, Holy'. His six followers were convinced that Naylor was to lead the faithful to a new Jerusalem.

James Naylor himself had no positive convictions. 'It was given me what I was to declare,' he said, 'and ever since I have remained, not knowing today what I was to do tomorrow.' His followers hoped to proclaim Naylor at a Quaker meeting in the town on the afternoon of their arrival, but before they could do this, they were arrested.

Under questioning he showed himself completely indifferent. When asked why he entered the city in so strange a manner, he replied: 'It was for the praises of my Father, and I may not refuse anything that is moved of the Lord.' When asked what his followers meant by singing 'Holy, Holy, Holy', he replied: 'They are of an age to answer for themselves.'

The Bristol justices turned him over to Parliament, which appointed a committee of fifty-five M.P.s to examine him. Before them he maintained that he was merely an agent of the Lord, and all that he had done was forced on him by his followers. 'There was never anything since I was born', he declared, 'so much against my will and mind as this thing, to be set up as a sign in my going through these towns, for I knew I should lay down my life for it. But it was the Lord's will, to give it unto me to suffer such things to be done in me, and I durst not resist it.' After ten long days of debate Parliament resolved by ninety-six votes to eighty-two to spare his life. He was adjudged guilty of 'horrid blasphemy' and sentenced to the pillory. His tongue was pierced with a hot iron, and on his forehead was branded the initial letter of his crime—the letter B. As an added disgrace, he was sentenced to be whipped through the streets of the city his followers had led him through in that sad triumph.

(2)

Naylor's case focused Fox's attention on the problem of how far an individual might follow his conscience against the opinion of others, and, over the next four years, Fox introduced a system of monthly and quarterly meetings covering the whole country. Conformity became the rule.

By the time Charles II was 'restored', Fox realized that the Kingdom of Christ was not coming as soon as he had hoped. So, in a more sophisticated epistle, he laid down *The time of right-*

eousness and justice stretched forth over all merchants: 'Do rightly, justly, holily, equally to all people in all things; and that is according to that of God in every man.' He still stressed the need for simplicity in dress and for restraint in all forms of recreation, since to him it was a practical way of trying to redistribute wealth more equitably.

The Quakers too, began to prosper as individuals and a marked discrepancy began to appear in their social backgrounds. Fox, therefore, issued injunctions about Poor Relief. As early as *The Vials of Wrath upon the man of Sin* (1655) he wrote: 'Ye that set your nests on high, join house to house, field to field, till there be no place for the poor, woe is your position . . . The righteous God is coming to give to every one of you according to your works.'

'To every one of you, according to your works.' The idiom is becoming strangely familiar. It was first applied in poor relief.

It was in the Quaker schemes of poor relief that many community projects arose. In this, as in their industrial undertakings, they insisted on corporate action. The anabaptist P. C. Plockhoy in a pamphlet *The Way to make the poor in These and Other Nations Happy* (1659) had urged the foundation of 'Little Commonwealths' to carry out his schemes of co-operative production and housekeeping, but their attempts have greater relevance to England.

Thomas Lawson, a clerk to a monthly meeting, who was employed at Swarthmore to teach Mrs. Fell's daughters, addressed Parliament on the subject in 1660. In an *Appeal to the Parliament concerning the Poor that there may be not a beggar in England* (1660) he set out a 'platform':—a labour office in each parish should provide information to the officers so that provision could be made for their employment. Nine years later George Fox, in his organization for the Society, laid down that 'Friends should have and provide a house or houses where an hundred may have rooms to work in, and shops of all sorts of things to sell, and where widows and young women might work and live'.

This was not possible in view of the number of prisoners to be catered for and here the 'friends' organized co-operative work especially for those imprisoned for their faith in York Castle.

John Bellers was specially employed in relief work; he was later made treasurer of a fund for employing the poor, and soon was active in putting forward various proposals. From 1679 (when he was only 23) till 1696 (when he was 40) his fertile imagination evolved numerous projects which he committed to paper. One of them was *Proposals for Raising a College of Industry of all Useful Trades and Husbandry* (1696).

This work has had an immense importance on the direction of social thought. A century and a quarter later Francis Place was so impressed by it that he took it to Robert Owen who reprinted it, observing that 'any merit due for the discovery calculated to effect more substantial and permanent benefit to mankind than any ever yet contemplated by the human mind belongs exclusively to John Bellers'. Later, in 1867, Karl Marx described it as a 'phenomenon in political economy', and his enthusiastic endorsement has been echoed by Karl Kautsky and Eduard Bernstein.

The essence of Bellers' proposal is quite simple. A community of some three hundred producers should be established, costing, he reckoned, £18,000, and run on a joint stock basis. Like his successors he saw it as: 'a Community something like the example of primitive Christianity, that lived in common, and the Power that did attend it, bespeaks its Excellency'.

His proposals were brought before the yearly meeting in 1697 and the committee circulated them to different monthly and quarterly meetings asking whether they would be willing to encourage it 'by a voluntary contribution'. The committee, envisaged 'one House or Colledge for a beginning' being 'set on foote by a Joynt Stock by Friends of Estates throughout ye Kingdom (severall having subscribed considerably already)'.

But the districts were cold. So a Bill was drafted to present to Parliament in which Bellers was active too. In only one district, London, was his proposal adopted—Clerkenwell in 1701 where a Workhouse was established for thirty inmates. Bellers originally proposed that men and women of all occupations should work a farm, but the Clerkenwell Workhouse was more like a factory. A suggestion was in fact made in 1712 that it should be formally converted into one. But the inmates were mercifully either too old or too young. So what might have been an experimental community became a hospital and nursery, producing yarn and mops on the side. It ultimately became a school.

For experimental Christianity, especially in the field of corporate secular life, had no more powerful practitioners than the Quakers. The community at Nent Head, near Alston, in the northern Fells, pioneered by the London Lead Company in 1692, was followed by numerous other industrial ventures in the eighteenth century.

At its end, two interesting communities were essayed by Quakers. One was in France, where Robert Grubb of Clonmel in Ireland, together with Jean Marsillac of Congénies, backed by English friends, applied to the Council of the Department of Loir et Cher for permission to establish an industrial, commercial and artistic community, together with a school, in the castle of Chambord. It was to house eighty or a hundred workshops and introduce 'new trades and particular cultures possessed until now by England'. The Minister of the Interior was sympathetic but the outbreak of war made the scheme impossible.

A second was at Milford Haven in Wales where a great shipper, William Rotch, who had previously tried to make a Quaker settlement at Dunkirk, came with other Friends to found a colony based on whaling. They had been ruined by the American War of Independence and saw in Milford Haven a fine opportunity for an experiment in industrial co-operation. It too failed.[1]

These 'static' communities have not received, nor need they receive, the same considerate attention from historians as the 'dynamic' communities established by the great Quaker ironmasters at Swalewell, Ebbw Vale, and Coalbrookdale. But we shall meet the idea again.

[1] Isabel Grubb, *Quakerism and Industry before 1800* (1930), 143–4.

4

◇◇

The Philadelphians

◇◇

THE other leading Digger, William Everard, was at one time a member of a community at Bradfield under John Pordage, the vicar.[1] All of them 'lived in the highest spiritual state' under 'Father Abraham' (Pordage), and 'Deborah' (his wife). One outsider thought they tried to carry the 'perfection of monastical life too far'. They 'lived together in community', wrote Richard Baxter, 'and pretend to hold visible and sensible communion with the angels'.[2]

In August 1649 Pordage, as a result of reading the work of Jacob Boehme received 'not only a clear leading convicting light' but 'likewise received from the Lord a stamp and strong impression of power moving our wills to follow the light through the death of all things, to come up into the perfect life and image of God'.[3] Others beside Everard, joined him. One such recruit Philip Herbert, Earl of Pembroke, took Pordage's teaching too literally, and became a convinced millenarian. Later in life he was to visit King Charles II and :—

[1] G. H. Sabine, *The Works of Gerrard Winstanley* (1941), 104 n., remarks 'It is credible that Wm. Everard may have been the man of that name who lived with Pordage and he may have made Winstanley acquainted with Pordage's mysticism.' See also Christopher Hill, *Puritanism and Revolution* (1958), 316.

[2] *Reliquiae Baxterianae* (1696), 387, 285.

[3] *Innocence Appearing through the Dark Mists of Pretended Guilt* (1655), 78.

kneeling told his Majesty that he had a great message 'to deliver to him, and that was, the end of the world would be this year, and therefore desired his Majesty to prepare for it.' 'Well,' said the king, 'if it be so, yet notwithstanding I will give you seven years' purchase for your manor of Wilton.' Pembroke replied, 'No an please, your Majesty, it shall die with me' and so went away, making his Majesty and the whole Court merry with this fancy.[1]

Four other members of the community cast fitful gleams in the dark gloom of provincial millenarianism. One of them, Ebenezer Coppe, was an anabaptist whose 'Fiery Flying Roll' was burnt by order of Parliament in 1650. A second, Thomas Tany, had already served a term in Newgate Prison for proclaiming the rebuilding of the Temple and himself as the high priest. He disappeared after assaulting men at the Parliament House. A third was Roger Crab, a vegetarian ascetic, who described Oxford and Cambridge as 'The whore's great eyes' and the Church 'a Bawdy House'.[2]

Pordage was ejected from Bradfield in 1654 for blasphemy and immorality: blasphemy in view of the 'revalations' he had received, immorality in having had improper intercourse with a woman in London. His reply was the pamphlet *Innocence appearing through the Dark Mists of Pretended Guilt*, which in turn provoked a pamphlet from one of his judges comparing Pordage to Satan at noon.

On the restoration of Charles II Pordage took a small congregation in London. There he was joined by Mrs. Leade, a 39-year-old mother of four daughters, two of whom had died in infancy. From her account, Dr. Pordage's group now numbered about a hundred. Because of the plague in 1665 Pordage returned with them to Bradfield. Mrs. Pordage died in 1668, and Mrs. Leade's husband died two years later. Pordage returned to London and found her poverty-stricken, as the man to whom her husband had entrusted his money proved to be a swindler. Poor as she was in this world's goods she began to experience rich 'visions' of the next; and duly recorded them in a spiritual diary called *A Fountain of Gardens*. These visions encouraged Pordage and her 'to wait together in prayer and pure dedication'.

Pordage was a mild chiliast, but Mrs. Leade was a strict one.

[1] Hist. MSS. Comm. (Hastings), ii (1930), 150.
[2] M. L. Bailey, *Milton and Boehme* (Oxford, 1914), 141.

To her the real advent of Christ, the resurrection and transfiguration of all believers and the establishment of the glorified Church on earth was imminent, as the title of her next work, *The Heavenly Cloud Now Breaking* (1681) shows. When Pordage died in 1681, she used his tracts (which he never published during his lifetime) to supplement her own.

Treading her lonely millenarian path, Mrs. Leade issued *Revelation of Revelations* (1683), which attracted a number of German readers. Indeed she became so well known there that in 1694 when some German settlers were emigrating to Pennsylvania in the steps of F. D. Pastorius, they visited her to exchange millennial convictions. In Holland, too, followers arose. One of them, a young English doctor from Leyden, Francis Lee, found her living at Lady Mico's College, a house of charity near London.

Francis Lee was 34 when he first met Mrs. Leade in 1694. A former fellow of St. John's College, Oxford, he had refused to take the oath of allegiance to William and Mary, and had gone abroad. He has left us an account of how he was asked by a Rotterdam merchant called Finley to visit her to get 'a transcript of her writings'. So many correspondents were anxious to read her works that, when she became blind, he undertook to write letters from her dictation and dispatch them. And so her writings increased. *The Enochian Walks with God* (1694); *The Laws of Paradise* (1695); *The Wonders of God's Creation, Manifested in the Variety of Eight Worlds* (1695) followed each other in rapid succession. Lee also bound himself by marrying her daughter.

The English disciples of Mrs. Leade soon formed a community of their own and called themselves the Philadelphian Society. In 1696 Mrs. Leade dictated *A Message to them Withersoever Dispersed over the Whole Earth* followed by *The Tree of Faith: or, The Tree of Life, springing upon the Paradise of God* (1696), *The Ark of Faith* (1696) and *A Revelation of the Everlasting Gospel Message* (1697).

Apart from Lee, the most striking convert to the Philadelphians was Dr. Richard Roach.[1] Not only did he live with them, but he partook of their visions and was 'visited from above with extraordinary communications'. He published, with Lee, a

---

[1] Some of his papers are in the Bodleian Library (MS. Rawlinson).

monthly periodical for the society entitled *Theosophical Transactions* consisting of 'Memoirs, Conferences, Letters, Dissertations, Inquiries, etc. For the Advancement of Piety and Divine Philosophy'. The *Theosophical Transactions* contained an account of a New Christ said to have been born at Gutenberg in Bayreuth, and even had a representative in Germany in the person of young Johann Dittmar. German literalism corrupted the mystical teaching of Pordage and Mrs. Leade, and one Eva von Buttlar and two adherents professed to be representatives of the Trinity. She preached complete community of goods and unlimited sexual intercourse for her followers; at her trial in 1706 she alleged that a writing of Pordage lay at the root of her ideas.

These transactions worried the Archbishop of Canterbury who summoned Roach to see him since Roach was vicar of St. Augustine's, Hackney. Roach was too 'rooted in his opinions' to retract. At Hungerford Gardens 'great opposition and violence from the rude multitude' prevented further public meetings of the Philadelphians so they adjourned to Westmorland House. There they drew up 'constitutions' and also an explanation of the proceedings, to serve as an answer to the many inquiries they were receiving. As a 'new sect with a hard name' they were often confused with Quakers, so they pointed out:—

> As to their difference . . . they were not so silly as to place Religioun in Thouing and Theeing, in keeping on their Hats, or in a sad Countenance, as the Hypocrites had in our Saviour's time . . . As to their peculiar Principles (they held) That the Coming of Christ was near at Hand; and therefore they think it their Duty to warn and awaken the World, that they may prepare for that great and solemn Time, by a good Life, Universal Charity, and Union among the Protestant Churches.[1]

Another chiliast who was attracted by the Philadelphian Society was Thomas Beverley who in a dozen or so pamphlets forecast the millennium for the year 1697. Roach, in his *Imperial Standard Advanced*, records the change of mind induced in him. 'Mr. B. desir'd, and had a conference with the Society; in which they speaking of the Kingdom first in Spirit, and Inward Power; and not expecting the great things which he did, at that Time,

---

[1] Nils Thune, *The Behmenists and the Philadelphians* (Upsala, 1948), 93.

and so nothing being found to Answer His Scheme of Things, he concluded Over-hastily against this Own Line of Time and Alter'd it to 1700.' The Germans (who took Mrs. Leade far more seriously than the English) numbered Beverley amongst the Philadelphians and translated one of his works.

The constitution was laid down in 1697. With German money, the Philadelphians could keep Mrs. Leade in full communion with the spirit world, and in 1699 she obliged with *The Sign of the Times, Forerunning the Kingdom of Christ and Evidencing what is to come.*

Lee himself explored the practical aspects of the Old Testament story. One of his tracts was *On Naval Architecture, as Applied to Noah's Ark, showing how it was Accommodated to Live in a Tempest of Waters.* His piety and energy had one good practical effect. It is generally believed that he suggested to Robert Nelson, F.R.S. (his friend, whose life he was commissioned to write), the foundation of Charity Schools.[1] That pattern was to become almost endemic amongst the mystics: if the new dispensation was not to be vouchsafed for their generation, it should be made possible for the next. Education was the invariable concomitant of Utopist endeavour.

The Philadelphians broke up in 1703 and Lee became a Roman Catholic just before his death in 1719. Roach lived on to spread the millenarian gospel, and in *The Great Crisis, or the Mystery of the Times and Seasons Unfolded* (1725) and *The Imperial Standard of Messiah Triumphant Coming now in the Power and Kingdom of His Father to reign with the Saints on Earth* (1728) extended Mrs. Leade's visions.[2]

Whilst Roach explored the clouds, another neo-Philadelphian did much to alleviate men's lot on earth. Mysticism demands a kind of asceticism, and by a singular chance this doctrine was assimilated by George Cheyne, a Falstaffian figure, 30 years old and thirty-one stones in weight, who came to London in 1701, lording it in taverns, eating and drinking till his bulk excited the

[1] 'He was the first that put Mr. Hoare and Mr. Nelson upon the founding of Charity Schools, upon the same plan as that of Halle in Germany, and was continually encouraging and promoting all manner of Charities.' F. Secretan, *Life of the Pious Robert Nelson* (1866), 70.

[2] An account of Lee and Mrs. Leade can be found in *Notes and Materials for a Biography of William Law* (1854), together with his correspondence with Henry Dodwell (pp. 188–258).

comment of those with whom he rioted. Part of his personal therapy was a course of Bath waters, part a regimen of abstemiousness. But, finding that appetite returned, and with it increasing corpulence, he became, by personal experience, a believer in vegetarianism. At the age of 49 he published *Observations concerning the Nature and due Method of Treating the Gout* (1720). Most of the English disorders, he said, began in immoderate diet, lack of proper exercise among the upper classes, and an uncertain climate, which closed the pores making normal perspiration impossible. Cheyne had begun to capitalize his own experiences, later to be graphically compiled in *The English Malady* (1733). Between his *Observations on the Gout* (1720) and *Essay on Health and Long Life* (1724) he practised his temperance and vegetarian theories on himself. The result was highly successful, and for the remaining nineteen years of his life (he died in 1742 at the age of 72), he was an enthusiastic apostle of food reform. He was also a successful one, for his *Essay on Health* ran to nine editions in thirty years, and was being published over a hundred years later. It was much cited by John Wesley, who used it extensively when compiling his own *Primitive Physic* in 1764.[1]

Cheyne introduced the works of Boehme to his great friend William Law [2] in whom the movement found its greatest mouthpiece. Law was so interested in Lee that he borrowed from Lee's daughter, Mrs. de la Fontaine, many of her father's manuscripts and copied several of them by his own hand. These he kept with him at King's Cliffe, a farm near Stamford where he retired in 1740 with Mrs. Hutcheson and Miss Hester Gibbon, the historian's aunt. One of the reasons why Law never married was revealed by himself just before he went to King's Cliffe:—

John the Baptist came out of the Wilderness burning and shining, to preach the Kingdom of Heaven at hand. Look at this great saint, all ye that desire to preach the Gospel. Now if this holy Baptist, when he came to Jerusalem and had preached a while upon penitence, and the Kingdom of Heaven at hand, had made an offering of his Heart to some fine young *Lady of great accomplishments,* had not this put an end to all that burning shining in his character?

[1] For a good study of Cheyne see C. A. Moore, *Backgrounds of English Literature, 1700–1760* (Minneapolis, 1953).
[2] J. H. Overton, *William Law* (London, 1881), 92.

For the next twenty-one years he and his two female companions tried to carry out the precepts of his *Serious Call*. Law was the great idealist and mystic of the early eighteenth century.

When another graduate of Leyden, Bernard Mandeville, a contemporary of Lee's, wrote the cynical analysis of eighteenth-century society known as *The Fable of the Bees, or Private Vices Public Benefits* (1714), showing that human beings are essentially depraved, pouring scorn on the charity schools founded by the S.P.C.K., Law refuted it in print. Mandeville's thesis, so fundamentally opposed to that of the millenarians, as indeed of all men who believed in revelation of any kind, needed refutation, and Law's was so successful that it was republished by F. D. Maurice in 1846.

Law's philosophy was contained in his *Serious Call*, a book which exercised a great influence over John Wesley. Though they quarrelled, Wesley acknowledged 'Mr. Law . . . was once a kind of oracle to me'.[1] 'Law came before the Gospel', said one of Wesley's friends.[2]

Law channelled Behmenist thought into the main current of English mysticism, and by his detailed work (in the study) at King's Cliffe after 1740, made it 'safe' to study. But the chiliastic element in it kept popping out to disconcert contemporaries and their successors.[3]

In paying tribute the 'fulness of heart and intellect' that 'burst forth in many a simple page' of Fox, Boehme and 'the pious and fervid William Law', S. T. Coleridge remarked:—

> the writings of these mystics acted in no slight degree to prevent my mind from being imprisoned within the outline of any single dogmatic system. They contributed to keep alive the *heart* in the *head*; . . . If they were too often a moving cloud of smoke to me by day, yet they were always a pillar of fire throughout the night, during my wanderings through the wilderness of doubt, and enabled me to skirt, without crossing, the sandy deserts of utter disbelief.[4]

[1] For the relationship between them see C. W. Towlson, *Moravian and Methodist* (1957), 14–16.

[2] Venn, *Family Annals*, 72.

[3] *The Works of Jacob Behmen. . . to which is Prefixed the Life of the Philosopher Left by the Rev. Wm. Law* (J. Richardson, 1764). B. M. Press Mark C. 126. K.1. Coleridge's main comments can be seen in vol. 1, pp. 125–7.

[4] J. Shawcross, (ed.) *Coleridge's Biographia Literaria*, (Oxford 1907) I, 98.

5

<hr style="border-top: dotted" />

Camisards

<hr style="border-top: dotted" />

(1)

THREE years after the mortal remains of 81-year-old Mrs. Leade had been laid to rest in Bunhill Fields cemetery by Richard Roach, the millenarian spirit revived at Purley in Surrey. According to him: 'several persons, who had been concerned in the First, appeard and bore their Testimony again, yet in such a Manner under the Conduct and Protection of the Spirit as not to be expos'd to Injuries and Insults as before'.[1] These new millenarians were Camisards from France, so called because they wore their shirts outside their breeches.[2]

To avoid being chained to the galleys or forced to expiate their heresies as exiles in New Orleans (at the mouth of the Mississippi), they either formed 'assemblies of the Desert' in France or fled to England. They taught that there were four

[1] Thune, op. cit., 136.
[2] The name Camisards has various explanations. Mountaineers wore their shirts outermost to distinguish each other during the wars of Louis XIII. Jean Cavalier, their leader, whose *Memoirs of the Wars of the Cevennes* were published in Dublin in 1726, says that his men carried two shirts, one of which they wore; and the other which they carried in their knapsacks. Being on the move all the time they had no time to wash their linen and used to leave it with their friends. See also Charles Tylor, *The Camisards* (London, 1878). H. Desroche, *Les shakers américains* (Paris, Ed. Minuit, 1953). See also G. H. Dodge, *The Political Theory of the Huguenots of the Dispersion, with special reference to the thought and influence of Pierre Jurieu* (New York, 1947), 158–64.

degrees of inwardness of the spirit. The lowest (*L'Avertisse-ment*) was the intimation that the spirit was about to descend, the second (*Le Souffle*) described the actual inspiration of the spirit. The third (*La Prophétie*) enabled the recipient to judge. The final stage (*Le Don*) signified that the recipient was so suffused with the spirit that he could perform healing miracles and withdraw from earthly affairs.

They despised learning. As a blessing pronounced on 18 July 1708 ran:—

> Tis not by University learning that thou shalt be qualified for the work I design thee to be engaged in; therefore, depend not upon it, for it will be of no use to thee in this particular. But depend thou alone upon the leading of the Holy Spirit, and thou shalt find that by the same thou wilt be better qualified for my work than thou could'st be by all the learning of both the universities in the land.[1]

Their leaders in England were Durand Fage and Elie Marion whose oratory and gestures were bizarre, violent. On one occasion Fage cried 'Mon enfant, je m'en vais répandre sur les ennemis mes jugemens terribles, et ma dernière sentence sera, tring, trang, swing, swang, hing hang.'[2]

Elie Marion, possessing *Le Don*, spoke darkly of the end of the world and the burning of London. His *Prophetical Warnings* (1707) so provoked the more established French churches in London that he and two of his helpers, John Daude and Nicholas Facio, were fined twenty marks and pilloried at Charing Cross and at the Royal Exchange. Marion had a paper attached to his forehead, advertising his crimes. It ran 'Elias Marion, convicted for falsely and profanely pretending himself to be a true prophet, and printing and uttering things as dictated and revealed to him by the Spirit of God, to terrifie the Queens People'.[3]

Their English converts were equally picturesque. The first, Sir Richard Bulkeley, was a humpbacked virtuoso, who had demonstrated to the Royal Society a model of a chariot he had

---

[1] Henry Nicholson, *Falsehood of the New Prophets Manifested*. Nicholson was a M.D. who correlated muscular motion with the pressure of the atmosphere.

[2] N.N. *An Account of the lives* . . . *of the Three French Prophets* (1708).

[3] Edmund Chishull, Appendix to a Sermon: *The Great Danger and Mistake of all new and uninspired Prophecies relative to the end of the World*: Being a sermon (on James V. 8) preach'd at Sergeants-Inn Chappell Nov. 23rd, 1707. This ran to more than three editions. Chishull was later to engage in controversy with William Whiston.

invented which could not overturn. Among the crowded audience which heard him giving a 'stupendous relation of what it had performed' was John Evelyn who remarked, 'There was only these inconveniences yet to be remedied; that it would not containe above one person; That it was ready to fire every 10 miles, & being plac'd & playing on no fewer than 10 rollers, made so prodigious noise, as was almost intolerable. These particulars the virtuosi were desired to excogitate the remedies, to render the Engine of extraordinary use', etc.[1] The second, John Lacy, formerly a wealthy member of the congregation of Edmund Calamy, the Nonconformist historian, wielded his pen on their behalf. The constant iteration of the past sufferings of the 'ejected' led Lacy to dream about the future of the 'selected', and an unsuccessful lawsuit discredited the efficacy of secular justice in his eyes. So in 1707 he gave the world *The Prophetical Warnings of John Lacy*. In this, he claimed miraculous powers. Bulkeley supported him, and resolved to sell his estate and give it to the cause, hoping that Lacy would cure him of his stone, his rupture and his hump back. The third Camisard convert, Thomas Emes, had derided Colbatch's theory that alkali was mortific and 'acid' was curative in *A Dialogue between Alkali and Acid* (1698). He had also argued in the same year *The Reasonableness and Union of Natural and the True Religion*. He now attained such a status amongst the Camisards that when he died on Christmas Day 1707, Lacy predicted his resurrection at Bunhill Fields on 25 May 1708. Lacy's prophecy excited wider attention than Marion's sojourn in the pillory; and the trained bands were called out to control the crowds assembled to witness the promised event. The Attorney General prosecuted Sir Richard Bulkeley and Calamy reproved Lacy in *A Caveat against New Prophets* (1708). In 1709 the House of Commons passed a Bill enabling foreign Protestants only to be naturalized if they took the oath of allegiance and received the Sacrament in a Reformed Congregation.

Marion also won the support of two energetic writers, Francis Misson and Abraham Whitro. Francis Misson was of French birth. He migrated to England in 1685 on the revocation of the Edict of Nantes and became tutor to the younger grandson of James, Duke of Ormonde. He subsequently made his name with

[1] E. S. de Beer (ed.), *The Diary of John Evelyn* (Oxford, 1955), iv. 483–4.

a racy account of life in London. His pen was turned to their service and in his *Théâtre Sacré des Cévennes, ou Récit des prodiges arrivés dans cette partie du Languedoc* (1707), he championed Marion with force; his work much impressed John Lacy who translated it into English. The second, Abraham Whitro, issued in 1709 *The Warnings of the eternal Spirit spoken by the mouth of . . . A.W.*, for which Sir Richard Bulkeley wrote the preface.

They spoke of the new heaven, the new earth, the first resurrection, and the New Jerusalem descending from above. As Thomas Brown wrote:—

> this great work was to be wrought by a spiritual power proceeding from the mouths of those who should, by the gift of the spirit, be sent forth in great numbers to labour in the vineyard, and their mission should be attested by sighs from heaven
> . . . they endeavoured to support their predictions by the many scripture prophecies concerning the millenium, or reign of Christ, and universal peace on earth. This message, they said, they were to proclaim to every nation under heaven, beginning first in England.[1]

'Prophecy' spread from London to the provinces. Stephen Halford of Birmingham was tempted to emulate Lacy until his friends confined him. Admonitions, reprimands and denunciations of these 'prophecies' publicized them even more. Dr. Josiah Woodward issued some sharp *Remarks on Modern Prophets* (1708), Francis Hutchinson gave to the world a *Short View of the Pretended Spirit of Prophecy* (1708) in which he sketched its rise from 1688 to the year 1708, and Nathaniel Spinckes issued *The Shortest Way with the French Prophets, or an Impartial Relation of the Rise Progress and total Suppression of those Seducers: The New Pretenders to Prophecy examined, and their pretences shown to be groundless and false* (1709); he followed these up with the *New pretenders to prophecy Re-examined, and their pretences shewn again to be groundless and false* (1710). Spinckes' wrath was called forth especially by Bulkeley and Whitro. It is interesting that Hutchinson became an Irish bishop and Spinckes a nonjuring bishop.

But before their translations Bulkeley had died. He was laid to rest, not in Bunhill Fields, but in a black marble tomb at

---

[1] Thomas Brown, *An Account of the People called Shakers* (Troy, 1812), 310.

Ewell, Surrey. Lacy, deprived of his position, deserted his wife and migrated with a certain Betty Gray to Lancashire. It was claimed that there were four hundred prophets in various parts of the country and Lacy wandered about 'sighing' and 'quaking'. [1]

One of those who was affected by the Camisards was William Whiston. He had a conference with them at his house in 1713.[2] Whiston was a Fellow of the Royal Society, and had succeeded Newton as Lucasian Professor of Mathematics at Cambridge. When the Camisards had first appeared Whiston had published *An Essay on the Revelation of St. John so far as it concerns Past and Present Times* (1706). In this he stated that the Holy City, the New Jerusalem and the Marriage of the Lamb are, as it were, one and the same thing. This State, he went on, is the same as the Binding of Satan and of the Reign of the Saints for a thousand years after the first resurrection. His unconventional theology led to his resignation of the chair in 1710.[3]

In fairness to him it must be said that Isaac Newton was suspected of 'ploughing with Behmen's heifer' and of 'shutting himself up for three months to search for the philosopher's stone in the writings of Boehme'. This, as has been shown, was unjustifiable.[4] William Whiston, F.R.S., was, if not a Behmenist, at least a millenarian. In 1710, he published *Primitive Christianity Revived*, and in 1715 started a society for promoting primitive Christianity in Cross Street, Hatton Garden. Amongst its members were John Gatty, Arthur Onslow, Thomas Emlyn and Thomas Chubb, all animated by Whiston's forecast that the millenium would occur in 1715. (Whiston later altered this). Gatty was a deist and Chubb became the first preacher to describe himself as a unitarian in England. By 1726 Whiston, still a convinced millenarian, had models made of the Tabernacle of Moses and the Temple of Jerusalem. He lectured on these at London, Bristol, Bath and Tunbridge Wells. He looked for the restoration of the Jews to Palestine and confidently predicted the millennium would occur in 1746 when the gaming laws would be

[1] See 'John Lacy and the Modern Prophets' in James Sutherland, *Background for Queen Anne* (London, 1939), 36–74.
[2] *Memoirs of the Life and Writings of Mr. William Whiston* (1753), p. 119.
[3] op. cit., 98–99.
[4] Arthur Wormhoudt, 'Newton's Philosophy in William Law', *Journal of the History of Ideas* (New York, 1949), x. 421–9, shows that Law and Brewster (Newton's nineteenth century biographer) were mistaken.

swept away. His translation of Josephus, first published in 1737, was a great success, being re-published many times and being quoted, amongst others, by John Minter Morgan. Whiston's placing of the millennium in 1746 was not a little influenced by this.[1] For all his eccentricities he left his mark; Goldsmith was said to have had him in mind when he wrote the *Vicar of Wakefield*, he was a friend of Addison and Steele, and Swift praised his honesty.

(2)

Whilst Whiston and Lacy were, in their distinct ways, evangelizing in England, a new adjutant of the Camisards appeared in London in 1731, Benjamin du Plan. Du Plan was a believer in the 'inspired' prophetesses—indeed he received his call from one of them. 'I have always maintained,' he wrote, 'both in public and private, that there have been amongst us, and still are, those who have received extraordinary gifts from the Holy Spirit. . . . I have known those who without study have spoken the wonderful things of God much more fluently and convincingly than those who have prepared themselves by study.'[2] In London, du Plan took 'great pains' to organize the Camisards and claimed by 1748 that his mission was on a solid basis.[3] E. D. Andrews says that there was a kind of 'loose federation' of the groups under his control. The 'Desert Meetings' in Picardy grew in number and strength as thousands flocked at night time to hear the inspired prophetesses, securing themselves by posting sentries to look for the approach of government troops.[4]

'Desert Meetings' is perhaps a strong term to apply to similar meetings held in England, yet in Lancashire such meetings were being held, if not on such a large scale. At Bolton-le-Moors, for instance, on the outer periphery of Manchester, the Camisards had a flourishing cell. In about 1747, two members of that cell received a 'further degree of light and power' which led them to separate from the Quakers. These two, Jane Wardley and her

[1] *Memoirs*, 333.

[2] D. Bonnefon, *Benjamin du Plan* (London, 1878).

[3] Tylor, op. cit., 2 and 3.

[4] E. D. Andrews, *The People Called Shakers. A Search for the Perfect Society.* (New York, 1953), 6. H. Desroche, *Les shakers américains. Néo-christianisme ou présocialisme* (Paris, 1955).

husband James, still used the techniques of the Quaker meetings, but their 'silent meditation' was interrupted by passionate, anti-clerical revelations. Jane Wardley, or 'mother Jane' would 'with a mighty trembling' walk up and down the floor declaiming :–

> Repent. For the Kingdom of God is at Hand. The new heaven and new earth prophesied of old is about to come. The marriage of the Lamb, the first resurrection and the new Jerusalem descending from above, these are even now at the door. And when Christ appears again, and the true church rises in full and transcendant glory, than all anti-Christian denominations—the priests, the church, the pope—will be swept away.[1]

The Wardley society at Bolton acquired adherents. One of them was a former Methodist, John Hocknell, another Ann Lee—a short, stout woman with a fair complexion, blue eyes and light brown hair. She was to become a mistress—messiah of a new faith. Ann Lee joined the Wardleys in 1758 when she was twenty-two.

Because the Wardleys danced and cried out in strange tongues, they were known as the Shaking Quakers, or Shakers. Ann Lee, their recruit, was the daughter of a blacksmith called Standerin. She soon forged ahead in a hot apocalypse, moulding souls for God in Manchester. The intensity of her evangel was conditioned by her strong revulsion from the earthly pleasures of being wife to a blacksmith for whom she had unsuccessfully borne four children. For ten years or more she led her followers, suffering imprisonment for her violent 'shakings' on the Sabbath, where she was fed with milk and other liquids by a tobacco-pipe stem through a keyhole.

It was in one of these periods of imprisonment that Ann Lee received a vision of the primeval sin of Adam and Eve, and emerged as an apostle of celibacy. From now on she was known as the 'Bride of the Lamb' or 'Mother Ann'.

In her new role she received another vision of a tree with shining leaves that told her to go to America where the Church of Christ's second appearance would be founded. So with her husband, brother, niece and some relatives, she left Liverpool in 1774. Here her title of Mother was really earned, for in the

[1] W. S. Warder, *A Brief Sketch of the Religious Society of People called Quakers* (London, 1818).

next and last ten years of her life she created a network of Shaker communities in the eastern states.

Eleven of these communities were organized before the end of the eighteenth century. Watervliet and New Lebanon both took shape in New York State in 1787, followed some years later by Hancock, and the two families at West Tittsfield in Massachusetts, all in 1793, and New Gloucester, Maine, in 1794. Of these by far the largest was New Lebanon, which until its dissolution in 1947 had a total membership of 3,202 people. Eight more communities and eleven para-communities were subsequently added in the nineteenth century.

These successful experiments excited the interest of, amongst others, Robert Owen, to whom W. S. Warder,[1] a Philadelphia Quaker, reported in 1816, and who incorporated Warder's report almost verbatim in Number 19 of the *Economist*.[2] Others whom we will meet again in these pages were impressed by the sacramental nature of the Shakers' regard for the Lord. Harriet Martineau,[3] James Silk Buckingham,[4] Charles Lane,[5] Mary Hennell,[6] were some of the many who made known to the English the community life of the Shakers. They were to continue that influence till the time of Tolstoy.[7]

[1] See Robert Owen, *New View of Society* (1818).

[2] 2 June 1821.

[3] Harriet Martineau, 'The Shakers', *The Penny Magazine* (London, 1887).

[4] James Silk Buckingham, *America, Historical, Statistic and Descriptive* (London, 1831).

[5] Charles Lane, 'A Day with the Shakers', *The Dial* (Boston, 1843).

[6] Mary Hennell, *An Outline of the various Social Systems and Communities which have been founded on the principle of co-operation* (1844).

[7] It is said that *The Millennial Church* (1823), was written at the request of a Russian Consul in New York for publication in Russia (Andrews, op. cit., 221). Tolstoy (whom we shall meet later) carried on a correspondence with Frederick Evans.

6

❖◇❖

Moravians

❖◇❖

(1)

Mrs. Leade's writings also influenced Count Zinzendorf in Germany who organized the pietists of Wittgenstein into a Philadelphian Society.[1] Zinzendorf was a great organizer. From his student days at Halle, when he had established the 'Order of the Mustard Seed', whose members wore a gold ring on which were engraved the words 'No man liveth unto himself' (Rom. XIV: 7), he had been busy. After getting married he bought an estate at Bertholdsdorf, near Great Hennersdorf in Upper Lusatia. He transformed this into a model village, with a school, a bookseller's shop, and a dispensary. Asked to give asylum at Fulneck in Moravia to some exiles who were being persecuted for their religion he founded Herrnhut ('The Place God will guard') for which he discovered and revived the ancient constitution of the Moravian Church. From now on he set himself to renew the life of the Moravian Church, vowing 'As long as I live I will do my utmost to see to it that the little company of the Lord's disciples shall be preserved for him until he comes'.[2]

[1] Nils Thune, *The Behmenists and Philadelphians* (Upsala, 1948), p. 149.
[2] For a general account of the Moravians see W. G. Addison, *The Renewed Church of the United Brethren 1722–1930* (1931), A. Bost, *A History of the Bohemian and Moravian Brethren* (1834), C. W. Towlson, *Methodist and Moravian* (1957), and G. A. Warner, *The Beginnings of the Brethren's Church in England* (1901). Some Moravian archives are in the John Rylands Library at Manchester.

Moravian ideas came flooding into England, first through a wealthy, inquisitive and conscientious Yorkshire clergyman, called Benjamin Ingham, who found them 'more like the Primitive Christians than any other Church now in the world'. Ingham was very impressed by their living 'together in perfect love and peace having, for the present, all things in common'. 'In their business', he wrote, 'they are diligent and industrious, in all their dealings strictly just and conscientious. In everything they behave themselves with great meekness, sweetness and humility.'[1] Ingham was a friend of John Wesley, having travelled with him to Georgia.

One of Zinzendorf's converts, Boehler, a Pietist trained at Jena, was received into the Moravian Church in 1737, and came to England a year later.[2] On 1 May 1738, he drew up rules for a 'society', enabling it to become a self-governing democratic body where 'everyone without distinction, submitted to the determination of his brethren'. It flourished under another friend of Wesley, James Hutton, who hired the Great Meeting House in Fetter Lane to accommodate members. This also impressed Wesley.

At Ingham's invitation a second missionary, John Toelschig, came to Yorkshire in 1739 and was followed by a third, Spangenberg, who made his headquarters at Smith House, near Halifax, where, every Saturday, Yorkshire Moravians would meet for a midday meal or 'love feast'. Three years later, in February 1743, Zinzendorf himself arrived and founded the first Moravian community in England. The story goes that he was visiting the sick child of a Moravian missionary at Pudsey when he found himself looking over a rough briar-covered tract known as Lamb's Hill. The vista so impressed him that he told Ingham, who promptly bought it in January 1744 for the Brethren, giving part for buildings and part on a yearly rent for cultivation (later he granted it to the community for five hundred years). This was the origin of the first Moravian community in Britain. Consecrated in 1746 with a chapel and organ it was reinforced by houses for labourers, sisters and the brethren. John Wesley, a one-time member of the Moravian community at Fetter Lane, described it as 'on the side of a hill, commanding all the vale

---

[1] Luke Tyerman, *The Oxford Methodists* (1873), 68.
[2] J. Hutton, *A History of the Moravian Church* (1895), 131.

beneath, and the opposite hill. The front is exceedingly grand, though plain, being faced with smooth white stone. The Germans suppose it will cost by the time it is finished about three thousand pounds. It is well if it be not nearer ten. But it is no concern of the English brethren. They are told (and patently believe) that "all the money will come from beyond the sea".'[1]

(2)

Fulneck, as this English settlement of the Moravians was called, was a real community. A clothing-business was begun in 1748, followed by a worsted and glove factory, a farm, a tailor's shop, and a shoemaker's: all operated by the men of the community. The sisters helped with needlework and hosiery. Each trade was called a diacony and conducted business for the benefit of the whole congregation. Thus James Charlesworth, a single brother, was appointed manager or 'deacon' of a cloth-weaving factory which not only kept a number of other single brothers actively employed but did a great trade with Portugal and Russia. Other diaconies were organized in the shape of a bakery, a glove factory, an inn, and a general store. The profits from these diaconies (for all engaged in them only received a salary) went to augment the funds of the congregation. Even single sisters made the community famous by their needlework and their marble-paper.[2]

Its frigid economic system was controlled by a rigid moral law. Only elders could allow a member to spend a night away from the community. Single brothers had to sleep in one dormitory, rise at the same hour and say prayers before breakfast. Single sisters had to wear the same uniform of black, grey or brown, with a white three-cornered shawl. A single brother could not lift an eye, much less a hand, to a single sister without permission of the elders.

These elders were the ministers, three 'labourers', one single brother, one single sister, and a widow. In monthly meetings they would judge by Christian precept or, where that was ambiguous, by 'lot'. This 'lot' was an old custom of the Moravians dating back to 1467, when they nominated their first synod

---

[1] *Journal of John Wesley*, ed. N. Curnock (1938), iii. 292.

[2] Wm. Cudworth, *Round about Bradford* (1876), 504–5; J. Hutton, *History of the Moravian Church* (1895), 262 ff.

by slips of paper placed in a vase. It was regarded as the authentic voice of God and was only abolished in 1857. It had been used by Zinzendorf when, on 7 January 1731, he had placed two texts in a box, 1 Cor. II. 21 and 2 Thess. II. 15, as to whether or no the Moravian Church should be renewed. The lot, as used at Fulneck, consisted of a box of Christian texts presented to the questioner, who thus selected the authentic, divine ruling on a moral problem. Zinzendorf believed in it so firmly that he always carried around with him a little green book with detachable leaves, each inscribed with a text, so that in a dilemma he could pull out a leaf at random for guidance.[1]

Below the elders in the hierarchy were the choir elders, an advisory body. These consisted of members of the 'choirs' also established by Zinzendorf. Each choir had its separate age and status group: married people, widowers, widows' choir, single brethren, single sisters, youths, great girls, little boys, little girls, and infants in arms. The 'choirs' of the womenfolk were distinguished by the ribbons in their caps: blue for married women, white for widows, pink for young women, and red for girls under 18. These choirs supplanted in many respects a normal family. All premises and finances were managed by a third body, the elective congregation committee. Descending the hierarchy from this came the large helpers' conference, consisting of the committee, the elders' conference and others. Finally came the congregation council, elected by the congregations. Needless to say all elections were confirmed by 'the lot'.[2]

Zinzendorf also tried to 'settle' the London congregation, so on 20 April 1750 he bought Lindsey House, and the adjoining Beaufort House. It had once belonged to Sir Thomas More, whose *Utopia*, published 234 years before, might well have provided the Brethren with an historical precedent. A chapel and a minister's house were built, the mansion itself renovated, and a cemetery laid out. Plans were laid to establish a settlement with choir houses and other dwellings. Over £12,000 was spent on making it a busy Moravian headquarters.

[1] A. G. Spangenberg, *The Life of Nicholas, Count Zinzendorf*, Trans. B. de la Trobe (1838).

[2] John Wesley used 'the lot' for advice about his proposed marriage with Sophia Hopkey. The establishment of the London Congregation as a separate society was effected through it in 1742 and for a long time no pupil could be admitted to a school unless his name was confirmed by the lot. Towlson, op. cit., 243–4.

From here Zinzendorf launched a campaign for the imposition of discipline, as opposed to religion, on would-be Moravians in England. In a *Consolatory Letter to Members of the Societies that are in Some Connection with the Brethren's Congregation* in 1752, he refused to accept converts who refused to join Moravian communities. Moravians, he said, could only receive brothers with caution, and could not accept converts from other churches who would not observe the strict socio-religious code he had prescribed.

(3)

But the communistic nature of these communities excited criticism. Even the open-minded Earl of Shelburne, known to his age as the 'Jesuit of Berkeley Square', was perplexed by them. Housing Germans with their strange names they were obvious targets for the xenophobic sniper. Soon accusations of treachery were levelled against them. At Fulneck, Gussenbauer was arrested, tried at Wakefield and imprisoned in York Castle. At Hadfield in Essex, where a Moravian school had been established, the brethren were accused of being adherents of the Young Pretender and of housing barrels of gunpowder; a mob from nearby Thaxted soon surrounded the Moravian school and tried to force an entry. Their communal meals or 'love feasts' were regarded as immoral; their conventual lives as Catholic aberrations. They were accused of kidnapping single women for their settlements, and of proselytizing for the Papacy or for a pope of their own. They were suspected as antinomians, who dismissed 'duties' as immaterial and regarded 'faith' alone as a necessary justification of life. One M.P. pointed out in the House of Commons in 1749 how dangerous it was to have Moravians discouraging their converts from bearing arms.

The charge of antinomianism was a severe one, and pressed home by John Wesley in *A Short View of the Difference between the Moravian Brethren, lately in England and the Rev. Mr. John and Charles Wesley* and *A Dialogue between an Antinomian and his Friend*.

Criticism was accompanied by a disaster. The English diaconies had invested £67,000 with a Portuguese Jew called Gomez Serra who in 1752 suddenly stopped payment. This loss, coupled with an existing debt of £30,000 incurred in their heavy building programme, led to Zinzendorf being accused of robbery and fraud, and his followers of practising rites not sanctioned by the New Testament.

One English bishop, Lavington, the Bishop of Exeter, in *The Moravians Compared and Detected* (1754) compared them to swine, and their feasts as debauches of the worst kind. John Wesley in *Queries to Count Zinzendorf* (1755) challenged Zinzendorf to explain himself. This Zinzendorf now did. So did Hutton. In eight pamphlets they disposed of the charges of forgery and debauchery. They also published a hymn-book, an important addition to Christian worship (since the Anglicans only sang psalms), which certainly had its effect on its day and age, and stressed the adoration of Christ in Christian worship. They also published the rules of their order, *Statutes: or the General Principles of Practical Christianity, extracted out of the New Testament* (1755). This pocket guide to souls for walking in the life of the Spirit was a necessary astringent. It marks the high tide of Moravian influence in England. And, to show their enemies just how strong they were, two more Moravian communities were founded.

The first began to take shape at Gloonen in Northern Ireland in 1755 where Cennick, a Methodist turned Moravian, had been active for nine years. Unfortunately the lease was a short one. Three years later, when Brother Horne got the opportunity of a long lease of 200 acres from Charles O'Neill, he took it. On 20 November 1759, the Moravians entered and began to build with great energy. A house for the single brethren was built first and by 7 November 1760 was occupied by brethren from Gloonen. This new site was renamed Gracehill. Land was levelled for larger buildings. In good weather on 12 March 1765 a special liturgy was held at Ballykennedy where the assembled choirs sang 'Oh how amiable thy habitations are!' A house for the single sisters followed in 1766, which held fifty sisters and two overseers. The original house for the single brethren was replaced in 1768 by another housing thirty brethren. A congregation shop was finished by 1783; enlarged seven years later and after another seven it had to find larger premises. Day schools were built in 1788, a girls' boarding school in 1790 (exempt from window tax), and in 1805 a boarding school for boys was built by Hartley and Montgomery. In 1819 a third larger building was erected for the single brethren. The community was housed in a large square, with cross-roads north and south from and to the open country. The centre was planted with shrubbery, bounded by beds with forest trees at intervals and gravelled walks. It became such an integral part of the landscape that it escaped pillage in the 1798 rebellion.

Its four schools—a boys' academy, a ladies' college, and two primary schools—had a number of distinguished pupils, one being John Nicholson, the hero of Delhi, whose statue stands in the market square at Lisburn. But their supervision, lamented an unnamed historian of the movement, 'very much engrossed the attention of the clerical faculty, and there was a partial collapse of that gospel spreading instrumentation which had brought the true light and God's saving health to the north of the Island'.[1]

(4)

A third English community, tentatively begun in 1743, at Dukinfield, near Manchester, with 'choirs' in private houses, was reorganized in 1757 when a house for single brethren was obtained. In 1758 houses for the single brethren and single sisters were built, then enlarged. A trombone band was formed, a school for girls built in 1760, and another for boys in 1766. By 1771 more land was necessary.

The brethren at Dukinfield had the same trouble as their brethren at Gloonen: land was leasehold and on a precarious life-lease at that. So they decided to settle elsewhere. After inspecting various sites Bishop Watteville bought a fifty-three-acre farm at Droylsden in 1779. Joseph Saxon and his family moved in, measures were taken to level the land, brick kilns were built, and Brother John Lees of Ashton undertook to be the inspector and paymaster of the work. The brethren of Dukinfield contributed generously, and seemed reconciled to the fact that their settlement was a gathering place preparatory to the accomplishment of the Lord's place elsewhere. On 9 June 1784 the foundation stones of the chapel and the choir houses were laid by Benjamin de la Trobe in the presence of a large crowd.

[1] *Moravian Chapels and Preaching Houses in Great Britain and Ireland* (Leeds and London, 1886–90), and Sir Douglas Savory, 'Fame of the four schools at Gracehill', *Belfast News Letter*, 8 December 1956.

The settlement, consisting of the chief buildings, burial ground, and thirteen (later seventeen) private houses, was completed in May 1785. The great exodus from Dukinfield to the new community could take place two months later.

The new community was called Fairfield. It cost £6,000, borrowed from Herrnhut.[1] In addition to this, several members built houses on their own account. It housed 110 communicant members, 22 single brethren, and 45 single sisters. At its formal consecration on 17 July 1785, a great divine service was held with two bands, one from Fulneck, the other from Fairfield.

Ten years later, the Fairfield community was inspected by Dr. Aikin, the Manchester historian. He found it had

the appearance of a little town. There is a large and commodious chapel with an excellent organ. The ground plot is laid out with great taste and judgement; it forms a large square. The chapel and some large dwelling houses well-built of brick form the front. On each side of the chapel are two deep rows of dwelling houses; on the back front, behind the chapel, is a row of elegant large houses. These, with the chapel, form a large square mass of buildings, round which is a broad paved street, and the whole is flagged round. On the other side of the street is another row of excellent buildings, which surround the whole, except the front; at a short distance from which is a fine row of kitchen gardens, and opposite to the chapel, a large burying ground, the whole divided and surrounded with quick-set hedges. One of the houses is a convenient inn with stabling, etc., for the accommodation of those who frequent the place. The neatness of the whole has a very pleasing appearance, and the place is frequented by numbers from Manchester. . . .

The cotton manufacture forms a principal part of the employment of the inhabitants, including spinning, weaving, etc. Tambour and fine needlework is carried to a great pitch of perfection and is chiefly sent to London; there are also in this settlement, tailors, shoemakers, bakers and a sale shop for most articles, as well as for the convenience of the settlement as for the neighbourhood. The Manchester, Ashton, and Oldham canal (completed 1794) comes close to this place, which will be of infinite advantage to it, as well for the carrying of goods to and from Manchester and Ashton, as for procuring a supply of coals nearly as cheap as at the port.

[1] Various names were suggested for it: Salem, Hope, Emmaus, Union, Unity and Fairfield. They were referred to the governing body of the church, which replied 'Fairfield'.

A boys' school had been built in 1790, Sunday schools in 1793 and a girls' boarding school in 1796. The first and third obtained new buildings in 1871 and 1876. Day schools established in 1796 persisted till 1854 when they and the Sunday Schools shared a new building.

As for the former settlement at Dukinfield, Dr. Aikin remarked, 'It now looks like a deserted village', adding: 'Between the lodge and the Dissenters Chapel lies a neat chapel belonging to the Moravians, furnished with an organ, adjoining it is a very extensive range of buildings, once inhabited by an orderly and industrious colony of that fraternity, who carried on a variety of trades and occupations, erected at great expence under promises that leases would be renewed'.[1]

Yet at Dukinfield a boys' boarding and day school was built, and thanks to Charles Hindley, later M.P. for Ashton, they obtained new buildings in 1844, whilst the chapel was twice rebuilt, in 1825 and in 1860.

(5)

The three communities of Fulneck, Gracehill, and Fairfield survived into the nineteenth century. Chelsea, for which Zinzendorf had such a grand design, was, with the exception of the chapel, minister's house, and burial ground, sold in 1774, and in a very real sense was the graveyard of Moravian hopes. There, Zinzendorf died in 1760, and there, Cennick, Hutton, Boehler, and La Trobe lie buried.

Benjamin de la Trobe was manager of the Brethren's English finances from 1760–81. His writings and his friendships healed the breaches between Moravians and Methodists. As a friend of Dr. Johnson, Rowland Hill, John Newton, Charles Wesley, Hannah More and Bishop Porteous, he made Moravianism respectable, but in doing so he cauterized its further growth by insisting, with the German brethren, on the principle of 'United Flocks', which virtually made the Church a subsidiary of the Establishment.

There were five other 'aborted' communities; Ockbrook (for the Midlands), Bedford (for the South Midlands), Haverfordwest (for Wales), Ayr (for Scotland), and Tytherton (for the

[1] J. Aikin, *A Description of the Country from Thirty to Forty Miles round Manchester* (1795), 232–3.

West of England). Yet they irradiated their regions and a number of preaching places were established. Had these preaching places developed into congregations, the Moravian Church might have had a history comparable with that of other dissenting denominations. But the Brethren refused to abandon community ideas. All full members of the church had to sign a 'Brotherly Agreement' not to proselytize from any other denomination, to do all in their power to help the Anglican Church, and to submit to the full discipline of the communities. Marriage, education, social welfare, and business were, for Moravians, to be under the control of the elders. The rules were to be read aloud to them once a year, and all who did not obey them were to be expelled. The 'lot' was retained, even for ascertaining whether or no a person had a vocation.

The economic life of the most prosperous of these three communities, Fulneck, vastly impressed John Wesley:—

'I see not what but the mighty power of God can hinder them from acquiring millions,' he wrote, 'as they buy all materials with ready money at the best hand, have above a hundred young men, above fifty young women, many widows, and above a hundred married persons, all of whom are employed from morning to night, without any intermission, in various kinds of manufactures, not for journeymen's wages, but for no wages at all, save a little very plain food and raiment; as they have a quick sale for all their goods, and sell them all for ready money.' 'But', he pondered, 'can they lay up treasure on earth, and at the same time lay up treasure in heaven?' [1]

But Wesley and the Moravians were, however, to be disappointed. The inn at Fulneck was given up in 1819, cloth manufacturing was abandoned in 1837, the bakery in 1846. Fulneck concentrated on education rather than production. It was as a school that it is perhaps now best remembered. With James Montgomery the hymn writer, Richard Oastler the factory reformer, Christian Ignatius La Trobe, the campaigner against slavery; Benjamin Henry La Trobe the famous American architect, it has a distinguished roll of old boys. [2] But its example survived. Thomas Evans, in his tract *Christian Policy the Salvation of the Empire* (1816) asked,

[1] *Journal of John Wesley*, ed. N. Curnock (1938), vi. 273.
[2] Talbot Hamlin, *Benjamin Henry La Trobe* (New York, 1956), iv.

Do not the societies of the Moravians and Quakers, whose policy is brotherhood and friendship extended to every individual of their communities afford an example what Christian unity is? What such policy is capable of producing is clearly shown from this circumstance, that none of the members of this community are ever known to want parish relief, or were ever forced to beg.[1]

Thirty years later when John Minter Morgan launched his scheme for 'self-supporting villages' under the 'superintendance' of the Established Church, he too looked to the Moravians as an exemplar. And it was one of Morgan's recruits, James Silk Buckingham who, at a meeting of the Church of England Self-Supporting Village Society on 27 May 1846 said: 'The benefits resulting, in the Moravian settlements, from a more intimate connection between secular and religious affairs . . . encourage a well-grounded hope that associations of the unemployed poor, under the direction of intelligent members of our own pure and reformed church . . . would realise advantages still more important'.[2]

Goodwyn Barmby, who had only read about them, saw their limitations. 'Although there is a happy excitement of corporative spirit and religious sentiment,' he wrote of their settlements, 'their system is far from being a system of perfect community.'[3]

It was in 1851 that Kingsley showed how he too, was influenced by them and wrote:—

> Suspecting that the true reason why all Socialist attempts at land-colonisation in England have as yet signally failed is because they have been undertaken in ignorance, and I fear also in hasty self-conceit. But the Moravian Socialist Establishments have not failed, and why? because they were undertaken in the fear of God, and with humility and caution; because the Moravians have believed, and acted up to their own creed, that they were brothers and sisters, members of one body, bound to care not for themselves but for the Commonweal. An establishment undertaken in that faith will surely succeed with common practical care.[4]

[1] In the Goldsmiths Library, University of London, p. 13.
[2] John Minter Morgan, *Letters to a clergyman* (1846).
[3] *Howitt's Journal*, 31 July 1847.
[4] Charles Kingsley, *The Application of Associative Principles and Methods to Agriculture* (1851), 64.

7

Revelations and Revolution

(1)

A BEHMENIST Anglican clergyman, Thomas Hartley, gave to Englishmen the news of a new dispensation, proclaimed as having taken place in 1757. Englishmen were introduced to it in 1778, by Thomas Hartley's translation of Emanuel Swedenborg's *Heaven and its Wonders, and Hell: From Things Heard and Seen*. This proclaimed the dissolution of Babylon in the spiritual world. In 1757 the old Church, according to Swedenborg, had perished and a new revelation was amplifying its lost truths, and a new spiritual age beginning. Swedenborg claimed to have visited the spiritual world as a preparation for understanding the word of God, and interpreting it at a higher level: a 'pure correspondence' between spiritual and material things. Every material thing embodied an eternal truth. As he said:—

> As often as I conversed with angels face to face, it was in their habitations, which are like to our houses on earth, but far more beautiful and magnificent, having rooms, chambers and apartments in great variety; as also spacious courts belonging to them, together with the gardens, pictures of flowers, where the angels are formed into societies. They dwell in contiguous habitations, disposed after the manner of our cities and streets, walks and squares. I have had the privilege to walk through them, to examine all round about, and to enter their houses, and this when I was fully awake.[1]

[1] *Heaven and Its Wonders, and Hell: From Things Heard and Seen* (Everyman ed.), p. 81.

58

Swedenborg saw three heavens, each consisting of a society. And on his doctrine of correspondences every earthly society was a heaven on a smaller scale. Heaven, was 'conjoined' to man by 'The Word'. 'The Word' was God's provision for restoring man to the heaven from which he had been sundered by the denial of direct revelation. Swedenborg developed his idea in *Arcana Coelestia*, in *The White Horse, mentioned in the Apocalypse* and in the appendix to *The New Jerusalem and its Heavenly Doctrine*. The crux of his doctrine rested on the Chapter 21, v. 11, 16–19 and 21 of the Apocalypse.

Thomas Hartley, his English interpreter, held that 'the blessed millennium' was 'on its way towards a speedy revival in the church'. In *Paradise Restored . . . A Short Defence of Mystical Writers* (1764) and his version of Swedenborg's *De Commercio Animae et Corporis* (1769), he bridged the gap between Boehme and Swedenborg. Boehme believed in an 'inward' opening but Swedenborg professed to have received an 'external' revelation. This difference between 'internal' to 'external' revelation should not, however, blind us to the many likenesses between the two: since both stressed that the spiritual and the natural, the visible and the invisible world, did correspond.[1]

As a result of reading Hartley's translation of *Heaven and Hell*, Robert Hindmarsh was converted and in 1782 opened his house for meetings.[2] After a year a public meeting was held in the London Coffee House on Ludgate Hill, on 5 December 1783. Amongst those who talked to Hindmarsh was John Flaxman the sculptor, who would repair with the Swedenborgians to

---

[1] Like the Behmenists, the Swedenborgians were enthusiastic pioneers in the education of the young. The 'New Church's' doctrine of correspondences, whereby every substance and form had a spiritual and moral counterpart, was suited for moral teaching. Thus a stone (truth), a circle (harmony) became, in the hands of Swedenborgians, instruments of moral instruction. One such teacher was to make a name as a pioneer of infant education in the early nineteenth century: James Buchanan. Of Buchanan's work one of his famous pupils, Barbara Bodichon, remarked, 'he insisted that we were angels'. (Hester Burton, *Barbara Bodichon 1827–1901* (London, 1949), 5–9). Buchanan's work in turn influenced Samuel Wilderspin who 'formed his system' from the Swedenborgians.

When Buchanan's first employer, Robert Owen, published a broadsheet tabling 140 sects and parties which a community could house, he began with 'Arminian Methodists and violent ministerialists' and, near the end, number 135, 'Swedenborg and violent Reformers'; Alex Cullen, *Adventures in Socialism* (Glasgow, 1910), 109. It is perhaps worth noting that the early treasurer of the Independent Labour Party, T. D. Benson, was a Swedenborgian.

[2] A. E. Beilby, *Rev. Thomas Hartley, A.M.* (London, 1930), 41.

worship in the chapel of the Asylum for Female Orphans in St. George's Fields. They did this for five years until, on 7 May 1787, they decided to form a separate body. By 27 January 1788 they opened a chapel of their own and convened a conference of all those who had read Swedenborg's works. With the circular convening the meeting, certain basic propositions for the New Church were issued of which Number 35 read: 'That the last Judgement was accomplished in the Spiritual World in the year 1757.'

Beginning on Easter Monday, the conference terminated on the following Friday with a series of resolutions. Of the sixty or so subscribers to these, Number 13 was William Blake and Number 14 his wife.[1]

(2)

Blake differed with Swedenborg in rejecting predestination, but absorbed Swedenborg's doctrine of 'correspondences', calling it 'Divine Analogy'. Blake believed that 'God is Man & exists in us & we in him'. Blake's symbols became part of the English thought.

> I give you the end of a golden string,
> Only wind it into a ball.
> It will lead you in at Heaven's gate,
> Built in Jerusalem's wall.

His story of Albion and Jerusalem, every man and every woman, man and the church is told in the *Four Zoas*. His identification of Albion and Jerusalem, with Albion both England as well as universal man and Jerusalem, the holy city as well as universal woman can be found in Milton. In a passionate evocation of the legend that Christ came to England as a young boy with Joseph of Arimathea, Blake asked,

> And did those feet in ancient time
> Walk upon England's mountains green?
> And was the holy Lamb of God
> On England's pleasant pastures seen?

> And did the Countenance Divine
> Shine forth upon our clouded hills?
> And was Jerusalem builded here
> Among these dark Satanic mills?

[1] J. G. Davies, *The Theology of William Blake* (Oxford, 1948), 34.

Bring me my Bow of burning gold:
Bring me my Arrows of desire:
Bring me my Spear: O clouds unfold!
Bring me my Chariot of fire.

I will not cease from Mental Fight,
Nor shall my Sword sleep in my hand
Till we have built Jerusalem
In England's green and pleasant Land.

He gave the answer in the last of his prophetic books: *Jerusalem*. England and Jerusalem were once united and can be again. His belief that this was so evoked :—

The fields from Islington to Marybone,
To Primrose Hill and Saint John's Wood,
Were builded over with pillars of gold,
And there Jerusalem's pillars stood.

Her little-ones ran on the fields,
The Lamb of God among them seen,
And fair Jerusalem his Bride,
Among the little meadows green.

Pancrass & Kentish-town repose
Among her golden pillars high:
Among her golden arches which
Shine upon the starry sky.

The Jew's-harp-house & the Green Man,
The Ponds where Boys to bathe delight,
The fields of Cows by Willan's farm,
Shine in Jerusalem's pleasant sight.

She walks upon our meadows green:
The Lamb of God walks by her side:
And every English Child is seen,
Children of Jesus & his Bride.

The salvation of man, Blake saw, lay in inspired art. The inspiration of the artist's activity is the building of the city of Golgonooza, from which the real nature of the world may be seen. This building is a perpetual process, in which Los (the

61

soul) and the Spectre join. The Saviour explains to Los the nature of life lived in 'the land of life' where each 'live in perfect harmony in Eden'. 'Let every Christian', Blake wrote in Book 4, 'as much as in him lies, engage himself openly and publicly before all the world in some mental pursuit for the Building up of Jerusalem.'

Blake's life was as intense and significant as any prophet's. His wife remarked, 'I see so little of Mr. Blake now. He is always in Paradise'.[1] And his vision of Paradise was to inspire more than Swedenborg's ever did. To W. B. Yeats he was one or 'the great artificers of God who uttered mysterious truths'.

(3)

As Blake was issuing his *Prophetic Books* in 1793, William Godwin's *Enquiry concerning Political Justice* appeared. This moving brief for happiness through reason rather than government, stirred an undergraduate who had enlisted in the army under the false name of Silas Tomkyn Comberback. When he reverted to his rightful name on being bought out of the army, Samuel Taylor Coleridge still burned to carry Godwin's precepts into action. At Cambridge (where he returned) or from his Quaker friends Charles Lloyd and Robert Lovell, Coleridge may have caught an enthusiasm for a community. The combination of all three, Godwin, Cambridge and diffused Quakerism, may have predisposed him to a scheme of Robert Southey's.[2]

For like himself, Southey was an undergraduate—at Balliol College, Oxford. Of the two, Southey with his hawk-face, hooknose and craggy eyebrows, was at first the leader. Coleridge,

---

[1] The extraordinary difficulty of understanding Blake has been materially assisted by the biography by H. M. Margoliouth (Oxford, 1951), and by Margaret Rudd, *Organized Innocence* (1956), and by D. V. Erdman, *Blake: Prophet against Empire* (Princeton, 1954).

[2] Sister Eugenia's hypothesis. See 'Coleridge's Scheme of Pantisocracy and American Travel Accounts', *Proceedings of the Modern Languages Association of America*, XLV (1930), 1069–1084; E. K. Chambers, *Samuel Taylor Coleridge* (Oxford, 1938), 20. J. Simmons, *Southey* (London, 1945), 232, who gives evidence for the meeting taking place at Worcester College. W. Haller, *The Early Life of Robert Southey, 1774–1803* (New York, 1917), 121. Mary Cathryne Park, 'Joseph Priestley and the Problem of Pantisocracy', *Proceedings of the Delaware County Institute of Science*: X (Philadelphia, 1947), 10. The Report referred to was Thomas Cooper, *Some Information respecting America* (Dublin, 1794), 75. See also Henry Wansey, *An Excursion to the United States of North America in the Summer of 1794* (Salisbury, 1796), 193.

thick-lipped and gasping (he found it difficult to breathe through his nose) regarded him as a 'nightingale among owls' and hung on his words. Southey's words were pure Rousseau: apostrophes of the noble savage, republicanism, and the nobility of life in a country where 'man's abilities would ensure respect'. The man who introduced them to each other was Robert Allen, and George Burnett, a Balliol contemporary, was another who joined them.

The fifth member of the group, Robert Lovell, a Quaker's son, knew all about Joseph Priestley's purchase of land at Loyal-oak on the Susquehanna River and had read the report on it by Priestley's son-in-law. Southey showed him how the whole scheme would establish: 'a genuine system of property . . . From the writings of William Godwin and yourself, our minds have been illuminated'.[1] To yet another recruit he wrote in the September of 1794: 'A small but liberalised party have formed a scheme of emigration. At present our plan is, to settle at a distance from Cooper's town, on the banks of the Susquehanna'.[2]

Both Coleridge and Southey behaved as if inspired. Coleridge confessed that he had 'positively done nothing but dream of the system of property' as he went walking in Wales. Indeed as he described the scheme to 'two huge fellows, of butcher-like appearance' at an inn, they danced 'like Wesleyan converts' as he talked.[3] Southey set himself to finish a poem, *Joan of Arc*, in order to raise money for travel and implements. 'This new pantisocratic scheme has given me new life' he exulted, 'new hope, new energy; all the faculties of my mind are dilated'.[4] Coleridge, not to be outdone, wrote a poem on 'The prospect of establishing a pantisocracy in America'.

> Where dawns, with hope serene, a brighter day
> Than e'er saw Albion in her happiest times,
> With mental eye exulting now explore,
> And soon with kindred minds shall haste to enjoy
> (Free from the ills which here our peace destroy)
> Content and bliss on Transatlantic Shore!

[1] A. R. Waller and A. Glover, *Collected Works of William Hazlitt* (London, 1902), ii. 278–9.

[2] W. G. T. Shedd, *Works of Samuel Taylor Coleridge* (New York, 1880), iii. 623–4.

[3] E. H. Coleridge, *Letters of S. T. Coleridge* (New York, 1895), i. 91–2.

[4] Edward Dowden, *Southey* (New York, 1880), 32.

Together they tramped through Somerset to see Southey's mother, and saw Thomas Poole, a well-to-do tanner at Nether Stowey, to whom they told their scheme. Poole was much intrigued having evidently heard the full scheme, for a month later he wrote to a friend describing it. As he saw it, twelve men and twelve women, already 'familiar with each other's dispositions', were to embark in April. The produce of each man's labour for two or three hours a day was to maintain the colony, which was to be communal. Leisure would be spent in study, discussion and the education of children. One hundred and twenty-five pounds would be provided by each man as initial capital. By this time, according to Poole, Coleridge was the leader of the project.[1]

On their way through Bath they stayed with one Fricker, a manufacturer of sugar pans. He had five daughters. One was engaged to marry Lovell, the fifth member of the pantisocratic group, another was engaged to Southey and a third had repulsed the proposal of George Burnett. Of the two remaining sisters, Sarah now got engaged to Coleridge although Coleridge was already attached to Mary Evans.

Coleridge was in London in September 1794 when at the *Salutation and Cat* he met an American land agent, primed with information culled from Cooper.

> He says that 2000 £ will do; that he doubts not we can contract for our passage under 400 £; that we shall buy the land a great deal cheaper when we arrive at America than we could do in England. That twelve men may easily clear 300 acres in four or five months; and that, for 600 dollars, a thousand acres may be cleared, and houses built on them. He recommends the Susquehanna, from its excessive beauty and its security from hostile Indians. Every possible assistance will be given us; we may get credit for the land for ten years or more, as we settle upon. That literary characters make *money* there.[2]

'That literary characters make money there': how this moved Coleridge during the next term at Cambridge. 'Pantisocracy!' he apostrophized. 'Oh, I shall have such a scheme of it! My head, my heart, are all alive.' Southey was no less exhilarated: 'We preached Pantisocracy and Aspheterism everywhere,' he

[1] Mrs. H. Sandford, *Thomas Poole and His Friends* (London, 1888), i. 95–102.
[2] M. C. Park, op. cit., 10.

told his brother. 'These, Tom, are two new words, the first signifying the equal government of all, and the other the generalisation of individual property'.[1] A date of departure—March 1795—was fixed, and in the intervening six months they resolved to acquire such knowledge settlers needed.

On 22 September 1794 they drew up plans, on lines laid down by Cooper in *Some Information*. 'By all means,' wrote Coleridge to Southey, 'read, ponder on Co(o)per, and when I hear your thought I will give you results of my own'.[2] Southey gave special thought to the logistics of the scheme and told his brother Tom,

> In March we depart for America, Lovell, his wife, brother, and two of his sisters; all the Frickers; my mother, Miss Peggy, and brothers; Heath, apothecary &c; G. Burnett, S. T. Coleridge, Robert Allen, and Robert Southey. Of so many we are certain, and expect more. Whatever knowledge of navigation you can obtain will be useful, as we shall be on the bank of a navigable river, and appoint you admiral of a cockboat . . . my aunt knows nothing as yet of my individual plan; it will surprise her, but not very agreeably. Everything is in fair train, and all parties eager to embark . . . my mother says I am mad; if so, she is bit by me, for she wishes to go as much as I do. Coleridge was with us nearly five weeks and made good use of his time . . . we are busy in getting our plan and principles ready to distribute privately . . . The thought of the day and the visions of the nights, all centre in America.[3]

And on the 14 October he wrote again:—

> We are now twenty-seven adventurers. Mr. Scott talks of joining us; and if so, five persons will accompany him . . . I wish I could speak as satisfactorily upon money matters. Money is a huge evil which we shall not have long to contend with.[4]

But Coleridge at Cambridge, having planned a 'Book of Pantisocracy' which should 'comprise all that is good in Godwin' spent his time chasing a Miss Brunton, daughter of a theatrical manager at Cambridge. Realizing he was making a

[1] G. C. Southey, *Life and Correspondence of R. Southey* (London, 1850), i. 218–19.
[2] E. H. Coleridge, op. cit., i. 91–92.
[3] G. C. Southey, *Life and Correspondence of Robert Southey* (London, 1850), i. 211.
[4] ibid., 1, 221.

fool of himself he composed, on 24 October 1794, a *Monologue to a Young Jackass in Jesus Piece*:—

> Innocent Foal! thou despised and forlorn!
> I hail thee Brother—in spite of the fool's scorn!
> And fain I'd take thee with me, to the Dell
> Where high soul'd Pantisocracy shall dwell.[1]

Southey was anxious to take Shadrach Weekes, a servant of his aunt, to the Susquehanna, not as a full member of the group but as a servant. Coleridge disagreed. 'SHAD IS MY BROTHER' wrote Coleridge in capitals to Southey, and indicated his perturbation that slavery was going to be introduced into the colony. 'This is *not our plan*, nor can I defend it.'

Coleridge then had doubts as to whether the women (except Edith and Sarah) were pantisocrats at heart. 'That Mrs. Fricker! We shall have her teaching the infants *Christianity*,—I mean that mongrel whelp that goes under the name—teaching them by stealth in some ague fit of superstition.'[2] The Fricker family was indeed at the root of Coleridge's growing dissatisfaction with Southey. Mary Evans was trying to dissuade him from the scheme and her words carried weight with Coleridge as he had no real desire to marry Sarah Fricker, and groaned to Southey: 'to marry a woman whom I do *not* love, to degrade her whom I call my wife by making her the instrument of low desire, and on the removal of a desultory appetite to be perhaps not displeased with her absence. Enough! These refinements are the bewildering fires that lead me into vice. Mark you Southey, *I will do my duty*.'[3]

Since their pens could not finance their removal to America, Southey began to lecture at Bristol in January 1795, and Coleridge asked to help him. If omen were needed, when Southey assented Coleridge once forgot to appear on the lecture platform at the appointed time. By February money was scarce and Coleridge had to apply to Joseph Cottle, the bookseller, for a loan. Cottle was delighted to help and confessed 'never did I lend money with such unmingled pleasure, for now I cease to be haunted day and night, with the spectre of the ship! the ship!

---

[1] E. K. Chambers, op. cit., 32.
[2] Haller, op. cit., 146.
[3] E. K. Chambers, op. cit., 42.

which was to effect such incalculable mischief'.[1] Cottle need not have feared losing the two for strong leading strings were holding them back. Southey confessed that, 'affection had one or two strong cords around my heart, and will try me painfully'.[2] By February his days were 'all disquieted, and the dreams of the night only retrace the past to bewilder me in vague visions of the future. America is still the place to which our ultimate views lend, but it will be years before we can go'. And so by March 1795, the month in which they should have sailed for America, they had changed their minds, and resolved to marry the Fricker sisters and retire 'into the country, as our literary business can be carried on there, and practising agriculture, till we can raise money for America, still the grand object in view'. Since Coleridge had been on a walking tour of Wales they hoped to take up farming there.

Piqued by the death of his friend Edmund Seward, Southey began to shun all company except that of Edith Fricker. Slowly he withdrew from the Pantisocrats and made, as Coleridge said, 'Self an undiverging Center'. Coleridge was very bitter: 'It scorched my throat. Your private resources were to remain your individual property, and everything to be separate except on five or six acres. In short, we were to commence partners in a petty farming trade. This was the mouse of which the mountain Pantisocracy was at last safely delivered!' On 1 September 1795 Southey left their College Street lodgings.

Southey, though he protested that he would go to Wales or whatever place Coleridge chose, surrendered to his uncle's desire that he should take orders. Coleridge was outraged: to abandon Pantisocracy in favour of an undertaking with an uncle was unthinkable. 'Southey', he wrote, 'Pantisocracy is not the Question; it's realisation is distant—perhaps a miraculous Millenium.'[3] Marrying Sarah Fricker on 4 October 1795 Coleridge took her, with Burnett and Martha Fricker, on a pantisocratic honeymoon to Clevedon. Southey married Edith Fricker on 14 November and immediately set off for Lisbon

---

[1] ibid., 35.

[2] Joseph Cottle, *Early Recollections: Chiefly relating to the Late Samuel Taylor Coleridge, during his long residence in Bristol* (London, 1877), i. 38–40.

See also George Whalley 'Coleridge and Wordsworth in Bristol', *Review of English Studies*, N.S. i (1950), 324–40.

[3] E. L. Griggs, *Collected Letters of Samuel Taylor Coleridge* (Oxford, 1956), i. 158.

alone, leaving his wife in charge of Cottle's sisters. To jettison even a pantisocratic honeymoon showed that Southey was, as Coleridge wrote, *'lost* to *me,* because you are lost to virtue'. He went on :–

> 'What plan was I meditating, save to retire into the country with George Burnett and yourself, and taking by degrees a small farm, and there to be *learning* to get my own bread by my bodily labour—and then to have all things in common—thus disciplining my body and mind for the more successful practice of the same thing in America with more numerous associates . . . my indolence you assigned to Lovell as the reason for your quitting pantisocracy. Supposing it true, it might indeed be a reason for rejecting *me* from the system. But how should this affect pantisocracy that you should reject it. And what has Burnett done that he should not be a worthy associate ? He who leaned on you with all his head and with all his heart : he who gave his all for pantisocracy, and expected that pantisocracy would be at least bread and cheese to him.[1]

Coleridge deserted Pantisocracy for the reading of Jacob Boehme. The results of this reading, fortified by experience, he publicly avowed twenty-two years later when he said of Boehme: 'He was indeed a stupendous human being. Had he received the discipline of education, above all had he possessed the knowledge which would have guarded him against his own delusions, I scarcely know whether we should have had reason to attribute greater genius even to Plato himself.'[2]

Coleridge became increasingly interested in applying the principles of the Bible to present distresses. This led him to a philosophy of history—especially to the workings of providence in human affairs. His *Long Sermons* nearly trod, as he put it, 'on the glowing embers' of Revelation. 'The elements of necessity and free will', he wrote, 'are reconciled in the higher power of an omnipresent Providence that predestinates the whole in the moral freedom of the integral parts.' Contemplating this drift to a near millenarianism one critic remarks that when Coleridge 'uses the Bible to throw light on contemporary events, he runs the risk of being compared with Richard Brothers or Joanna Southcott'.[3]

[1] E. H. Coleridge, op. cit., 140.

[2] Kathleen Coburn (ed.), *The Philosophical Lectures of Samuel Taylor Coleridge* (London, 1949), 329. For the perseverance of pantisocratic ideas in Bristol see G. Carnall, *Robert Southey and his Age* (Oxford, 1960), 29.

[3] John Colmer, *Coleridge: Critic of Society* (Oxford, 1959), 134.

(4)

The comparison is an apt one because Richard Brothers was in the navy, just before Coleridge joined the army. It was in the navy that Brothers discovered the incompatibility of Christian principles and military service. And as Coleridge became pantisocratic, Brothers became prophetic. In *A Revealed Knowledge of the Prophecies and Times* Brothers explored the dispersion of the Jews and his own lineal descent from King David. Arrested on 4 March 1795 for treason and confined in a private asylum, he wrote more prophetic tracts in which, like the early Quakers, he claimed illumination from an inner light. He commissioned plans for the 'New Jerusalem' from a Scotsman, John Finlayson, who secured his release from prison, supported him and printed many of his works.[1]

Brothers' 'New Jerusalem' had 56 squares, 320 streets, 4 temples, 20 colleges, 47 private palaces and 16 markets. They excited interest amongst a number of people, but not as many as listened to the more exotic prophecies of his contemporary, Joanna Southcott. She also experienced an inner light of prophecy, and obtained the support of two of Brothers' disciples, Colonel Basil Bruce and William Sharp the engraver. They in turn secured the adhesion of three Anglican clergymen.

With their support she took a house in Paddington in 1802 and began to issue certificates for the millennium. With these she attracted other followers of Brothers, like George Turner of Leeds, and soon chapels were opened in her honour. No less than 14,000 persons were 'sealed' for Salvation in five years. 'Trials' of her writings were held. By 1813 she announced that Shiloh would be born from her body and to mounting excitement she went into retirement[2] to prepare for the event.

By 27 December 1814 she was dead. After her death George Turner of Leeds inherited her followers. He also prophesied that a new world would begin and offered to his followers places in it. He even gave a year—1817—and the names of the new Cabinet promising that everybody's 'powers' would be maximized a hundredfold. The failure of this prophecy to materialize

---

[1] Cecil Roth, *The Nephew of the Almighty* (1933).
[2] Alice Seymour, 'The Express', *Containing the Life and Writings of Joanna Southcott* (1909).
Charles Lane, *Life and Bibliography of Joanna Southcott* (Exeter, 1912).

contributed to the rising influence of the man who was to depose him: John Wroe.

Another Southcottian group under John Wood—a former Sandemanian—became convinced that the year 1826 marked the new dispensation. Wood as 'Zion' or 'Shiloh', visited Nottingham, Sheffield, Barnsley, Worksop and Birmingham, voicing his version of the 'inner light'. He owed much to George Fox and Ludowick Muggleton.[1]

(5)

Not all the prophets of this troublesome time were quite as false, nor as irrational. The aggressive Northumbrian, Thomas Spence, after witnessing an attempt made by the Newcastle Corporation to take over the Town Moor some four years earlier, became a secular crusader in 1777, hawking his views about the streets. Thomas Evans (father of the editor of the *Manchester Observer*) wrote 'If there has lived since the days of the Redeemer, one person more than another, that has imitated what is related of that great character in the Scriptures . . . it has been this friend of his species . . . the admirable Thomas Spence!'[2]

Last of the orgiastic chiliasts, Thomas Spence preached the virtues of land nationalization and the rights of man, as outlined in *The Rights of Man, as exhibited in a lecture . . . at Newcastle*. In this he described his ideal state of Spenceonia where land was vested in the corporate ownership of the parish, and occupiers, accepting it on a parochial lease, paid rent, the only tax. In Spenceonia, the parish council governed the community: fairs, schools, industries and the militia all coming within its surveillance. Embroidered in later pamphlets the essence remained the same: land was to be nationalized and only one tax was to pay

[1] C. B. H[olinsworth], *Memoir of John Wood* (1881).

[2] Thomas Spence owed much to the followers of John Glas who held that the Church should be responsible for the maintenance of all its members. In 1733 Glas moved to Perth, where he built the first meeting-house of the church, and was joined by Robert Sandeman, then a young man of twenty, who married his daughter Katherine and virtually succeeded him as leader of the sect, which is often known as Sandemanian. Other sects, like the Johnsonian Baptists and the Walker Separatists, stemmed from the original Glassite root. There was a singular diffusion of Glassite ideas to the north of England, largely through the migration of Scotsmen across the border. One of those who came south was Spence's father—a net-maker and shoe-maker.

for its occupation. As with land, so with language: he also proposes a revised alphabet based on the principle of one letter, one sound.

After a stint as a schoolmaster in Newcastle he went to London. For his great 380-page *Grand Repository* 'intended for the use of everyone who would acquire a complete knowledge of the English language with the least waste of time and expense', followed by a cheap anthology of famous authors translated into his Spencean English, did not have the appeal which he thought it deserved. So, instead of hawking them and his political writings around the streets of Newcastle, he had set up a stall at the east corner of Chancery Lane and Holborn.

A Bow Street runner was soon on his tracts, and bought one, thinking it contained Paine's *Rights of Man*. Finding it was written by Spence, he returned and bought what he had intended to do the first time. So Spence appeared before the justices on a charge of selling seditious literature. His little stall was closed, and he was committed to Clerkenwell. This inspired yet another pamphlet.

Arrested four times in two years on similar charges, he drifted from Chancery Lane to 8 Little Turnstile, High Holborn, where he wrote still further of his scheme: *The Rights of Man* was republished, followed by *The Meridian Sun of Liberty*, *The Rights of Infants*, and the *Perfect Commonwealth*, an account of the constitution of Spenceonia. In his first stall in Chancery Lane, he had supported himself by selling saloop, a drink made from sassafras. In his second, he traded in coins and tokens on which his own ideas were stamped, and would jerk them on the pavement before the feet of passers-by in the street. By the turn of the century, he was in the street himself, hawking his pamphlets from a barrow.

But though he appeared to have been ploughing a lonely furrow, there were signs that he had not wasted his time. The disinherited sons of Adam were beginning to realize that he was indeed their unfee'd advocate. In 1801, he was once more tried for sedition and found guilty, but this time the proceedings were watched with interest by both Cobbett and Francis Place. In gratitude to these and others whose interest he felt, he published an account of his trial in his special alphabet. Little Spencean clubs began to meet in the public houses, spreading the crude jingles which Spence wrote for them. By 1812 there was a Society of Spencean Philanthropists, for whom Spence was to edit a new periodical called *The Giant-Killer* or *Anti-Landlord*. Profounder figures began to feel the draught which he was causing: Coleridge commented on their apprehension of 'half the truth', Parson Malthus felt impelled to contradict them, and Southey admitted that they were 'men who know distinctly what they mean, and tell us honestly what they aim at . . . infinitely more respectable than the shallow orators who declaim about reform'.[1]

Spence's chief disciple, Thomas Evans in *Christian Policy the Salvation of the Empire* (1812) categorically maintained that the division of land would 'render the world a paradise, a heaven on earth'. We have already met him as one impressed by the Moravians whose works he probably read as the librarian to the Spencean Society. Later he succeeded his father as editor of the *Manchester Observer*.[2]

Spence himself died before the effect of his teaching could bear fruit. Soon the Government planted a spy in their midst. Francis Place tended to poke fun at them. 'Poor harmless Spenceans,' he wrote, 'with their library consisting of an old Bible and three or four small publications, a high priest under the name of librarian, and some forty or fifty followers, were held out as a bugbear to all men of landed property who were to succumb to these formidable and numerous speculators, and be compelled to resign their lands to the parishes for the use of the whole community'. But the spy saved the assassination of the Cabinet and Spenceanism disappeared, until H. M. Hyndman rediscovered it to enrich the tradition of English Radicalism.

(6)

Mystical, poetical, political: the dimensions of the New Jerusalem needed fusing with the practical. Communications being poor in those days, one wonders what animated the inhabitants of Longridge Fell, seven miles north-east of Preston, to form in 1793 a Society 'for the purpose of building a New

---

[1] Olive D. Rudkin, *Thomas Spence* (London, 1927).
[2] In *Something to the Purpose: A Receipt to Make a Millenium* he dilated on the Spencean plan. He too was excited by the opportunities for agrarian communities or 'agrarian fellowship' offered by the United States of America.

Town'.[1] It belongs to a stirring, perhaps of some Moravian leaven. It certainly indicates that millenarian and meliorist activity was working in places far removed from Bristol, London or Newcastle. But then Preston was to be the scene of the inauguration of a yet greater millenarian movement, some thirty years later, as we shall see, whilst in Manchester the great secular millenarian Robert Owen was, at this very time, sharpening his ideas.

After meeting Robert Owen in 1816, Southey remarked that he was 'neither more nor less than such a Pantisocrat as I was in the days of my youth'. 'Had we met twenty years ago', Southey mused, 'the meeting might have influenced both his life and mine in no slight degree'.[2]

But by this time Owen was influencing other people.

[1] Seymour J. Price, *Building Societies: Their Origin and History* (London, 1958), 43.

[2] William Haller, *The early life of Robert Southey, 1774–1803* (New York, 1917), 166.

The Owenite Apocalypse

1

<hr>

The Genesis of the Parallelogram

<hr>

(1)

A T New Lanark near the Falls of Clyde on 1 January 1816, in an annex to a cotton factory, a 45-year-old cotton miller delivered an address: 'What ideas', said Robert Owen,

> 'individuals may attach to the term Millennium, I know not; but I know that society may be formed so as to exist without crime, without povery, with health greatly improved, with little, if any, misery, and with intelligence and happiness increased an hundred-fold; and no obstacle whatsoever intervenes at this moment, except ignorance, to prevent such a state of society from becoming universal.'

To overcome that obstacle, this two-storied annex had been built, a school museum, music hall and ballroom. It reflected the desire of the miller to increase the happiness of his work-people a hundredfold.

Owen, a Welshman, had managed them for sixteen years with great success and before that had spent thirteen years in Manchester.[1] He talked with Coleridge and lent money to Robert Fulton, the American steamboat pioneer. He (with others) bought the New Lanark Mills in 1799, since when he had improved the working conditions of the pauper children and increased the housing accommodation.

[1] W. H. Chaloner, 'Robert Owen, Peter Drinkwater and the Early Factory System in Manchester', *Bulletin of the John Rylands Library* (1954), XXXVII, 78–102.

As early as 1812 in his *New View of Society* he had first put forward the idea of this New Institution, or as he called it, the Institution for the Formation of Character, but his partners opposed him, so he bought them out with the help of a second group. These partners also raised objections, and so on 31 December 1813, with the help of a third group he bought the works and the Institution together for £114,100.

This third group consisted of Quakers, William Allen, John Walker, Joseph Fox and Joseph Forster, together with Michael Gibbs, an Anglican.

Of these the most influential and important was William Allen, a chemist who was both a Fellow and a member of the Council of the Royal Society. In the larger laboratory of life Allen refused a contract to supply the Russian Army with drugs, because he disapproved of war. He denied himself sugar for forty-three years of his life because it was produced by slave labour. Impressed by his integrity and ability, the debt-ridden Duke of Kent asked him to undertake the management of his affairs.

Allen's passion for social justice was as strong as Owen's. In 1810, at the age of 40, he had issued the first number of *The Philanthropist* 'to show that all, even the poorest, may render material assistance in ameliorating the conditions of man'. To this end he made no less than eight long journeys abroad, recording both in his diary and in print impressions of other continental experiments in social amelioration. He inspected the educational communities established by Fellenberg at Hofwyl and Pestalozzi at Yverdun in 1816, and in the following year visited the Quaker 'colony' at Congenies (near Avignon).

This joint venture of theirs, the New Institution, took children as soon as they could walk to the lower floor. There in three rooms they would play and go on to the rudiments of learning. At the age of 6 they rose to the second floor to begin school. This floor was also used in the evenings as a lecture room and chapel.

The children were under a gentle Swedenborgian teacher, James Buchanan, who joined in June 1814 and began work in November of the following year. As a Swedenborgian, he used the doctrine of correspondences in his teaching: every substance or form had for him a spiritual or moral counterpart. Thus a stone corresponded to truth, a circle to harmony and so forth. One of his pupils remarked 'These were not always comprehensible but he seemed to have a great reliance on them in his discipline'. He insisted that his children were angels and would humour them in every possible way. Unfortunately, this gentle soul parted company with Robert Owen two years later, when he was invited to start an infant school at Brewers Green, Westminster. He later went to Vincent Square. From his work grew in 1824 that of Samuel Wilderspin and the Infant Schools Society.

(2)

Owen's ideas grew, too. The end of the Napoleonic wars left many unemployed so his 'New Institution' soon expanded in scope. Asked to draft a report, first by the Archbishop of Canterbury, then by a Parliamentary Committee, he responded by proposing a planned community. The diagram of this, published by the Parliamentary Committee on the Administration of the Poor Laws and inscribed 'A view and plan of the Agricultural Villages of Unity and Mutual Cooperation', triggered off a series of experiments which have no parallel in British history.[1]

Southey in a letter to John Rickman on 14 September 1816 wrote:–

> As to Owen, he is far gone in metaphysics, but neither rogue nor madman. We must see Lanark before we can fairly appreciate what he has done. In his views of society he is an enthusiast, and most imprudently blurts them out, when they can answer no possible purpose but that of raising an outcry against him, and injuring him in every way. I myself have a much stronger inclination to believe him right in the opinion, that to a community of lands we must come at last, than I should choose to avow; but in my view of things, it can only be arrived at as the result of the greatest possible improvements in society: it is a *little* in favour of this system that it is the point upon which most Utopia-framers have agreed; and that it does not necessarily deliberate the character is proved by Sparta, the men of which were not men-children, but men indeed. Let us leave this where it ought to be left,—among good hopes and harmless speculations.[2]

[1] For the influence of Jeremy Bentham and J. M. Gandy on the general format of the Utopian schemes of this time see Helen Rosenau, *The Ideal City* (1959), 131.
[2] J. W. Warter (ed.), *Selections from the Letters of Robert Southey* (1856), iii, 45.

This community, of from 500 to 1,500 persons, was to be a quadrangular structure, three sides of which were to consist of flats of four rooms each; the fourth taken up by a dormitory for all the children above 3 years of age. A section in the middle of the first side was to be for the professional men (schoolmasters, clergymen, and doctors) of the community, and other sections were to be used as schools, dining-rooms and chapels. The whole was to be surrounded by stables, factories, farms and laundries. The community was to be self-supporting, the members engaging in various branches of manufacture and agriculture. Its total cost would be £96,000, raised either by private subscription, parochial charity or central funds. William Allen was sympathetic: No. XXV of his *Philanthropist*, carried a full exposition of the Report. So did *The Times* and the *Morning Post* of 9 April 1817. The latter by 5 May was obviously impressed by it.

So much favourable comment was elicited that on 24 July 1817, a meeting of wealthy merchants was convened at the George and Vulture, a London tavern, to give Owen a chance to explain his plan. Owen took it. He was so persuasive that a committee was formed to consider the scheme and collect subscriptions.

But not all the comment was favourable. Robert Southey attacked it as irreligious. Owen replied in a five-column letter written the day after the tavern meeting, and published in *The Times* five days later, stressing the economic practicability of the scheme. In a second letter to *The Times* on 9 August, occupying an entire page, he pointed out how 'the proposed villages will ever be the abode of abundance, active intelligence, correct conduct and happiness'.

Five days after his second letter to *The Times* Owen addressed a meeting in the City of London Tavern, calling for a committee to investigate his plan asking for subscriptions to begin an experiment. He had already received an offer of 1,500 acres from an anonymous donor as a site for a pilot community. Insisting that the plan was now 'so fixed and permanent' that its adoption was a mere matter of time, he prophesied that it would supersede the existing arrangements of social life. 'I look forward', he told his auditors, 'to ending my days as an undistinguished member of one of these happy villages, living upon twenty pounds a year and earning it.' But no one at the City of London Tavern spoke in favour of the plan, even though many of them were 'reformers'.

Radical editors, like Thomas Wooler of the *Black Dwarf* and Hone of the *Reformist's Register* (23, 30 August 1817) rightly pointed out that there was nothing new in Owen's plan, Thomas Spence had already suggested it, so Hone called it 'The Spencean plan doubly dipped'. Owen himself agreed, in his first long letter to *The Times* after the 'George and Vulture' meeting, that he owed much to John Bellers, the seventeenth-century Quaker and further emphasized his debt by reprinting Bellers' pamphlet in 1818.[1]

Modest as he might be in acknowledging the origins of his plan, Owen was the very reverse when it came to advertising its merits. He bought 30,000 copies of the newspapers containing his letters and speeches and posted them to every clergyman in the kingdom. This cost him, during the months of August and September 1817, some £4,000. On one occasion his newspapers caused the mail coaches a delay of twenty minutes.

Such a formidable publicity campaign was the prelude to a third public meeting, held on 21 August 1818. This marked a turning point in Owen's career. This time he put forward his plan for a community, but in the course of a rhetorical question to his audience as to why the plan had not been adopted in the past, he said :—

> hitherto you have been prevented from knowing what happiness really is, solely in consequence of the errors—gross errors—that have been combined with the fundamental notions of every religion that has hitherto been taught to men. And, in consequence, they have made man the most inconsistent, and the most miserable being in existence. By the errors of these systems he has been made a weak, imbecile animal; a furious bigot and fanatic; or a miserable hypocrite; and should these qualities be carried, not only into the projected villages, but into *Paradise itself*, a *Paradise would no longer be found!*

This was untoward aggression, and *The Times* commented on the following day 'Mr. Owen promised a Paradise to mankind, but, as far as we can understand, not such a Paradise as a sane

---

[1] James Jennings wrote an article in the *Monthly Magazine* (Jan. 1818) showing the affinities of Owen's scheme with Pantisocracy. See Carnall, *Robert Southey and His Age* (1960), 29.

man would enjoy, or a disciple of Christianity could meditate without terror.'

Rebukes stung Owen to more violent language. By 10 September 1817, he hit out in a letter to the papers against the 'fatuity and weakness' of his opponents. Furthermore, instead of advocating communities as a solution to the problem of the unemployed, he claimed that they would effect the salvation of society. The able-bodied working class, property-owning classes, and the rich, all were to be organized in a network of communities embracing every permutation of religion and politics. To put the new and larger scheme into operation he announced, on 19 September, that the New State of Society Enrolment Office would open in Temple Chambers, Fleet Street, and that books of enrolment would be found at all the leading publishers. To deal with the applications, Dr. Wilkes was appointed, whilst Owen himself went back to his business, and in the following year, undertook a continental tour.[1]

(3)

As Owen visited the continent, others visited New Lanark. One of them was Dr. Henry Gray Macnab, physician to the Duke of Kent, who arrived after Buchanan had left for Brewers Green. 'The government of the New Lanark Colony', he remarked, 'is founded on the social relations of man. Everything anti-social is banished.' His report, published in the same year acknowledged that. Of the schools he wrote:–

> The children and youth in this delightful colony are superior in point of conduct and character to all the children and youth I have ever seen . . . What must these children feel, and how forcible must their example be on the minds of parents, particularly in cases which are not uncommon at New Lanark, of old and infirm parents supported by the industry of their children.

He went on:–

> the greatest regularity and decorum prevailed. We heard children

---

[1] For the best account see A. Podmore, *Life of Robert Owen* (1905). It should be supplemented by M. I. Cole, *Robert Owen of New Lanark* (1953), not by R. H. Harvey, *Robert Owen, Social Idealist* (Univ. of California Publications, XXXVIII, 1949). *Robert Owen 1771–1858, Catalogue of an exhibition of printed books held in the Library of the University of London, October–December 1958* (London, 1959), gives a good bibliography; Asa Briggs, *Robert Owen in Retrospect* (Loughborough, 1959), a good assessment.

of four years old read well in the Testament; others of five read, and that well, historical pieces from various authors. The writers and counters were industrious, the writing was in good style; and the ladies who were with us said the sewing and marking were very good.

Owen, fortified by his travels and reading (especially on the Shaker settlements in America) returned full of vigour in 1819. His *A New View of Society* (1818) consisting of his reports and letters to the press, together with an account of the Shaker communities, was in the bookshops. He himself, thanks to work on a Factory Act with Sir Robert Peel, was in the public eye, so in April 1819 he stood for Parliament in the constituency of Lanark, Selkirk, Peebles and Linlithgow. An *Address to the Working Classes* which was published in the *Star* on 15 April, and in the *Examiner* ten days later, explains why he was defeated. The rich he declared were limited by the habits and sentiments traditional to them. This tradition was now to be modified: 'The past ages of the world', he concluded, 'present the history of human irrationality only, and we are but now advancing toward the dawn of reason, and to the period when the mind of man shall be born again.'[1]

Owen made a model of his proposed community for exhibition. He also illustrated the social structure of England by making eight cubes corresponding to the statistics in Colquhoun's *Resources of the British Empire* (1814). The longest and base cube (representing the working classes) had a side of $3\frac{5}{16}$ of an inch, the smallest and top cube (representing the Royal Family and Peerage) had sides of $\frac{3}{16}$ of an inch. Placed in tiers they gave a graphic picture of his ideas.

Since he had failed to get a voice in Parliament, he now turned to the Royal Family. Henry Grey McNab, whose report on New Lanark had just been written, was the honorary physician to the Duke of Kent. On 26 June 1819 the Duke of Kent himself presided over a meeting at the Freemasons' Hall to appoint a committee to examine Owen's plan. The committee included David Ricardo the economist, and Sir Robert Peel, Owen's ally in factory legislation. It issued an appeal for

[1] For the emotional response to his gospel see E. J. Hobsbaum, *Primitive Rebels* (Manchester, 1959), 126–49, and J. L. Talmon, *Political Messianism. The Romantic Phase* (1960), 140, 208.

subscriptions on 11 August so that a pilot community could be organized, hoping to raise £100,000. To sway the doubtful, an address was published on 23 August testifying to their belief in Owen's plan. To disarm the cautious, the committee went to great pains to point out that the project was neither godless nor communistic, but a joint stock venture paying interest on capital invested and wages for labour. After three months of struggle to gather support, they had in the end to acknowledge defeat. This was on 1 December 1819.

One last attempt was now made to get the community under way. Sir William de Crespigny, a member of the Duke of Kent's committee, moved on 16 December for the appointment of a select committee to inquire into Owen's proposals. Lord Brougham and Ricardo were amongst its supporters, Wilberforce and the Chancellor of the Exchequer amongst its opponents. Crespigny's motion was lost by 141 votes to 17.

Economists had meanwhile been questioning the viability of Owen's communities. How, it was asked, would they cope with market fluctuations? The *Edinburgh Review* of October 1819 carried a trenchant presentation of their case. Owen, to fight back, laid a report before the committee of the County of Lanark. He seized on the subject of spade as opposed to plough husbandry. His excuse for doing this was the citation of a Gateshead farmer's experiments by some visitors from Leeds to his New Lanark Works, and he seriously argued that 'the introduction of the spade, with the scientific arrangements it requires, will produce far greater improvements in agriculture than the steam engine has effected in manufactures'. The spade became, in Owen's eyes, the instrument of salvation, the analogue in agriculture of what the steam engine was in industry. Coupled to this he put forward, as a remedy for the currency troubles of the time, a labour theory of value. His report, considered on 1 May 1820 by a general meeting of the county, was referred to a select committee which wanted to see a trial experiment in spade cultivation. Hamilton of Dalzell offered 700 acres of land as a site, together with a subscription.

(4)

An acute observer later remarked:

When Mr. Owen showed that men, brought by certain contrivances

84

under a laborious, kindly, self-denying superintendence, would be more happily situated than those who were merely treated as animals capable of producing a certain quantity of cotton twist, the demonstration was not the less valuable because the result of it might have been anticipated. But by a process (alas! most natural) he went on to the conviction that the whole secret lay in the particular machinery which he recommended: then, by another step, to the further conclusion that such a machinery was in itself capable of producing every desirable moral result. That rubicon once passed, it needed only a mind somewhat more generalizing, daring, and self-conceited than that which is found in the majority of men, one withheld by no historical knowledge and few intellectual impediments from experiments for the disorganization of society, to produce a preacher of the doctrine that men are mere creatures of circumstances, and that by a re-adjustment of circumstances their condition may be completely reformed. The necessary corollaries from these propositions worked themselves out by degrees, without the help of any intellectual subtlety, as the obstructions to the new scheme made themselves manifest.[1]

This mechanistic gospel was most assimilable—especially Owen's own model. Its possibilities for revitalizing and maximizing community life shone more brightly against the dark obsession and turgid resentment of those whose community life was vanishing. The promise of miniscule welfare states reached, at times, the height of apocalypse. From 1820 to 1830, co-operation and communities were regarded by the thinking classes as G. J. Holyoake said as 'the religion of industry'.[2] It reverberated through the decades. For it both gave an explanation of what was happening, and enabled those who understood to feel a sense of mastery and responsibility for their fate. As F. D. Maurice wrote in 1838:–

When the poor men say, 'we, too, will acknowledge circumstances to be all in all, we will cast away any belief in that which is invisible, this world shall be the only home in which we will dwell', the language may well appal all who hear . . . Nevertheless . . . it is the 'we will' . . . which imparts to the dry chips of Mr. Owen's theory the semblance of vitality.[3]

[1] F. D. Maurice, *The Kingdom of Christ or Hints to a Quaker* (ed. Alec Vidler, London, 1958), 199–200.
[2] G. J. Holyoake, *A History of Co-operation* (1906), 71.
[3] Maurice, op. cit. The point is also made by Canon V. A. Demant in *Religion and the Decline of Capitalism* (1949), 27–28.

This opportunity of mental mastery over their fate, compensating as it did for the loss of responsibility and sense of significance in work, even without great practical results, has been a profound influence in the growth of socialism.

(5)

Owen's 'peculiar opinions' were no secret to William Allen. As early as August 1814, he and Fox had made the use of the Holy Scriptures in the New Lanark school a condition of their support. Later, in 1818, as Owen helped Sir Robert Peel promote his Factory Act, an anonymous pamphlet referred to 'Mr. Owen with the Millenium dawning over the ruins of Christianity in a cotton-mill'.

Allen's intimations of uneasiness were increased. He had no wish to see the Millennium dawning over the ruins of Christianity in New Lanark. For Allen was not only a good business man but had a considerable knowledge of such experiments. He had been travelling abroad too. In Russia in 1819 he made friends with the 69-year-old General Contineas, the superintendent of the Crimean Colonies, a friendship that lasted for the next eleven years. Allen learnt much from Contineas: seeing the Mennonites at Gorlitz, Greenenthal and Altona; the Dukhobors at Terpania and the Malakins at Simferopol. By 1821 he had his own plans for a community which he discussed with the Emperor Alexander. The Emperor was so impressed that he borrowed Allen's plans with a view to modifying arrangements in the Crimean colonies.

With his own community to foster, Allen refused to co-operate further in making New Lanark 'an infidel establishment'. On 21 January 1824 he secured as treasurer of the British and Foreign Schools Society control of the New Lanark Schools, thereby releasing Owen for other projects. In this year he received a visit from George Flower, who had founded a settlement in Illinois. Thinking that America was a more suitable field of operations, Owen sent his son Robert in the autumn of that year to negotiate the purchase of a ready-made community established by a German, George Rapp, at Harmonie, on the Wabash River between Illinois and Indiana. There, as we shall see in Chapter 6, he was to make yet another experiment.[1]

[1] Gladys Scott Thomson, *A Pioneer Family: The Birkbecks in Illinois* (1953).

2

✦✧

Experiments at Brighton

✦✧

(1)

ALLEN's scheme for a colony was stimulated by the poverty-stricken appearance of the village of Lindfield near Brighton. With its church a dilapidated wreck, the tithes owned by a lay impropriator, and no school, it was an eye-sore. He employed an investigator to supplement and enlarge his own findings in the area. He also launched, in 1822, a successor to his journal *The Philanthropist*. This was *The Inquirer*, a significant change of name. He also began to explore the best ways in which a poor man and his family could best live on two acres of land.

Five months after he had taken over the New Lanark Schools, Allen called on several of the inhabitants of Lindfield to explain his views. He was 'well received', and found willing co-operators in Stephen Wood, the Earl of Chichester and John Smith then M.P. for Buckinghamshire. This was in July 1824.

They first built a school on the ground opposite the west part of the common, open to pupils of any religion, equipped with a farm, a printing office and workshops. Boys paid 3*d*. a week, girls 2*d*. and infants 1*d*., but these fees were progressively reduced according to the number of children in a family, and according to the number of attendances made by each child. Thus if there were four children in a family or an only child attended every day in the week, no fees were payable.

87

Such a success did this prove that in 1825 when John Smith visited it, he bought the 100 acre estate of Graveley for Allen's 'colony'. There, twelve cottages were built, with an acre and a quarter of land to each: six to rent at 2s. 6d. a week and six at 2s. Though both types had three bedrooms and a kitchen, the more expensive had stuccoed fronts and slate roofs and the other plain walls and thatched roofs. Both types were built in sets of two with a long line of outhouses tailing to the rear like the upright of the letter 'T'. These outhouses each faced outward so that each tenant had his own wood-house, wash-house, bake-house and piggery. On larger holdings of five to six acres, six more cottages were built to let at 3s. a week and Allen took one of these for himself.

Allen, as a Fellow of the Royal Society and friend of Humphry Davy the famous chemist, was the ideal man to direct an enter-prise built on land so poor that the original owner described it as only 'fit for colts'. By 1827 Allen felt confident enough to publish a pamphlet *Colonies at Home*. Outlining his scheme for providing every poor family with a piece of land and enabling them to cultivate it to the greatest advantage, he proposed that voluntary associations of benevolent persons in certain districts should provide capital loans and corresponded with farmers all over England in order to put the poor in the way of providing for all their wants by their own industry to enable them to procure an education for their children; and thereby generate in them 'a moral and independent feeling'. After the colony had been in operation for nine years it established its own paper, the *Lind-field Reporter*, actually printed by the 'Schools of Industry' where boarders were enrolled.

(2)

Allen's example infected others: James Cropper built an Agricultural School; Samuel Gurney bought seven acres of land at West Ham and divided it up into allotments. Further experi-ments were begun at Ballinderry near Lisburn in Ireland and Lastadie near Stettin in Germany. Allen argued that 'home colonies' were a remedy for poverty far superior to Owenism or emigration. Emigration, in his view, merely removed the best and left the worst.

Allen's own colony prospered. The cottages with their bake-houses, wash-houses and piggeries were so delectable in the light of living conditions elsewhere, that his settlement was nicknamed 'America', a name that survives today in America Lane. Allen himself is remembered in Allen Road and his daughter in Hanbury Park. Like Cropper's at Pinhead, Allen's school still survives to this day though as a private house.[1]

In Somerset and Devonshire, public meetings were held at Bridgwater, Tiverton and Exeter to raise money for an experiment. The Hon. Lionel Dawson and a Mr. Vesey were the two promoters of the scheme which got off to a fine start on 37 acres of land in 1826. Cottages were prepared for the 'co-operators', and it was hoped to house 400 families. Though in January 1827 the editor of the *Co-operative Magazine* (a journal which had started in January, 1826) reported that Downlands Devon Community had been abandoned, the colonists secured another farm and by 1827 had got under way again. They held a public meeting in August 1827 but thereafter vanish from record.[2]

(3)

Two years after Allen began his experiment at Lindfield, Dr. William King, son-in-law of the rector of Rottingdean, settled in Brighton. Originally intending to enter the Church, King found an outlet for his energies helping to found the Brighton Provident Society, an infant school and the Brighton British Schools. Helped by Allen, he was also the confidant and advisor of Lady Noel Byron, who came to share his social enthusiasms.

By 1827, King and one of his working men friends, William Bryan, became convinced that a co-operative shop could painlessly provide the money to finance a community. This was a great advance on the idea mooted in London that goods of co-operative productive societies should be sold in bazaars. A benevolent fund association was founded in the old Mechanics' Institute, and, to provide practical instruction, King issued a journal known as *The Co-operator*—a four-page monthly selling for a penny. The shop became the centre of a number of social activities. A piece of land was taken over some nine miles from Brighton on which several members grew vegetables for the

[1] H. Hall, *William Allen* (Haywards Heath, 1953).
[2] Podmore, op. cit., 377–9; Holyoake, op. cit., 71.

store. So successful was this project that a second society was formed, known as the Sussex General Co-operative Trading Association.[1]

We are fortunate in having an admirable synoptic view of their society in a letter which Robert Southey wrote from Keswick to Walter Savage Landor on 22 August 1829 :–

> Owen's political opinions have begun to germinate, and will very speedily produce fruit after their kind, which will be of two sorts. Some of the labouring classes have gone to work in the right way. Under the direction of some clear-headed promoter of the scheme (one of their own class), a certain number of working-men at Brighton, by clubbing sixpence a week each, which they vested not in a benefit society, or saving-bank, but, as soon as it amounted to a sufficient sum, in a little grocer's shop, carried it on by one of their members, for the benefit of the whole. Of course all the members purchased their goods there. The profits and the continued subscription were next invested in a mackerel boat; then in a garden of 28 acres: thus far the experiment had gone when I obtained my account of it. Their intention is to go on till every member of this society is employed in the service of the whole, and then they consider their society to be complete. They publish a weekly paper explaining their principles and progress, at one penny each; and of this paper 12,000 copies are sold. Already seventy such societies have been formed. One at Leicester has set up a manufactory of stockings, from which all the other societies buy. Thus far all is well; and the immediate advantage of such unions to the persons engaged in them so great, manifest, and undeniable, that it is no wonder they would multiply as fast as they are multiplying. But in another of their papers, which is published by a co-operation society at Birmingham, they declare that their vesters aim at nothing short of a community in land and in goods. The men who write these papers are plain, practicable, strong-headed men. Very soon such fellows as Cobbett will take up the principle, and use it as an engine of mischief,—the most tremendous that has ever yet been brought to bear upon society.
>
> Momentous as this is, it has not yet engaged the attention of a single public writer. There will be a paper upon it in the next 'Q.R.' by my friend Dr. Gooch, who happening to be at Brighton got acquainted with the facts; and who has looked hitherto at the bright side of the question. I agree with him in all his hopes and

---

[1] S. Pollard, *Dr. William King: A Co-operative Pioneer* (Loughborough, 1959), 17–33.

feelings; and when next we communicate, I doubt not but he will partake in my darker apprehension. Yet if we can keep this principle within its proper bounds, so as to secure the well-being of the whole lower order, without pulling down the higher orders, leave full scope for that desire of bettering our own condition, which is the main-spring of improvement in every thing, and at the same time prevent that desire from making way to its own gratification by injuring or defrauding others;—if this could be done, I should then indeed gladly sing my *Nunc dimittis*! At present the ship is driving fast toward the breakers, and it behoves those who know their duty, to cast about in what manner they may best construct rafts from the wreck (they who may survive), when they shall have stood by it to the last.[1]

Dr. Gooch's article was duly published in the *Quarterly Review* in November 1829. It gave a most favourable account of the experiment. Southey's less pessimistic premonitions were themselves confirmed by the last number of the *Co-operator* to be published (August 1830). For it gave the startling information that no less than 300 similar societies had been formed throughout the kingdom; and that several of them had written to the Brighton Society for advice.

As for Southey, he was more stimulated than his biographers have given him credit for, since he began to write his *Sir Thomas More: Or, Colloquies on the Progress and Prospects of Society*, which appeared in 1829 and 1831. And, singularly enough, his old partner in Pantisocracy was also affected by another great impulse towards community founding—St. Simonism—to which we will turn. Before doing so, we had better follow Owenism for a little while.

[1] John Wood Warter (ed.), *Selections from the Letters of Robert Southey* (London, 1856), IV. 146–7.

3

<hr/>

Spa Fields

<hr/>

Before Allen got busy on his colony, a Scots disciple of Owen's launched an experiment in London. George Mudie came from Edinburgh where he had, in 1812, been a member of a discussion group which used to meet in St. Andrew's Chapel. He had tried to persuade the group to start a newsroom; but the majority of the members were apparently against it.[1] As a result, he had left in disgust for London where he published *The Modern Athens, London* and (according to Lord Henry Cockburn) 'various other personal and vulgar works'.[2] He became editor of *The Sun*.

Meeting at Mitchell's Assembly Rooms, London, on 23 January 1821, with a group of printers, he outlined a plan for a community. A committee appointed for the purpose began to meet at the Medallic Cabinet, 158 The Strand, to raise money. To help them Mudie issued a weekly journal, the *Economist*. It appeared for the first time on 27 January 1821 with the motto *Homo Sum: Humani nihil a me alienum puto*, and aimed at explaining 'the new system of society projected by Robert Owen, Esq., and . . . a plan of association for improving the condi-

[1] G. Mudie, *A Few Particulars Respecting the Secret History of the Late Forum* (Edinburgh, 1812).

[2] MS. in frontispiece of the copy, *A Few Particulars*, at present in the British Museum. I cannot trace the work to which Lord Cockburn refers.

tions of the working classes during the continuance at their present employments'.

Soon the real plan of a 'Co-operative and Economical Society' was formed to work for the establishment of a community of 250 families. Each male member was to contribute a guinea to the central fund and from this fund the community would feed, clothe and educate its members. A common kitchen, a dining-hall and school, together with the manufacture of articles used by the community would save, according to the calculations of the committee, some £8,000 a year. These calculations were published in the *Economist* and encouraged the intrepid experi-menters to say they were 'satisfied that the collective sum will provide the whole establishment with all the necessaries and many of the comforts of life in abundance, and at the same time furnish a power for the purposes of production and traffic'. Mudie felt confident that they would become independent.

The community was to be no Owenite village, nor a spade paradise, but located in the city itself. A co-operative store was established on members shares 'with a view to facilitate the dis-tribution of goods and for other social purposes, as many of the members as can conveniently quit their present residences, do live as nearly as possible together, in one or more neighbour-hoods'.

By warm editorials, Mudie did his best to incubate the pro-ject. Hammering away at the iron predestinarian gloom of the Malthusian economists, he published long moral dialogues showing that, as yet, no society had been held together by any-thing more sophisticated than force. He cited the examples of the Shaker settlements in America,[1] the Moravian settlements in Europe[2] and Fellenberg's experiment at Holfwyl.[3] He under-lined the enormous increase of productive power since 1792. He cited movements going forward in his native Scotland—at Motherwell, where Hamilton of Dalzell had issued a prospectus for a community. He opened his columns for letters like that from a Woolwich workman, telling the story of the successful experiment in co-operation initiated at the Arsenal there in

[1] e.g. in No. 6 (3 March 1821), quoting Corbauld's account; No. 18 (26 May 1821), quoting Mellish, and No. 19 (2 June 1821).
[2] e.g. in No. 6 (3 March 1821).
[3] e.g. in Nos. 8 and 9 (17 and 24 March 1821) citing the reports of Capo d'Istrias and M. Renagger.

1816. He reported the debate on Owen's schemes initiated by Maxwell in the House of Commons in June 1821 and began to include excerpts from his other paper *The Sun*. By 22 September he was reporting the formation of a co-operative society amongst the builders and by 22 December the flourishing state of Abram Combe's 'The Practical Society' in Edinburgh, which had seventy members and was growing rapidly each week.

The 'Spa Fields Congregational Families' whose minutes Mudie published had now begun to live together. The women worked from six in the morning till eight o'clock at night and the children were kept busy 'without a moment's intermission'. Mudie himself took on extra duties. To that of editor of the *Economist* he had added (after 1 September 1821) that of printer, too.

By 17 November 1821 the Spa Fields society had taken several houses at the corner of Guildford Street East, Bagnigge Wells Road, and Spa Fields, and a large room to hold a hundred persons. Several families went into residence. A fixed charge for maintenance was decided—married couples paying 14s. 5d. a week, those with children slightly more. Some women worked within the community, others outside, but they pooled their wages to provide for the advancement of communal life. All domestic arrangements like meals, recreation and education, were communal. They advertised by circular that they would execute cobbling, haberdashery, hardware, painting, craft and household work, and announced that a school, run on approved Fellenbergian lines, would be opened.[1]

To stimulate 'self criticism' in the members, monitors were chosen from the fellow members to 'admonish' those whose behaviour offended against 'the general harmony and goodwill of the families'. Each monitor looked after one person and acted as his 'confessor'.[2] The community also established a dispensary. As No. 51. of the *Economist* announced :–

> The Society is fitting up a laboratory, from which medicines will be administered under the direction of a practitioner engaged to make regular visits to the Establishment. From his Reports, and those of the various Committees, I shall be enabled to lay before the public sets of tables, accurately representing the condition and progress of

[1] *The Economist*, No. 45 (December 1821).
[2] *The Economist*, No. 50 (19 January 1822).

a community, as respects birth, marriages, and deaths; the ascertained or probable causes of disease and death . . . and the age at which dissolution takes place . . . the development of their mental and bodily powers and the means pursued for the formation of good and prevention of bad habits of their body. . . .

This was a remarkable anticipation of the Peckham Experiment of a century later.

The *Economist* itself became a community venture: naturally enough since most of the men were in fact printers. Proofs sometimes got so slovenly that Mudie was constrained to apologize on 2 March 1822: 'The late numbers, having been from unavoidable circumstances left to the charge of an inexperienced and incompetent person, have abounded in so many blunders that I am ashamed of them.'

Whether his shame prevented any more numbers of the *Economist* appearing is not known, for it ceased publication. The last number appeared on 9 March 1822. The Society itself seems to have lasted for another two years, with some twenty-one families—mainly working class and Mudie's own. Ultimately, the proprietors of the *Sun* (of which he was still editor) compelled him either to abandon the community or resign from his editorship. He chose the former, and the Spa Fields community dispersed.[1]

Soon afterwards Mudie left the *Sun* for another adventure in community—at Orbiston.[2]

---

[1] F. Podmore, *Life of Robert Owen* (1905), 354.

[2] Mudie's subsequent career is difficult to trace. By his own admission he published the *Political Economist and Universal Philanthropist* (London, 1822), and *The Advocate of the Working Classes* (Edinburgh 1826–7). He was not heard of again until 1840 when he was living at 243 The Strand. Here he taught and published *The Grammar of the English Language truly made Easy and Amusing by the Invention of Three Hundred Moveable Parts of Speech* (London, 1840). He claimed to have invented an 'illuminated temple of letters' wherein a child could learn the alphabet in a day. From here he also announced a 'musical and mechanical key to the Infant Soul' whereby 'the precise degree of sensibility of Infants from one month to eighteen months old, may be accurately measured and determined'. He was also taking an interest in mechanical shorthand writing. He cropped up again in 1848 with a reply to Lamartine entitled *A Solution of the Portentious Enigma of Modern Civilization* (London, 1849), in which he equates the national workshops with parochial workhouses. He was then living at 23 Parr Street, Hoxton, London.

4

<hr/>

Orbiston

<hr/>

Mudie's experiment was a far less exciting affair than that of
Abraham Combe's at Orbiston. To Abraham Combe, the road
to New Lanark was what the road to Damascus was to St. Paul.[1]
When this 35-year-old tanner went over in October 1821 to see
Robert Owen's model industrial community at New Lanark he
was so impressed that he returned to wager that the Royal
Circus in Edinburgh would be pulled down, within five years,
to make room for a community. This revelation from 'the Great
Governing Power of the Universe' led him to found a Practical
Society of which Mudie wrote. Here members could meet together, establish a school for their children, and a store to buy
their goods. Combe mended his habits too and became a
vegetarian. The Practical Society did not live up to its name
and soon dissolved. Combe then decided to set up a community
in his own farmyard. A profit sharing venture was organized,
dormitories and kitchens were built. It failed too. He began to
write. But Owen was off to America, and something had to be
done in England. So, with the support of Hamilton of Dalzell,
another wealthy Owenite, he organized a joint-stock company,

<hr/>

[1] G. J. Holyoake said he 'deserves to be ranked with Mr. Owen for the cost to
himself with which he strove to prove co-operative life practicable'. *The History of
Co-operation* (1906), i, 173.

which purchased 291 acres of land on the banks of the Calder, nine miles east of Glasgow, known as the estate of Orbiston. Here his third and most famous experiment got under way.

(1)

The first stone of the Orbiston experiment was laid on 1 March 1825. A vast stone building, four storeys high was designed to house a thousand persons at a cost of £50,000. Communal living was its aim. There were to be common kitchens, common dining and amusement rooms and common schools. Only adults' bed-sitting rooms were not common.

The north wing was completed in six months. A store was stocked to supply the workmen. A meeting of the proprietors was held in one of the common rooms on 17 October and were so impressed that some of those present offered to double their subscriptions. Already 125 shares of £250 each had been taken up, and £5,119. 8s. had been spent.

Inhabitants for the large block were sought by newspaper advertisements. Combe conducted the first applicants—some weavers from the town of Hamilton—round the premises himself, explaining the principles of his system. They duly chose their rooms and were admitted as tenants. To give greater publicity to the venture he now published a weekly periodical: *The Register for the First Society of Adherents to Divine Revelation at Orbiston in Lanarkshire. N.B. with a circumstantial account of the rise and progress of the first British Community founded on the important principles of Co-operative Self-Directed Labour*. The first number appeared on 10 November 1825. It was unpopular. Even the superintendent of the store at New Lanark refused to sell it, whilst one bookseller in returning the copies, said that he did not wish his name to be coupled or in any way connected with it.

The community was nicknamed Babylon. To those who watched the five-storey block rise near the river it may well have looked so. With weavers and blacksmiths on the ground floor, joiners, cabinet makers, and wheelwrights on the second, and printers, painters, shoemakers, tailors, and harness-makers on the third and fourth, it had with some apartments cost £91,963. 16s. Of this £1,313 9s. 6d. was due for payment and £4,560 still remained to be paid by the subscribers.

On the first anniversary of the community the tenants held a meeting under Abraham Combe to discuss self-government. They decided to convene a general meeting every Wednesday evening at eight o'clock. Departments were to be established, temperance and cleanliness observed and the private rooms made sacrosanct. The ethical principles of the Sermon on the Mount, were unanimously agreed upon as a code of conduct. The tenants also promised to finish the building themselves, so the workmen hitherto engaged marched out of Orbiston on 8 April 1826, with a band playing and their tool kits on their backs, leaving the building for the tenants to finish. Two days later, on 10 April, the communitarians formally took over.

For convenience, each member was given a number by which he or she was to be known—a necessary expedient since there were now a hundred. They also hoped to be given wages and when these were not forthcoming on the first Saturday night, Combe's office was besieged. He tried to convince them that such old-world habits were not acceptable in Orbiston and summoned a meeting urging them to work so that they might produce to eat. At this meeting each member was to value each hour of his work, and this would be examined by a committee of governors.

To help arrive at some form of classification, departments of agriculture, manufacture, domestic economy and education were organized.

To set an example Combe himself seized a spade and spent several hours a day in a field by the river. But his spadework did not extend to the feeding arrangements which gave certain advantages to the proprietors and the non-manual workers as opposed to the labouring poor. It also made him so ill, that he had to go to Edinburgh for treatment, leaving the colony in the hands of other proprietors. One of these, Captain O'Brien promptly suggested that a number of slackers should be expelled.

This Combe, on his return, was unwilling to do. The divine nature of his mission did not allow of the use of force. Here an intelligent inhabitant called William Sheddon came to his aid and suggested the establishment of an ironfoundry. Combe agreed. Soon there joined the colony Alexander Campbell a joiner,[1] William Wilson a turner, and Robert Hicks, a carriage-wheel maker. This ironfoundry was to be financed by the proprietors as an autonomous venture. The investors were to receive a discount, and the workmen in it were to have preferential treatment. A building for it was obtained by converting an old flax mill on the other side of the river.

As ironfounding became a success Combe organized other ventures, like a market-garden, a cobbler's shop, a printing press, a dairy and a building concern. To superintend them more effectively Combe moved out of his farmhouse at Orbiston Mains to a living-room on the ground floor of the community block. With him moved the *Register*, hitherto issued from Edinburgh. From 19 August 1826 it was printed at the Orbiston Press as a house journal for the promulgation of his views on noise and intemperance, particularly intemperance. Numbers had risen to 250.

(2)

At this point Combe fell ill for a second time. Instead of Captain O'Brien taking the lead, a powerful theoretician, Henry Kirkpatrick, became the dominant influence, probably because he now editored the *Register*. Kirkpatrick had opposed the establishment of the foundry company as a dilution of the principles of full community. By 16 September 1826, he was pressing in the *Register* for absolute equality, and full community of property amongst all members.

This irritated the foundrymen, and delighted the others, who were not doing so well. So two parties formed. The foundrymen on one side defended their incentive system of paying the workers in proportion to what they produced. On the other the Kirkpatrick party said full communism would ensure that all would be equally interested in, and active in producing for, the community, since moral compulsion, not personal profit, would operate as an incentive. Kirkpatrick's party now approached the proprietors with the request that 'all members of the society unite together to produce a common stock, out of

[1] 'His voice', wrote G. J. Holyoake, 'sounded like a truce.' Campbell worked for the *Glasgow Sentinel* and his son-in-law was a bookseller. He claimed to be the first to advocate division of profits—to the Glasgow Co-operative Bakers in 1822 and at Rochdale in 1840. op. cit., i, 211, 236 and 278.

which all our common expenditure, here after to be agreed on, will be paid; and that an equal share of the surplus of labour be placed to the account of each member of the community according to the time occupied by each'.

A. J. Hamilton of Dalzell, the proprietor from whom the land had been purchased and who now stood in for Combe, was anxious to favour the Kirkpatrick party and at a meeting of the proprietors gave it his support. But the foundrymen's leader, William Wilson, advised him to proceed cautiously and not to agree to the equal division of produce. Because of the foundrymen's opposition, the Kirkpatrick party appointed superintendents over the various departments in the belief that the approval of the proprietors would be forthcoming. They also wrote to Abraham Combe, still ill, in Edinburgh, informing him of their intention.

On 3 October 1826 the proprietors met again. Before accepting the proposals of the new 'rules' drafted by the Kirkpatrick party, they insisted that each member should be subject to a ballot before readmission. They also insisted that, before being admitted, each member should testify that man was the creature of circumstance, that 'character is *formed for*, and *not by* the individual, as taught in the writings of Mr. Owen'. The purpose of the ballot was to purge the community of undesirables. It occupied four hours, and at the end all were accepted. The proprietors then decided, under Hamilton's inspiration, that the property should be leased to the tenants with the option of purchase, and the deed was prepared.

(3)

Thus began a real era of community at Orbiston. To celebrate it, a band was engaged for a social evening. In the orgy of speech-making and dancing it was thought fitting to thank the absent Abraham Combe for his good wishes: 'We are more than ever convinced' wrote the celebrants 'from the experience we have had, of the soundness of the principles, the truth of which we came here to prove; and we have no doubt but that a short time will show to the whole world, that the best way for mankind to promote their own interest is to do unto others, in every respect, as they would be done unto.'

But Abraham Combe was almost past addressing. So William

Combe his brother was appointed vice-president of the community.

But the 'community party' of Kirkpatrick had only triumphed for a brief time. The redoubtable Captain O'Brien who had taken over during Combe's first illness and urged that a number of settlers should be dismissed, had not only invested money in Orbiston, but was living there with his wife and four children. He made no secret of his contempt for the slackers. Consistently he had urged Abraham Combe to purge them. Now he came forward to advocate the establishment of a boarding school for 100–200 children. He confessed that he had not been aware that he was 'to be impressed into a Society under the nickname of "Adherents to Divine Revelation" where nothing else was meant but natural religion, to the exclusion of revelation as received amongst mankind'. The boarding school, he argued, would be both 'a manufactory of mind, and a school of labour; by the latter, these children could be made to pay much of the expense of keeping them, and the profit arising from the school fund would have afforded ample means, not only of extending the best education to the community's children, but also of defraying every expense attending them, even their diet and clothing, under twelve years of age, to the entire relief of their parents'.

The Captain's Pestalozzian enthusiasm led him to become the general agent of the schools and take the whole risk upon himself. He proposed therefore to allow the children to sleep in the upper storey of the present building until the new wing was finished.

The school was duly established, and managed by Miss Whitwell, whose skilful hand had adorned the Main Hall at Orbiston with a symbolic painting. She bent her energies to getting the children to attend school, assisted by Alexander Campbell, the joiner who had arrived soon after the foundry company was established. Monitors were appointed, dramatic productions were encouraged, and so successful were her efforts that the *Glasgow Free Press* sent a representative to hear her lecture early in November 1826.

One index of the growth of the community (now 290 strong) was the need for water and drains. So a reservoir was built to the west of the building; and drainage by use of septic tanks was organized. Solids from the sewage were manuring the fields, and the liquid decanted on the kitchen gardens. Rules for sweeping the stairs and passages had been laid down and kept. The north part of this scheme was completed and the avenue block was begun.

Three of the departments were flourishing, printing, food growing and the foundry. The *Register* was appearing once a fortnight, and both the food-producing department, and the foundry group, were so busy that they began to abstain from the weekly meetings. The food-producers cultivated seventy-five acres and had planted a vegetable garden and an orchard. They had even found time to make roads and walks round the building. By June 1827, thirty-five acres of oats were rustling in the summer breeze, a wheat crop was in full ear, blossom was on the fruit trees, vegetables were in the garden and the herbaceous beds were a riot of colour.

The foundry group took advantage of the plentiful supplies of coal and iron in the neighbourhood. With moulding sand from the estate, they began to work a new cupola, melting thirty cwt of iron at a time, blowing the flames by means of a bellows attached to the old water wheel of the mill. Twelve men were actively employed and, according to the circular issued, they were willing to execute orders to make anything from a steam engine to a scale of standard weights. Their water wheel was also geared to a saw mill where planks were made for extending the building and farm houses.

(4)

The only sections not prospering were those acting in the spirit of true communism: weavers, tailors and shoemakers, who were very annoyed because others were most uncooperatively buying boots and clothes outside the community. So they issued an order that all members should in future wear Orbiston clothes. They were supported by the women, who, unfortunately, concentrated on embroidery rather than clothes-making.

The success of the farmers, foundrymen and printers provoked such jealousy that one night their tools were stolen. To prevent this happening again three men patrolled the grounds with guns. Further trouble arose over the communal feeding tables, so a common table was instituted and the whole expense of cooking was divided. A mess man, John Reid, was appointed, and given two female assistants. As a result 221 returned to eat in the mess room; but 77 preferred to draw their rations and cook for themselves. The disparity in consumption was startling. The 221 communal feeders only consumed 97 pecks of meal in a week but the 77 private feeders consumed 103 pecks. The same story was repeated in the case of the bread, sugar and meat. The proportions were, if anything, increased when one examined the consumption of salt and butter, for the 77 took three times as much as the 221.

The new editor of the *Register*, Stephen Fenner, thundered against the conspicuous consumption of the private feeders, and accused them of selling their rations to the outside world for alcohol and tobacco, and thereby making it impossible for the community to save at all.

By March 1827 the colony was on short rations. Several began to leave and those who stayed behind only did so to grumble. Countercharges against the advocates of equal distribution were made, and Alexander Campbell was accused of having an apartment more luxurious than that of a proprietor.

On top of all this, Abraham Combe became so ill that William Combe was forced to manage the community by himself. He found it beyond him, and convened a committee of the proprietors. These had already decided not to go ahead with the communal kitchen and bakehouse.

Meanwhile, that intrepid Irishman, Captain O'Brien, had been blasting away at the principle of equal distribution within the community, and had enlisted supporters. He prophesied that Orbiston 'could not stand, and that a break up amongst its members must soon take place'. This cooled off the enthusiasm (already much diminished) of other proprietors. Only A. J. Hamilton was proof against his jeremiads.

O'Brien sapped the morale of the most successful section of the community; the foundrymen. One of them sold his shares at half price and left. William Wilson himself could not find a purchaser for his stock, so he took the matter to a solicitor. Influential backers, like the Scottish Union Insurance Company, increased their interest charges.

A close scrutiny of the productive potential of each member was instigated by the committee of management in June 1827.

This resulted in piece-work being adopted. Superintendents of departments were given power to regulate wages. A sharp reminder was given to members to make 'economy and industry their watchword'. This drastic abandonment of the basic purpose of the colony was followed by Abraham Combe's death three months later. A. J. Hamilton fell ill.

(5)

The end came suddenly. The bondholders pressed William Combe so hard that in December 1827 he gave orders to the members to leave. He himself went to America with a number of them, leaving behind a party under Alexander Paul to look after the lands for the proprietors. The creditors, led by the Scottish Union Insurance Company, were anxious to obtain their pound of flesh and secured the committal of Alexander Campbell and William Sheddon to gaol. The land was sold on 7 December 1830, for £15,050, to the owner of the neighbouring estate, Mrs. Cecilia Douglass of Douglass Park. She had always resented the gaunt community building which reared itself so near her own house, and had it demolished. Some of the stones were used to make houses in Bellshill and Motherwell.[1]

The failure of the scheme in no way damped the enthusiasm of its leading members. Alexander Campbell, later to play a part in another community, agreed with A. J. Hamilton, who wrote in his private journal 'The experiment at Orbiston was no fair test of Pantisocraty [sic]'.

[1] A full account is in Alex Cullen, *Adventures in Socialism, New Lanark Establishment and Orbiston Community* (Glasgow, 1910). See also Benjamin Jones, *Co-operative Production* (Oxford, 1894), i, 56–62.

5

◇◇◇

Ralahine

◇◇◇

In the same year in which Orbiston was sold, the Lord Lieutenant made a military progress in County Clare in May 1830 to survey the troubles. These troubles were perhaps best symbolized by the conditions prevailing on the Ralahine estate of John Scott Vandeleur, a landowner in County Clare, whose 618-acre estate lay midway between the two main roads from Limerick to Ennis and twenty miles from each. Half the estate, some 300 acres, consisted of cultivated land, a bog of sixty-three acres used as a fuel source, a lake for water power, and a small stream. Vandeleur's peasants walked up to six miles in order to work under a harsh and brutal steward, who on one hot summer's day, at reaping time, when some of them had stopped to take a drink of water from a can in the corner of the field, angrily kicked the can over, saying that it was merely an excuse for wasting time. The peasants took their revenge. At midnight, they held a meeting in Cratloe Wood on the borders of the lake and swore to kill him. Lots were drawn and, soon afterwards, as the steward was bolting the door of his house, he was shot in cold blood.

A number of the peasants on other estates were condemned to death and, before the sentences could be executed, they went underground, forming themselves into gangs. These gangs with names like 'Terry Alts', 'Whitefeet' and 'Lady Clare's Boys', roamed the county. The law was powerless to control them; even the priesthood lost all moral control over them.

(1)

Having heard of Robert Owen's experiments at New Lanark, Vandeleur decided to salvage his estates by undertaking a similar experiment at Ralahine. To do so, it was essential to find a collaborator. To find one, he went to Manchester. There at a hotel at the corner of King Street he met E. T. Craig.

Craig was a singular character.[1] At the age of 11 he had been a member of the Manchester Mechanics' Institute and at the age of 30 was editing the *Lancashire Co-operator*. He was also no stranger to Ireland, having travelled there in 1828—on foot, visiting Wicklow, Dublin and Limerick. Concerned with the neglected state of the River Shannon he reflected: 'The absence of cranes on the tidal part of the river caused great impediments to trade and traffic. Ships laden with merchandise would ride as near inshore as practicable during high tide, and then drop anchor. At low water, porters would take their horses and carts to the vessel, and for a short interval help to discharge the cargo. The tide would soon return, and thus many days would be wasted in waiting for the fall of the tide to resume the work . . . The Shannon was then waiting for "Government help". Some Lancashire lads I know, would have made short and cursory work of waiting for Government. "D—— the Government! Why wait for them? Let us co-op, and do the work for ourselves." Some would fetch wood, some stone, some iron, so that in a short time a captain would be able to float his vessel at a pierhead and in a single day would unload his ship.'

To 'co-op' he went in 1831 to Ralahine—which also lay on the banks of the Shannon.

This, he reasoned, would provide a great moral stimulus to Owenism. He confessed himself 'strongly impressed with the frankness and apparent sincerity' of Vandeleur, and agreed to go to Ralahine 'as soon as possible to prepare the people and frame the regulations and make the organization necessary for the expected change'.

[1] For a life of E. T. Craig, see the *Republican*, July–August 1883.

Vandeleur's sincerity was borne out by the preparations he had already made for the experiment. A large building had been erected—30 ft. × 15 ft. intended as a dining-hall, with a room of the same size above it. At right-angles to these, six cottages were being built. Not far away stood the old castle of Ralahine with its promise of yet further accommodation when needed.

At first Craig was suspected as a spy imported to discover the murderer of the steward. Even Vandeleur's family were opposed to 'the new system', while the servants treated him to a barrage of jokes and ridicule. Yet Craig bore himself with equanimity and poise, mingling with the people, visiting their cabins, and obtaining their opinions on his proposed 'regulations'. He learned enough Irish to respond to rough and cheery greetings. He even saw the humour of one of his early sponsors telling him to reply to every greeting with the phrase, 'Tharah ma dhoel' (Go to the Devil). He won the confidence of the peasants by successfully treating a coachman who had met with an accident. He and Vandeleur pressed ahead with the completion of houses, dining-rooms, lecture-hall, store-room and premises, and the old castle of Ralahine was made available for temporary accommodation.

(2)

By 7 November 1831, he and Vandeleur could convene a meeting of the peasants to outline his scheme for a community. The draft objects of the association were outlined. All of them were to be parceners of a common capital. Each of them was to obtain security against poverty, sickness, infirmity, and old age. All children would be educated, and the standard of living would rise by many degrees.

Vandeleur had every interest in seeing the scheme operate, partly because he hoped to obtain higher rents for his land and partly because he hoped to pacify the peasants. The pacification involved their participation and to secure it, a ballot was held. Vandeleur addressed his tenants:

My friends,
  Before I give the rules for adoption, I find it necessary to have each member submitted to the ordeal of a ballot, because I have

reason to suppose that some persons of one class have an unkind feeling towards others of another class and are also opposed to the system. I could now, before the rules are adopted, or the agreement signed, turn out any or every person that I supposed was not cordially inclined to co-operate for the benefit of each and all. So that now the only terms on which I will allow the rules to be passed will be that each person on the list, according as they are alphabetically arranged, shall be balloted for, and if any person should unfortunately happen to be rejected by a majority of the persons voting, I must, however disagreeable to my feelings, dispense with the services of that individual; and I cannot any longer suffer that person to continue in the establishment. I am aware that some strangers are here, but Mr. Craig expresses a strong desire to be elected or rejected by ballot, as it would be more agreeable to him to be admitted by the general body than that you should have it to say that I forced him on you. Then, when the members are elected, we will adopt the rules and sign the agreement; and I trust that those who now oppose the society will find it in their interest to carry the rules into effect.

Forty adults and twelve children subsequently were admitted by ballot to the Society. Each of these was given a number, so were animals and implements and duties. Slates, on which daily tasks were detailed by number, were hung on the walls of the public dining-room.[1]

These duties were arranged by an elected committee, not a steward, and if bad weather prevented outside work, other jobs were found for them by a small subcommittee. A suggestions book was placed in the committee room and at a weekly general assembly of the members entries in it would be discussed. At one of these weekly assemblies the constitution was discussed. Vandeleur was president with the right to choose the secretary, treasurer and storekeeper. As rent for his land he was to receive, delivered to Ralahine, Bunratty, Clare or Limerick, 370 barrels of wheat, 240 of barley, and 50 of oats; 10 cwt. of butter, 30 of pork and 70 of beef; hay at 30s. a ton and manure at 1s. a load. The members agreed to this arrangement on 10 November 1831.

---

[1] Compare this with the experimentally created 'social climates' of the twentieth century described in the *Human Relations*, especially the work of Kurt Lewin and W. R. Bion. Elliot Jaques, *The Changing Culture of a Factory* (London, 1951), gives an interesting account of a modern version of this democratic control.

As money, the committee issued printed cardboard labour vouchers for each day's work. They were worth 8*d.* and were about the size of a gentleman's ordinary visiting card. Fractions of these, down to sixteenths, were recognized and so of course were multiples which were printed in red.

Each child in the Association had to be brought to the infant school at six in the morning (including Sundays), 'thoroughly cleaned, combed and washed', where it remained till six in the evening. No parent could take a child away during these hours.

(3)

The Ralahine Agricultural and Manufacturing Association, as it was known, attracted attention. John Finch, a Liverpool merchant, came over for a three-days visit, and published a favourable report in a Liverpool journal. Finch was so impressed by the work of the Association that he testified before a select committee of the House of Commons in 1834, saying, 'I am determined to devote a considerable portion of my time to the promulgation of the arrangements and laws of Ralahine'. Another visitor was the brother of Archbishop Trench. Ralahine deserved its friends. Agrarian terrorism, though on the increase in other counties, practically ceased (if later accounts are to be believed) in County Clare. *The Times* and other London newspapers took notice and published short appreciative reports. These induced one young man, Joseph Cox, to make his way to Ralahine to join the fifty members. The honesty and sobriety of the community (for under the articles of association, no liquor or tobacco could be purchased) impressed the Catholic priesthood, and one of them told Craig so. Well might Craig say of his experiment, 'It is no longer a theory of Utopia, as in the days of Plato and of More, but a real, tangible verity, waiting only for prudent, practical development and extension by those who comprehend its purpose, and can organize the men and materials necessary for success'.

Craig's part in this was considerable. He ensured that each married couple had a separate house, he saw to it that youths shared dormitories and sitting-rooms. He took special care about sanitation, since in Limerick there was an outbreak of cholera in 1832. He also was an enthusiastic advocate of mechanical aids to farming, introducing the first reaping machine into Ireland at Ralahine. The machine was not introduced without misgivings, as looms had previously been destroyed in the district and Vandeleur had to write an address to the neighbourhood justifying its appearance.

So well were things going that Craig took time off to visit the first Co-operative Congress which was held at Manchester. On his return he found fever and cholera raging on the lands outside the society. This led him to take a hand in the education of some of the young men—a ticklish task, since all of them were Catholics, but an essential one, as he wished them to understand the processes of agriculture.

He began with some simple chemical experiments on air-pressure and went on to illustrate the phenomena of plant life. Craig was an enthusiast for industrial training. The use of tools, drawing from fine objects, and instruction in the use of implements, alternated with moral instruction. Indeed, so important did the school become that in 1832 he brought back a wife to look after and develop the infant side of it.

Mrs. Craig, in addition to running the school, taught the society how to bake bread—an acquisition appreciated at their first Harvest Home. Certainly her support to the social life of the community impressed visitors. One was William Thompson, another was Robert Owen. The former, the Socialist owner of large estates in Cork, told Craig that he wished to establish a community on the model of Ralahine, and on leaving, presented him with a copy of his work on forming communities. Robert Owen's visit was most welcome, for it was his experiment at New Lanark (as reported on by Dr. Macnab) that had drawn Craig to experiment. A third visitor was William Pare, who not only published a book on the Ralahine experiment, but was appointed, on the death of William Thompson in 1833, an executor of his will.

For two years all went well. Then a catastrophe occurred. Vandeleur was a gambler. As Craig relieved him of the responsibility of running his estate, he spent more and more time at his club. His debts mounted and he absconded. All Craig's efforts were needed to cash the labour notes in which the peasant proprietors had been paid before Vandeleur's creditors sold the estate: on 23 November 1833 the experiment came to an end with the last general meeting of the Association. Craig left for England with his wife.

(4)

In 1844 Craig organized, for Lady Noel Byron, an industrial school at Ealing Grove in London, which he modelled on Fellenberg's Academy at Hofwyl. This venture met with more success than his Ralahine experiment and attracted the attention of, amongst others, the Rev. C. W. Woodbridge, editor of the *American Quarterly Journal of Education*, and Sir James Kay Shuttleworth, then secretary of the Committee of the Privy Council on Education.

He became editor of the *Star in the East*, a periodical owned by James Hill at Wisbech, where he witnessed the establishment of another community at Manea Fen. He became a pillar of the Co-operative Movement, a pioneer of ventilation. But none of his later work quite matched his experiment, as a young man of 29, in Utopia-founding: an experiment which left its mark on the social thinking of nineteenth-century England. Enoch Craggs, in Disraeli's *Endymion*, had obviously heard of it; so had many of the Irish land reformers of the later nineteenth century.[1]

Ralahine had a great place in the community tradition of the century. Accounts of it were published in the *New Moral World* early in 1840, and, apart from Craig's own numerous articles, the great apostle of land nationalization, Alfred Russell Wallace held up its practice of self-government as 'a practical and conclusive answer' to the critics of his plans.[2] To Wallace, its kindergarten was a pioneer venture, its sanitary and dietary regulations a model. 'At Ralahine', he wrote 'it was found that the most ignorant of the labourers were sometimes able to make suggestions of value to the community . . . it shows that sufficient business capacity does exist among very humble men

---

[1] E. T. Craig, *The Irish Land and Labour Question, illustrated in the history of Ralahine and Co-operative Farming* (St. Quentin, 1882); E. T. Craig, *An Irish Commune. The History of Ralahine* (Dublin, 1920); William Pare, *Co-operative Agriculture: A solution of the Land Question as exemplified in the history of the Ralahine Co-operative Agricultural Association, County Clare, Ireland* (London, 1870); G. J. Holyoake, *A History of Co-operation*, (London, 1906), i. 178–81; G. D. H. Cole, *A Century of Co-operation* (Manchester, 1944), 22–23, 34, 341.

[2] A. R. Wallace, *Studies Scientific and Social* (1900), ii. 455–77.

as soon as they have an opportunity of practising it.' It inspired William Morris, and influenced General Booth.[1]

[1] Craig became an inveterate educator. By 1858 he was editor of the *Leamington Advertiser*. He founded the *Brighton Times* and also during his life edited the *County Express* and the *Oxford University Herald*. Like many contemporaries he was immensely interested in phrenology. He wrote *Phrenological chart of the propensities, moral sentiments, and intellectual faculties of the human mind* (1845) and also contributed to the *Phrenological Magazine*. He tried to apply these studies to men of genius as his *Shakespeare's portraits phrenologically considered* (1875) shows. But his real interest lay in promoting the cause of co-operative farming, and at 78 he published *The Irish Land and Labour Question*, which was translated by Marie Moret. At 81 he wrote *Competitive Society Illustrated, showing how the producers of wealth are fleeced by non-producing consumers* (1885), and in the following year, *The Irish Labourers Land Act* (1885), and *A Memoir and in Memoriam of Henry Travis, M.P., English Socialist* (1886), together with *The Portraits, Bust and Monument of Shakespeare* (1886). At 88 he could be justified for publishing *History of a Great Discovery in the Prevention of Premature Death by the power to restore the fluidity of the vital current, in cases of inflammation of the blood* (1892), and addressing Gladstone on his experiences with *The First Example of Profit Sharing and Home Rule. A letter addressed to the Rt. Hon. W. E. Gladstone* (1892). His fertile mind seemed never still, for in the same year he issued *The Triangular carriage, for moving through the air . . . for the prevention of war . . .* (1892), and *Ralahine idealised, or organised production, distribution and consumption* (1892). His last publication was perhaps his aptest. It was a book of verse entitled *Friends in Need* (1893).

6

William Maclure and New Harmony

In 1825 an experiment, inspired by John Gray, was initiated by the London Co-operative Society. Gray, at the age of 26, had just published his *Lecture on Human Happiness*.[1] This attempted to prove, on the basis of figures given in Colquhoun's *Treatise on the . . . Resources of the British Empire* (1814), from which Robert Owen had built his 'cubes', that labour was being robbed of four-fifths of its produce. What he said in his *Lecture on Human Happiness* was enough for the London working men. They drew up articles of agreement for the formation of a community based on principles of mutual co-operation, calculating that if £20,000 were subscribed, they could go ahead at once. Interested parties were invited to get in touch with James Cross at 108 Strand, London, for further information.

[1] John Gray, *A Lecture on Human Happiness* (London, 1825). Reprinted in facsimile by the London School of Economics in 1931. 'The plans to which we allude, are altogether different from those proposed by Mr. Owen, and we willingly admit, that they are altogether inferior to them; but we entertain a hope that they will be useful in proving to the world, that unity of interest is in every way consistent with individuality and distinctions of property, and at a period like the present, when we hesitate not to say, that society is on the eve of relinquishing for ever the commercial principles on which it has hitherto acted; we think that too many modifications of the same fundamental principles cannot be laid before the public; for out of each something advantageous may perhaps be selected.' (p. 71.)

(1)

One of the interested parties was William Maclure, a 63-year-old Scotsman who had emigrated to America forty years before.[1] Settling in Philadelphia, he first made a modest fortune and then a name as a geologist. When he tired of combing Europe for rocks, he combed it for ideas. His most fruitful harvest was gleaned at Hofwyl, the educational colony established by J. H. Pestalozzi. Here he spent seven years and tried to persuade Pestalozzi to emigrate to Philadelphia. Failing in this, he persuaded one of his lieutenants, Francis J. N. Neef, in 1805. Five years later, Maclure secured another adherent, this time the geologist Gerard Troost. Both flourished by transplantation: Neef as a teacher and Troost as a scientist. Neef wrote the first pedagogical work in the English language to be published in the United States and founded a Pestalozzian school; while Troost established a pharmaceutical laboratory, an alum manufactory, and ten years after his arrival, became a professor of mineralogy.[2]

On 20 July 1809 Maclure read a paper to the American Philosophical Society on the geology of the United States. This he expanded eight years later by another paper on the same subject presented to the same body on 16 May 1817. This second paper, published as a separate pamphlet, undoubtedly made Maclure's name known beyond the immediate circle of his American friends. Maclure was elected president of the local academy and held the post for the next twenty-two years. He

[1] Address by Samuel G. Morton, delivered to the Philadelphia Academy of Natural Sciences in 1841, *A Memoir of William Maclure* (2nd ed., Philadelphia, 1844), and the article by George P. Merrill in the *Dictionary of American Biography* (20 vols., New York, 1943), xii. 135–7, it seems to be presumed that he was a botanist, since of twelve representative encyclopaedias consulted, all give the plant Maclura, but only five give a short note about him. He published the report of a mission to settle the accounts of Americans who had claims against the French Republic in 1807: *To the People of the United States* (Philadelphia, 1807).

[2] For Troost, see Henry G. Rooker, 'A Sketch of the Life and Work of Dr. Gerard Troost', in *Tennessee Historical Magazine*, Series II (3 vols., Nashville, Tennessee, 1930–7), III (1932), 3–19. For Neef see Ada Carman, 'Joseph Neef: A Pestalozzian Pioneer', in *Popular Science Monthly* (New York, 1872–), XLV (1894), 373–5. His popularization of the work of Condillac, *The Logic of Condillac* (Philadelphia, 1809), shows how sensational psychology was taking root. Mind, as the product of sensation, has no independent existence as Locke would maintain. This is a significant anticipation of Spencer, more striking by the fact that Condillac would have the child repeat the experiences of the race.

was a good friend to them: a considerable portion of the first part of their journal was printed in his own house, while he presented its library with over 1,500 volumes. Benjamin Silliman (sixteen years his junior and a professor at Yale), who was well qualified to judge, said of Maclure's work this time: 'Few men have seen so much of the structure of our globe, and few have done so much with such small pretensions.'[1] The *Edinburgh Review*, in 1818, spoke of it in its Wernerian context: 'His general views are much more enlarged and philosophical, than is usually met with in the geologists of that school; and, like most of those who have had opportunities of extensive observation, he has found that the theory of the Freyberg Professor Werner is of a very limited application.'[2]

Maclure was also a pioneer of *geo politik*. He divided the known United States into three regions (the Mississippi Basin, the Alleghenies, and the Atlantic slope), and prophesied their future. The first was destined, on account of climate and soil, to become a country of immense agricultural possibilities. Since ships of war would not be able to pass up the river, he argued, it would be safe; a nation of agriculturalists would flourish, whose rulers would be deprived by nature of keeping a fleet or army 'which hitherto have always produced the ruin of free and equal representative governments'. 'On this earth, or in the page of history, it is probable no place can be found of the same extent, so well calculated to perpetuate a free and equal representative government, as the basin of the Mississippi, both from its physical advantages and the political constitutions on which the state of society is bottomed.'[3] For the peoples of what he called the Atlantic slope, he had no such rosy views. They would become a military people, he forecast, since their accessible coast and numerous rivers would involve them in numerous wars. The third, or Allegheny region, he thought, would be the last part of the continent to be thickly inhabited.

[1] In his *American Journal of Science and Arts*, I. 209–13, he placed him beside Saussure, who explored the Alps; Dolomieu, who formulated the volcanic laboratory analogy; Humboldt, who examined Mexico, and Werner himself, whose theories were elaborated within the confines of his native Saxony.

[2] See review of William Maclure's book, *Observations on the Geology of the United States of America* (Philadelphia, 1817), in *Edinburgh Review*, XXX (1818), 375.

[3] Maclure, *Observations on the Geology of the United States of America*, 126.

(2)

Restless and searching, Maclure was perpetually on the look-out for fresh talent to add lustre to his own intellectual enterprises. His third major recruit was a naturalist, Charles Alexandre Lesueur, who had explored the coasts of Australia in the opening years of the century and brought back 100,000 zoological specimens. Lesueur was most reluctant to leave his native land, and it took much persuasion by Maclure to induce him to change his mind.[1] The offer of 'untraitément annuel' of 2,500 francs no doubt helped Lesueur to make his decision. The two of them embarked for the United States via the West Indies in August 1815, accompanied by two more Pestalozzians: M. Schaer and M. Alphour. Maclure himself, with characteristic energy, took the opportunity to survey the West Indies, publishing a report on his return. These observations, dated 18 October 1817, marked Maclure's return to Philadelphia, where, as has been already noticed, he assumed the presidency of the Academy of Natural Sciences. There Lesueur settled down for the next nine years, with Troost: Neef having removed in 1814 to Louisville, Kentucky. All three retained their membership in the academy.

Maclure himself did not settle. The picture presented by the European progressives was discouraging. Pestalozzi's work at Yverdon seemed to be coming to an end: he had lost his wife in 1815, and in the same year, sixteen of his teachers left him in a body as a protest against his retention of an unpopular teacher. Johannes Niederer, Hermann Krusi, and Johannes Ramsauer, his three chief assistants also left, and lawsuits, hostile pamphlets, and misrepresentation looked like drawing a curtain on a great experimental drama. All this, to an enthusiast like Maclure, must have looked disastrous, and it is not surprising that he characteristically set about continuing the work himself.

(3)

The site which he selected for his operations was Spain. There, at Alicante, he planned a great agricultural school on the

---

[1] Mme. Adrien Loir, *Charles-Alexandre Lesueur, Artiste et Savant Français en Amérique de 1816 à 1839* (Le Havre, 1920), 15, said that her subject was 'sollicité depuis longtemps par William Maclure', also, that Maclure promised he would return after two years.

lines of Hofwyl or Yverdon. In it, physical labour was to be combined with moral and intellectual culture. It was to do for the education and training of the young what Fellenberg and Pestalozzi had failed to do in harmony. Maclure's enterprise secured him an estate of 10,000 acres, he repaired the buildings and put the whole estate in order.[1] He visited various parts of southern Spain with a view to scientific investigation. Unfortunately for him, the liberal dawn which he so confidently expected to illuminate the country did not materialize: the estate was confiscated and returned to the Church, and Maclure received no compensation. But that did not prevent him from continuing his geological studies.[2] His fierceness was not only directed against bad geologists, but also against the tiresome natives of Spain. In a letter to Silliman in 1823 he wrote :–

> I have been much disappointed by being prevented from executing my mineralogical excursions in Spain, by the bands of powerful robbers, that have long infested the astonishingly extended surface of uncultivated and uninhabited wilds, in this naturally delightful country; not that I require any money worth the robbing, to supply me with all that I need—for the regimen which I adopt, for the promotion of my health, in my excursions, demands nothing but water, and a very small quantity of the most common food; but these barbarians have adopted the Algerine system of taking you, as a slave, to the mountains, where they exact as a ransom, as many thousands of dollars, as they conceive the property you possess will enable you to pay.[3]

Nor were the bandits of Spain the only menace to his freedom. At Paris, the editor of the *Revue Encyclopédique* asked him to contribute some essays. Maclure wrote six, but they were excluded by the censors of the press as too democratic. They were afterwards translated into Spanish and published at Madrid.[4]

These years in Spain crystallized his interests around the formation, not of rocks, but of character. More and more was education becoming uppermost in his mind. This is shown in a

[1] Morton, *A Memoir of William Maclure*, 18.
[2] *American Journal of Science and Arts*, VII. 256.
[3] ibid., VIII (1825), 187.
[4] Maclure, *Opinions on Various Subjects, Introduction*. These essays were subsequently published, with others, at New Harmony.

remarkable letter which he wrote to Silliman on 19 October 1822:—

It is an axiom with me that it is the positive and real interest of every individual in society to have as many friends and as few enemies as possible. To obtain them he must do as much good and as little harm as possible. In reflecting upon the absurdity of my own classical education, launched into the world as ignorant as a pig of anything useful, not having occasion to practice anything I had learned, . . . I had been long in the habit of considering education one of the greatest abuses our species were guilty of, and of course one of the reforms the most beneficial to humanity, and likewise offering to ambition a fair field. Almost no improvement has been made in it for two or three hundred years; there was immense room for change to put it on a par with other functions of civilization. The task appeared easy, and the credit to be acquired by any considerable, for nearly the same reasons. I adopted rock-hunting as an amusement in place of deer or partridge hunting, considering mineralogy and geology as the sciences most applicable to useful practical purposes, but, like most of the things of the greatest utility, neglected,—having long given up all idea of changing the opinions of man as a labour far above my abilities. I have been endeavouring, for some twenty years, to change the education of children, and stumbled by accident about eighteen years ago on the school of Pestalozzi in Switzerland, which subserved the useful purpose that I have formed to myself of a rational education. I have been ever since doing something towards propagating and improving the scheme, and the success in the fruits are more than I expected, for it has won some of the most promising men in our country, such as Henry Sybert &c., &c., but has not been able to penetrate deep into the crust of prejudices which is early interwoven with our self-love, so as to make the greatest part of mankind jealous and inveterate enemies of any system that gives knowledge on cheaper terms than they themselves paid for it; though I have little doubt that in time some such system will generally prevail in our country, where the power, being in the hands of the people, through the medium of our popular governments, renders a diffusion of knowledge necessary to the support of freedom, and of course the necessity of an almost equal division of both property and knowledge, which the advantages given to those who can afford to send their sons to colleges very naturally counteracts.[1]

---

[1] G. P. Fisher, *Life of Benjamin Silliman* (New York, 1866), II. 40–43. This letter is worth quoting *in toto* because of Silliman's own acknowledgement in the *American Journal of Science and Arts*, X (1826), 145–50, that 'The Pestalozzian system of instruction has been introduced into this country by the public spirit and liberality of Mr. Maclure'.

To offset his Spanish tragedy, he opened a school in his house in Paris. In it 'Boys from eight to ten years old become good mineralogists and chemists, almost equal to the analysis of rocks, and speak and grammatically understand three to four modern languages, mathematics in all its branches, are good arithmeticians, and in short before the arrival of that critical time, the age of puberty, they will possess more useful knowledge than they could have had by the old system at the age of thirty or forty'.[1] His little school served as a magnet for yet more teachers. William Phiquepal and Madame Fretageot, both Pestalozzians, followed the path that Neef, Troost, and Lesueur had taken before them, and, by 1821 were also in Philadelphia. Once there, Maclure's ready pen secured them the advertisement they deserved, and in the *American Journal of Science*, volume X, he wrote an article on 'The Epitome of the Improved Pestalozzian System of Education, as Practised by William Phiquepal and Madame Fretageot, formerly in Paris, and now in Philadelphia'. But before Maclure himself left Paris, he wrote once more to Silliman.

He had discovered something new.

(4)

This something new was John Gray's pamphlet. He told Silliman: 'A Prospectus of the British establishments, with the first lecture on human happiness, by John Gray, has been published: it places the state of society, in a new and highly interesting point of view, extremely favourable to liberty'.[2] He also declared 'our disgrace and humiliation would be much aggravated, if the two establishments now forming in Britain were to succeed, and the attempt now making in America were to fail'.[3]

To prevent this, he determined to throw in his lot with Robert Owen, and ensure that 'the American one' would succeed. The two men were no strangers to each other: Maclure had

---

[1] Fisher, *Life of Benjamin Silliman*, ii. 43.

[2] *American Journal of Science and Arts*, X, the letter dated 2 May 1825, from Paris. With this he informed Silliman that he had bought the whole edition of Michaux's *North American Sylva* in order to present them to various agricultural societies. He also said that he had bought past numbers of the *Journal de Physique*, the *Revue Encyclopédique*, and the *Westminster Review* for presentation to the American Geological Society, 165, 167.

[3] *American Journal of Science and Arts*, X. 165.

visited New Lanark, Owen's Scottish social experiment, while Owen had visited Philadelphia. Owen was anxious to inaugurate his new moral world as far away from the corrosions of the old one as possible, Maclure wished to try the Pestalozzian methods of instruction on human beings who had known no other. It was but natural that they should get together, especially as Maclure's considerable wealth enabled him to play the part of joint patron. The agreement was that each should provide the sum of $150,000 towards the joint community.

Maclure had one asset for Robert Owen which is acknowledged by a recent writer: his alliance with Robert Owen 'partially counteracted' the 'unfortunate publicity' which Owen's public utterances brought upon the embryo community.[1]

Maclure took to community building with enthusiasm. He forwarded to New Harmony his private library, philosophical instruments, and collections of natural history, 'designing', as his biographer said 'by these and other means to make that locality the centre of education in the west'. Moreover, he rounded up his scientific associates to meet Robert Owen at New York by early November 1825. They assembled (with the notable exception of Neef, who came later) and took wagon and carriage to Pittsburgh. There, since they could not get a steamboat, the party purchased a keel-boat, and fitted it up for the journey. This was the famous boat-load of knowledge about which so much has been written, and which arrived at New Harmony on 26 January 1826.

Maclure was 63 years old: Owen eight years younger. Owen was in a hurry to establish his 'half-way house to the social state', but Maclure was anxious to promote a more gradual system.[2] It was the age-old tug-of-war between the evolutionary and revolutionary personalities. Owen soon found this out, and set up a system of education different from that of Maclure. Indeed, when Owen was washing the dirty linen of his quarrel

[1] Richard W. Leopold, *Robert Dale Owen, A Biography* (Cambridge, Massachusetts, 1940), 27.

[2] George P. Merrill, *The First One Hundred Years of American Geology* (New Haven, Connecticut, 1924), 33, quoted Maclure as saying 'land in the cities can no longer rise in value. The Communistic society must prevail, and in the course of a few years Philadelphia must be deserted; those who live long enough may come back here and see the foxes looking out of the windows'. It looks as if Maclure was not anxious to invest money in real estate in Philadelphia.

with Maclure in public, he naïvely confessed: 'Mr. Maclure went out to establish a favourite system of education at New Harmony; and I had heard so much of the Pestalozzian system, and of Mr. Maclure's exertions for its promotion, that I did expect the social system would be aided with it, and by the assistance of those he would take with him. The population of New Harmony waited week after week, and month after month, with more patience than I ever saw exercised on any similar occasion. I was myself disappointed that he could not organise his operations.'[1] He attacked Maclure's brother as 'a mere tradesman who knew but little except *to buy cheap and sell dear*', and continued: 'I had, I suppose, somewhat irritated Mr. Maclure; for I had commenced a system of education different from his own— and I therefore made my arrangements independently of him, and commenced my system under the direction of a Mr. Dorsey.'[2]

Maclure paid $40,000 and a balance of a further $5,000 and Owen admitted defeat on 13 April 1828, leaving the field clear for Maclure, who now got into his stride. Earlier he had written in the *American Journal of Science* his manifesto: 'The great and fundamental principle is, never attempt to teach children what they do not comprehend, and to teach them in the exact ratio to their understanding it, without omitting one link in the chain of ratiocination proceeding always from the known to the unknown and from the most easy to the most difficult, practising the most extensive and accurate use of all the senses, exercising, improving, and perfecting all the mental and corporeal faculties by quickening combination: accelerating and carefully arranging comparison; judiciously and impartially making deductions; summing up the results free from prejudices, and cautiously avoiding the delusions of imagination, the constant source of ignorance and error.'[3]

(5)

Maclure was at last able to establish what he had failed to do in Spain: an educational community. It was to be an advance on Fellenberg's agricultural community at Hofwyl, for it was to be

---

[1] See Robert Owen's speech delivered at Philadelphia on 27 June 1827, which was printed in the New Harmony, Indiana *Gazette*, 8 and 15 August 1827.

[2] ibid.

[3] *American Journal of Science and Arts*, X. 145.

more democratic. Neef took over the higher school, assisted by his four daughters and one son. In this, children from 5 to 12 were to be reared: arithmometers, trigonometers, machines, skeletons, and flowers were to serve as realistic bases for the study of various subjects, and the children were to print and publish their own textbooks. It was on this school (not the infant department, which was Owen's idea) that Maclure devoted all his thought. An industrial department was grafted on to the school, so that the child should pay for its maintenance, and gain self-respect by so doing. In this the child chose his trade, and if he had no positive choice, Neef was to assign him to one for which he displayed a special aptitude.[1]

There were two other schools: one leading to this higher school, and the other leading from it. The former would be called an infant school and the latter a vocational course. The junior school, as might be expected, was under Madame Fretageot, and the vocational school under Phiquepal d'Arusmont. Numbers, according to Owen's son, were 130 before Maclure arrived; afterwards, according to Maclure, they were nearly tripled.[2] Maclure's estimate was: 100 in the junior school, nearly two hundred in the higher school, and 80 in the vocational department. What is even more important is that the educational society had purchased from Owen no less than 900 acres of land for an experimental farm, several houses, two large granaries, and a public building which was being converted into a workshop. This public building had been a church used by the former Rappite members of the community.[3]

Maclure's educational venture was the real core of the enter-

---

[1] The first number of the New Harmony, Indiana, *Gazette* contains an advertisement of the school. From the first, the schools appear to have been run as a separate society, called Macluria. The literature is enormous, the best accounts being George B. Lockwood, *The New Harmony Movement* (New York, 1905), and Will S. Monroe, *A History of the Pestalozzian Movement in the United States* (New York, 1907). Maclure seems to have believed in vocational guidance.

[2] Robert Dale Owen, *Threading My Way, An Autobiography* (London, 1874), 260. Maclure's letter dated 4 July, 1826, and addressed to the editor of the *Revue Encyclopédique* is given in Frank Podmore, *Robert Owen* (London, 1923), 313.

[3] Nothing has been said of the previous settlers at New Harmony, whose leader had sold the settlement *en bloc* to Robert Owen. Prudence Hanks wrote of Owen at this time 'He has already had near a thousand persons join him, American and English—he is an agreeable and very benevolent man, but visionary—he wants to *set the world to rights* and does not know it is a work beyond his powers.' Gladys Scott Thomson, *A Pioneer Family* (1953), 100.

prise, for it drew into its service the distinguished foreigners who had accompanied Maclure down the Ohio. Troost and Lesueur both taught their respective disciplines to the boys, and a third scientist, Thomas Say ('the father of descriptive entomology in America'), also added his efforts.[1] Say was 39 when the New Harmony educational experiment began: a Philadelphian like the others, but with a wider periphery of American experience. He had accompanied Major Stephen Long's expedition to the Rocky Mountains seven years before, and had geologized in Minnesota. The community were indeed lucky to have such a further star among their illuminati: especially as he anchored himself in 1827 by marrying Lucy Way Sistaire, one of three sisters who had come on the boatload of knowledge.

With Owen gone, the community shook off his political ideas and settled down as a happy family. Intermarriage drew them closer: Neef's daughter married Owen's third son, David Dale Owen; Professor George Davidson married Robert Fauntleroy's sister; Jane Owen (Owen's daughter) married Robert Fauntleroy, and d'Arusmont married Frances Wright, a transient member of the community who made her name elsewhere.

Owen's sons seem to have been infected by Maclure's geological enthusiasms rather than by their father's politics. For, with the notable exception of Robert Dale Owen, the eldest, they all played their part in the schools, teaching and researching.[2] Indeed, the extremely critical Mrs. Trollope, whom nobody could accuse of communistic leanings, thought it a good idea to send one of her sons, Henry, to school here. Other travellers in America, like the Duke of Saxe-Weimar, were similarly impressed. The Duke wrote: 'All the boys and girls have a very healthy look, are cheerful and lively, and by no means bashful. The boys labour in the field or the garden, and were now occupied with new fencing. The girls learn female employments;

[1] For Say and a number of letters from Maclure, see Harry B. Weiss and Grace N. Ziegler, *Thomas Say, Early American Naturalist* (Springfield, Illinois, 1931).

[2] Robert Dale Owen, a rolling stone, nevertheless did great work for education in Indiana, and, as a member of Congress, introduced the Bill for the founding of the Smithsonian Institution. William died at New Harmony in 1842. David Dale arrived in New Harmony in January 1828, and eleven years later made it the headquarters of the United States Geological Survey. Richard, who arrived in New Harmony when he was 18, died at New Harmony when he was 81, having, in the meantime, taught in the schools, run a steam flour-mill, and been professor of natural science at Western Military Institute of Kentucky.

they were as little oppressed as the boys with labour and teaching; these happy and interesting little children were much more employed in making their youth pass as pleasantly as possible.'[1] The research, always a concomitant of good teaching, went on at a very high level. Troost, it is true, moved to Nashville, Tennessee, in 1827 with his large collections of natural history, and was, the following year, made professor of geology, mineralogy, chemistry, and natural history at the university. But the technique he followed was Maclurian; he built a large museum (the best west of the Appalachians) just as Maclure had done in Philadelphia,[2] and, as the State geologist of Tennessee, he did much to make its resources known. Lesueur, on the other hand, spent the next twelve years of his life teaching drawing in the community school at New Harmony, engraving plates, and sketching the specimens of St. Louis, New Orleans, and near-by states. As his biographer acknowledged 'les rêves de New-Harmony ont laissé Lesueur indifférent'.[3] He piloted the Prince of Wied around,[4] and executed the illustrations for the work of Thomas Say. It was Say's work, written at New Harmony, on the conchology and entomology of the United States that Maclure subsidized most heavily. Madame Fretageot was delegated by Maclure to run the little community of scholars and teachers, as Maclure found yet another place where he could live.

According to Silliman's account on 17 November 1828, Maclure appeared at a meeting of the geological society 'decidedly marked by age and infirmity'. Silliman remarked 'the brilliant man whom I first saw twenty years before had now hoary locks; he stooped as he walked, and an ulcer on his leg

[1] Karl Bernhard, Duke of Saxe-Weimar Eisanach, *Travels Through North America during the Years 1825 and 1826* (2 volumes in one, Philadelphia, 1828), ii. 106–23.

[2] Maclure's work in helping the Academy of Natural Sciences was acknowledged at his death.

[3] According to Loir, *Charles Alexandre Lesueur*, he was making voyages with his sketch-book, and in the library of the museum at Le Havre, where he returned after the death of Say in 1834, there were no less than 700 drawings. He published at the New Harmony Press in 1827 his work *American Ichthyology, or Natural History of the Fishes of North America, with Coloured Figures Executed From Nature.*

[4] Prince Maximilian von Neuwied with his corps of scientific explorers spent the winter of 1832 at New Harmony. With Teutonic thoroughness, he had an artist and taxidermist with him. He published the account of his journey in *Reise in das innere Nord-America in den Jahren 1832 bis 1834* (2 vols., Coblentz, 1839–41).

made him lame'. Maclure had struck up a friendship with Thomas Cooper, a man of as radical an outlook as his own.[1] Maclure declared that he was now living in Mexico, and was intending to bring back a number of young native Indians in order to have them educated in the United States, that they might diffuse the benefits of instruction among the people of their own race. But what is even more significant is that P. L. A. Cordier, author of *Essai sur la Température de l'Intérieur de la Terre*, should have considered Maclure important enough to send him a copy for his opinion. Cordier was a member of the French Academy, and the doyen of French geologists.[2]

Before leaving for Mexico, Maclure had organized his 'school of industry'. 'Utility shall be the scale on which we shall endeavour to measure the value of everything' he announced, and, on 16 January 1828, the *New Harmony Disseminator* first appeared to ventilate his ideas 'edited printed and published by the pupils of the school of industry'. In this octavo fortnightly, Maclure's opinions were given to the world. From Mexico he would communicate them, while at New Harmony Madame Fretageot acted as his lieutenant, cosseting Say, ensuring that d'Arusmont did his job, and ordering the numerous talent that had congregated at New Harmony. The first number of the *Disseminator* announced: 'These sheets will contain observations on the possibility of improving practical education, by separating the useful from the ornamental, and thereby reducing the labour and fatigue of instructing youth, and we will endeavour to prove that children can educate, clothe and feed themselves by their own labour when judiciously applied to produce articles of real value.'

His friend Silliman thought he was too modest in his management of the enterprise: 'I have always wished', he wrote to

---

[1] Thomas Cooper (1759–1839), subject of a biographical study by Dumas Malone, *The Public Life of Thomas Cooper, 1783–1839* (New Haven, Connecticut, 1926), had also emigrated from England. He was a friend of Priestley, and Jefferson had wanted him to become the cornerstone of the University of Virginia. But Cooper preferred to hold the chair of chemistry at the University of South Carolina, to which he was elected in January, 1820. See *ante* p. 64.

[2] P. L. A. Cordier, 1777–1861, had been a pupil of Dolomieu, whom he accompanied to Egypt with Napoleon in 1797. On his return he was made inspector of mines in the Appenines. In 1819 he obtained the chair of geology of the museum, and in 1822 became a member of the academy. He had sent his essay addressed to Maclure at New Harmony.

Maclure', that there might eventually be an establishment on that subject *to bear your name*, and to diffuse knowledge and benefit to this country, when you and I are gone. Even a posthumous dedication of a small portion of your fine Western or Spanish territories would accomplish the object without seriously interfering with your great and interesting undertaking at New Harmony. Forgive this liberty . . .' [1]

(6)

Maclure now broke his connexions with New Harmony. Say died in 1834, depriving Maclure not only of one of his closest associates, but also of one of his dearest friends. Neef, who had left New Harmony in 1828, returned in 1834, but this was counterbalanced by the loss of Lesueur, who in 1836 went back to Paris, whence he became director of the museum at Le Havre. But perhaps the greatest blow of all was the loss of Marie Louise Duclos Fretageot who had managed his affairs so well since 1828. Not for nothing was she the wife of a colonel of hussars in Napoleon's army: for five years she had mothered the little group of advanced students, acting as midwife to all their literary productions. Her death in 1833 caused a serious break in the chain of communicative control by which Maclure kept his hand on affairs in New Harmony.

Maclure now left his Mexican resting place, and in the autumn of 1835 gave his New Harmony Library to the Academy of Natural Sciences at Philadelphia. The 2,259 volumes which went afforded a complete coverage of every department of useful knowledge, especially natural history and fine art. In addition, he gave to the academy a $10,000 claim against the Spanish government which he possessed, following it up with a gift of another $10,000 in 1838. Such munificence enabled the society to build on the corner of Broad and George Street a building in which they could hold their meetings. The first meeting, held on 7 February 1840, marked the year of Maclure's death in Mexico.

(7)

The surge and tug of the ideas which Maclure manipulated, the ambience of the men he brought to the west, and the domi-

[1] Fisher, *Life of Benjamin Silliman*, ii. 44. Evidently Silliman did not think that New Harmony was going downhill.

nant impress of his own enthusiasm weaned Owen's sons from their father's political activities, and set them in the careers that they followed. David Dale Owen's indication of the mineral riches of Iowa, his classification of the subcarboniferous strata of Indiana (a name that he coined) and his official reports, are themselves tributes to Maclure, whose infectious enthusiasm made New Harmony the real centre of United States geology till the transfer to the Smithsonian Institution took place.

Maclure's contempt for antiquarians stemmed from their invariable opposition to the general good, their 'supporting and enforcing arbitrary maxims of what now may be called despotism; obstructing by sophistry and miscalled logic, all the roads to the comfort and happiness of the millions; reasoning that because the ancients, whom they call our masters, did not arrive at the same height of perfection, it is impossible for any of the moderns to improve. I would not give a single new fact of the operations of the laws of nature, for all the antiquities that exist.'[1]

The light that radiated from New Harmony was a very real one, shining in all sorts of places where it is difficult to follow.[2] The little friendless Irish boy, Edward Murphy, thought so much of it, that when he became a man of substance, he left large sums of money to establish a library. Horace Mann's cousin, Josiah Mann, was living here in 1850, and his three daughters married into the Owen family.[3] Bronson Alcott, then teaching in the centre district school of Cheshire, Connecticut, corresponded with the New Harmonists.[4] Perhaps the most exciting whiff of what was happening on the Wabash passed to young Abraham Lincoln: who is not only said to have seen the colonists pass up the river on their way to New Harmony, but also to have begged his father to let him join them (not because he was interested in their political ideas, for he would certainly never

---

[1] Maclure, *Opinions on Various Subjects*, 229.

[2] Donald C. Peattie, *Green Laurels* (London, 1937), 264–88; Louis Martin Sears, 'New Harmony and the American Spirit', *Indiana Magazine of History* (Bloomington, Indiana, 1905–), XXXVIII (1942), 225–30; and Arthur Deen, 'Early Science in the Ohio Valley', ibid., XXXIII (1937), 32–44, have essayed to do so.

[3] Elfrieda Lang, 'The Inhabitants of New Harmony According to the Federal Census of 1850.' ibid., XLII (1942), 355–394 for an analysis of the census returns of 1850.

[4] Odell Shepard, *The Journals of Bronson Alcott* (Boston, 1938), 4.

have heard of them, but because they had books—and he was desperate to learn).[1]

Maclure took good care that the light should shine after his death, for by his will, no less than 160 libraries were set up or supplied from a fund which he provided for the purposes of aiding instruction. The importance of these libraries in stimulating thought among ordinary people when such institutions did not exist has yet to be calculated. Visitors like Constantine Raffinesque (1783–1840), John J. Audubon (1785–1851), Joseph Leidy (1823–91), Leo Lesquereux (1806–89), George Engelman (1809–84) made the place a scientific Mecca, to which such a world-famous geologist as Sir Charles Lyell had to pay his respects. Major Sidney Lyon, who superintended the geodetic survey of Kentucky, Professor H. A. Worthen, the State geologist of Illinois, Professor E. T. Cox, the State geologist of Indiana, and Dr. J. C. Norwood, who participated in the geological survey of New York, were all, in a real sense, New Harmony men.

Something of the infectious enthusiasm that must have prevailed at New Harmony in the years 1825–6 can be gathered from the lament of the county clerk of Greene County, who wrote to the governor that the two associate judges had abandoned the county and attached themselves to the new community on the banks of the Wabash. One left in November 1825, and the other in April 1826.[2] We can only recapture it if we look at Maclure's own testament, his fiery *Opinions on Various Subjects*, peppered with the commas which scar his prose and make his meaning so opaque. Gathered in these two volumes are all his newspaper articles on education, his political essays, and his philosophy. Breathing through them all is his fervid patriotism: as he urged 'we still continue to copy Britain in spite of fifty-one years of independence. The mechanism of our minds, like a clock wound up under the old colonial system, goes on without being changed by external circumstances. But in no slavish imitation of the follies of Europe, have we been so essentially injured in our vital principles, as in the copy we have taken and still continue to take,

---

[1] John Strachey, *The Theory and Practice of Socialism* (London, 1936), 290. He told Jesse Fell that in Indiana 'there was absolutely nothing to excite ambition for education'.

[2] Dorothy Riker, ed., *Executive Proceedings of the State of Indiana, 1816–1836* (Indianapolis, 1947), 447. This is volume XXIX of the Indiana Historical *Collections*.

of their absurd, monkish system of education'.[1] To this theme he returned again and again. He guaranteed that he could teach geology in five lessons with properly ticketed specimens.[2] His enthusiasm for the spirit of the Pestalozzian system, and the healthy economy of Fellenberg's industrial schools never blinded him to the basic needs of a democracy: positive knowledge. Without that, despotisms could trample as they had done in Europe. He was no doctrinaire socialist, but a pioneer in the scientific movement in the West: one of the creators of the new humanism.

[1] *Opinions on Various Subjects*, 105.
[2] ibid., 51.

7

The Religion of Community

(1)

Owen's departure from the English stage left it clear for others. Quite a body of people of one kind or another were interested in forming communities. There was, for instance, John Minter Morgan who first heard Robert Owen at the London Tavern on 21 August 1817 expound his gospel that 'national education and employment could alone create a permanent, rational, intelligent, wealthy, and superior population, and that these results could be attained only by a scientific arrangement of the people, united in properly constructed villages of unity and co-operation'. As Owen became more aggressively atheistic, Minter Morgan became more conciliatory and Christian. Minter Morgan had supported the Duke of Kent's Committee, established in 1819 to raise subscriptions for the establishment of an experimental 'parallelogram' or 'Village of Unity and Co-operation', by publishing an enthusiastic pamphlet entitled *Remarks on the Practicability of Mr. Owen's Plan to improve the Conditions of the Lower Classes*.[1]

Morgan was concerned with the moral consequences of indiscriminate industrialization, and having a substantial income,

---

[1] His importance has been recognized by Max Beer, *History of British Socialism* (1929) i. pp. 126, 180, 184, 228–30. G. D. H. Cole, *Socialist Thought: The Forerunners 1789–1850* (1953), 51, describes him as 'the first to take up Owen's plans of 1817 and advocate their adoption, while rejecting Owen's hostility to religion'.

130

devoted it to projects of social amelioration. In 1826 when he was 44 years old he published *The Revolt of the Bees*. Serialized by the *Co-operative Magazine*, this was much read by working men, who bought it for their Mechanics' Institutes. Harriet Martineau read it too. Taking as his model the text of that cynical eighteenth-century Freud, Bernard Mandeville, he turned the image of the hive to other purposes. Mandeville had used it to illustrate his thesis that private vices were public virtues; Minter Morgan used it to show this was wrong. He described a hive that went through five revolutions, from 'noble savagery', through 'pastoral occupations', 'farming' and 'industry', to a fifth revolution pioneered by 'the wise bee'—Owen. This fifth revolution affected a beneficial redistribution of the fruits of wealth and knowledge to all the bees. The idea caught on. He followed this by publishing in the following year *An Inquiry Respecting Private Property and the Authority and Perpetuity of the Apostolic Institution of a Community of Goods* (1827), showing that the original function of a deacon was that of custodian of the 'communal property' of the early Christians.[1]

Apian as Minter Morgan's own industrious eclecticism was, his energies were from now onwards directed to harness the power of the Church of England to the cause of community founding. He addressed the Bishop of London in 1830 on the importance of this. 'Through the insufficiency of knowledge and experience in their respective eras,' Morgan wrote, Plato, More and Bacon 'were unable to perfect a system'. 'Yet', he continued, 'their general principle was true and has at length assumed a practical and durable form'. This 'practical and durable form' was that 'each class of society could derive great advantages (from a community) without the surrender of their present habits and opinions'. He asked the Bishop of London to sanction and commend communities as 'an advance towards a superior state of society'.[2]

To enable each class to preserve 'its present habits and opinions' he proposed that there should be communities based on class. A 'college', as big as one of the largest squares in

---

[1] This work shows how the Essenes (p. 121), Spenceans (p. 132) and Shakers (p. 134) and Moravians (p. 134) coloured thought on the subject. He republished it in the Phoenix Library in 1850.

[2] *Letters to the Bishop of London* (1830).

London and surrounded by a park and gardens, was to be built for the upper classes. Each of the 1,000 families it would house were to pay a rent of £100 a year. The cost he estimated at £800,000. He described this upper-class community as combining

> the pleasures of town and country residence, for besides procuring, in a superior degree, their present objects including education for their children, they could have libraries, theatres, and philosophical apparatus for lectures, music and ballrooms, baths, gymnasia, and whatever belongs to the highest physical and moral cultivation . . . Increased attention could be given to scientific enquiry by magnificent orreries, globes lately exhibited at Paris, superior solar microscopes, and other aids to philosophical illustration, and such as no private fortune, however great, could command. The powerful impulse which such exhibitions and aids would have in stimulating the useful curiosity of the children, must be obvious. The concerts also could be conducted upon a scale of magnitude, and with an effect beyond the reach of any private entertainment. The Association would enable the children of the middle and higher classes of society to enjoy the benefit of an infant school, which has hitherto been confined to the working classes.[1]

Morgan had a model of this 'college' made and placed in the saloon of the Colosseum in Regent's Park. For the other two classes, more modest communities were projected. 'Squares' were to be erected seven miles outside London and centred round a school. The unemployed would have a 'settlement' to provide work.

For those not in community, Morgan suggested that churches should be opened on workdays as community centres and in the evenings for lectures. Even here he was careful to add, 'There would be no premature mixture of classes, as each class could occupy the same pews and seats as on a Sunday.'

(2)

Minter Morgan was in close touch with Stedman Whitwell[2] and William Thompson.[3] Both published analogous schemes in

[1] ibid.

[2] Stedman Whitwell was at New Harmony (Indiana) with Owen from January to August 1826 where he published a new nomenclature suggested for communities in *New Harmony Gazette*, 12 April 1826, and published an account of it in the *Co-operative Magazine* (London) in January 1827.

[3] R. K. P. Pankhurst, *William Thompson, 1775–1833* (London 1954).

the same year. Stedman Whitwell's *Description of an Architectural Model . . . for a Community upon a principle of United Interests, as advocated by Robert Owen* (London 1830), described one three times as large as Russell Square, covering thirty-three acres with a quadrangle of twenty-two acres. A diagonal line of this vast structure was to coincide with the meridian to ensure equal distribution of light and be convenient for astronomical and geographical purposes. Each side of the parallelogram was to be of 1,000 ft. long. Each apartment was to have a ground and a first floor, two sets of sitting-rooms, a chamber, a closet and hot and cold water. Dormitories were to be provided both for the unmarried and for children. The whole building was to be internally heated. There were to be libraries and public rooms with large staircases leading throughout the building. It was a Fourierist phalanx anglicized.

Thompson went one further than mere proportions by issuing *Practical Directions for the Speedy and Economical Establishment of Communities* (1830) a copy of which he gave to Ralahine. He thought that communities could be founded as easily as 'the establishment of any ordinary manufacture', by a joint stock company. Communities, he considered could arise out of any of the 300 co-operative ventures then existing in England. From such co-operative nuclei, communities of 2,000 people could take shape. His sanitary, agricultural and economic ideas included a suggestion for regulation of the birth rate. He died three years later leaving £10,000 to some socialist trustees for the purpose of establishing Communities. As the legacy was inadequate and creditors were pressing, the plan came to nothing.

Thompson's plan captured the imagination of co-operators; at the Manchester Co-operative Conference of 1831, it was resolved 'upon the plan laid down by Mr. Thompson' to establish communication with 199 other Co-operative Societies in order that 'an incipient Community of two hundred persons, with a capital of £6,000 may immediately be formed in some part of England'. A committee was duly formed in October of that year to carry out the plan. 'Immediacy', however, was the stumbling block. Owen (who had returned to England in 1829) discouraged the project, and at the 1832 Congress in London the Committee reported that they had only secured support from two of the societies. Travellers from America, who had seen communities forming, fed the enthusiasm of T. Wayland, who in his *Equalization of Property and the Formation of Community* (1832), revealed that he was much encouraged by their tales.

(3)

Thompson was in turn influenced by St. Simonian ideas. The eponymous founder of this faith was a Frenchman who, like Swedenborg, tried to reconcile science with Christianity. His followers, again like the Swedenborgians, treated his gospel as a new revelation. They founded a monastery at Menilmont, near Paris, and arranged to travel to the shores of the Bosphorus to look for a 'Female Messiah'. The story of how they built a canal in the Nile Delta does not concern us here, since before these eccentricities began, St. Simonism was working through English social thought.

One of the English exponents of St. Simonian ideas was James Elimalet Smith who in 1833 averred that Christianity was not yet established, nor could it be unless an equality of rank and privilege and a community of goods was acknowledged. To Smith a true Christian was 'one who turns the world upside down'. Christ's disciples were true Christians because they had established 'a happy little community and only failed to be happy in the fellowship of one common mind and interest when they departed from the elementary principles of their Master's faith, and retreated into the old prevailing system of society around them, in which the interest of the community was overlooked in the separate and conflicting interests of private individuals'.[1]

As Smith saw it 'the establishment of the social system is nothing but the Christian millennium; it is the last part of a great plan of nature, and circumstances will occur to further its advancement in spite of hostility of priests and lawgivers'. And again, 'The *seed* of Christianity is the doctrine of SOCIAL LOVE, the *fruit* is the establishment of the SOCIAL SYSTEM.' To emphasize the importance which St. Simon attached to 'La Femme Libre', the publishers of his lecture enclosed a coloured engraving of 'a St. Simonian Free-Woman' which could be detached and framed for contemplation.[2]

[1] The only study of him to date is W. A. Smith, *'Shepherd' Smith the Universalist* (cf. pp. 138 and 175) (London, 1892). He edited *The Shepherd*, a complete file of which, beginning on 30 August 1834, is in the Library of the University of London.
[2] *A lecture on a Christian Community* (1833).

It was to spread St. Simonian ideas that Smith founded *The Shepherd* in 1834. It was edited solely by Smith till July 1837 after which others helped him. A lively preoccupation with messianic precedents animated the contributors.[1] They dismissed both Joanna Southcott (whose followers had 'no brotherhood amongst them') and Richard Brothers as bogus. Of Anne Lee, the founder of the Shakers, however, they had many good words to say. She was described as 'one of the finest types of the new system of Christianity which exists'. 'Of course', they went on, 'as a type it is full of imperfection, but the brotherhood, community of interest, industry and prosperity and stability which characterize the institution (of Shakers) place it in the foremost rank of the millenial precursors. It is merely a political type however, no new truth was made known to it'.[2]

Smith himself preferred to advocate the doctrines of St. Simon. In this he was not alone. John Stuart Mill confessed that he was inclined to think that 'under some modification or other' the 'St. Simonite system' was 'likely to be the permanent condition of our race'. Carlyle was more entangled: he prepared a translation of St. Simon's *Nouveau Chrétianisme*, but was unable to find a publisher for it.[3] James Elimalet Smith also translated it, and found a publisher.

In his translation (*New Christianity*, 1834), Smith pointed out that 'industry can ameliorate the condition of the poor far more than any of the measures hitherto taken by temporal or spiritual powers'. For Smith, science could repeat the miracle of the loaves and fishes by making men 'happy not only in heaven, but on earth'. Smith made available for English readers the St. Simonian idea that religion was 'a human invention . . . the sole political institution tending towards the organisation of humanity'. Together they had published *St. Simonism in London* (1833), giving the substance of the St. Simonian creed.

Industry must from henceforth be the basis on which the government will rest; and the organisation of industry must be the end to which the science of government must aim. Competition and

[1] Smith himself had been influenced by John Wroe, for whom see *infra* pp. 274–6.
[2] For the influence of the Shaker Communities in America on English social thought see E. D. Andrews, *A People called Shakers, A Search for the Perfect Society* (New York, 1953).
[3] D. B. Cofer, *St. Simonism and the Radicalism of Thomas Carlyle* (London, 1931).

antagonism must give way to association and community of interests. Industry in itself is peaceful, averse to broils and quarrels, opposed to oppression and war; it becomes only a hostile power when oppressed.

And again :–

The whole state must gradually be transferred into one large establishment, directed by the most enlightened among the industrious classes; and the government must transform itself into the chief manager of industry and commerce.

It was a convincing creed. 'I defy anyone to answer the arguments of a St. Simonist', said Samuel Taylor Coleridge on 1 August 1831, whilst that sturdy sceptic, Harriet Martineau, saw that it offered 'a new law of love and human equality in place of that Christian one which it assumed from existing appearances to have failed'. She went on: 'Many listened, with new hope and a long-forgotten cheer, to the preaching of the golden rule of this new faith—that everyone should be employed according to his capacity, and measured according to his works . . . work was to be worship and affectionate co-operation was to be piety.'[1] Even across the Channel, at Le Havre, the young German poet Heine was writing :–

'Tis on this rock that we shall build
The Church's third foundation;
Our sufferings are over now,
For new the dispensation.

That Holy God is in the light
And in the darkest places;
And God is everything there is,
God is in our embraces.[2]

Among the English converts were the Swedenborgian preacher Rowland Detroisier[3] and Mrs. Wheeler.[4] People in

---

[1] R. K. P. Pankhurst, 'St Simonism in England', *Twentieth Century*, CLII (1952), 330–40; 498–512; CLII (1953), 47–58, and *The Saint Simonians Mill and Carlyle* (London, 1957).

[2] The translation can be found in E. M. Butler, *Heinrich Heine* (London, 1955).

[3] G. J. Holyoake, *History of Co-operation* (London, 1906) i. 227–8, who knew him, thought that 'he was a man of greater promise than any who lived among the political and co-operative classes'. He filled his pulpit at Hulme with geological specimens, electric and galvanic machines, was the founder of the Banksian Society at Manchester and of mechanics' institutes at Hulme and Salford (Holyoake says 'the first two ever established in England'). He impressed not only Carlyle and John

London, Liverpool, Manchester, Birmingham, Dublin, Glasgow and Edinburgh displayed interest, and a special chapel in Manchester was mooted. Two St. Simonian apostles, Prati, and Fontana, hired the Burton Lecture Rooms in Burton Crescent, started a school and issued pamphlets. They met and talked with Robert Owen and George Grote.

Though anxious to rescue labour from the toils of capital, St. Simonians opposed small-scale co-operative communities. In their opinion these offered 'no common life, no motive of action, no spirit of order, no method in the distribution of labour, no compass for the retribution of the worker, no standard for fixing employments and gradations among the members'. Small-scale communities to them were 'a mere chance medley composition, or at best an unwieldy corporation . . . witness the decay of several labour exchanges and incipient communities founded here and elsewhere upon a false and metaphysical principle of non-responsibility and mathematical equality'. In place of such communities, St. Simonians hoped to establish a 'true association' with men of great moral principle; a religion which should be used as social policy. *De chacun suivant sa capacité: a chacun selon ses oeuvres*, ran their text, and it was to re-echo down the nineteenth century.[1]

Basically they were chiliasts. The clergy in St. Simonian eyes had only given men a celestial paradise, but the growth of industry now made it possible to establish a paradise on earth. According to their English interpreters, the two great stages of human progress corresponded to the two great divisions of nature: material (the law) and physical (the gospel). These

---

[1] By invoking the spirit of Christianity against its institutional leaders he employed, as F. E. Manuel, *The New World of Henri Saint-Simon* (Cambridge, Mass., 1956), 349, writes, 'a tactic destined to have a long history amongst utopians and revolutionaries in modern times, from Cabet's *Le Communisme c'est le vrai Christianisme* to recent identical slogans paraded by world communism in Catholic countries'.

Stuart Mill, but Lady Noel Byron, and Jeremy Bentham as well. He was the secretary of the National Political Union (formed in 1831) to secure the passage of the 1832 Reform Bill and later the lecturer at the New Mechanical Hall of Science at Finsbury. Characteristically he died in the service of education, having caught a bad chill on the opening of the Mechanics Institute at Stratford.

[4] Mrs. Ann Wheeler was a member of a St. Simonite Circle at Caen in 1818 and also a friend of Jeremy Bentham and Robert Owen. She introduced Fontana and Prati to James Elimalet Smith. R. K. P. Pankhurst, op. cit.

were embodied in the male and female principles which, when joined produced 'The New World'. The St. Simonian social system would unite the two. 'Of all the social systems ever promulgated', wrote Smith, 'St. Simonism, has proved the most electrical in its influence upon the imagination.' He also deployed the view of all the principal Utopists: Plato, More, St. Simon, and Fourier. Readers were expected to 'fill of the vacua of one by the verbosity of the other'. One of the contributors was Charles Lane, a Pestalozzian, who wrote 'Education Practically Considered' for the issue of 12 August 1837. Education was one aspect of community building, communities themselves needed building.[1]

(4)

Smith soon obtained a patron, Mrs. Chichester, and on 31 July 1838 he wrote 'Mrs. C. and myself felt much interested in several of the members of the aesthetic fraternity who associate together for mutual instruction at Mr. G's lodging ("our mutual friend *J. P. Greaves*")'. Greaves was a mystic and a friend of Charles Lane, who, wrote Smith, 'has sent out a useful pamphlet on betrothal. Everything is good that will break up and break down the present laws, systems, and arrangements of marriage, which, as now existing in every grade of society, are most vicious.'[2] Mrs. Chichester was also a vegetarian for, as Smith said, 'she wants Lane to co-operate with our efforts to bring eating animal flesh and blood, and the butchery trade altogether, into thorough disgrace and contempt'.[3]

Thanks to Mrs. Chichester, Smith was able to hire a hall in London to found a new journal called *The Penny Satirist*. Amongst his audience was J. A. Heraud, who with F. F. Barham edited the *New Monthly Magazine*.

[1] He quoted with approval from a review of Cooper's *Excursions in Italy*, 'Let there be a company formed to erect buildings of great size, to lodge the labouring mechanics and manufacturers. Such an edifice might be raised on arches with composition floors. It might enjoy every facility of water and heat, and even of cooking and washing, on a large scale, and, of course economically. The price of rooms could be graduated according to means and space obtained for the exercise of children in the greater area of so many united lots. Entire streets might be constructed on this community plan, the whole being subject to a common policy. Here however, the community principle should cease, and each individual be left to his own effort.' *The Shepherd*, 10 March 1837.

[2] W. A. Smith, *Shepherd Smith the Universalist* (London, 1892), 198.

[3] op. cit., 199.

Heraud impressed Emerson who described his editorship of the *Monthly Magazine* as a

'bolder and more creative spirit than any other British Journal'; and Emerson lamented that 'papers on the highest Transcendental themes were found in odd vicinity with the lowest class of flash and so-called comic tales', but excused it as 'a necessity, we suppose of British taste, made these strange bed-fellows acquainted, and Mr. Heraud had done what he could'. Emerson was particularly impressed by ' Foreign Aids to Self-Intelligence . . . especially the papers on Boehme and Swedenborg. The last is, we think, the very first attempt to do justice to this mystic, by an analysis of his total works; and though avowedly imperfect is, as far as it goes, a faithful piece of criticism'.[1]

Emerson's views were definitely not shared by Thomas Carlyle who regarded Heraud as 'a loquacious, scribacious little man, of middle age, of parboiled greasy aspect, whom Leigh Hunt describes as "wavering in the most astonishing manner between Something and Nothing".' 'To me' Carlyle wrote to Emerson,

he is chiefly remarkable as being still—with his entirely enormous stock of vanity and very small stock of faculty—out of Bedlam. He picked up a notion or two from Coleridge many years ago, and has ever since been rattling them in his head, like peas in an empty bladder, and calling on the world to 'list the music of the spheres'. He escapes *assassination*, as I calculate, chiefly by being the cheerfulest, best-natured little creature extant. You cannot kill him, he laughs so softly, even when he is like killing you. John Mill said 'I forgive him freely for interpreting the Universe, now when I find he cannot pronounce his *h*'s. Really this is no caricature; you have not seen the match of Heraud in your days. I mentioned to him once that Novalis had said "The highest problem of Authorship is the writing of a Bible". "That is precisely what I am doing" answered the aspiring, unaspiring.'[2]

(5)

Meanwhile in Lancashire the community idea was pursued with almost messianic zeal.[3] Elijah Dixon of Manchester

[1] The *Dial* (Boston, 1842), 231.

[2] *The Correspondence of Thomas Carlyle and Ralph Waldo Emerson*, Ed. C. E. Norton (Boston, 1883), i. 277.

[3] 'Gracious Father of universal nature!' apostrophized the *Lancashire and Yorkshire Co-operator* on 1 October 1831, 'hasten the glorious day; let thy kingdom come on earth that all men may love thee and love one another.' Quoted Neil J. Smelser, *Social Change in the Industrial Revolution* (1959), 258.

attacked the existing land monopoly and sponsored a 'Social Community Company' in 1832. This was to buy land on capital raised by weekly subscriptions with which a co-operative community could be established. One of the members made 'a beautiful model' of the scheme. It has been suggested that this company built a farmhouse west of Manchester at Chat Moss and tried to farm 600 acres of waste land. Then again the Reverend Joseph Marriott of Warrington said he 'would give up his profession and with his family enter such a society'. William Carson of Pemberton near Wigan went on record as saying that 'many persons in Lancashire had serious intentions of forming a Community' at Worsley and Liverpool. At the first co-operative congress, held at Manchester in May 1831, and at the second at Birmingham in October 1831 and at the third in London in April 1832, these and other Lancashire delegates spoke out strongly for immediate steps to be taken to establish a community.[1]

But it was Owen who brought community out of congress and into the arena. His paper the *Crisis*, first issued in 1832, carried a picture of a community on its title page. Two years later as the *New Moral World*, it carried numerous suggestions for communities, 'J.C.', for instance, writing in the fourth number of the *New Moral World*, proposed a 'Floating Co-operative Community', arguing :–

> As the preservation of the human species depended on the ark, why may not the regeneration of society arise from the waters. The very deluge which destroyed the imperfections of anti-diluvian society, may become instrumental, by the aid of modern science, in establishing the foundation of a new moral world by giving a local habitation and a name to what has been contemptuously called the visionary system of Mr. Owen.

'J.C.' suggested that an old warship should be purchased on the Thames where such an experiment might be initiated.[2] Another correspondent, 'E.L.', suggested a week later that a community should be established.[3]

As Owen re-entered the English scene, Morgan intensified

---

[1] A. E. Musson, 'The Ideology of Early Co-operation in Lancashire and Cheshire', *Transactions of the Lancashire and Cheshire Antiquarian Society*, LXVIII (Manchester, 1958), 122–7.

[2] *New Moral World*, 22 November 1834.

[3] ibid., 29 November 1834.

his educational and mystical work. He was increasingly drawn to Greaves who, as Pestalozzi's chief English disciple, he held in high regard, remarking in *Hampden in the Nineteenth Century, or Colloquies on the Errors and Improvement of Society* (1834), that 'among the numerous advocates for various improvements, there was not one who exceeded him in personal sacrifices to what he esteemed a duty'.

When in 1834 the *New Moral World* was issued, its opening sentences struck a new millennial note: 'The time is therefore arrived when the foretold Millennium is about to commence, when the slave and the prisoner, the bondsman and the bonds-woman, the child and the servant, shall be set free for ever, and oppression of body and mind shall be known to no man.' This challenging overture marked Owen's emergence as a Utopist proper; his alliance with trade unions, co-operators and political reformers dissolved for ever. He told his friends (among them Francis Place), that 'within six months the whole state and condition of Society in Great Britain would be changed'. Having crossed his Rubicon (and he used the very image) Owen, like most prophets of a new dispensation, went on a missionary tour, began writing an account of his life, and above all, establishing a 'church'. This Church, 'The Association of All Classes of All Nations formed to effect an entire change in the character and condition of the Human Race', was established on 1 May 1835 to 'carry into practical operation' his 'system of society'. A fund was floated to form a community.

The quickening interest of his adherents pulsates through the pages of the *New Moral World*. Thus W.H.S. from Birmingham wrote on 8 October 1836, to 'whet the blunted purpose', and 'Socialist' on 10 December 1836 wrote 'Let me entreat you to take the subject really into hand and to establish a community'. Joseph Smith of Salford and James Charlesworth of Bolton wrote to similar effect. James Hind on 7 January 1837 declared that 'a community should be speedily established, as a nucleus for the world'. On 6 May 1837, L. Pitkiethly, the famous Huddersfield Radical, was reported as resolving to collect the scattered disciples of the Rational System in the West Riding together to establish a community. A substantial number of contributing delegates came forward from over a dozen of the northern manufacturing towns, when the annual co-operative congress was held in Manchester in 1837. The Society was registered and Owen appointed 'Rational Service Father'. A secretary and editor, G. A. Fleming, was appointed and the congress resolved to 'create a new public opinion in favour of this entire change in the character and condition of man by public meetings, lectures, discussions, missionaries, cheap publications, mutual exchange of productions upon equitable principles without individual competition'. They insisted however, that their main objective was to found 'as soon as possible, Communities of United Interest'. And to show they meant business, the delegates formed a 'National Community Friendly Society' to initiate the work.

The Missionaries were duly and promptly appointed and in 1838 began to tour London, Birmingham, Leeds, Manchester, Liverpool, and Glasgow. All were enthusiastic communitarians: Lloyd Jones, Rigby, Green, Buchanan, Campbell and Hollick. Campbell we have already met as an active member of the Orbiston community and shall meet again. Green we shall meet again. They and their colleagues soon formed nearly sixty 'branches' before they had been in office for a year. Meanwhile the society inspected sites for a community.

By 1838 a 'Christian Community Society' was being formed and the *New Moral World* of 26 September 1840 reported that 'the impetus which has given form and consistency to the scattered efforts of this school of Communists seems to have emerged from Coventry and is principally to be attributed to Joseph Squires'. Squires was a teacher in the infant school at Gosford Street, Coventry, and acted as corresponding secretary to the Christian Community Society, other members of which were Thomas Barlow (of 28 Hardman Street, Manchester), and Elijah Dixon of (Woodward Street, Manchester). They too wished to settle their members on the land.

It was time for the Owenites to begin, and they did.

(6)

On 11, 12 or 13 July 1838, Owen went to stay with James Hill of Wretton near Wisbech whose estate had been selected by the National Community Friendly Society in 1837 as the site for their first experiment. Hill's insistence that he himself should direct the experiment led them to abandon this idea. Hill was married to the cause of social improvement; his second wife was the daughter of Southwood Smith, and his daughter, Octavia Hill, was to distinguish herself as a housing reformer. Hill's paper, the *Star in the East*, cast a fitful and intermittent millenarian light over the Fen Country.[1]

In 1839, the two societies—the Association of All Classes and the National Community Society—amalgamated as the Universal Community Society of Rational Religionists and registered as a friendly society. A second site was inspected—at Tytherly in Hampshire—and it was proposed to take both it and the Norfolk estate for community purposes.

They were encouraged in this by the great success of the missionaries who, in their second year of office, had increased their diocesan areas to include 350 towns and had brought in 50,000 adherents. These adherents were being organized into 'Social Institutions'—sometimes called Halls of Science. The first of these Social Institutions was opened in Sheffield under the leadership of Isaac Ironside.

In these Social Institutions, services and socials were synonymous. They possessed a hymnal, *Social Hymns*, a collection of 150 stirring songs. Some of them like Nos. 65, 129, and 148, were literally hymns to community.

> Community is labour blessed,
> Redemption from the Fall,
> The good of all by each possessed,
> The good of each by all.

> Community doth all possess
> That can to man be given;
> Community is happiness,
> Community is heaven.

In these Halls of Science adherents would discuss the *Book of the New Moral World* (then currently being published in seven parts) or a précis of it entitled *Human Nature or the Moral Science of Man* written especially for this purpose by Samuel Cornish. From these they learned that 25 million men could supply the wants of 600 millions. Only existing methods of producing and distributing wealth, the emphasis on profit, the

[1] C. E. Maurice, *Life of Octavia Hill* (1913), 5–6.

practice of isolating families, and separating family interest prevented this. Villages of Co-operation and Equality would solve the difficulty. Owen even suggested that the government should purchase the new railways and the land by the side of them up to six miles broad so that communities could be established as the railways developed. But the irresistible groundswell of sentiment bore him on. The first communities were now taking shape almost in spite of him.

8

Manea Fen and Tytherly

(1)

'THERE has been some writing, and much preaching, and the
world requires much more of both, to create a powerful influential public opinion in favour of united exertions, and means of
enjoyment of health and happiness; but one successful and well
conducted agricultural experiment would be more serviceable
than either'.[1] This 'one serviceable experiment' was now to be
made by William Hodson, a farmer of Brimstone Hill, Upwell,
near Wisbech. He had heard Robert Owen speak. Having spent
six years afloat, he had few qualms about the unchartered seas
of community founding. His natural vivacity of temperament
prevented him from becoming, as he told his friends, 'a sober
saint or a formal anchorite'.[2] He had been a Methodist lay
preacher, but ran into trouble because he married his deceased
wife's sister; a heinous moral offence to those who were aware
of the civil and canon law as it then stood. The United Advancement Societies at Wisbech were behind him. He claimed that his
experimental community would solve not shelve the problem of
class: 'The present distinctions in society are the cause of more
envy and strife than anything which has ever been produced in
the world. In order to avoid this calamity, there will be no
distinction, no individual property, the motto will be "Each for

[1] *New Moral World*, 25 August 1838. (Henceforth referred to as *N.M.W*).
[2] Holyoake, *A History of Co-operation*, i. 63, 180.

all".' In his community food was to be cooked by a special scientific apparatus. There was to be a common dining-room, a large schoolroom. Machinery 'hitherto (been) for the benefit of the rich' would be 'adapted in the colony for lessening labour'. A steam engine would be erected for thrashing and grinding corn. Land would be let at a moderate rent, and before anyone could be dispossessed, a common vote (in which women would participate) would be taken. Fifty houses for members were to be erected as quickly as possible 'so that fifty families may form a community. These houses will be constructed with flues so as to heat them to any required temperature, thus avoiding the labour of making fifty fires, to consume an immense fuel besides dirtying the room you live in and also removing the possibility of your children being burnt to death.'

The *New Moral World* blew coldly on the scheme by quoting the Town Clerk of Ephesus: 'Let us do nothing rashly.' E. T. Craig also prophesied 'failure and disappointment' if a community was formed with 'the raw materials and men which Mr. Hodson has at command at present'.[1] But the Owenite branches hailed Hodson's manifesto. In London, Branch 16 held a public meeting 'to consider the best means of promoting the success of this important experiment'.[2] At Birmingham the Secretary of the Cambridgeshire Community, S. Rowbotham, told an audience:—

> Many of you, no doubt, have concluded from the accounts which have some time since appeared in the *Star in the East* and *The New Moral World*, that the situation is unfit for the purpose and the attempt must end in failure. Such were my opinions. But I can now assure you, from personal inspection and residence upon the spot for nearly a fortnight, that the place is in every respect well calculated for a community, and that with the preparations already made, the devotedness and practical knowledge of Mr. Hodson and your concurrence and assistance, we will succeed.[3]

[1] *N.M.W.*, 15 September 1838. It is interesting that the National Community Friendly Society, formed by the orthodox Owenites in 1837, looked for an estate in Norfolk and actually contracted to buy the Wretton estate, near Wisbech, of James Hill, who, however, demanded the right to carry it out (Holyoake, op. cit., 188). For Hill's interest in social reform (his second wife was the daughter of Dr. Southwood Smith) see C. E. Maurice, *Life of Octavia Hill* (London, 1913), 5–6.

[2] op. cit., 22 September 1838.

[3] op. cit., 12 January 1839. *The Star of the East*, published at Wisbech, was edited by James Hill.

And so it seemed. Hodson's estate at Manea Fen, which was
1¼ miles long and ¼-mile wide, would maintain fifty or sixty
people until the community was established, and it would,
through trustees, be able to own the estate in twenty years. The
community building, Rowbotham went on, would be finished
in a week and the wheat, pigs, and cows offered adequate
guarantees of the necessities of life. Moreover, the Bedford
River, which ran close by the estate, 'would form a beautiful
promenade in the summer evening'. The prospect of acquiring
another 500 acres in a few years would spur the colonists on to
make the community a perfect square. The whole project,
Rowbotham concluded, 'would teach a lesson to our radical
friends'.

But more loyal and orthodox Owenites disagreed. G. A.
Fleming, secretary of the National Community Friendly
Society, said in *The New Moral World* on 12 January 1839: 'It is
all under the entire controul (sic) of Mr. Hodson and has no
further connection with the body of the Socialists than they
individually may think it proper to form.' Owen himself held it
was too small; in his view the minimum size of a community
was 500. Yet at the same time he expressed 'cordial sympathy'
for the project; and rather patronizingly remarked that it might
'become a useful auxiliary to more important and conclusive
experiments upon a new principle of society'.

Amongst such divergencies of opinion, the Owenites of
Salford were determined to make up their own minds and
dispatched A. Hutchinson to Hodson's land for three days. He
returned with a favourable report. Instead of 'a vast extent of
black, moorish looking waste where the eye would be spent as
if looking on the ocean', he saw much fertile land, forty acres of
wheat, peat for burning, and larks, snipe and wild duck in
abundance. Above all, he was impressed by the 'clear, concise
and business-like nature of Mr. Hodson's arrangements'.

On this evidence, the Salford Owenites resolved 'to the
utmost of their power, to give encouragement by purchasing
the various articles they (the colonists) might manufacture or
produce', and requested the land committee of the National
Community Friendly Society (of which Fleming was the
secretary) 'to take into their serious consideration the eligibility
of the 700 acres adjoining Mr. Hodson's land, for forming a

community'. Both these resolutions were laid before the central board of the Owenites. The secretary of the Hodsonian experiment, S. Rowbotham, was present at this meeting in Salford, as he had also been at another at Birmingham and as he was also to be at Rochdale on 21 January 1839. Rochdale, needless to say, followed Salford in passing similar resolutions.

And so Manea Fen received its first recruits in the Christmas of 1838. Some were a poor lot. One of them, Charles Crawford, of Garnet Street, Stockport, returned beggared on 1 April 1839. 'I am without home and without bread', he told the Salford Owenites four months later, 'as the tools by which I earned my bread have not reached their destination.' [1] He claimed that in his three months in the community he had received no wages. But a more convinced supporter of Hodson, E. Wastney, gave cogent reasons for this:

> They commenced finding fault with one another and with everything about them. At the time of our arrival the first general split had taken place, there had been a fall spent on nothing but useless discussions; previous to this split there were no less than 7 females and 4 males constantly engaged to manage the household department which at that time consisted of about 30 persons. . . . All they (the first colonists) did was look to the provisions, this I assure you was done in the most disgusting manner possible . . . they paid much more attention to the beer shops and the company of the lowest prostitutes that were to be found in the district.

Wastney painted a Hogarthian picture of the drunken riots—lasting the whole night—and concluded, 'a worse selection of persons for carrying out any great object of this description than the parties who have left this establishment it would be impossible to make'.[2]

(2)

Since the Owenite journals were so hostile, Manea Fen decided to establish a weekly of its own, 'to defend the Community, report its proceedings, and form a medium of communications between the society and the people'. Using Minter Morgan's metaphor, they called it the *Working Bee*, as it was

[1] *N.M.W.*, 4 May 1839; see also Crawford's letter in the same paper on 8 June 1839.
[2] The *Working Bee*, 3 August 1839. (Henceforth referred to as *W.B.*)

'intended to be devoted to the best interests of the Industrious Classes'. As the announcement ran: 'The *Working Bee* will be commenced by a Society of Working Men, associated to carry into Effect Practical Communities of Equality of Duties, Rights, and Means of Enjoyment, the Establishment of which will give Universal Suffrage, and the whole Produce of their Labour, to all who are now robbed of their Political and Social Privileges.' 'He who will not work neither shall he eat' ran the sub-title, and the publishers (the Trustees of the Hodsonian Community Society) delegated the editorship and printing to John Green, a former Missionary for Owen's National Community Friendly Society at Liverpool. He brought out the first number on 20 July 1839.[1]

The person responsible for recruiting such undesirables, S. Rowbotham, was dismissed, and a more messianic call went out that future recruits should renounce 'the old world' as 'false, hollow and rotten . . . in error alike in its religion, its morals, economics and politics'.

Describing themselves as 'Communionists' (the word was their own) the Manea Fen trustees defined the term as meaning 'All amongst us is ours'. They continued :–

> No mine or their is here in our community but universal common-alty of interest is felt and expressed throughout our establishment . . . Amongst us are no drunkards, no swearers, no prostitutes, no tradesmen and no thieves. We have no such places as St. Giles, London; Angel Street, Manchester; or Lace Street, Liverpool; contrasting their filth and ignorance, with the princely mansions, and sons and daughters of fashionable life.

The trustees announced their intention to refuse admittance to anyone except those who had first served as hired individuals. Referring to their 'file of applications' they declared themselves aware of the 'heart cries' of those who were prejudicing their jobs in 'the old world' by propagating the truths of 'communionism'.[2]

---

[1] He was the author of *The Emigrants* (Manchester, 1838) and *Casper Hauser or the Power of External Circumstances exhibited in forming Human Character* (Manchester, 1840). Holyoake, who does not mention his interest in Manea Fen, recalled (op. cit., i. 237), that 'he was a useful lecturer. . . . He afterwards went to America, where, before he had acquired the faculty of seeing two ways at once, necessary in that land, he was cut in halves by a railway train. He held some official position on the line.'

[2] *W.B.*, 27 July 1839.

On 27 July 1839 conveyance of the estate to the trustees was announced. They numbered four: John Green, editor of the *Working Bee*, Edmund Wastney, who had defended the expulsion of the undesirables as being 'penniless in pocket and bankrupt of moral qualifications', Thomas Doughty and William Cutting.

With Doughty as architect, four houses were started, twelve others began to rise, with a railway, some 200–300 yards long, connecting them to the brick kilns. A kitchen (with larder, wash-house and oven), dormitories for hired labourers, single men and six married couples, a dining room for fifty people and a library were soon finished. There was a compositors' room (9 ft. × 9 ft.) for the press, a barn for the joiners and a six-roomed cottage. The clay pit (40 ft. × 12 ft.), now some twenty-two feet deep, had yielded clay for 100,000 bricks, for which the kiln had been built, and was drained by an 'Archimedean screw'.

A further set of some seventy-two cottages in the form of a square, the fourth side open to the banks of the Bedford River, was announced. This, the first of a series of from six to eight squares 'as circumstances may determine', would enable them, to 'classify our members according to time of membership, congeniality of mind, knowledge of our principles, and amiability . . . preparatory to the erection of a final community'. Less remote was the intention to build a windmill of eight horse-power to drain the clay-pit, without which such plans would never mature.[1]

Thirty-five acres of wheat, twenty-seven of oats, twenty-four of grass, a hundred of fallow, with fifty acres ploughed in the preceding week was no small achievement.

The most singular feature of Manea was an observatory on the top of which floated a tricolour with the Union Jack—indica-tive of conquered tyranny—'cowering below it'. This had two platforms—one housing forty people for tea, and the other sixteen.

That old veteran of Ralahine, E. T. Craig,[2] was installed in the library with his class. A gymnasium was in use and a cricket ground had been laid.[3] But perhaps the most surprising venture under active consideration was a laboratory. Well might

[1] *W.B.*, 3 August 1839.
[2] He had formerly been teaching at Hill's infant school in Wisbech.
[3] *W.B.*, 10 August 1839.

one correspondent tell a friend in far-away Penzance: 'My dear fellow, in seven years from this, Manea Fen will present the appearance of Paradise'.[1]

(3)

To the conservative Fen farmers, however, Manea Fen was no Paradise. One of them wrote to the *Cambridge Advertiser*, in early August saying it

> may have the effect of inducing pious and well-disposed persons to take IMMEDIATE steps to counteract the sting of the *Working Bee*. If this is not done, I fear we shall, before long, find that the fearful scenes of 1816 will be again enacted in this place and neighbourhood; for when once the religious principles of the people are undermined, what security is there for life or property . . . It is clear the editor and his correspondents ridicule the idea of future rewards and punishments, and entertain very lax notions of morals and the intercourse of the sexes.[2]

Another local, but more vocal, critic was the Christian Advocate to the University of Cambridge, the Rev. G. Pearson, who expressed his horror both at the ruling doctrine at Manea Fen—that man was not responsible for his actions—and at the concubinage which he professed to find there:—

> It is impossible to say how much mischief such a body of men may not be capable of doing amongst the more ignorant and depraved part of the native population, by personal exertions, secretly and cautiously employed, and by the distribution of cheap publications of an infidel and revolutionary character.[3]

He went on:—

> I am informed, on good authority, that the colony at Manea Fen is very assiduous both in preaching and in dispensing small tracts, in the propagation of their infidel and revolutionary doctrines, and that, after the harvest, they purpose to undertake a lecturing tour, for the purpose of making their opinions more extensively known.

Calling on the clergy to be on their guard, he continued:—

> As the existence of these infidels in this country may not be generally known much less their contemplated scheme of making proselytes amongst the rural population, I trust that the clergy and

[1] *W.B.*, 10 August 1839.
[2] *W.B.*, 14 August 1839.
[3] *W.B.*, 28 September 1839.

religious persons of every description, will excuse the liberty which I have taken of drawing their attention to the subject . . . and be on their guard against the extension of these emissaries of infidelity among the country parishes, and may take measures to avert these flagitious and wicked attempts.

(4)

Meanwhile the orthodox Owenites had finally purchased some land at Tytherly in Hampshire. On a hill facing south, with plenty of trees, it seemed the ideal spot. Owen suggested that John Finch of Liverpool, Heaton Aldam of Derbyshire and Frederick Green of London be the triumvirate of management under the Board, with Finch as the Acting Governor and Aldam as Director of Agricultural Operations.

The branches rallied with subscriptions to float it. Each branch giving £50 secured a nomination. Some gave gifts in kind—books, tools, implements and furniture. Generous as the branches were with money and goods, they did not rally with equal fervour to nominate men who could farm the land, and Aldam found himself appealing for ploughmen, hedgers and ditchers, carpenters and smiths.

Recruits came in, full of millenarian enthusiasm. A new chronology was adopted by the enthusiasts. It dated from 1 October 1839, the date when the property was taken over. Like their counterparts in the old immoral world, they budgeted their time, rising at 5 a.m. for a mathematical class, before tea and 'public business'. They finished at 6 p.m. and spent the evening from 6-30 p.m. to 8 p.m. in dancing, drawing, music or the study of geography, agriculture and botany. Sundays were free.

Fifty-seven 'colonists', men, women and children, took up residence. They worked hard to build a large new dining-hall with bedrooms above, to decorate it with engravings and paintings and adorn it with stained-glass windows. But when they finished it, it proved too small for them. Many had left northern industrial towns for what they hoped was paradise, but Tytherly was no paradise. Both Governor Finch and the Director of Agricultural Operations, Aldam, were ill, and had to resign in May 1840. Congress appointed replacements, but Aldam died soon after his appointment. The colonists began to drift away and, by the end of the summer of 1840, there were only nineteen colonists left, eight men, four women and seven children. To help gather in the harvest fifteen to twenty labourers had to be hired. Over £316 was lost, for the expense of employing hired labourers was greater than the charge of supporting the colonists, even though labourers in Hampshire only earned 8s. per week.[1]

(5)

Manea, on the other hand had been going from strength to strength under Hodson as President and Agricultural Director, and his six colleagues: Green (of the Press), Joseph Davidge (of stores), William Cutting (of the smiths), Thomas Doughty (of the bricklayers) and Edmund Wastney as secretary.

The editor of the *Working Bee* was purged after a complaint by Doughty (the Architectural Director) that he had received 'brutal and disgraceful treatment' from Green. A public meeting was called in the evening of the same day and Green offered to leave in twenty-four hours. He was described as 'issuing from his office, using the most violent language towards an unoffending fellow-creature, accompanied by threats, which, in the old state of society, would have subjected him to the laws of his country'. He was given £2 to go away. Green's departure was unfortunate, and he regretted it, since he left his wife and child behind. He voiced it in a poem *I left in Grief*, one verse of which ran :–

> Adieu dear Fen, in thee are hearts,
> From which I ne'er would wish to sever.
> Whose love, too deep to be effaced,
> Is stamped *within my heart for ever*.[2]

W. H. Bellatti was chosen to succeed Green as editor and S. Collinson to act as Director of the Printing Establishment.

Wastney, the secretary, had been recruiting other personnel. An advertisement appeared above his signature in the *Working Bee* of 23 November 1839, asking for candidates and specifying that 'they must be first-rate workmen, and well acquainted with the principles of socialism, and of the following trades, viz., one Wheelwright, one Cabinet Maker, one Printer, two Joiners and

[1] Podmore, *Life of Owen*, 531–74.
[2] B. Jones, *Co-operative Production* (1894), i. 71–75. *W.B.*, 16 November 1839; *W. B.*, 23 November 1839; *W.B.*, 7 December 1839.

one Gardener'. They got a number of replies and were able to select accordingly.[1]

The new Director of the Printing Establishment, Samuel Collinson, of Rochdale, inaugurated a scientific column in the *Working Bee*. He had joined the community five months earlier, in June, having left Rochdale the previous March. He was also probably responsible for the recruitment of two more Rochdale men by the community: Cropper and Heywood. Certainly the defections from that quarter seemed to annoy Fleming who attempted to dissuade them from going.[2]

Some Owenites were anxious that Manea Fen would not divert enthusiasm from their own community at Tytherly. One of Owen's most vocal and powerful supporters, Isaac Ironside, builder of the Hall of Science at Sheffield,[3] came down in person to visit Manea Fen, and left with the community's builder. Manea Fen was furious :–

> This gentleman (i.e. Ironside), decoyed our builder . . . he sent a letter to the director of the brick-making establishment informing him that he is chosen to go to Tytherly and must leave us forthwith and repair to Sheffield to receive instructions prior to going there . . . were we actuated by the method pursued by inhabitants of the old world, of dealing with offenders according to their deserts, we should give Mr. Ironside a very different reception if he ever honoured us with any more of his 'social visits'. It is the conduct of such men as Mr. Ironside that does so much injury to the great cause in which we ought to be engaged rather in assisting than injuring each other.[4]

Little injury, however, seems to have been done.

Because the windmill was finished on the very day in which the 'communionists' received their enrolled rules from the revising barrister, it was ceremonially named Tidd Pratt, then the Registrar of Friendly Societies.[5] This source of power

---

[1] *W.B.*, 3 November 1839.

[2] *W.B.*, 7 November 1839.

[3] Isaac Ironside, 1808–70, was Owen's most active supporter in Sheffield and became one of the promoters of the Tytherly establishment. See *infra* 6 (3).

[4] *W.B.*, 30 November 1839.

[5] Tidd Pratt, 1797–1870, who was counsel to certify the rules of savings banks and friendly societies from 1834–46. His vigilance on behalf of the public was known and he would disclose, as far as official restraints allowed, the unsound condition of any benefit or friendly society which he found.

enabled water to be pumped out of the clay pit; a circular saw of 36-in. diameter to be worked; a lathe and grindstone to be turned; and, perhaps the greatest refinement of all, circular brushes for cleaning boots and shoes, or knives and forks, to be operated.[1] As the news of the Tytherly community came in through the columns of the *New Moral World*, the Manea Fen community could proudly boast: 'Our houses are now rapidly approaching completion and we hope in a short time to see every member and candidate comfortably lodged. Our school will be finished in a few days and we have formed ordinances for its government'.[2] A thousand fruit trees were purchased, and the members agreed to work from 6 a.m. to 10 p.m.

Financially, the situation was equally encouraging. The communionists had already repaid William Hodson £600 of the money he had loaned them. At this rate they looked like owning their 200 acres of land free of debt in three years. Hodson himself acknowledged that it had ceased to be dependent on him since it was governed by regulations which could not be altered except 'by the consent of the members'. 'I would impress upon all parties', he told them, 'that I can have but little influence over the society I have had the pleasure of forming.' With Wastney as secretary and the stalwarts Cutting, Davidge, Doughty, G. Dunn, and D. Jones as trustees, it looked so prosperous that they decided to fan out and establish branches. So they issued a manifesto. 'We are anxious to extend the benefits we have received', wrote the editor of the *Working Bee*, 'to all who feel desirous of co-operating with us in the noble and benevolent cause in which we have engaged.' Branches were to be 'chartered' in each town where there were more than ten sympathizers. These branches were 'to disseminate as extensively as possible the principles of co-operation, by circulating the *Working Bee* and such publications as may, from time to time, emanate from this society, and to establish *Depots* for the sale of such articles as may be manufactured for sale by members of this Establishment. From these Branches, we shall, in future, select individuals as members to fill up vacancies, extend our operation, and augment our numbers'.[3]

[1] Probably a shaft attached to the steam engine drove them.
[2] *W.B.*, 14 December 1839.
[3] *W.B.*, 28 December 1839.

Hodson made a lecture tour of the Midland Counties. On Boxing Day, 1839, he spoke at Leicester, with some effect, at the festival of their Institution, securing six recruits who joined Manea Fen in the following February.[1] On 27 December he spoke at Nottingham 'in a chapel', and reported: 'I saw here an invention for weaving stockings by power made by a Mr. Barton[2] formerly of A.1 Branch, London. This gentleman must not be long out of community, he must either be with us or at Tytherly. The Rational Religionists would do well to secure his services'.[3]

From Nottingham he travelled to Lincoln, where he spoke at the Guildhall on 28 December to an audience which included 'Lawyers, Clergymen and Physicians' who 'appeared paralysed with the novel views' they heard. Here he was sharply questioned by a local Methodist minister, the Rev. Mr. Roebuck who, said Hodson, 'wished to draw me out upon Religion, but could not, for my object was to teach the people how to live happily, his to teach them how to die. My replies to him on the Marriage question seemed to give satisfaction.' Here Hodson 'engaged a gentleman who for many years was connected with a provincial paper' as well as Charles Bates, an ironmonger.[4]

One of the more interesting by-products of Hodson's tour was to stimulate the formation of yet another community—this time at Pant-Glas in Merionethshire, by John Moncas and a Liverpool body who described themselves as 'The Community of United Friends', which we shall meet later. Moncas showed where his real inspiration lay by sending reports of his communitarian experiment to the *Working Bee*, and looking to Manea Fen as his model.[5] Even more interesting was its aggravation of John Brindley, formerly a master at the National School of March, Cambridgeshire, who emerged at this time as

---

[1] These consisted of Slingsby (a joiner) and his wife and child; Baker (a wheelwright) and his wife; and Green (a bricklayer and plasterer). These brought the strength of the community up to forty-two.

[2] For whom see W. H. G. Armytage, *A. J. Mundella, 1825–1897: The Liberal Background of the Labour Movement* (London, 1951), 22.

[3] *W.B.*, 4 January 1840.

[4] His speech was well reported in the *Lincoln Gazette*, 30 December 1839, but the *Lincolnshire Chronicle* of the same date described it as a 'blasphemous effusion' and Hodson as 'a minion of mischief'.

[5] It was reported in the *Working Bee* of 3 February 1840, and other accounts appeared 24 April, 8, 15 August, and 9 September. See *infra*, pp. 240–3.

a formidable peripatetic anti-socialist lecturer and seems to have taken a particular dislike to the Manea Fen community.[1]

On Hodson's return the Directors began to envisage a community of 700 people.[2] Certainly the number of people who came to look round the colony became so large that they had regretfully to announce that they could no longer serve refreshments without payment. Among these visitors was G. A. Fleming, who visited them on behalf of the orthodox Owenites. The secretary of the community was by now W. P. Throsby. D. Jones had retired from the directorate and had been replaced by Slingsby, a joiner, one of the recruits obtained at Leicester during Hodson's missionary tour. The *Working Bee* was to be transformed into 'an effective organ for the dissemination of social principles and a source of profit to the community'. From this time onwards they began to share copy with the *New Moral World*.

The goodwill of the Universal Community Society of Rational Religionists, as the main body of the Owenites, now seemed fairly assured. For, in an article entitled 'A look around us' in the *New Moral World*, the author wrote of the Manea Fen colonists :–

Their establishment has been in existence upwards of 12 months; it has, however, made comparatively speaking, but a small progress owing to the unfavourable circumstances under which it was commenced, and which, during a considerable portion of the first year, continued to attend its management. None regretted these drawbacks more than we did nor would have more gladly assisted in their removal; but a misapprehension at the commencement prevented both parties from understanding each other; and we were, therefore, content to leave its rectification to Dr. Time, who, as a correspondent wittily remarks, 'is a physician who gives most successful prescriptions in cases of disagreement'. The obstructions to the progress and good management of Manea Fen have, we understand, now been removed, and the greater portion of these difficulties incident to all new undertakings surmounted.[3]

He quoted from the *Working Bee* of 29 February 1840 :–

[1] John Brindley's past activities were constantly exposed in the *Working Bee*.
[2] *W.B.*, 29 February 1840. On 28 March that year they actually numbered fifty-two.
[3] *N.M.W.*, 14 March 1840.

A wide stretch of country lies between Tytherly and Manea: it must be the object of both colonies to unite them by a chain of happy community; and however much we may now smile at the idea of doing so, let us recollect, that not many years since, several miles intervened between some of the Shaker establishments in America, which are now separated by two or three fields. A close cordial union among the friends of socialism, and mutual assistance, will effect wonders.

Fleming himself was impressed :–

The building and agricultural operations are proceeding with great vigour and determination; the winter sown crops are looking well, though there is as yet that unfinished appearance about the place which may be expected from large works in the process of execution; it is evident that the colonists possess a command over very substantial advantages and their steady well-directed efforts will speedily effect all that can be desired. Another harvest will place the success of the establishment beyond doubt, and afford an example to capitalists which we earnestly hope many of them will follow.[1]

The healing of the breach between Manea and Tytherly was symbolized by the appearance of Hodson at the Co-operative Congress in May 1840, when he appealed for union. Explaining that the average population of Manea Fen over the past year had not been below twenty, that they had built twenty-four houses and some workshops, he urged that the Rational Society should join forces with Manea Fen: Tytherly becoming an educational, and Manea Fen an agricultural community. His proposition was discussed but the old guard of the Rational Society refused to co-operate. Yet Hodson was not downcast. On the contrary, on Whit Tuesday he was to be found at Highbury Barn at a grand tea and ball in honour of Owen.

A completely new *Working Bee* was issued on 6 June 1840 with the motto 'United to support; but not combined to injure'. It contained information of the Board's plan to erect a 'Machine Establishment' at Manea Fen for the manufacture of thrashers and drills. They informed their supporters that they had been offered a cast iron moulder, blow furnace, a steam engine and 'every other requisite for carrying on a foundry'. To enable this to be operated they appealed for the help of first-rate mechanics and when these were forthcoming, they would commence the

[1] *N.M.W.*, 28 March 1840.

building required. They also appealed for two bricklayers and individuals from the Staffordshire potteries who could make chimney pots, flower pots, and other refractory products. In the same issue they offered building bricks, flooring tiles, drain pipes and pantiles for sale together with worsted and other stockings. All goods would be delivered by boat.[1]

These boats were multi-service craft. In May, the colonists sailed up the Bedford River to Walney 'enlivening the way with stirring songs', in a six-oared cutter named *The Morning Star*. In June, they attended a Ranters Meeting and quite stole the show. For as the *Working Bee* proudly confessed, everyone turned to look at 'the colonists'. 'A great improvement is manifested in the manners of the people towards us', it continued, 'we receive no insult from them now, or nothing worth calling such.'[2]

Money was abandoned in the community—labour notes being issued for work done and cashed at the store. 'This plan saves us the trouble of getting cash . . . money is merely the representation of wealth', Hodson told the Co-operative Congress.[3] At a special meeting a uniform was adopted: tunic, trousers, and straw hats (with caps in the winter time) for men; dresses for women. Chemistry was consistently studied on wet days.[4]

So many visitors were attracted that a 'conductor' was appointed. One of the curious was the former Agricultural Superintendent of the Tytherly community—Heaton Aldam, who the month before had resigned his post there. It was, perhaps, the euphoria generated by such continued expatiation on the merits of Manea Fen that led the Directors, in announcing their intention to build three lime kilns, to say 'These additions to our premises will soon give us all the appearance of a town'. Certainly they seemed to be forging ahead: a school was flourishing, and on 27 June they were able to announce 'the first birth in the community'—a daughter to William Hodson.[5] And

---

[1] They also announced the accession of Hodges (a knitter), his wife and four children and Ward (also a knitter), together with his wife and two children: all from Leicester.

[2] *W.B.*, 13 June 1840.

[3] *W.B.*, 30 May 1840.

[4] *W.B.*, 13 June 1840.

[5] A death had already occurred, also in Hodson's family (of his daughter), on 15 January 1840.

to the visitors must be added the invitations sent by Bradford, Northampton, Wigan, and Hinckley to William Hodson, offering lecture rooms so that he could explain the community to sympathizers. Hodson announced that as soon as a sufficient number were obtained he would 'lay down an itinerary'.[1] Probably one reason for this interest was Hodson's insistence on the fact that dissatisfied socialists had no need to emigrate to the backwoods Utopias of the United States of America, or to settlements in the colonies.[2] As he said, 'The schemes of that class of men who think it better to go abroad than to produce at home, have often struck us as absurd . . . These incorporations (i.e. communitarian settlements) would be far more likely to prove successful than attempts to colonise Van Diemen's Land or New Zealand'.[3]

Unusually fine weather marked the harvest of 1840, enabling the communionists to gather mustard and oats worth some £900.[4] To this task all hands were turned, for as the *Working Bee* said, 'in the ideal communities of Sir T. More, and in the existing communities of America, the plan is said to be adopted at harvest time of all hands leaving their customary occupations to gather the corn'. Even the 'gymnastic apparatus' was put aside.

The desire for union with Tytherly persisted. 'Union, Union!' cried the *Working Bee* of 5 September. Three weeks later, lamenting that Tytherly was to be abandoned (for the dissensions there had become so acute that C. F. Green had been instructed to reduce the membership), the *Working Bee* was plaintively asking its readers to 'take goods manufactured by the hands of co-operators. If, my friends, you will do this, without any other subscription, we soon shall be able to offer a model community to you.'

Certainly Manea Fen seemed healthier than Tytherly, where numbers had now sunk to nineteen—of which seven were children of 10 years of age and under. To this some fifteen or so hired labourers should be added, making the total thirty-five. Manea Fen, on the other hand, had fifty 'in community'—and

[1] *W.B.*, 11 July 1840.
[2] For the most comprehensive account of these see A. E. Bestor, *Backwoods Utopias* (Pennsylvania, 1950).
[3] *W.B.*, 11 July 1840.
[4] *W.B.*, 29 August 1840.

showed how they were deployed: fifteen in thrashing oats for market, eighteen in claying the land, six on the *Working Bee*, three gardeners, a schoolmaster, brickmakers, and the remainder employed in various tasks. All that was needed was a market for their products.[1] Hodson argued:—

> What can be made or effected in community, let it be purchased by Socialists. The profits accruing therefrom would enable us to start some other branch of manufacture, more than we have now. If every Socialist wore the stockings made in community, very soon would we be enabled to send cotton and linen goods to wear, and thus bring into community many of that injured race existing in the manufacturing districts.

Referring to his approaching tour—the prelude to a society independent of the Owenites with auxiliary branches of its own, Hodson wrote: 'I shall in my tour form societies, the members of which will stand pledged, so long as they continue members, to purchase all articles of our manufacture, without injury to their interest. Depots will be formed, conducted by trustworthy and creditable parties, with a Grand Central Depot in London—to and from which all transactions will proceed.'

This courageous, forward-looking policy attracted those who had found the dissensions in the two other communities unbearable. From Tytherly returned two craftsmen who had previously belonged to the Manea Fen community: Storey, a brickmaker, and Collinson, a printer; while from the Pant Glas community (now broken up) came Robert Reed, and another, Horner, a printer, applied to return. The *Working Bee* with a hint of sanctimony announced: 'Sincerely do we hope we shall be enabled to provide an asylum to those who have been debarred from continuing their exertions elsewhere.'[2]

There seemed to be an open challenge to Robert Owen and the old guard of the Rational Religionists being formulated. B. Warden attacked 'the social priesthood' of Owen's 'missionaries' and suggested that they would be more useful in a community than on a lecture platform. Yet at the same time Hodson was negotiating with the Owenite Central Board for a union on the basis of self-governing communities. He was probably induced to do this because Owen, William Galpin, and F. Bate

[1] F. Podmore, op. cit., 537; *W.B.*, 26 September 1840.
[2] *W.B.*, 26 September 1840.

(who had engraved a picture of the Manea Fen community) had formed 'The Home Colonization Society' to provide funds for Tytherly without straining the finances of the Central Board. Hodson's idea was that the Central Board should raise money to lend, and that all future communities should emanate from those already in existence. His proposal was defeated by sixteen votes to four.[1]

(6)

The rejection of Hodson's overtures threw the Manea Fen colony back to its own resources—and the coming winter. How were they to sell the products of their labour? The *Working Bee* suggested that if every one of its 5,000 readers bought a pair of stockings it would keep three stocking makers active for a year.[2] But this alone would not repay the outlay—some £6,000 —on the blacksmith's shop, the printing office, the file shed, the brick kiln, the windmill, the twenty-four houses, the dining-rooms, the kitchen, the sleeping apartments and the outhouses.

So the members of the community held a meeting in order to solve the problem. Hodson agreed to give up the presidency (he preferred to do so) in order to travel for the community and 'live to carry forward the good cause of communities'. From what he said, it was largely due to his wife that he took this decision, for, he confessed, 'Mrs. Hodson is not a Socialist'.[3]

He was described by a reporter for the *Liverpool Albion* who visited the community at this time as 'a man well fitted for the enterprise he has undertaken: in the prime of life, with an athletic frame which fits him for the physical difficulties of his situation. He possesses a mind of great energy and high intellectual capabilities'.

The reporter was impressed by the spirit of the community too; its teetotalism and sobriety, its adherence to majority rule, and its business-like nature. For the members, he went on, hold the estate on a twenty-one-year lease, paying 5 per cent interest on the purchase money as rent. Hodson was described as having advanced £2,000 for which he held notes-of-hand, and as having spent £3,000 on the buildings. 'There is no lack of exertion', commented the writer, indicating the fifty-five acres of oats, the

[1] *W.B.*, 3 October 1840.
[2] *W.B.*, 10 October 1840.
[3] *W.B.*, 31 October 1840.

eight stacks of wheat, and the seventeen acres of mustard, and continued, 'Amidst all their wordly-wise proceedings it would seem they have a dash of romance about them . . . all proceed to the fields with music at their head.' He was much impressed with their two boats, their project for a railway, the chemical enthusiasm of Hodson himself—made manifest in the evening classes, and especially the uniform dress: 'The men wear a green habit . . . presenting an appearance somewhat like the representation of Robin Hood and his foresters, or of the Swiss mountaineers. The dress of the females is much the same as the usual fashion, with trousers, and the hair worn in ringlets . . . They are quite the lions of the villages round about.'[1]

Six years of maritime life had endowed Hodson with a tendency to speak out when things displeased him and he had earlier asked the colonists that, if at any time they observed 'too great a levity' in his proceedings, he 'would esteem it a favour to be corrected by them'.[2] The significance of these remarks was now borne in upon the colonists as the winter closed in about them. With his non-Socialist wife at his elbow, Hodson's stock of both money and patience, seemed to run out. Distrusted by the editor of the *New Moral World*, his overtures rejected by the Central Board, faced with the prospect of having to finance the community from his own resources, and deprived of the comfortable security of his friend James Hill's bank (which failed in 1840), he seems to have run into personal difficulties and a circular was issued by the trustees of the community concerning his conduct. The *New Moral World* remarked that this 'raised so many questions of business and law that we must make ourselves fully acquainted with the facts and bearings of the case, before we can venture to do more than thus allude to the matter'.[3]

The grisly end of the whole experiment was soon painfully documented. The members of the community, convinced of Hodson's unfitness for the post, were powerless to force him out because they depended on him for 'pecuniary advances'. Three days before Christmas 1840, Hodson gave orders to the meat contractors to stop deliveries to the community. A public meeting of the communitarians decided to take over management, do

---

[1] *W.B.*, 28 November 1840.
[2] *W.B.*, 5 February 1840.
[3] *N.M.W.*, 9 January 1841.

away with hired labour, dispose of the lighters and to consult a solicitor. Hodson's reply was to seize the books. Another members' meeting was convened on Christmas Day, and condemned his action. There, however, unanimity ended. A pro-Hodson party formed and when, four days later, another meeting was convened to ask for the books, Hodson pointed out that he possessed the money obtained by the sale of the crops, and when they demanded it, he replied that it was in the hands of 'a gentleman in March'.

Tension mounted. The *Working Bee* ceased publication. The leader of the anti-Hodsonians was the oldest member of the community, William Davidge. He was obviously the main target for Hodson's anger and on 30 February, one of the pro-Hodsonians shot at him with a gun. What is worse, the pro-Hodsonians formed a kind of terrorist group. The *New Moral World* reported that 'men with bludgeons have constantly been about the premises; the shops and rooms have been broken into and their contents taken out. Nearly all the members have now resigned. The remainder are determined to obtain possession if they can'.[1]

It was a hopeless task which they soon abandoned. Ten years later, Robert Gardner could write: 'From 100 to 200 of the disciples of Robert Owen, commonly called Owenites, located themselves here for about 12 months, within the last few years. They occupied 150 acres of land, had everything in common, according to their system; and published (whilst here) a paper or pamphlet called the *Working Bee*. But alas! for the mutability of human institutions, the Socialists have fled'.[2]

And today, the only memorial of their lively presence at Manea Fen is the name Colony Farm.

(7)

With Hodson's failure the newly formed Home Colonization Society had now only one experiment to worry about: Tytherly. Bate and Galpin gave generously, so did Owen.

Salford loyalists turned to help. Joseph Smith travelled about the country collecting sheep. He would rise at the end of a

---

[1] *N.M.W.*, 20 February 1841.
[2] Robert Gardner, *History, Gazetteer and Directory of Cambridgeshire* (Peterborough, 1851), 497.

socialist meeting and propose that all who had passed the resolutions should there and then subscribe for the purchase of a sheep. To ensure a response he always arranged for the exit doors to be locked. His mixture of metaphors had an intoxicating effect on his audience. He would warn them of the 'abysses hanging over their heads', into which they would fall unless they contributed. And as the money jingled on the platform he would promise them the unique experience of 'sailing into port on the top of their watch-towers'.[1]

These and other measures had their effect. New farms were leased till the community were working over one thousand acres. A three-storey red brick building was built to house the residents, designed by Joseph Hansom, eponymous inventor of the famous cab. This was palatial. The kitchens had mahogany wainscots several feet high, and a little railway on which food was taken to the dining-hall. The main building, set in promenades and lawns, had the letters C.M. where the date should have been signifying 'Commencement of the Millennium', carved above the main door.[2]

Partly to rear the next generation according to his principles and partly to get some return for money Owen started a school. Its pupils were divided into four classes. The first, from birth to 5 years old, were to be trained to feel confidence in all around them. The second, from 5 to 10, were to help in the domestic work and keep the house and gardens in order. The third, from 10 to 15, were to direct the activities of those below them, and study science. The last class, from 15 to 20, were to marry and produce all the wealth required by the community.

The schools for these future Utopians were ready by 1843. They began with their sixty-one pupils, thirty-five of whom were fee-payers. The total number of adults in the colony was now forty-three, and Owen increased their number to 300. So far the experiment had cost £11,667 3s. Now to equip the buildings with a dairy, a farmstead, another boarding-house, workshops and a printing establishment, a further £8,000 was called for.

To raise this, Owen issued a prospectus, inviting the public to subscribe £25,000 to provide Tytherly with equipment and

[1] G. J. Holyoake, *History of Co-operation* (1906), i. 229.
[2] F. Podmore, *Life of Owen*, 543.

also an industrial school for 500 children. But he obtained less than a tenth of this—some £1,900—which enabled another farm to be leased and the number of children to be raised to ninety-four (of whom sixty-four were fee-payers, paying £25 a year).

But the wells of sympathy were not bottomless. Phillpotts, the Bishop of Exeter, could be ignored as a figure of fun, but not so the *Comic Almanac* to which Thackeray contributed. This published a cartoon and a lampoon ridiculing moral communism of Harmony:

> They've everything in common, so they say:
> Even not uncommon wives: perchance they may;
> And, if the principle they carry through,
> The babies may be sometimes common too;
> Making it puzzling, rather,
> For some of them to find their father.

On its economic basis the *Comic Almanac* continued

> And then how very strange
> Their labour they exchange!
> The cobbler who would like a dish
> Of fish,
> Goes to the fishmonger and heels a shoe,
> Then carries off a sole or two.
> The lawyer wants a coat—a decent fit
> To pay the tailors bill
> He need but make the tailor's will,
> Or serve him with the copy of a writ.

Yet, as the rhymster admitted

> It is a sect, I vow,
> That's much run after now;
> And Socialists are followed more
> Than ever they had been before.[1]

This was the bitterest cut of all, for the sheer exhaustion of their funds now vitiated the movement. The Social Institutions or Halls of Science, which the provincial branches had now in many cases erected, lacked social missionaries to keep the members together, because in 1844 the Congress had decided, in view of the heavy calls of Tytherly, to discontinue their appointments.

[1] G. Cruikshank, *Comic Almanac 1835–43* (London, n. d.), 382–4.

Because of this Owen resigned. In his place the Congress elected John Finch of Liverpool to the chair. Finch had visited and written about Ralahine and in 1839 he had published a series of essays on the millennium. As governor of Tytherly, John Buxton of Manchester was elected, whereupon two of the existing board of directors, G. A. Fleming and F. Bate, resigned. This was a further blow, as Bate had given over £12,000 to the community.

When the new management took up office in May 1844, they not only inherited a deficit, but found that an investment of further capital was needed to secure the tools necessary to work the farm. So, after the report of a select committee appointed by Congress, it was decided to wind up the enterprise in August 1845.

The result of the whole experiment was that the leases of the farms were taken over by William Galpin, a Salisbury banker, and Isaac Ironside of Sheffield. Robert Owen went to America. The builders were left in charge of Buxton and his family for a year.

After a squabble between the trustees (Finch, Green, and Clegg) Harmony Hall was advertised for sale in *The Times* as a lunatic asylum. Ultimately it was leased as a school, and continued in its old role as Queenwood College, to provide for the instruction of the young. The headmaster, George Edmondson, conducted his school on most modern principles with an 800-acre farm attached to it for the scientific study of farming operations.[1]

The quarrels between the trustees and enthusiasts like William Pare continued up till 1861, when, after a hearing before the Master of the Rolls, the property was sold and the proceeds divided amongst the shareholders. The hundreds of small subscribers to the original fund received nothing at all.

[1] D. Thompson, 'Queenwood College', *Annals of Science* XI (1955), 246–54.

PHASE III

The Heyday of Experiment

1

❦❦❦❦❦❦❦❦❦❦❦❦❦❦❦

Ham Common and the Transcendentalists

❦❦❦❦❦❦❦❦❦❦❦❦❦❦❦

(1)

Flitting through the Utopian underground of those who did not agree with Owen's particularly environmentalist creed was the mysterious figure of James Pierrepont Greaves. He had drunk at more spiritual fountains, and to Thomas Carlyle was 'a humbug'. 'I know old ——— myself', Carlyle told Emerson, 'and can testify, if you will believe me, that few greater block-heads (if "blockhead" may mean "exasperated imbecile" and the ninth part of "a thinker") broke the world's bread in my day.'[1] The extraordinary thing about Greaves was that he was a semi-invalid for these last years of his life when, clad in a grey dressing-gown, he wielded great influence from his home at 49 Burton Street, near Heraud, who lived at No. 28. There were others, unlike Carlyle, who considered Greaves a major influence in his day. He converted Charles Lane who considered him 'a gigantic mind, bestriding the narrow world like a colossus'. To F. F. Barham he was 'a greater man than Coleridge';[2] a revealing comparison. Even level-headed G. J. Holyoake found him 'the most accomplished, pleasant and inscrutable mystic which this country has produced'. Holyoake gave him credit for possessing

[1] *The Correspondence of Carlyle and Emerson, 1834–72*, Ed. E. E. Norton (Boston, 1883).
[2] F. F. Barham, *An Odd Medley of Literary Curiosities* (London, 1845).

171

'competence, which enables a man to be unintelligible, and yet respected'.[1] H. G. Wright described him as possessing 'a lofty forehead, a well-defined contour, a nose inclined to the aquiline, a deep, slightly sonorous voice, a stature rather above the middle height, and a marvellous eye. Mystery, God, Fathomlessness, all were written upon him.'[2] Emerson wrote of him in the *Dial*: 'Pestalozzi declared that Mr. Greaves understood his aims and methods better than any other observer . . . He has been a chief instrument in the regeneration of the British schools.'[3]

Formerly a merchant, who had been ruined by the Berlin and Milan Decrees of 1806, Greaves became interested in J. H. Pestalozzi's work at Yverdun, where he had migrated in 1817 at the age of 40. In four years he had absorbed Pestalozzi's teaching, living abstemiously on biscuits and water.[4] Though they never learned each other's language, a strong affection grew up between the two men. After leaving Pestalozzi, Greaves spent another four years teaching English, first at the University of Basel, then at Tübingen, where the noted Strauss was one of his pupils. In 1825 he returned to England and founded the London Infant School Society. As its secretary he published *Three Hundred Maxims for the consideration of Parents* in 1827 and *Physical and Metaphysical Hints for Everybody*, and began to issue *The Contrasting Magazine* in the same year. This, as its name implied, held up contrasting passages of thought for readers to sharpen themselves upon.[5]

In 1832 he tried to alleviate social distress at Randwick in Gloucestershire by securing work for the unemployed whereby they were paid in labour 'tokens' made interchangeable for goods.[6]

Greaves held that there subsists an externally, sensibly realizable connexion between the human Soul and Deity; that

---

[1] G. J. Holyoake, *The History of Co-operation* (London, 1906), i. 153.

[2] ibid.

[3] The *Dial* (Boston, 1842), iii. 228.

[4] Thirty-three letters of Pestalozzi to Greaves, written from Yverdun between 1 October 1818 and 1 May 1819 were published as *Letters on Early Education, addressed to J. P. Greaves, Esq., by Pestalozzi* (London, 1827).

[5] His helper on these three enterprises was G. E. Biber, who not only revised his work but himself published a life of Pestalozzi in 1831. J. A. Green, *Pestalozzi's Educational Writings* (London, 1912), p. 211, considers that Biber also translated the letters referred to in Note 4 above.

[6] A. Campbell, *Letters and Extracts from the Writings of James Pierrepoint Greaves* (London, 1843–5).

God ever impregnates it with new seeds of love, intelligence and virtue; that the development of these seeds is an awakening of divine interest in humanity; and that the fostering of this connexion should be the proper objects of both theory and practice in society.

The group which gathered round the sage of Burton Street were all privateers on the seas of mysticism. They were described as 'young men, with more aspiration than power, and who, with the egotism of youth, thought in their hearts that they were levers destined to move the world . . . a mutual admiration society, sadly inarticulate in their teachings, deficient in that clearness of expression and directness of aim that usually characterize deep thinkers'.[1] There was John Westland Marston, a young man barely out of his teens, who edited *Psyche*, a periodical which specialized in the mystical, and later became a dramatist.[2] Another was Richard Henry Horne, editor of the *Monthly Repository* from 1836 to 1837, and later a literary lion.[3] A third was Charles Lane, described by Emerson as 'for many years manager of the "London Mercantile Price Current", a man of fine intellectual nature, inspired and hallowed by a profound faith. This is no man of letters but a man of ideas. Deep opens below deep in his thought, and for the solution of each new problem, he recurs, with new success, to the highest truth, to that which is most generous, most simple, and most powerful; to that which cannot be comprehended, or overseen, or exhausted. His words come to us like the voices of home out of a far country'.[4] A fourth was 30-year-old Christopher Walton, a large sententious man, without a spark of humour, one of the

---

[1] Camilla Toulmin, *Landmarks of a Literary Life* (1893), ii. 79.

[2] John Westland Marston (1819–90), together with Greaves and Charles Lane, was writing at the end of 1839 to Alcott 'letters of love and encouragement'. R. L. Rusk, *The Letters of Ralph Waldo Emerson* (New York, 1939), ii. 231. He began a long and successful career as a playwriter in 1841 with *The Patrician's Daughter*. He was much praised by Dickens and was the chief exponent of poetic drama on the English stage of his day.

[3] R. H. Horne (1803–84), for whom see E. H. Partridge (ed.), *Orion . . . with an introduction on Horne's Life and Work* (London, 1928), and Eric J. Shumaker, *A Concise Bibliography . . . of the Complete Works of R. Henry-Hengist Horne* (1943).

[4] The *Dial*, op. cit. He later wrote in a private letter: 'I find it hard to talk with Lane, tedious, & it would soon be insupportable: yet he is a preacher of righteousness, & accuses & arouses me, so that I find in him more valuable company than a man of information, a mere scholar who will give my fifty new propositions on the

secretaries of the Strangers' Friend Society, a silk mercer, whose collection of mystical writings led up to a biography of William Law which is now in Dr. Williams' Library in Gordon Square.[1]

The woman member of the group, Camilla Toulmin, who had so tartly described them as imagining themselves as 'levers destined to move the world',[2] considered J. A. Heraud the greatest egotist she ever saw.[3] Yet Heraud[4] and F. F. Barham[5] were also disciples of Greaves: Heraud made the *Monthly Magazine* a platform for his ideas, and F. F. Barham, organizer of the Syncretics or Alists (as the group was sometimes known), collected materials for the biography of Greaves.[6]

(2)

As a *point d'appui* for anti-Owenites, Greaves now became important. J. Minter Morgan published the letters which Greaves received from Pestalozzi and wrote of him: 'among the numerous advocates for various improvements, there was not one who exceeded him in personal sacrifices to what he esteemed a duty'.[7] Alexander Campbell, originally a member of the community at Orbiston[8] and later as a missionary of Owen's

---

[1] Christopher Walton (1809–77), author of *Outline of the Qualifications for a Biography of William Law* (1847–52), *Notes and Materials for a Biography of William Law* (1854), and *An Introduction to Philosophy* (1854).

[2] *Landmarks of a Literary Life, 1820–92* (1893), loc. cit.

[3] op. cit., 284.

[4] Heraud (1799–1887) had previously been assistant editor of *Frazer's Magazine* and editor of the *Sunbeam*. He later became dramatic critic and a contributor to the *Athenaeum* (1843–68), and the *Illustrated London News* (1849–79).

[5] F. F. Barham (1808–71) said that his system 'included and reconciled divine truths wheresoever found'. He later published a revised edition of the Bible in 1848.

[6] F. F. Barham, *An Odd Medley of Literary Curiosities* (London, 1845).

[7] *Hampden in the Nineteenth Century or Colloquies on the Errors and Improvements of Society* (London, 1834), ii. 23.

[8] Alex Cullen, *Adventures in Socialism, New Lanark Establishment and Orbiston Community* (Glasgow, 1910), 230, 246, 248, 278–80, 299, 318.

---

same platform I already occupy, but never a new platform . . . we are wonderfully the debtors of these men when we look into the road & woe who goes by cart & coach; or look into the newspaper & see how the mankind buys & sells, rules & votes . . . perhaps they will stimulate our downy thought until we exist a stronger will & seeing how much we are agents in the tremendous game of cause and effect that is played around us, we shall come to abandon things less, & know that we do the wrong which we permit'. R. L. Rusk, *The Letters of Ralph Waldo Emerson* (New York, 1939), iii. 207.

Society of Rational Religionists had met Greaves at Cheltenham in 1838. It was, he wrote 'an incident I shall ever deem as one of the happiest in my life. At our first interview, both felt friendly sympathy and an affectionate attachment for each other, even though I could not then fully comprehend the peculiar language in which his ideas were spoken.'[1] A third Owenite convert gained by Greaves was Samuel Bower, of Bradford, whose reading of Owenite ideas and American Communitarian projects had led him to publish *Competition in Peril: or the Present Position of the Owenites, or Rationalism considered: together with Miss Martineau's account of communities in America* (London, 1837), and *The Peopling of Utopia: or, the Sufficiency of Socialism for human happiness: being a further comparison of the Social and Radical Schemes* (Bradford, 1838). Following in their footsteps came James Elimalet Smith. To him Owenism had by 1841 become 'the ultra negative'.[2]

Greaves had also become well known in American transcendental circles as a result of his *Exposition of the Principles of Conducting Infant Education* being read by Bronson Alcott. Alcott was so inspired that he compiled for William Russell's journal an article on 'Pestalozzi's Principles and Methods of Education',[3] and went on to write *Record of a School* and *Conversations on the Gospels*. These were given by Harriet Martineau to Greaves who on 21 September 1837 wrote a long letter praising him 'almost fulsomely'. This was a prelude to a series of long letters.[4] Alcott replied by sending Greaves twelve copies of his *Conversations on the Gospels*, but his letter failed to reach Greaves. Greaves' adjutant in his correspondence was William Oldham, who told Alcott that 'any instructions and monitions or divine sympathies' which he wished to forward would be 'thankfully received and used for the universal good'.[5]

(3)

Oldham had established in 1838 a school at Ham Common

---

[1] A. Campbell, *Letters and Extracts from the Writings of J. P. Greaves* (London, 1843–5), i, iii, iv.

[2] W. A. Smith, *Shepherd Smith the Universalist* (London, 1892), 198.

[3] Odell Shepard, *Pedlar's Progress, the Life of Bronson Alcott* (London, 1938), 86.

[4] op. cit., 208.

[5] F. B. Sanborn and W. T. Harris, *A. Bronson Alcott, His Life and Philosophy* (Boston, 1893), i. 313.

called 'Alcott House', based on Bronson Alcott's Temple School at Boston, with H. G. Wright as headmaster. Wright, a bachelor who conformed to Greaves' doctrine of inflexible celibacy, was an active and lively spirit. He advertised in the *New Moral World*, and addressed the Co-operative Congresses in 1840 and 1841 on his educational ideas. Alcott was impressed when he met him. He told Emerson :—

> You have never seen his like—so deep and serene, so clear, so true, and so good. His school is a most refreshing and happy place. The children are mostly under twelve years of age, of both sexes; and his art and method of education simple and natural. It seemed like being again in my own school, save that a wiser wisdom directs, and a lovelier love presides over its order and teachings. He is not yet thirty years of age, but he has more genius for education than any man I have seen; and not of children alone, but he possesses the rare art of teaching men and women. That I have dreamed and stammered and preached and prayed about so long, is in him clear and definite. It is life, influence, reality. He cherishes hopes of making our land the place of his experiment in human culture, and of proving to others the worth of the divine idea that now fills and exalts him![1]

Indeed Alcott regarded Wright as being 'the first person whom I have met that has entered into this divine art of inspiring the human clay, and moulding it into the stature and image of divinity. I am already knit to him by more than human ties, and must take him with me to America, as a coadjutor in our high vocation, or else remain with him here. But I hope to effect the first.'[2]

Wright also edited a journal called the *Healthian*. From 1 January 1842 to February 1843, it provided the ideas of the hydropathist Vincent Priessnitz and was, after the first number, published by Vincent Torras 'at the Pestalozzi Press'. It was the organ of the Health Association. Alcott also admired these aspects of Wright's work. '*The Healthian* is edited here by Mr. Wright and Mr. Lane, and they are contributors to almost every reform journal in the kingdom. They are not ignorant of our labours in the library at Alcott House—your own works, those

---

[1] ibid., i. 320–2.

[2] F. B. Sanborn, *Bronson Alcott at Alcott House, England, and Fruitlands, New England 1842–1844* (Cedar Rapids, 1908), 16–17.

of Mr. Graham—besides foreign authors, not to be found with us.'[1]

Alcott's visit to England took place four months after Greaves' death. Arriving late in May, having read Wordsworth's *Excursion* on the way and dreaming of 'planting Edens, fabling of worlds, building kingdoms and men', he stayed four months. His first night was spent at the London Coffee House in Ludgate Street, which coloured most of his subsequent visits:

'I have no love of England, nor England's sons and daughters.' He told his wife 'There is here no repose or gentleness, nor grace. Strife and violence mar all things, all men. Hercules stands at every corner with sanguinary club, grim in iron mail . . . I will not turn on my heel to see another man (Beast I meant). And the women are tragic all—Mrs. Carlyle, Fox, Heraud all are tears of sorrow.'[2]

Rejecting London as a 'huge den . . . wherein Beelzebub whelps' he made for Wright's School, now called Alcott House, where on 5 July 1843 a gala was held for 'all those interested in human destiny'. Two meetings were held, one at 3 and one at 7 p.m., both under the chairmanship of Alcott. Sixteen or twenty assembled on the lawn at the back of the house. At this meeting, Wright, Lane and Alcott presented three 'scriptures', dealing with 'Reformation', 'Transition' and 'Formation'. In the heady atmosphere of a Surrey summer, talk ran high and Alcott went on record with a sturdy vegetarian testament:

Our trust is in purity, not in vengeance. Together with pure beings will come pure habits. A better body shall be built up from the orchard and the garden . . . From the fountain shall we slake our thirst, and our appetite shall find supply in the delicious abundance that Pomona offers. Flesh and blood we will reject as 'the accursed thing'. A pure mind has no faith in them.[3]

Another convention on the 7 September discussed whether private property should be abolished.

[1] ibid., p. 18. Sylvester Graham (1794–1851), advocated the consumption of bread at least twelve hours old made of unbolted flour, sleeping on hard mattresses, open bedroom windows, cold baths, looser and lighter clothes, daily exercise, vegetables and fresh fruit diet, and other simplifications of living. Emerson referred to him as 'the poet of bran bread and pumpkins'. Graham's *Lectures on the Science of Human Life*, published in 1839, was well received.

[2] Odell Shepard, op. cit., 310.

[3] Sanborn and Harris, op. cit., 342.

Alcott returned to the United States in October. With him went H. G. Wright, Charles Lane, and his son William. Both Wright and Lane believed that 'On a survey of the present civilised world, Providence seems to have ordained the United States of America, more especially New England, as the field wherein this idea [of a new Eden] is to be realised in actual experience.'[1] They took with them Greaves' Library of 1,000 volumes, and arrived in Concord on 21 October 1842. There, as Emerson wrote 'All day and night they hold perpetual Parliament . . . Mr. Greaves has been the teacher and mover of these men, and it will be long before they outgrow that influence . . . Greaves is a great man. I have a book full of his sentences on my table which is like some Menu transmigrated into Burton Street, London.'[2]

(4)

The exodus of Wright, the Lanes, and Bower to America precipitated the reorganization of Alcott House first outlined in *The Idea of founding an Industrial Harmonic Educational College for the benefit of such parties as were ready to leave the ignorant selfish strife of the antagonistic world* (1841). This was a prospectus for what was to be called the First Concordium. A Concordium was defined as 'the dwelling of those who desire in all respects to be in concord with the Triune Universe Spirit and its creations'. The site was described as formerly the Alcott House School, 'healthy and picturesque', near Richmond Park, midway between Richmond and Kingston and two miles from each, and from Hampton Court and Bushey Park. The members, to be called Concordists, were to unite for the purposes of submitting to the universal law until they 'accord or concord with it'. Here in the concordium, the triune law of goodness, wisdom

[1] ibid., 343.

[2] Ralph L. Rusk, *The Letters of Ralph Waldo Emerson* (New York, 1939), iii. 97. Emerson wrote on 26 October 1842: 'Alcott and his friends Lane and Wright have safely arrived & we expect Mr. Lane & son (a boy of nine or ten years) to spend a few weeks with us. Lane seems to be quite a superior person. He is the author of the two pieces on Greaves & on Cromwell in the last Dial. They have brought out a thousand volumes, chiefly mystical and philosophical books—which I saw safely through the Customs House forms yesterday & tonight this cabalistic collection arrives in Concord. We shall scarcely need the moon any longer o'nights. They have brought 9 or 10 volumes of Mr. Greave's MSS, and some casts & prints of him & others, & what with these, & their wonderful selves, they hardly believe they have left anything behind them in England.'

and power, 'the most lawful, intelligent and efficient conditions for divine progress in humanity' would be worked out. The regimen was based on the spartan rules of life enunciated by James Pierrepont Greaves: 'Pure air, simple food, exercise and cold water are much more beneficial to man, than any national doctrinal creeds, or any churches, chapels, or cathedrals'.

And a stern regimen it proved to be. Members rose at 5.30 a.m. and after repairing to the bath-house went for their morning run; at 6.15 a bell rang summoning them to their occupation. They breakfasted at 8 a.m. on brown bread, or Scotch oatmeal bread, figs and cold vegetables, returning at 9 a.m. to their occupations. The children lunched at 12 noon, the adults at 1 p.m., and during each meal there would be reading. At two o'clock in the afternoon they would return to work, continuing till half past four. The last meal, signalized by the ringing of a bell, took place at 6 p.m., and after this there was a lecture.

The meals were spartan. The consumption of flesh, butter, cheese, eggs, mustard, vinegar, oil, spices, beer, wine, tea, coffee, and chocolate was banned; and the school (with fees of £5 a quarter) specialized in shoemaking, carpentry and gardening. Friendly visitors were accommodated on Sundays and Mondays at 6d. a meal and 6d. a bed. One of these visitors (on 28 April 1843) was Robert Owen. The dress was equally utilitarian: each member wore a brown holland or cotton blouse, a neat check shirt without neck cloth or any other clumsy wrapper round the neck. Hats and caps were rarely worn on the premises. But, living as they did near the metropolis, concessions had to be made: 'When going out each dresses rather more in accordance with the world without, which to them is more like a foreign country than their native abode.'[1]

One of the principal objects of the Concordium was to prepare missionaries for the cause. A new monthly, *The New Age*, first published in May 1843 from 'the Concordium Press' stressed the importance of employing the people on the land. In the same month, the Director of the Concordium, William Oldham ('Pater' to the inmates) left on a missionary tour with two Concordists. This tour covered 100 miles and embraced Romsey,

---

[1] *The New Age*, 6 May 1843. It began as a penny weekly but on 1 July 1843 became a twopenny monthly. It was published at 'The Concordian Press', Ham Common, Surrey.

Southampton, the Isle of Wight, Portsmouth, Chichester, and Brighton. 'Their simplicity, the peculiarity of their dress and the simplicity of their manners', reported the *New Age*, 'attracted all those with which they came into contact.'[1]

The Concordium gained the support of many old Owenites too. Owen himself visited them in April 1843. Now as their treasurer they secured F. Bate, who had already given all he had —some £12,000—to the abortive community at Tytherly in Hampshire.[2] William Galpin, who, like Bate, was a member of the 'Home Colonization Society', also came to address them.[3] And the faithful Alexander Campbell, on his return from Scotland, in August 1843 embarked on a missionary visit for them in the Midland Counties.[4] Perhaps the most eloquent testimony of the value of the Concordium to the Owenite reformers was the fact that it assumed responsibility for the widow and two daughters—Theophila and Hypatia—of Richard Carlile.[5]

The Concordium certainly had few pretensions. 'Persons disposed to assist us', ran an appeal in *The New Age*, 'may much aid by giving orders for printing, clothing, boots and shoes etc. We ask not money so much as useful employment. Our work is equal in style and workmanship to any found in London or elsewhere.'[6]

(5)

Buoyant, optimistic and messianic, the Concordium welcomed the return from America of Henry Gardiner Wright. 'His sympathies', reported *The New Age*, 'are not all in harmony with their democratical government; neither the love and character of the Americans generally so far please his taste as to induce him to stay in that country.' Wright was perhaps responsible for the renewed emphasis on food reform; for the Concordium now became active in forming the British and Foreign Society for the Promotion of the Abstinence from Animal Foods, as well as collecting subscriptions for the great

---

[1] ibid., 20 May 1843.

[2] F. Podmore, *Life of Robert Owen* (London, 1923), 559.

[3] *The New Age*, August 1843.

[4] *The New Age*, September, 1843.

[5] Richard Carlile (1790–1843) issued *The Republican* from 1819–26 and numerous controversial tracts. He had opened a hall for free discussion in 1830 and was subsequently imprisoned for refusing to pay church rates.

[6] *The New Age*, 10 June 1843. It also carried advertisements.

American vegetarian, Sylvester Graham, to visit England.[1]
Their buoyancy was reflected in an optimistic appeal in the
New Age for September 1843.

> We trust associations will be brought into practice in many other
> localities and have had some pleasure in hearing that a small experi-
> ment has commenced near Sheffield, and that one is contemplated
> near Manchester. Another effort on a small scale, is also in practice
> at Hanwell, by our good friend Goodwyn Barmby, under the name
> of the Moreville Communitorium, where persons desirous of pro-
> gress upon universal principles are received in affection and
> intelligent fellowship.

The spartan nature of the régime provoked G. J. Holyoake to
laughter. Holyoake bore Greaves no ill-will, but when he visited
the Concordians after Greaves' death, with Maltus Questall Ryall,
he

> found it, by observing a tall patriarchs' feet projecting through the
> window. It was a device of the concordium to ensure ventilation
> and early rising. By a bastinade on the soles of the prophet with
> pebbles, we obtain admission in the early morning. Salt, Sugar, and
> tea were alike prohibited, and my wife, who wished salt with the
> raw cabbage supplied at breakfast, was allowed to have it, on the
> motion of Mr. Stolzmeyer, the agent of Etzler's 'Paradise within
> the Reach of All men'. When the salt was conceded it was concealed
> in paper under the plate, lest the sight of it should deprave the
> weaker brethren. On Sundays many visitors came, but the enter-
> tainment was slender. On my advice they turned two fields into a
> strawberry garden, and for the charge of ninepence each, visitors
> gathered and ate all they could. This prevented them being able to
> eat too much at other meals, for which they paid, and thus the
> concordium made money.[2]

Two passages from the *New Age* show how difficult it was
proving to found a New Jerusalem in Surrey:–

> We think the period has arrived when we should pay attention to
> the superior cultivation of the land as the chief manual duty in which
> we can be engaged; and we have to thank some of our correspon-
> dents for the interest they have taken in informing us of small
> estates that are yet to be disposed of. We have looked at several,

[1] Wright had become discontented with the Alcott household and on his return
to England wrote on 30 July 1844 to Emerson introducing John Chapman as a
publisher for Emerson in England. Chapman, Wright wrote, bowed reverently
'at the shrine of certain Transatlantic Discoursers on "Nature" and transcendental
"Essay" writers'. Rusk, op. cit., iii. 265. He died in March 1846.

[2] G. J. Holyoake, *A History of Co-operation* (London, 1906), i. 265.

but have not yet seen such a one as we should like to remove to: and our Pater is now on a tour with the view of looking for anything suitable for us. . . . our chief requisites are, pure air, plenty of good water, and from twenty to fifty acres of land of average quality, freehold, and if possible, title free, situated in a locality well adapted for the growth of fruits, Corn, and flax or hemp . . . (House not essential), for we are prepared to labour before we desire to be partakers of the fruit.[1]

And then:

With regard to association, our views are somewhat modified. We still see the advantages of the good, the wise and the powerful associating together as instruments of the general Good, but we likewise see that this can only be done in proportion as persons are in some degree fitted to associate: and that the work of submission must be confined to no locality or arrangement, but that in every place and in every act this great duty must be the beginning, the middle and the end of all the efforts that are made.[2]

(6)

Meanwhile, what of Charles Lane? With Alcott (and for a short time H. G. Wright) he had leased an attractive but unproductive site on a hillside near Harvard, where in June 1843 he had begun to live a life of manual labour, varied by almost frenzied bursts of writing for the *Dial*. This social experiment— for so Fruitlands can be called—suffered from the almost insuperable handicap that the hens and the bees which they kept should not be robbed of the fruits of their labour.[3] Manual labour and authorship might have been a therapeutic for some but not for Lane or Alcott. 'They have no repose', wrote Emerson, 'no self-satisfaction, but as quick as they have conceived a thing they are wretched till it is published.'[4]

The frosts of winter had barely begun to nip the community before Lane found himself in gaol for non-payment of taxes. Both he and Alcott now became thoroughly disillusioned with Pestalozzian ideas as likely to 'oppose the establishment of the community which stands on universal love'. By January 1844 he had broken with Alcott, and took himself and his son off to the Shakers, putting Fruitlands up for sale. Two years later, it was

[1] *The New Age*, November 1844.
[2] *The New Age*, December 1844.
[3] Rusk, op. cit., lists Lane's contributions to the *Dial*, vi. 495.
[4] C. E. Sears, *Bronson Alcott's Fruitlands* (1915).

sold, but only under a mortgage, for $1,700 of which $400 seems to have been paid in cash.[1]

Late in 1846 Lane returned to England, his wonderful library being packed and sent to Emerson, who had also agreed to act as Lane's agent for the collection of interest on the Fruitlands mortgage. Naturally, Lane returned to Ham, where he either continued, or restarted the school. He addressed the Co-operative League in London on 27 January 1847 'giving many interesting details concerning the settlements of the Shakers, all confirming the practicability of the system of co-operation.'[2] Emerson dined with him at Ham and found him full of friendliness and hospitality. The school then numbered sixteen children, one lady as matron, and Oldham. 'This is all the household' wrote Emerson. 'They look just comfortable.'

In 1848 the Concordium came to an end. The *Reasoner* reported it had 'passed into new hands. Its present use is that of an educational asylum for orphans whose parents have died of cholera.' The school was run on vegetarian principles and Lane published *Dietetics: An Endeavour to ascertain the Law of Human Nutriment* in 1849. The last glimpse we have of Lane is a melancholy one. By December 1854 he had lost touch with Emerson, who asked a friend to look him up in London

> & satisfy yourself as exactly as you can of his condition & purposes. The Shakers wish to know, & I wish to know of him. A portion of his library still remains on my shelves; nor have I sold any book for the last few years. Alcott thinks they are not Lane's to sell. My practice, I think must not be bound by A's casuistry, and if Lane is suffering or is uneasy about them, I would make a final sale of them, though there is not I suppose a value of $50.[3]

And then Emerson added :—

> There came from Marcus Spring, I believe, some unpleasant rumour, as if in solitude, & sickness L. had found some irregular indulgences. He is a man of so much ability & of so respectable aims and stoutness that he ought to be visited & cherished.[4]

---

[1] Rusk, op. cit., iii. 214, 231, 235, 240. Lane had written 'A Day with the Shakers' for the *Dial* of October 1843, and Emerson had written as early as August 1843: 'Mr. Lane is very much engaged with the Shakers & will write of them for the Dial, & perhaps may join them.' iii. 196.

[2] *Howitt's Journal*, 27 February 1847.

[3] Rusk, op. cit., iii. 425, iv. 117, 158, 226, 287.

[4] ibid., iv. 178–9.

2

❖◇❖◇❖◇❖◇❖◇❖◇❖◇❖◇❖◇❖◇❖◇❖◇❖◇❖◇❖◇❖◇❖◇❖◇❖

Hugh Doherty and the Phalanstery

❖◇❖◇❖◇❖◇❖◇❖◇❖◇❖◇❖◇❖◇❖◇❖◇❖◇❖◇❖◇❖◇❖◇❖◇❖

(1)

ANASTOMOSING links between these little cells are visible in the next group, that congregated about Hugh Doherty in the 1840s.

To Doherty, Fourierism was 'Universalism', 'Humanization' and 'Solidarity'. He warmed to Fourier's educational ideas— that children learned by doing the things they like—and he published an *Introduction to English Grammar on Universal Principles* in 1841. In the same year he published a memoir of Fourier and a translation of A. L. E. Transon's essay on *C. Fourier's Theory of Attractive Industry*.[1]

Fourier's educational ideas make him, as G. D. H. Cole pointed out, 'an important anticipator of modern ideas of education, especially in its vocational aspects'.[2] Doherty not only assimilated these but also Fourier's ideas on work and incentives to work.

Fourier was a newly departed saint to Doherty, having died only three years before, foretelling a period of harmony which would last for 35,000 years, when the world would be organized in autonomous groups of 1,800 people called 'phalanxes'. These

---

[1] Hugh Doherty, author of a *Memoir of C. Fourier* (1841), *Organic Philosophy* (1864–78), and *The Philosophy of Reason* (London, 1865). He later qualified as a doctor and died in 1891.

[2] G. D. H. Cole, *Socialist Thought, The Forerunners* (London, 1953), i. 65.

phalansterians would be property-owning, polyandrous, petit-bourgeois. Having lost his own small inherited income during the French revolution, Fourier's system of society was designed to prevent revolution and was therefore graded in classes, or groups. He saw the will of God pervading the world in all its movements: material, organic, and social. This pervasion he called the law of universal attraction. From this law he deduced his universal analogy: everything in one part of the world has a parallel elsewhere. Mankind, as he saw, was oppressed by civilization (a collective term for evil) and needed release so that human passions (hitherto repressed) could have free play. These passions he classified as sensitive (sight, hearing, taste, smell and touch), affective (friendship, ambition and familism) and distributive (emulation, alternation, composition). The harmonizing of these passions, effected by their free play, would be analogous to producing the colour white from a combination of colours. This harmonizing, he concluded, would need new social arrangements, or 'phalanxes'.

Individuals would be arrayed in groups of seven or more; the groups arranged in series of twenty-four or more, and the series arrayed in a phalanx. Each phalanx would live in a phalanstery where labour would be made attractive by considering the likings and capacities of each individual and by allowing changes. Common labour would produce a common stock which would be distributed, a basic minimum going to each member and the remainder divided according to labour (five–twelfths), capital (four-twelfths) and talent (three-twelfths). The highest paid labour would be the most necessary, and the lowest the most pleasant.

So much did Fourier believe in his system that he foresaw a time when the whole world would be a federation of Phalanxes with Constantinople as the capital. In France both a Fourierist paper and a phalanx were begun. The phalanx, on an estate near the forest of Rambouillet, failed but the newspaper, *Le Phalanstere*, after a shaky start, got on its feet in 1836 as *Le Phalange* and by 1843 had become *La Democratie Pacifique*.

(2)

In 1841 there was published a book which seemed to offer Doherty the very instrument whereby Fourier's ideas could be realized. This was a work by J. A. Etzler entitled *The New World: or Mechanical System to perform the Labours of man and Beast*. This, a sequel to a more general work which Etzler had published five years before entitled *The Paradise within the reach of all men, without labour, by powers of nature and machinery* (1836), gave Doherty a lead.

Etzler preached the necessity of using mechanical slaves, and in *The Paradise* had pointed out there were 'powers in nature sufficient to effect in one year more than hitherto all men on earth could do in many thousands of years . . . and the most profitable, shortest and easiest way to put them into operation for such great purposes, is, to form "associations".'

In a series of brief imaginative sketches he outlined means whereby the winds,[1] the tides,[2] the waves[3] and the heat of the sun[4] could be harnessed to supplant the labour of man. His conception was symbolized in the phrase 're-acting power' by which he meant that natural forces once harnessed would need very little superintendence. Thus the heat of the sun, captured and concentrated in great 'burning mirrors', would enable foundries and 'vitrifying establishments' to operate continuously, producing the machines and prefabricated buildings for the 'Paradise'. He also envisaged the utilization of natural substances, like wood, for food, and the manufacture of synthetic fibres.[5]

Etzler outlined a revolution in the technique of living. Large apartment houses, where each person would have his or her own rooms for sleeping, bathing and dressing were planned, with flat roofs, pipes for warm and cold water, gas, scents and air-conditioning. These were to be 1,000 ft. long, 200 ft. high and 100 ft. wide, and were to have 'boxes that move up and down' to transport inhabitants to upper floors, as well as artificial light.[6]

Four phases in this great change were envisaged. The first would involve the organization of an association to collect funds

[1] *The Paradise Within Reach of all Men, without Labour by Powers of Nature and Machinery* (Pittsburgh, 1833), 6.
[2] ibid., 10.
[3] ibid., 16.
[4] ibid., 27.
[5] ibid., 64–65.
[6] ibid., 71–73.

and sponsor a pilot community on the Atlantic seaboard, and would necessitate the taking over of existing farms to establish it. The second would see the successful operation of the experiment. The third phase would see the Mississippi lands divided 'in community', each of not less than 1,000 people, and with 100 communities forming a state. These communities would begin along the Pacific coast where the forces of the winds, the tides, the waves and the sun would be easily available, and for them he sketched a government, not the 'tax-gathering and tax-expending' governments of his day, but one in which the whole community met once a week to approve of the work of its five committees of provisions, health, instruction, pleasure and police. The fourth and last phase of the Etzlerian Paradise would see the linking up of these communities by 'artificial roads of vitrified substances' along which vehicles would run at the rate of forty miles an hour, the establishment of foundries, and fabricatories of plastic substances for supplying wants, and the utilization of great lakes as food-producing areas. This last enterprise would be effected, he declared, by the use of 'floating islands' built of wood bases with earth on top.

Etzler was convinced that this Paradise could and would be attained within five or ten years after the first association had been formed as he indicated. Population of almost unimaginable density would be sustained. The expectation of life would increase to 110 or even 170 years, and moral problems would cease to exist. He appealed to all intelligent men:–

> If you want to choose the good and glorious road, you have to do it now, or your chance may soon be lost forever. In the contrary case, other nations or governments will use the offered means for the dominion over you. It will then depend from your masters what blessing or what curse the new means are to bring upon you . . . Americans, it is now in your power to become within ten years a nation to rule the world; your territory can contain from 200–300 million. You have it in your power to receive the most intelligent part out of all nations . . . you may cause a migration of nations, unparalleled in history.

He even addressed his appeal to the Senate and to President Andrew Jackson. But in his own time and in ours, few people in America paid any attention to him. True, his book has recently been described as 'one of the first American Utopias . . . (it)

187

forecast plastics, synthetic fabrics and air-conditioning. Henry Thoreau read this thin little volume and, repulsed by the picture it presented of a mechanical civilization, was confirmed in his preference for simple living.'[1] But for all its novelty, Americans were unmoved. As Etzler sadly confessed: 'I thought I had given to the public nothing but matters of fact . . . applying both to high and low people for examination of the subjects and offering models and everything required to see and understand the things I there treated of but they shook their heads in their own wisdom and declined to see or know anything of it'.[2] So Etzler moved to the West Indies, and after a short stay returned to the United States, this time to New York and Philadelphia, where as he says, 'I found some partners to aid my cause—the cause of the world hereafter.' One of these partners was the bookseller and publisher C. F. Stollmeyer[3] of 64 South Fourth Street, Philadelphia, who published Etzler's next tract *The New World or mechanical system to perform the labours of Man and Beast by Inanimate Powers* (1841), in which Etzler gave an account of his multi-purpose plough-bulldozer 'The Satellite'. This, as its name implied, operated in a circle from a point of stationary power. A plate at the back of this pamphlet gave details of its construction. 'There are certainly a few passages which verge on the utopian,' said a British working-class paper, 'but then there is quite enough of the *practical* to induce us to pronounce Mr. Etzler's projects deserving universal consideration.'[4]

(3)

Etzler seems to have come to England in 1840 with his partner Stollmeyer. Stollmeyer was living at 6 Upper Charles Street, Northampton Square, in 1841, and in 1842 an edition of

---

[1] A. E. Morgan, *Nowhere was Somewhere, How History makes Utopias and Utopias Make History* (Chapel Hill, 1946), 160–1.
V. L. Parrington, *American Dreams, A Study of American Utopias* (Providence, 1947), does not mention him.

[2] *Two Visions of J. A. Etzler . . . A Revelation of Futurity* (Ham Common, Surrey, 1844).

[3] Stollmeyer confessed that he was, whilst in Philadelphia, an active member of the Anti-Slavery Society. When he was editor of the *German National Gazette*, one of his stinging editorials (after a mob had tried to burn a public hall) led to his being threatened. See *The Sugar Question Made Easy* (London, 1845), 10.

[4] *The English Chartist Circular*, No. 128, p. 304. In 1844 *The Paradise* was translated into German and published at Ulm.

Etzler's original work, *The Paradise Within Reach of All Men*, was published in England.

At this point Doherty obtained the services of Shepherd Smith, whom he commissioned to translate Fourier's works for publication early in 1841.[1] Doherty also recruited James Young, a mechanical inventor after Etzler's own heart, and Arthur Young who wanted to establish a Fourierist experiment in France, near Dijon, where he had bought an estate.[2] He also started a weekly paper called the *Phalanx* for which James invented a new machine on which it could be printed.

With James Young, Etzler demonstrated another invention, patented on 12 April 1842: 'a car destined to transport materials and for other objects, moved in the method invented by Mr. Etzler'.[3]

In September 1841, a company was formed of which Stollmeyer was a director to promote such inventions. One of these was for a ship to navigate the ocean by the power of the waves and the wind. The London *Phalanx* reported that models of these inventions had been made and that 'there was not the slightest doubt of their efficiency'. On 23 October 1841 it reported that Stollmeyer had returned from the Continent where he had secured patents on the models and announced that they could be inspected from 11 a.m. to 4 p.m. at No. 70 Cheapside, admission being obtainable from the offices of the London *Phalanx*, 3a Catherine Street, Strand. And when the English edition of Etzler's *Paradise Within Reach of All Men* was published in 1842, Etzler could be said to have been fairly well launched.

(4)

Yet another English convert to Etzler's technological Utopia was Luke James Hansard, the 56-year-old senior partner of the famous firm of printers to the House of Commons. In 1843,

---

[1] 'I am at present translating one of Fourier's works from the French which is to be published at intervals in a new weekly stamped paper at 6*d*. I will also write an article in it every week. It is to be called *The London Phalanx*.' L. A. Smith, op. cit., 212.

[2] op. cit., 212.

[3] J. A. Etzler, *Mechanical System in its Greatest Simplicity, for Agricultural Works, Formations of Ditches, Canals, Dams and any Excavations . . . and other works* (London, 1844).

under the pseudonym of Hugo Minor, Hansard published a three-volume work called *Hints to Railway Travellers*. Hansard, or 'Hugo Minor' as he chose to call himself then, was an enthusiastic advocate of the Fourierist principle of 'a union of interests *not* a community of goods', arguing 'in the same manner that an Insurance Society provides against loss by fire or sea, so does a phalanx offer security against poverty, in case of sickness and a home for the indigent . . . a true fraternal feeling between man and man, not an equality of grade; a strict and tolerant adherence to the Divine Law . . . the application of machinery, the arts, and sciences, to the comfort and aid of every class'. He proposed that 6,000 acres should be set aside on which a phalanstery should be created, with a suite for each family, public rooms, bathrooms, servants' quarters, a hospital and school. To look after this, a governor should be appointed with a minister and surgeon to help him. This, argued Hansard, was far more important than meddling with Corn Laws, Chartism, or Repeal Unions. For, with Etzler's inventions, the land would yield abundantly. Here was the Fourierite dream in full: an ideal society based on groups, with the groups constituting a series, and a number of series the phalanx.

But in 1842 Doherty was far too obsessed with Etzler's wonderful ship to worry about a phalanx. Shepherd Smith lamented on 18 October 1842 :–

> Doherty is keenly employed upon an automaton vessel at present, and expects to go to sea this month in it. It moves the paddles without steam, by means of wind and wave. This vessel has a float attached to it of equal specific gravity with the water. It is below the keel, and as the vessel heaves, the float resists with a power equal to the weight of the vessel—minus the resistance of the water— and moves the paddles by a simple machinery. The heavier the sea, the stronger the power. In rivers, the power is insufficient, and in still water zero. He is in high hopes of making a fortune and superseding steam. But I suspect that he is doomed to some bitter disappointment.[1]

So he was. Two months later, Doherty's boat sank. As Smith described it :–

> The float pulled it in head foremost and Stollmeyer had to jump for his life. Doherty has never spoken to me of it, but I heard it, and

[1] L. A. Smith, op. cit., 215.

that he lost his razors, etc., which he had put in it, intending to take a trip to France. He was not in it when it sunk. It cost £15 to raise it, and there is about £30 of damage done. They are repairing it. Stollmeyer says it was merely an accident, as the float was not fixed at both ends. I used to bother him long ago with the idea of its going down, when he invited me to go to France in it. I asked him if France lay at the bottom of the sea.[1]

(5)

When Smith posed this mocking question, Doherty took offence. The London *Phalanx* was soon a scene of uproar. He came in and gave all the hands a holiday, and shut it up: 'a piece of ill nature', remarked Smith 'for which he will yet pay, most likely. He seems quite ill-tempered; his boat sinking, and nobody caring for his Fourierism, makes him quite out of humour, and this only makes matters worse. The present number of the *Phalanx* is a most extraordinary production and shows that he is going into the wilds of the desert of thought.'[2]

Yet Doherty had enough energy left to start a Phalansterian Tract Society and act as its secretary. James H. Young was the president and William Tailor the treasurer. They met to dine at the Piazza Hotel, Covent Garden, on 7 April 1843 and agreed that it was high time to press for an experiment in phalanx founding.

They appealed to both Parliament and the Establishment to provide a million pounds with which to try a comparative experiment of the Owenite, Etzlerian, and Phalansterian plans. If, they argued, £300,000 were to be spent on a pilot project of each, the remaining £100,000 could be utilized by the Government to cover the costs of assessing and inspecting the results obtained. The final blow came on 13 May 1843. Smith described it: 'The *Phalanx* office is now shut up. The *Phalanx* is dead. The machine is stopped. The *Herald* is now printed in the old way. Doherty and I have had a fall-out about Fourier. He seems crestfallen about the failure of his attempt. But he must learn to be more universal, and give up the worship of dead men and their bones'.[3]

[1] ibid., 216.
[2] ibid., 221.
[3] ibid., 222.

(6)

With the cessation of the London *Phalanx*, Etzler and Stollmeyer had to turn elsewhere for support and they found it amongst the disciples of James Pierrepont Greaves. William Oldham invited Stollmeyer to lecture in July 1843.[1] Stollmeyer had moved (according to *Kelly's Directory*) to 3 Northampton Terrace, City Road, in 1843 and in the following year we find Etzler himself listed in *Kelly's Directory* as occupying 266 The Strand.

The collapse of Doherty's paper and the failure of Young's Fourierist Colony near Dijon led Etzler to propose yet another scheme: the colonization of Venezuela.[2] This was outlined in *Emigration to the Tropical World for the Melioration of All Classes of People of All Nations,* published by the Concordium Press, at Ham Common.[3] Stollmeyer's talk probably won over two other enthusiasts connected with the Ham Communitorium, Goodwyn Barmby and James Elmzlie Duncan. Barmby we shall meet later.

Etzler's other supporter, James Elmzlie Duncan, published *The Sun Beam.*[4] This contained the first instalment of a novel 'Edward Noble—the Utopist' in which some of the personalities of the time figured—O'Connor, Owen, W. J. Fox, Greaves and Cobden, with the inevitable addition, of course, of Etzler. In the only editorial ever published, Duncan affirmed that his columns would be 'especially devoted to making known the scientific and societarian plans of J. A. Etzler, the greatest man ever of this enterprising and wonder-working age . . . and the interests of the society now formed to carry out his system, The Tropical Emigration Society'.

He also informed them that:–

The satellite is now in progress of construction under the super-

---

[1] The Ham Communitorium published for Etzler two pamphlets in 1844: *Two Visions of J. A. Etzler* and *Emigration to the Tropical World.*

[2] The *Dial* (Boston, 1842), 86, reported in July of that year that 100 labourers had sailed from Le Havre to Santa Catharina, described as 'fifty miles from Rio', and that 1,900 more were to follow. It is not clear whether these were, in any way, associated with a French version of Etzler's scheme to colonize the tropics.

[3] Etzler also published, whilst in England, *A Dialogue on Etzler's Paradise, Between Messrs. Clear, Flat, Dunce and Grudge* (London, 1843).

[4] For whom see T. Frost, *Forty Years Recollections* (London, 1880), 50, who gives the name of his paper (wrongly) as *The Rising Sun.*

intendence of a skilful engineer, and within a few weeks will be in practical operation on the land. This machine, the most important that has ever been invented and which cannot fail to produce a greater effect on the world than any which has preceded it, a simple machine to supersede animal and human labour in that most vitally important of the business of human life AGRICULTURE.

The peculiar feature of the satellite is that it admits with little loss of power in the transmission of being worked and set in loco-motion by stationary power of either water or steam; situated at a distance from it, from a few feet or more.

He was especially anxious to inform his readers that Etzler's Paradise could be established, thanks to its use of mirrors to concentrate solar heat, and to 'its floating island' for as little as £7,000. This was 100 times cheaper than Owen's estimate of £700,000 for one of his parallelograms. 'Etzler', exclaimed Duncan, 'could build his Paradise for the sum Owen required for one of his towers.'

(7)

In this new project, Stollmeyer and Etzler won the attention of groups in the West Riding of Yorkshire. An Etzlerian move-ment was on foot there in January 1843 and Stollmeyer was writing for the *Northern Star* in August, September and October of that year. By August of the following year Etzler himself was writing for the *Northern Star*. Indeed Etzler came up to speak on 2 November 1844 and there is, in the *Northern Star*, evidence that there were Etzlerian branches in Bradford, Newcastle-on-Tyne and Bingley by December.

The constitution of the society was reformed in February 1845 and the *Northern Star* announced that it would carry a report of Etzler from Caracas on 19 July. A soirée was held to push the transit arrangements in January 1846 and from then on the project is shrouded in obscurity.[1]

Only one glimpse of the Venezuela project has been afforded to us, and that by Stollmeyer in a pamphlet *The Sugar Question Made Easy* (1845), dedicated to Don Alego Fortique, Minister Plenipotentiary of the Republic of Venezuela to the Court of St.

---

[1] *Northern Star*, 3 December 1843, 6 January, 13 January, 24 February, 9 March, 16 March, 30 March, 29 June, 6 July, 13 July, 27 July, 10 August, 2 November, 9 November, 16 November, 23 November, 7 December, 14 December, 1844, 4 January, 15 February, 12 July, 1845, 3 January, 10 January 1846.

James, 'in due respect of his Excellency's diplomatic ability', he struck hard at the West Indies lobby in the House of Commons. Since Etzler had succeeded in crystallizing sugar without heat or boiling at far less than the cost of making it in the usual way, he maintained that slave labour and all that went with it was unnecessary. He announced that: 'The inventor together with two other gentlemen have embarked for Venezuela in the month of February last, on behalf of themselves and a society in England for the purpose of selecting a proper locality for the said society, one of whose chief branches of industry will be the cultivation of sugar.'[1]

(8)

Doherty turned to flirt with the Swedenborgism of his new ally, James Garth Wilkinson, who wrote in 1846: 'Dr. Hugh Doherty is merging Fourier to the New Church, giving the former, however, masculine character in the compact.' Wilkinson was the great English writer on Swedenborg. 'It is the morning brightness of the world's day' he wrote, expressing his hope that with Doherty, he would 'carry forward the views of Swedenborg and Fourier' instead of being, as heretofore, 'the mere turnspit of those central fires'.

Though Wilkinson was not confident that the time for 'Association' had yet come, he was none the less a firm believer that it would. 'I look upon Fourier as the first worthy historian of animal man!' he exclaimed. In 1848 Doherty and Wilkinson went to Paris, where they met Brisbane (the American Fourierist), Dana, and Robert Owen. Wilkinson had considered emigrating to America and had consulted his friend and fellow Swedenborgian Henry James (the father of Henry the novelist and of William the psychologist) but James had advised against it. In 1849, when Emerson came over to Britain on a lecture tour, he met Wilkinson and found that they had a mutual interest in Swedenborg. For it was Wilkinson's unique function to translate much of Swedenborg for English readers. He was, in addition to being a trained scientist, a good journalist (in 1850

---

[1] *The Sugar Question Made Easy* (London, 1845), 17. Stollmeyer was evidently in New York in April 1844 where he participated in a great Fourierist meeting organized by Alfred Brisbane. See A. E. Bestor, 'Albert Brisbane: Propagandist for Socialism in the 1840'ties' in *New York History*, 1947, 28, 31.

he was the English Correspondent for a number of New York papers). Emerson was much impressed by Wilkinson's efforts and wrote in his *Representative Man*, 'This startling re-appearance of Swedenborg after a hundred years in his pupil is not the least remarkable fact in his history.' Whilst in *English Traits* he said 'Wilkinson, the editor of Swedenborg, the annotator of Fourier, and the champion of Hahnemann, has brought to metaphysics and to physiology a native vigour with a catholic perception of relations, equal to the highest attempts, and a rhetoric like the armoury of the invisible knights of old. There is in the action of his mind a long Atlantic roll not known except in deepest waters.'

But of Doherty, Emerson thought less, for after meeting him in Paris in 1848 he wrote 'a man of talent but not, I think, the great man Wilkinson thinks him'.[1]

[1] Rusk, *Letters of Emerson* (1939), iv, 75.

3

The Hanwell Communitorium

(1)

THERE had been a long Atlantic roll reverberating throughout the decade of the 1840s.

'We now and in the future shall apostolize for communisation, deeming it imperative that some communitarian arrangement should be adopted to meet the demands of the present progressive society. Our theme henceforth will be association.'[1] These sentiments, expressed in a pamphlet published by the Central Communist Bureau from 77 Norton Street, Portland Place in 1841 were voiced by Goodwyn Barmby, then a young man of 21, with four years of heavy political experience behind him. At 17 he associated with a revolutionary group in London; at 20 he was in Paris. Now he had organized the Central Communist Propaganda Society, to promote communitarianism as the 'crowning edifice' of life. Barmby offered to translate Morelly's *Code de la Nature* for a publisher, Thomas Frost. Frost was much impressed by his 'gentlemanly manners and soft persuasive voice, light-brown hair in a muddle and a collar and necktie à la Byron'. He was well read, with a hydroptic thirst for socialist ideas that was to make him one of the most restless characters in a restless age. Frost regarded him as 'conversant with the whole

---

[1] G. Barmby, *The Outlines of Communism, Associality, and Communisation* (London, 1841).

196

range of Utopian literature from Theopeompus and Euhemerus to Weitling and Albrecht'.[1]

(2)

Barmby set about trying to form his own community. The Central Communist Propaganda Society (or Bureau) was to be the agent by which this was accomplished. In this he was helped by Henry Fry of 8 Northfield Terrace, Cheltenham. Fry issued in November 1841, the *Educational Circular and Communist Apostle*—a monthly with a circulation of 1,000 copies, urging the immediate formation of a communitorium or social house, 'for the free exponency of the loveful, the intelligent, the beautiful'. Plans were mooted and it was hoped that they would be soon 'worked into actuality'. In this the meetings of the Central Communist Propaganda Society were reported. At the first, held on 13 October 1841, a memorial had been composed to the Archbishop of Canterbury condemning the 'hierophantic pomp of rich phylacteries and splendid equipages', and observing :–

> Your memorialists, moreover, cannot but behold the inutility of the Church. It teaches but from two books, and those it does not illustrate by the discovery of science or the creations of genius. It assists not but wages war against the poor . . . Your memorialists are desirous that your Grace should follow the example of Christ, and live after the manner of the poor while poverty remains. They also wish you to resign your annual incomes for the establishment of manufacturing and agricultural communes, assuring you of a generous pecuniary allowance, and they likewise are desirous that every church should become a temple of science, and every priest a scientific expounder, and that you yourself should set the first example.

The central council of the Central Communist Propaganda Society met again on 3 November 1841 to establish 'the Universal Communitarian Association', to operate through five territorial groups. The first or the central group was centred on the London area; the second round Cheltenham; the third round Ipswich, the fourth round Merthyr Tydfil, and the fifth round Strabane in Ireland. These branches were to be kept together by Thomas Heaviside, the secretary, and George Bird,

[1] T. Frost, *Forty Years Recollections* (London, 1880), 54–74.

the treasurer. Under the chairmanship of Goodwin Barmby, they were to be provided with lecturers 'properly authorised by diploma to avoid quackery and deceit'. In addition 'an organ of the press for the whole society' was to be issued weekly to supplement the monthly of Henry Fry. This weekly, *The Promethean or Communitarian Apostle*, was to report progress on an experimental community. 'The reign of the critic is over', Barmby announced, 'the rule of the poet commences. All Messiahs will be acknowledged.'

Barmby, in common with many of his generation, put forward a philosophy of history. According to this mankind had evolved through four ages, each of which was subdivided into two phases. The first age (called the age of Paradisation), manifested itself in pastoralism and clanism and found its archetypes in Moses, Ovid and the Vale of Arcady. The second (that of Barbarization), manifested itself in the feudal and later the municipal systems; the ideals of the St. Simonians. The third age (that of Civilization), was marked by Monopolism (or negative association) and Association (the positive form). Both monopolism and association were transitory and ascensive states, preceding the fourth and last age, which was that of Communization.[1]

This fourth or final age of communization, it was, of course, his mission to explain. This he did in a 'Communist Temple' established at the Circus, Great Marylebone, where on March 1842 he outlined his theory of a community. As he saw it there were four stages in its foundation. The first, or imperfect stage, was the club or lodging house; the second, or perfect stage, was the common production and consumption centre; the third was the complete city community and the fourth the country community. He pointed to the early Christians as examples of the community founders in history. Barmby was also a health reformer. Every community was to have its own Baptistery or Hydropathic centre, complete with Frigidary, Calidary, Tepidary, and Frictionary. He was also a food reformer and wrote *New Tracts for the Times* or *Warmth, Life and Food for the Masses*, in which he preached a vegetarian creed. Raw vegetables were to be the staple diet for three months in summer, with hot

---

[1] *Educational Circular and Communist Apostle*, January 1842.

cooked vegetables in the winter, and a mixture of both in the spring and autumn. Brandy, whisky and wines were banned (though wine made in the communitorium might be used) and indigenous herb drinks were to take their place. Sugar was only to be eaten in the form of honey.

The title of his *The Promethean or Communitarian Apostle* (which ran for three months as a monthly and then became a quarterly) was avowedly taken from Shelley, and Barmby tried most ostentatiously to line himself behind those whom he considered were his spiritual ancestors: Euphemorus, Panchaia, Plato, More, Campanella, Defoe, Fénelon, Bacon, Harington, Morelly, Hall, Retif de la Bretonne, St. Pierre, Swedenborg, Kant, Etzler, John Minter Morgan and Mrs. Manley.

(3)

In 1843 he founded the Moreville Communitorium, his first experiment. It was started in a house at Hanwell, taken on a lease of ninety-nine years, with an 'archon' and an 'archoness'. It was especially concerned with adult education, industrial training and with 'juvenile education for both sexes'.

Around this nucleus bigger things were to grow and in the *Promethean* Barmby urged: 'Unitedly let the genii embrace communism, unitedly let the capacities apostolise for Communisation. Let them strive heart with heart, shoulder to shoulder, and arm in arm to emancipate the world from the mercantile competition and the spiritual and material discord which now pervades it.' His millenarian enthusiasm led him to initiate a new chronology, beginning with 1841 as the year 1, N.D. But as Goodwyn Barmby lamented, 'few availed themselves of this opportunity and these were minds who were unprepared for the practice of the principles'.

Preaching and further propaganda were necessary, so to these he now bent his energies, and converted the Communitarian Society to the Communist Church. 'At the Moreville Communitorium', he wrote, 'I saw from practical results the importance of the religious basis, of the idea of duty, and the foundation of the Communitive State. It was there that, finding the small number and the unprepared condition of those who had hitherto professed Communism, I saw the necessity of more largely diffusing its principles among the public, before continuing further practical proceedings'.[1]

This 'diffusion of principles' led Barmby to issue the *Communist Miscellany* which consisted of a collection of tracts for the times forwarded to various parts of the country. He also issued another newspaper that succeeded the *Promethean*. This was the *Communist Chronicle and Apostle of the Communist Church*. It was followed in turn by *The Communitive Life*.

(4)

`As editor of the *Communist Chronicle* Barmby came into touch with William Weitling. 'The thoughts of Weitling are commingling with ours, and flying abroad like down-winged seeds over our common earth of green and gold',[2] he wrote in 1843 when Weitling was imprisoned in Switzerland. The 'commingling' of which Barmby wrote was no new process, indeed, Barmby himself had almost certainly met Weitling in Paris some years before, when Weitling had taken a role, if not the leading one, in the establishment of the League of the Just, an association of German exiles.[3]

Weitling, twelve years older than Barmby, came to Paris in 1835. Like Barmby, he had been much influenced by F. N. Babeuf, the French Communist after whom he named one of his sons. He too had read Saint-Simon and Fourier, and met (whether at this time or later) Étienne Cabet. For the League of the Just he had written *Die Menschheit, wie sie ist und wie sie sein sollte*: a manifesto calling for spiritual renewal and a rekindling of the 'inner light'. He invoked Christian precept against private property, inheritance, nationalism and sectarianism. On its publication he had gone to Zurich, still working at his trade as a tailor, living a most ascetic life, and editing a journal.

Weitling's activity as an initiator of *Arbeite vereine* in the

---

[1] A. E. Bestor attributes 'the naturalization of practically all these new terms in English to Barmby', *Journal of the History of Ideas*, XI (1948), 280. See also E. M. Tilton, 'The term "Communitarian" in the nineteenth century', *American Letter of History of Ideas*, II. (1956), 15. Bronson Alcott met Barmby in 1842 (*Journals*, 168–9), and absorbed some of his outlook.

[2] *Communist Chronicle* I, No. 11, p. 121.

[3] For which see Leopold Schwartzchild, *The Red Prussian, The Life and Legend of Karl Marx* (New York, 1947), 92; Carl Wittke, *The Utopian Communist, A Biography of Wilhelm Weitling* (Baton Rouge, 1950).

various Swiss towns that led Barmby to refer to the spreading network of communitarian 'cells' in Switzerland. So when Weitling started a journal (later called *die Junge Generation*) it found 100 subscribers in England. Joseph Moll, his old comrade, was now in London and he must have helped. This paper was so dangerous that Guizot ordered it to be seized in France and forbade its conveyance to England.

As expressed in *Die Junge Generation*, Weitling published articles on Owen, on the Rappist colony of Harmonie, and on the progress of science and invention. His masterpiece *Garantien der Harmonie und Freiheit*, was, though published in secret and by subscription, quickly seized by Metternich's spies. It advocated the establishment of a community of skilled workers, a *Familienordnung* of a million people, subdivided into *Familien Kreis* and below them *familienvereine*. Both *Kreis* and *Vereine* were to be governed by elected boards, each *Kreis* selecting a Congressman, the Congress a Senate and a supreme triumvirate administering the whole. In the summer of 1844, Weitling arrived in England to join former members of the League of the Just like Schapper, Bauer and Moll, for he had printed their articles.

Goodwyn Barmby, in the *Promethean*, and later in the *Communist Chronicle*, printed accounts of Weitling's work, and regarded him as an 'intelligent, clear and contemplative theoretician'.[1] The forty-four various national groups in London combined to welcome Weitling. The French, the German, and the publisher of the *New Moral World* all spoke, and Weitling delivered a stirring address on the international character of the movement. He kept himself alive by working at his trade, and at a universal language.

A great festival was organized in London on 22 September 1845 to commemorate the fifty-third anniversary of the birth of the French Republic. This congress was, in a very real sense, a forerunner of the International Working Men's Association, and the speeches were in French and German as well as English. In addition, Italian, Polish and Swiss delegations from their various 'groups' in London were present, together with a Hungarian and a Turk. Weitling spoke for the Germans,

[1] *Promethean*, March 1842, 54; *Communist Chronicle* 1, No. 5, 80; 13, 144, No. 14, 149. *Young Germany, An Account of the Rise, Progress and Present Position of German Communism* (London, 1844).

Thomas Cooper for the English (he also acted as president), and a disciple of Cabet's—Dr. Berrier-Fontaine—for the French.[1]

Whilst in England, Weitling was most active in the London Society of Communists, and increased its membership from 70 to 130 in ten months. He also became acquainted with the Christian Socialists, heard Charles Kingsley speak and knew Newton, the trades union leader.

The Germans in London at this time wanted to publish a journal for Weitling to edit, but he preferred to speak on the progress of mechanical inventions or to drink beer in a tavern in Leicester Square with his friends. His emotional and religious approach to communism became anathema to Schapper and the others, who had been much affected by English Chartism. So it was not long before the two of them quarrelled, especially since Weitling was very interested in emigration societies and model colonies. Indeed Weitling considered Owen's system was the best of all, and he said so at London meetings of the group.[2] He began to absent himself from the group, and also from England, which he left for good in January 1846.

After vainly trying to persuade Marx and Engels to modify their rigid materialism at a Conference in Brussels, he emigrated to America in 1847. Returning to participate in the German revolution in 1848, he only stayed for a short time. His second visit to the United States was for good.

(5)

Barmby meanwhile had established relations with a new sect which had sprung up in Ireland under the influence of Joshua Jacob and Abigail Beale. Jacob had been disowned by the Dublin Quakers in 1838 and had founded his sect in 1843. Under Goodwyn Barmby's influence (he visited them in 1843 and 1845) they progressed steadily towards a community. In five years they numbered thirty persons, children included. 'It was at one time still more extensive' wrote a reporter in *Howitt's Journal* on 18 September 1847, 'but the increasing strictness of their rules has caused the lukewarm and unworthy to fall away.'[3] He said they were regarded on one side as 'a set of harmless

[1] C. Wittke, op. cit., 101.
[2] C. Wittke, op. cit., 103.
[3] *Howitt's Journal*, 18 September 1847. Alexander Campbell also visited it, as did Joseph Barker (*The People*, III, No. 25).

enthusiasts, who thought to establish a kind of Utopian Republic in which all property was to be held in common', and on the other as 'archheresiarchs, who promulgated the most abominable doctrines and gloried in their crimes'. They wore a uniform of white Russia duck trousers, with shoes the colour of the original leather. Their community was in the estate of Lord Kilworden, and furnished with plain polished deal, with wicker flower stands. They ate a vegetarian diet of wheaten bread, butter, cheese, raisins, almonds and dried fruit. They rose at four to weave and sew whilst one member read aloud to them. After breakfast they worked in the fields, cultivating their farm and living according to the Carlylean maxim. They were sustained by a millennial hope that the time was approaching 'when this factitious state would pass away, and the whole family of men live together in a state of perfect harmony, worshipping the same God and redeemed by the same Saviour'.

In the autumn of 1845 Barmby travelled through Warwickshire, speaking at Bedworth,[1] and Coventry on 'Societary Science' and 'The Elements of Communitive Life'. At Birmingham he spoke both in the pulpit at the Christian Chapel, New Hall Street, and from the desk at the Literary and Scientific Institution. His reception at Birmingham and Coventry led to his remaining in those parts till 6 March 1846, building up a following around Nuneaton, Coleshill and Chilvers Coton.

(6)

We have seen how Emerson admired the Ham Common group. Barmby's own regard for Emerson was modified by his neglect of what Barmby called 'societary rectification'. 'It seems' wrote Barmby 'that Emerson slights this. We think wrongly . . . on this head there is a confusion in Emerson's writings which does not obtain in his heroic trumpet-blasts, in his stoical aphorisms, or even in his mystic improvisations . . . He does not categorize . . . He does not understand the law of the series.' Barmby did not warm to Emerson's prescription of self-improvement based on individual culture and temperance and lamented his 'slight to the social work'.[2]

---

[1] Two years later the 'Bedworth Group of the Communist Church' referred to him as their 'Pontiffarch', *Howitt's Journal*, 31 July 1847.

[2] *Howitt's Journal*, 13 November 1847.

Barmby looked to America with restrained enthusiasm. On his return he devoted himself to building up the East London Communist Group at Poplar. For the rest of 1846 and the first part of 1847 he was to be heard at the Cotton Street Chapel, Poplar, at the Farringdon Hall, London, and other places.

He was already a friend of Lewis Masquerrier of New York, the linguistic expert,[1] and early in 1847 he was approached by John O. Wattles of Cincinatti, editor of the *Herald of Progression* and founder of a 'Communist Church'. Wattles wished 'to put the wheat and corn of the west into the hands of the people of your country and keep it out of the hands of speculators'. Wattles' group of twenty-four young men met at the Melodeon, 'one of the most splendid halls' in Cincinatti,[2] and he told Goodwyn Barmby that their united capital was $200,000 'which they were going to invest in a community project known as "Excelsior".'

The medium envisaged for the exchange was the Co-operative League which early in 1847 hired the Farringdon Hall, King's Arms Yard, Snow Hill, for a shirt manufactory, and had embarked on a vigorous propaganda programme with lectures, including one by Charles Lane on Emigration. After some months of correspondence Wattles wrote that 'we are not prepared to move just yet; we are not sufficiently consolidated with ourselves, nor with you on that side of the water'. Worse was to follow. On 15 December 1847 the Excelsior Community, to which two Scottish communitarians, James Walker and James A. Mackison, had gone, was literally swept away by a flood. As the letter ran:—

> The waters of the Ohio rising, sapped the foundation of the building in which they were, and seventeen lives were lost, fifteen were saved. John O. Wattles and wife are safe. J. Walker was with material falling from the building knocked four times down in the water, and with desperate effort only, rescued his life. Mackison must have been covered with the falling bricks and wood etc. of the building.[3]

---

[1] Barmby was quite knowledgeable on schemes for universal language and wrote for *Howitt's Journal* of 13 February 1847, a good article on Isaac Pitman's phonography.

[2] *Howitt's Journal*, 27 March 1847.

[3] ibid., 12 February 1848.

Of this the Co-operative League were entirely ignorant as they sat down, eighty strong, to their vegetarian Boxing Day dinner, 'a farinaceous feast and a physiological feast', from which animal substances, as well as fermented drinks, were altogether excluded.

(7)

In July 1847, Goodwyn Barmby, together with Charles Sully, convened a meeting in the Literary Institute, John Street, Tottenham Court Road, to organize a communist emigration committee.[1] This was to promote the Icarian scheme of Étienne Cabet, a Frenchman who, during a five-year exile in London from 1834–9, had conceived such an admiration for Owen and the English that he published in 1839, *Le Voyage et Aventures de Lord William Carisdall en Icarie*.

In the elaborate scheme of formal human relationships which this fictional English peer explored during his travel to the Utopia of Icaria, there was much to attract. Cabet had his qualifications for such essays in political theory: as attorney-general of Corsica (a post given to him for his part in the revolution of 1830) and as an editor of *Le Populaire* (a left-wing journal whose tone he made so radical that he had to take refuge in England to escape two years' imprisonment), he had learnt much of the limitations of governments. Icaria was free from any such faults and Cabet, by presenting its constitution in the form of a journal kept by the observant Englishman, succeeded in making it seem a feasible experiment.

Cabet, as befitted one born in the year before the French Revolution began, looked to a benevolent despot. Icar was the benevolent despot who originally founded Icaria. But Owen's influence can be seen in the very structure of Icaria: a highly organized community run on New Lanark lines. The country was divided into a hundred provinces, and each province was subdivided into ten communes. The capital city was Icaria, which seems to have been an idealized Paris, bisected by a river which branched out into two arms at the centre of the city enclosing an island. This island was the civic centre. Icaria was itself divided into four quarters, and each quarter into fifteen communes. It had fifty horizontal avenues, intersected by fifty

[1] ibid., 17 July 1847.

vertical avenues. The houses were on the models of the older London Squares, fifteen to a block. All the pavements were covered with glass, all the factories were on the outskirts of the city, all the sanitation was on the most modern and approved lines.

The Icarians would breakfast each morning on a diet planned for them by a committee of scientists. They worked at professions for which their aptitudes best suited them, wearing the dress suitable to that profession or occupation. From the age of five to that of adulthood (eighteen for boys, seventeen for girls) their education was supervised by another committee. For those twelve years, this education was to be 'moral': only beyond that time could the vocational element begin. They chose their professions according to lists published by the State. No occupation was overcrowded and all enjoyed a smooth flow of recruits. At the mating age (usually three years after they had begun to work) Icarians were allowed a six-months' court-ship. They worked till the age of 65 (women till the age of 50), when they could retire.

The imagination of a number of Cabet's fellow-countrymen was quickened, and from the date of its first publication in 1839 many regarded it as a serious political probability. The noiseless windows of Icaria seemed to look on a better world than that ruled by the umbrella-carrying King of the French. For his fol-lowers Cabet issued an *Almanach Icarien, astronomique, scienti-fique, pratique, industriel, statistique* in 1844, and before another five years had passed he had an estimated following of nearly half-a-million. During these ten years Cabet's pen was busy on histories of France, revaluations of the gospel message like *Vrai Christianisme* (in which he based communism on the faith of Jesus), and other approaches to the sensibilities of potential Icarians. Nobody who joined his movement seemed to notice that in it the three principles of the French Revolution were significantly inverted: fraternity and equality came first, with liberty limping a long way behind.

At the age of 60, Cabet determined to put the Icarian theory to the test. He got the land (an extensive area in Texas), and made preparations to embark with his followers. 'We can send out', he wrote, 'from ten to twenty thousand men to create a new nation in America.'

By 18 December 1847, Howitt was reporting in his *Journal*, 'There is a considerable number of this class of communists residing in London, who have issued from their committee-room in Newman Street, Oxford Street, a pamphlet which they state to be their first English number of the harbinger of pro-gress'.[1] For this group, the call 'To your tents, O Israel' ran 'Allons en Icarie', and they repeated with fervour Cabet's address, inviting his followers to go to Icarie: 'we have the words dream and Utopia continually thrown in our face; let us, in answer, establish and realise Icarie'. It went on :–

> There will not be any obstacle in our commencing everything on the most perfect systems which modern science can offer to us; the plans and positions of our roads, towns, and manufactories, will be laid out from the beginning in a most advantageous manner; we shall aim at perfection in our workshops, our dwellings, our furni-ture, our clothing . . . in fact in everything.

The group announced that 'a large body of settlers from France and England, not less than ten thousand', would proceed to Icarie in the midsummer of 1848. The announcement created some stir. One correspondent in *Howitt's Journal* of 8 January 1848 warned them of the unsuitability of Texas, and the insta-bility of land titles there. Even more stirring was the news of Cabet's arrest and subsequent release. When, on 3 February, Dr. Roviga left France with an advance guard of sixty-nine Icarians, Sully had meanwhile sailed to New Orleans to receive them, arriving on 8 February to be greeted, amongst others, by William Weitling.[2]

(8)

The eventful year 1848 saw Barmby at work in the south of England, in Poole, the Isle of Wight and Southampton. It was whilst he was in Southampton that he heard of the revolution in Paris and he speedily departed thither as the representative of the Communist Church. There he had interviews with Cabet and other leading communists and addressed the Phalansterian Club.

He returned to find that a communist conference which he had convened was meeting at the Farringdon Hall, London. Delegates attended from the Leeds Redemption Society, the

[1] ibid., 18 December 1847.
[2] ibid., 25 March, 1848.

Co-operative League, the Icarians, the Phalansterians and other associations. An address was issued calling on the government to restore the land confiscated by Henry VIII from the Church, for the establishment not of monasteries but communisteries. The conference also proposed to establish an Apostolic College which should serve the Communitive Life and, by preaching and writing, induce others to do so too.

After 1848, Barmby became a Unitarian, probably due to the influence of W. J. Fox, M.P., who, it should be noted, was a friend of Eliza and Sara Flower, the two daughters of the Benjamin Flower who had established an 'English colony' in Illinois many years before. After ministeries at Southampton, Topsham, Lympstone and Lancaster he went to Wakefield where his writings toned down, and his contributions to *Howitt's Journal*, *The People's Journal*, *Tait's Magazine*, *Chambers' Journal* and other papers were less dithyrambic. Yet, though the remaining thirty years of his life were channelled in more orthodox grooves, he still showed flashes of his communitarian salad-days in organizations like the 'Band of Faith'.

4

<hr>

John Minter Morgan's Schemes

<hr>

(1)

ONE summer's day, 22 June 1841, 59-year-old John Minter Morgan launched a scheme to establish 'self-supporting villages' under the superintendence of the Established Church. It was a stirring attempt and it secured a respectable response. An admiral (Sir G. Scott), a general (George Norton Eden) and a respectable muster of clergy, mainly from the Ham, East Sheen and West Molesley districts, all attended.[1]

By assiduous promotion and activity, Minter Morgan persuaded William F. Cowper, the nephew of Lord Melbourne, to present a petition to Parliament in July 1842.[2] Though it came to nothing, his scheme was given some further publicity. He also sought for, and obtained, the approval of the Vice-Chancellor of the University of Oxford.

[1] His audience included the Hon. Alg. G. Tollemache, Rev. Jas. Hough, M.A., Capt. Blanchford, Gordon Forbes, Admiral Sir G. Scott, Gen. George Norton Eden, Rev. Thomas Hore and Capt. Roberts., R.N., all of Ham; the Rev. Dr. Walmsley and Rev. J. A. Emerson, M.A., of Hanwell; Rev. Geo. Hope, R.N., Rev. G. Trevelyan, M.A., of Malden; Rev. F. J. H. Reeves of East Sheen; Rev. E. A. Ommaney, M.A., of Mortlake; Rev. J. P. Mills, A.B., of West Molesley; Dr. Arnott, of Bedford Square; and G. Craik, Esq.

[2] The text can be found in Morgan's *Christian Commonwealth* (1850), pp. 97–98. W. F. Cowper later (in 1848) married Georgina Tollemache of Ham, whose cousin was another of Minter Morgan's supporters. She edited *Memorials* of his life (privately printed, 1890). From this we learn that in 1838 he was reading Law's *Spirit of Love* and 'liked it very much'. He was a friend and supporter of Laurence Oliphant.

Public meetings were organized in various parts of England. At Cheltenham the Rev. Francis Close expatiated upon his plan.[1] At Sheffield, the clergy assembled in April of 1843 to hear Minter Morgan himself in the Cutlers' Hall. As the *Iris* reported

Church of England Agricultural Self-Supporting Institution

During the past week Mr. John Milner [sic] Morgan, of Ham Common, in Surrey, has been exhibiting before the clergy and other inhabitants of the town, a very beautiful transparent painting at the Cutlers' Hall of a Self-Supporting Institution, the principles and economy of which, he states, might be applied, with the necessary modifications, to existing manufacturing establishments, having such an extent of land as might afford a healthful and profitable resource to the workmen and their families, especially in times of commercial difficulty. According to the prospectus, it is proposed to form, in the centre of an adequate extent of land (not less than one thousand acres) arrangements in connection with the Church of England, in which, under efficient direction three hundred families may be established, by the produce of their own labour, not only to support themselves, but to defray the expenses of the Establishment. In these expenses would be included the interest of capital advanced. The chief employment of the aggregated body would be agricultural, combined, at the discretion of the Committee of Management, with handicraft and mechanical pursuits. The whole concern looks very beautiful on canvas, but we doubt very much its practicability. We understand that Mr. Morgan purposes returning to Sheffield during the summer, when the subject will be brought before a public meeting.[2]

A similar meeting, six months later, at the Wakefield Mechanics' Institute called forth tart comment from the *Leeds Mercury*: 'The plan is very similar to that proposed by Mr. Robert Owen, with the addition of a church and a resident minister. We understand that the law of marriage, as at present understood, is proposed to be adhered to in the Modern Eden.'[3]

In the following year Morgan explained his scheme at the Clerical Library, and the Collegiate Sunday School, Liverpool, at the Athenaeum and St. Ann's schoolroom in Manchester, at

[1] Rev. Francis Close, 1787–1882, was a diligent pamphleteer who had published his 'Sermon to the Female Chartists at Cheltenham' in 1839 and issued a sermon 'On insipid sermons' in 1867.
[2] *The Sheffield Iris*, 15 April 1843.
[3] *Leeds Mercury*, 28 October 1843.

St. George's schoolrooms, Bolton, and at a large public meeting in Derby.[1]

Those who did not attend such public meetings were regaled by the issue of a large illustrated folio volume entitled the *Christian Commonwealth* (1845). In this he outlined his philosophy, citing Plato, Bacon, More, Harington, and the Gaudentia de Lucca (which he ascribed to Bishop Berkeley) as 'speculators on better systems of polity'. He added that his own times were far more auspicious than theirs as 'the idea of commencing *de novo* with a detached portion of the community, and illustrating their principles by an epitome of society, had not then occurred: but in modern times the principle of Association has often been resorted to for the accomplishment of many important objects'.

His two lieutenants, the Rev. Joseph Brown and the Rev. Edmund R. Larken, were also active. Brown was the chaplain to the Poor Law Schools at Norwood, and used to bring poor London children down to Ham Common each year.[2] E. R. Larken deserves fuller consideration.

(2)

The Rev. E. R. Larken was the rector of Burton-near-Lincoln in 1843. He had a large beard,[3] and flirted with a christianized version of Fourierism. As a 32-year-old social investigator in 1842 he said he had met 'with sights and sounds of distress enough to freeze the blood within my veins'. He was a devoted advocate of Association upon Christian principles, 'wherein, each labouring for all, the exertions of each will receive their due and proper reward—wherein the weak shall be aided and supported by the strong'. In 1843 he had preached a sermon at Horbling 'on behalf of the distressed manufacturers' from Galatians VI. 2: 'Bear ye one another's burdens'. The sermon, printed by J. Young as *Christian Sympathy* (1943), contained a sketch of the industrial system of Fourier.[4]

[1] J. Minter Morgan, *The Christian Commonwealth* (1845).

[2] He published a *Sketch of the State and Progress of the Poor Law Schools at Norwood with reference to Religion* (1843).

[3] So described by G. J. Holyoake, *Sixty Years of an Agitator's Life* (1893), i. 237. He had married the daughter of Lord Monson and his rectory was in his father-in-law's park. W. J. Linton, *Memories* (1895).

[4] An excellent account of his life (to which I am most indebted) is contained in J. F. C. Harrison, *Social Reform in Victorian Leeds* (Thoresby Society Monographs, III, 1954).

In 1845, with James Hole and David Green of Leeds, he helped establish, on 8 September, a Leeds Redemption Society. This, in January 1847, issued a paper the *Herald of Redemption*, later known as *The Herald of Co-operation, and Organ of the Redemption Society*.[1] Like other radical papers, it used printing and publishing facilities in the Isle of Man to avoid the stamp tax. Amongst the contributors was Goodwyn Barmby, and James Hole the editor who wrote on Ralahine, Communism and other topics. Hole lamented the class war: 'So accustomed have men become to pursue their own isolated interests apart from and regardless of that of others', he wrote, 'that it has almost become an acknowledged maxim, that when a man pursues his own interests alone, he is most benefiting society.' He criticized Robert Owen for confusing the idea of a Community with moral and metaphysical questions. Since the Leeds Redemption Society was to 'unite the labour of all for the benefit of all' and create a class of 'labouring capitalists', the paper took as its motto 'Labouring Capitalists not Labourers and Capitalists'.

To William Howitt, editor of the *People's Journal*, they had it within them 'to carry out for themselves the substantial portion of the plans of Owen, St. Simon or Fourier'. Howitt took the chair at the first anniversary meeting of the society on 7 January 1847. Five hundred people including Samuel Smiles (the apostle of self-help) and 'a fair proportion of females', attended to hear, amongst other things, a letter read from Mazzini, the Italian patriot, asking to be enrolled as a member.

Larken addressed this meeting by giving a spirited history of the co-operative principle. He showed it was embodied in the Mosaic Law, foreshadowed in the institutions of the Promised Land, and practised by the Essenes. He then went on to trace the principle to his own day. Larken also mentioned that Minter Morgan was at present in Italy gathering information for what Howitt significantly referred to as '*his* views for popular co-operation'.[2]

Like other movements in this decade, the Leeds Redemption Society threw off branches, one in Shoreditch (London) and others nearer Leeds at Birstal and North Cave. Yet more were envisaged at Newport, Monmouthshire, Cambridge, Barnsley, and Manchester.

[1] A file is in the Manchester Central Library.
[2] *Howitt's Journal*, 23 January 1847.

Six months later in July 1847 the Society was offered an estate at Garnlwyd, eighteen miles from Carmarthen and eight from Swansea 'on certain conditions'.[1] These conditions were that a community settlement should be established comprising some 220 acres of which ninety were immediately available. The soil was described by David Green, a member, as

'rich loam,—not deep, but capable of producing good crops. Only part of it is at present under cultivation, the rest growing nothing but gorse, which serves as fodder for cattle.' It had water 'pure and limpid, and probably suitable for printing', and a waterfall of from 6 to 9 feet, which 'might be useful for manufacturing purposes'. There was within a mile of the estate a seam of coal 9 feet thick, limestone suitable for building, and clay.

Then Green concluded:

'The timber upon the land is small, but this may be brought to within three miles of the estate by canal, and we understand that a railway is in progress at no great distance. Being a hilly country, the roads are steep, but they are in good condition. The scenery is very fine, and the locality very healthy. Land situated as this is, is more subject to vicissitudes of the seasons; but the communitive system here presents a compensating advantage over the individual system—as all persons on the estate could be enlisted on an emergency, a crop would often be saved which would be lost to the farmer. On the whole, the estate seems very suitable for both agricultural and manufacturing purposes.' [2]

This 'splendid gift' was rapturously accepted. One hundred and fifty pounds was immediately raised, to be paid by instalments. Howitt reported :–

We are now setting to work in good earnest, to thoroughly agitate the town and districts, and we hope others will imitate us in other districts; we must have no sleeping any more, people must labour, and the reward will be soon and great. We shall appoint one of the first scientific agriculturists in England to project the improvements with a view to immediate operations, and we shall have to elect our labourers in about two months.

The opportunity of Garnlwyd excited him

We should save immensely in the matter of manure, which is now

---

[1] Harrison, op. cit., says it was offered by a Mr. Williams who had returned from America 'enthusiastically in support of the community idea'.

[2] *Howitt's Journal*, 7 August 1847.

lost to agriculture; we should likewise save greatly in the difference between making goods for show instead of use, and the saving will be greatest of all by producing by a combined people working together for one great object, instead of a disintegrated nation's labour in confusion, one undoing what another has done. It is almost certain, that once fairly established, a community will be able to double itself annually. Let everyone who may know of any gentleman that he thinks will be inclined to aid us, send his address to 166, Briggate, Leeds, for it is our intention to send a properly prepared circular to all such in the kingdom.

The day for doubt and despair is passed, and the time has come for action. Men of England sleep no more; the day of your redemption has dawned, and onward is now the watch-word of the world.[1]

Houses and factories were to be built. Labourers (or associates) were to be selected from amongst the subscribers to work at Garnlwyd where they would eat from communal dining-tables. 'The position of each, with respect to dwellings, food, clothing, and education' announced the Society would be 'superior to that enjoyed by working men under the present competitive system, and will expect that each will do his duty to it in return.'[2]

At first, hired labour was employed to lay drains as the land was waterlogged, but by the following year the first manufactures—shoes—began to trickle back to Leeds, together with farm produce.

The Garnlwyd community was then only fourteen strong. To expand it a national congress was summoned on Whit Monday, 1851. The Rev. E. R. Larken took the chair and a target of £1,000 was decided upon, to be raised in £1 shares. To raise it, a fourteen-day propaganda campaign was launched under the direction of a full-time secretary with voluntary assistants. A copy of the directions to the missionaries, *Fourteen Days' Propagandism: What to Say*, exists today in the Library of the University of London. The 'line' laid down for the missionaries to follow shows that the previous experiments were in the forefront of their minds. 'Should your friends object that other such plans had failed, you must say, "True, but others have also succeeded—and ours is succeeding".' And if the unconverted

---

[1] *Howitt's Journal*, 4 September 1847.

[2] Jones, *Co-operative Production*, gives a brief account but the best is contained in Harrison, op. cit.

were to mention the land plan of Feargus O'Connor, the missionaries were to reply that 'it was *founded upon a totally different idea from ours*'. Their place in the great communitarian tradition was clearly stated: 'community of property is no untried theory, but a *system* that has been in practice for more than sixty years among a people called *Shakers*'.

The missionaries bent to their work. Meetings, and public discussions were held in Leeds and the surrounding districts. In November a great festival was celebrated by 400 people when Larken and other members of the Society delivered addresses.

It was to provide an outlet for the produce of the Garnlwyd experiment that a store was opened at No. 5 Trinity Street, Leeds. True it was only a shop over a stable, tended by one member in the evening and it was said that the principal article sold was 'blackberry jam'. Holyoake added that the blackberries were picked by children and sold to the colonists.[1]

Such an exiguous outlet, coupled to the difficulty of implementing the original programme, led to the Leeds Redemption Society being wound up in 1855. Unlike others, it had a surplus.

(3)

Another figure in the loosely-knit net of Utopians whom Minter Morgan enlisted for his Self-Supporting Village society was W. F. Cowper who also helped the Society for the Improvement of the Conditions of the Labouring Classes, established on 11 May 1844 from the old Labourers' Friend Society.[2] As such, it promoted schemes for model houses and agricultural cottages, allotments and 'planned dwellings'. Operating with greatly increased financial resources the Society for the Improvement of the Conditions of the Labouring Classes exhibited model houses in Streatham Street, Bloomsbury, where forty-eight families were housed, a building known as 2 Charles Street, Drury Lane, where eighty-two single men lived, and another at 76 Hatton Gardens housing fifty-nine single women. It had no

[1] G. J. Holyoake, *Jubilee History of Leeds Industrial Co-operative Society Limited* (1897), 2.
[2] See *The Labourer's Friend*, June 1844. The Labourer's Friend Society was formed in 1831 and had already published *Facts and Illustrations demonstrating the important benefits . . . derived . . . from possessing small portions of land etc.* (1831) and *Cottage Husbandry: the utility and national advantage of allotting land for that purpose* (1835).

less than seven designs for agricultural cottages in pairs. To this widening scope of operations, the Society issued a journal, The *Labourers' Friend*, which was to record similar promotions and activities for the next forty years.

W. F. Cowper promoted a Parliamentary Bill in 1845 for enabling vestries and local authorities to acquire land for letting it out in allotments: a measure opposed by the utilitarians like J. A. Roebuck, as unrealistic.

Morgan's travels abroad, to which Larken referred in his speeches to the Leeds Redemptionists, also took him to France where he met some English workmen at Boulogne in 1845 and (literally) unfolded his scheme to them. According to him they agreed 'it was the best remedy for the disorders of society they had yet heard of, and better than O'Connor'.[1] He also talked to the Fourierists, Considérant and Doherty. He interviewed Étienne Cabet, who gave him a copy of his famous book. So convinced was he of the essential wrong-headedness of Fourierist schemes that he devoted Letter 12 of *Letters to a Clergyman* (1846) to a severe criticism of them. Morgan also visited the Moravian settlements at Herrnhut in Saxony, Neuweid on the Rhine and Zeist in Holland. At each the bishops and managers recommended the speedy establishment of similar communities. In his travels he met the Baron von der Recke in Dusseldorf, where an old monastery was being used as a social community.[2]

The most impressive meeting organized by Minter Morgan was staged at the Exeter Hall on 27 May 1846. W. F. Cowper, M.P., once more in the chair flanked by powerful and distinguished Tories, compared their activities in the business of community founding to 'the situation of people digging in a field for a treasure which we believe to be somewhere about, but know not exactly where'. With another singular analogy, he continued, 'The Clubs of London show how the principle of combination can be applied to the increase of luxury. Palaces are reared containing comforts for a large body of men which they could not have individually and separately. But the benefits to be derived from combination have not yet been extended as they might be to the social existence of the hard labour classes.'

The audience was a large one, larger than had been expected,

[1] *Letters to a Clergyman* (1846), 5.
[2] ibid.

and the Bishop of Norwich rising to express his 'satisfaction' at this, outlined his own 'conversion' to Morgan's scheme:—

> I can well recollect that when I first heard of this institution, and mentioned it to others, prejudices were excited immediately; because Mr. Morgan talked of squares and parallelograms, immediately the ghost of Mr. Owen's plan rose up before people's imaginations; and I believe that that phantom very nearly nipped the whole scheme in the bud. He now simply proposes to establish a village, no matter what its form shall be, whether square, or circus or streets, but an aggregation of buildings, which shall accommodate 300 families, which, taking four or five to a family, we may consider to amount to 1200 or 1500 individuals.

After expatiating on the virtues of 'combination and concentration' as principles for improving the standard of living, the Bishop continued:—

> It appears that the ruling principle which Christianity enjoins in the intercourse between man and man has never yet been fully applied to the social and industrial arrangements of a country; these have hitherto not been directed by the spirit of love and mutual participation in different wants and cases. We have gone upon the old principle, which I fear still prevails among Christians . . . of each looking to his own interest and trusting that the interest of the whole would be secured by each member caring for himself. Now I am anxious to attempt something of a different sort.[1]

When the Bishop stressed that 'among the cluster of cottages, first, and above all, the spires of a Church of England should rise', cheers and 'a solitary hiss' greeted him.

James Silk Buckingham moved a resolution 'that the benefits resulting in the Moravian settlements, from a more intimate connection between secular and religious affairs, and the rapid accumulation of wealth in some religious societies constituted on a similar principle in America, encourage a well-grounded type that associations of the unemployed poor, under the direction of intelligent members of our own pure and reformed Church, with all the facilities and scientific appliances this country affords, would realise advantages still more important'. He quoted the Shakers and Rappites in support of his thesis, also the example of the Irish Waste Lands Society formed in

---

[1] For a full report of the conference, ibid., 153–92, *The People's Journal* I. (1846), and *Annals of Industry*, 46.

1841 under the Earl of Devon, then cultivating 18,000 acres of land with 2,000 people, and paying a dividend of 7½ per cent. Buckingham suggested that they might begin on the 'associative principle' with waste land on Hounslow Heath or Salisbury Plain.

The Rector of St. Johns, Clerkenwell, the Rev. Hugh Hughes, confessed that he knew of 'no other plan that is likely to meet the emergencies of Society'. 'The present miserable and destitute state of the working classes of this country', he went on, 'is far beyond the reach of any measure hitherto attempted for their amelioration.' Mr. Hughes vented some rousing socialistic principles which were loudly applauded when he said that 'the very necessity of these institutions would cease to exist if men were remunerated for their labour as they ought to be'. 'Our most holy faith repudiates the spirit of exclusive competition for wealth which marks the present generation.'

It was left to the Rev. E. R. Larken to propose the formation of the Church of England Self-Supporting Villages Society. Its aims were defined as for 'promoting the religious, moral and general improvement of the working classes, by forming establishments for three or four hundred families, in which instruction may be allowed, and religious ordinances administered, on the principles of the Church of England, and combining agriculture with manufacturing employment, for their own benefit'. One thousand acres, and £45,000 were wanted, and the Society set about raising it.

(4)

One of the speakers at Morgan's Exeter Hall meeting, James Silk Buckingham, suggested that the Church of England might begin its operations on Hounslow Heath or Salisbury Plain. Buckingham had been impressed and went on to exploit Morgan's ideas in a pamphlet of his own called *National Evils and Practical Remedies*, published in 1848. This is now recognized as the first complete and concrete scheme for a garden city, the first practical blueprint for a planned town. The very name of this model city—Victoria—was Minter Morgan's.

It was to be an iron city with glass-covered streets. Teetotal and non-smoking, with no pawnbrokers' shops, it was to cover a square mile and would house 10,000 people in ten classes, blending both agricultural and industrial elements in its economy. The streets were to be 100 ft. wide, all leading somewhere, as Buckingham deplored blind alleys which might lead to 'the morose defiance of public decency which such secret haunts generate in the inhabitants'. In plan it was rectangular. The centre of the town to be a large green park, with the main public buildings grouped round it. The houses, themselves in broad avenues, were to be in square belts around this civic centre, till they lapped the great green fringe outside the town itself. In these houses on the outside fringe of the town, nearest the green belt, were to be the workers' dwellings.

All the streets were to be covered galleries to keep those travelling to work from bad weather. His factory and workshop area covered forty acres. To relieve the drabness of his rows of houses, a liberal intermixture of open spaces and parks was suggested.

Buckingham proposed to launch it by means of a company with a capital of £4 million. This would build houses to sell at prices ranging from £30 to £300. The council of the town was to be elected by the shareholders, and in order to prevent anyone obtaining a monopoly, the number of shares to be held was limited. Certain features of his scheme seem surprisingly modern. One was that all married families with children were to have not less than three rooms. Another was that the children should stay at school till they were 15 years old. Medical service was to be free, with the doctors paid by the community to prevent disease rather than to cure it. Moreover, he suggested that it would be a good thing if as many of the inhabitants as possible took their meals in the large public halls provided for the purpose—a striking forecast of the civic restaurant[1] of the war years.

(5)

R. W. Emerson attended one of Morgan's meetings in 1847. He found the audience 'mainly socialist', and remarked on the 'huge coloured revolving view' with which Morgan explained

---

[1] Buckingham was not only a pioneer town planner in England (Lewis Mumford, *The Culture of Cities*, London 1940, 394), and the first M.P. for Sheffield, but a pioneer of self-government for the colonies (*Cambridge History of the British Empire*, Cambridge, 1940, ii. 405). He was also a notable publicist and founded *The Athenaeum*, *The Sphynx* and *The Oriental Herald and Colonial Review*.

his views of the future social organization of the country[1]
Morgan was also financing the publication, in this year, of
W. G. Walton's *Law and other Mystics* together with further
extracts from Greaves journals *New Theosophic Revelations* and
The New Nature in the Soul.

There is no doubt that Morgan's scheme was well known in
working-class circles. For when Thomas Carlyle was invited by
that model landlord, Sir Harry Verney to his house in 1847, he
met Thomas Cooper, and the conversation turned on the
imminent translation of the Chartist programme into fact.
Verney was so stirred that he asked Cooper for further information on 'Minter Morgan's plans, Fourierism and communism':
a combination which shows how confused the upper-classes
were on the implications of the first.[2]

(6)

Morgan's own books had meanwhile been having an effect
beyond his own efforts. As Canon Raven has shown, they were
in the library of J. M. Ludlow, who was the logistic genius of
the Christian Socialist Movement.[3] William Cowper, presenter
of the 1842 petition and a speaker at the Exeter Hall meeting in
1846, became an early supporter of the Christian Socialists in
association with Thomas Hughes.[4]

After the collapse of the Chartists and the rise of the Christian
Socialists, Morgan intensified his efforts to raise £50,000 for
his scheme. He issued a collection of his writings in the Phoenix
Library.[5] But few took him seriously. The *Illustrated London
News*, on 24 August 1850, condemned his project as 'dooming
men to an oyster-like level of morals and manners' and looking
'more like a lunatic asylum than the ordinary abodes of rational

---

[1] Rusk, *The Life of Ralph Waldo Emerson* (1949), 352.
[2] D. A. Wilson, *Carlyle on Cromwell and Others* (1925), iii. 406.
[3] C. E. Raven, *Christian Socialism* (1920), 140.
[4] Writing to Lady Cowper-Temple on 29 October 1888, Thomas Hughes said,
'It is all but forty years since we first met in Lincoln's Inn Chapel, in the early
days of Christian Socialism, of which movement then so vehemently and widely
denounced, he was from the first an avowed and liberal supporter, and from his
social and public position, ranked more than all the rest of us put together.'
Memorials (printed for private circulation, 1890), 151.
[5] It is significant that he included his friend Charles Hall's *The Effects of Civilization* (1805) in the series. Hall, who died in 1820, was practically unknown till
Morgan produced this edition. G. D. H. Cole, op. cit., 35.

men'. 'It reminds us', continued the *Illustrated London News*, 'of Bridewell, or some contrivance for central inspection, not of the sunny or shady lanes in which the rose and honeysuckle-decked cottages of our native land are so happily nestled. . . . The idea is obviously borrowed from the unsuccessful efforts of the State to correct the people by bridewells, workhouses and prisons—substituting a gentler kind of control for meagre diet, ships, dungeons and fetters . . . Mr. Morgan does not conceal his desire to organize the "destitute people" and the whole society in Reductions (formal villages) similar to those by which the Jesuits drilled the Indians in Paraguay and made them fit for the despotism and desolation of Dr. Francia.'[1]

Not only Paraguay, but New Harmony, Snigs End and Icaria were held up as typical examples of what would happen if the non-competitive, highly regulated society of Morgan's plan was brought into operation.[2]

Nothing daunted, Morgan proceeded with the publication of his testament, *The Triumph, or the Coming Age of Christianity* (1851). This was a collection of enthusiastic supporters of community life from Bacon to Thompson. From our point of view, a most interesting extract is that from Whiston's translation of Josephus on the Essenes. Amongst others were Buckingham and Mrs. Martineau on the Shakers, Beattie on the Elysian age and Langford on the age of gold.

(7)

One of those whom Morgan quoted in this anthology was his friend Robert Pemberton, and it was Pemberton who, in the year before Morgan's death, carried his ideas literally a stage further away from reality by publishing *The Happy Colony* (1854). Described as 'the result of twenty years study', *The Happy Colony* is dedicated 'To the Working Men of Great Britain' and divided into three parts: a Philosophical dialogue, an Address to the Workmen of Great Britain, and a description of the 'Elysian Academy or Natural University'. Two large plates are included in the text. Pemberton intended his colony

---

[1] *I.L.N.*, 24 August 1850.

[2] It should in fairness be said that there were a number of similar schemes in the air. In 1845 a London architect called Moffatt proposed to form an association for the erection of villages within four to ten miles of the metropolis to house 350,000 people at a cost of £10 million.

to be taken seriously, for his book includes a prospectus for its formation.[1]

'Why is man not happy?' asked Pemberton, and replied 'The cause is that every child is bred into slavery.' The remedy, he continued, was for the workers to found a Happy Colony under the sovereignty of Queen Victoria in an island of the Pacific,

[1] Pemberton, in this plan, shows himself a disciple of John Minter Morgan, for not only did he quote Morgan in *The Happy Colony* in 1854 (on p. 209) but by his *Address* of the following year, *To the Bishops and Clergy of all denominations and to all Professors and Teachers of the Christian World*, he shared Morgan's hope that the Established Churches would come to his aid in the project. Indeed, he shows his allegiance, by mentioning Morgan as his friend on p. 21 of this work. Before the *Happy Colony*, Pemberton had written three other tracts. *The Attributes of the Soul from the Cradle, and the Philosophy of the Divine Mother, Detecting the false basis, or fundamental error of the schools, and developing the perfect education of man* (1849); *The Natural Methods of Teaching the elements of grammar for the nursery and infant schools* (1851); and *The Natural Method of Teaching the Technical Language of Anatomy for the Nursery and Infant Schools* (1852). Afterwards he wrote six more: *An Address to the Bishops and Clergy of all denomination, and to all professors and teachers of the Christian World, on Robert Owen's proclamation of the millennial state to commence this year* (1855); *The Infant Drama: a model of the true method of teaching all languages* (1857); a letter by R. Pemberton on his system of teaching languages (1857); *Report of the proceedings at the inauguration of Mr. Pemberton's new Philosophical Model Infant School, for teaching languages . . . on the natural or euphonic system* (1857); *The Science of Mind Formation, and the reproduction of genius elaborated; involving the remedy for all our social evils*(1858); *An Address to the people on the necessity of Popular Education, in conjunction with emigration, as a remedy for all our social ills* (1859). As might have been expected from these, Pemberton's main interest lay in education. His *Address to the Bishops* said: 'Our present civilisation, under the boarding school system, is obtained at the cost and sacrifice of health, and muscular and nervous energy, producing empty heads and useless hands. All must be genteel, and consequently useless; and every species of useless occupation must be invented for the educated classes; but the burden of feeding, clothing, and housing this multitude of useless beings falls on the workmen. This state of villainy or corrupt imbecility cannot last. Every child of man is worth all the stars and worlds in the heavens; but every man that is bred to genteel idleness, is worse than a savage and does indirectly more mischief to society, by reason that others follow like a flock of sheep, the bad example.' As to the future he was very gloomy: 'Excess of population in Great Britain will of necessity bring about a dreadful crisis sooner or later. The gentleman-and-lady imbecile education, by which the nation is of necessity governed, combined with our commercial gambling mania, will if continued, produce ruin and destruction to Great Britain.' The only tangible result of his labours was the establishment of a school at 33 Euston Square, N.W. . . ., opened on 22 August 1857, where his son Robert Markham and his two daughters, Charlotte Delia and Elizabeth Mary, taught. This school essayed to practise the ideas embodied in his writings. Languages were to be taught by sound. 'Sound', he wrote, 'will become the giant power that will harmonise the human race.' He said that his school possessed a 'chromatic barrell organ' to accustom the child to music from birth, and a system of cards for teaching grammar.

'where the land is open and ready to receive the best and most scientific system of dividing and laying it out'. This best and most scientific system Pemberton outlined in his Queen Victoria Town—an interesting and novel garden city, planned on circular lines—as opposed to the rectangular fancies of James Silk Buckingham. Pemberton envisaged an inner ring of fifty acres with four colleges, each with conservatories, workshops, swimming baths and riding schools. These were to be surrounded by an outer ring containing the factories, public hospitals and gardens of the community. Outside these again was to be a park; the outer rim of this was to be three miles long.

The whole project was to cradle the new labour kingdom based on Creation and Love. Labour was to be the basis of the economic system. 'All truths must emanate from the people', Pemberton argued; 'the emancipating power must proceed from the labour kingdom.' He rejected the contemporary world of his own day as 'the germ of every sin and error, and the very root of all corruption, unhappiness and misery in every class of society . . . Wealth is the tyrant of labour and the destroying angel of the happiness of the human race'. Unlike Buckingham, who envisaged the establishment of his model city through a joint-stock company, Pemberton proposed to grant plots of land to its occupiers. Just how they were to obtain the capital for the enterprises is left unexplained.

Morgan died early in 1855 with much of the enthusiasm he had generated amongst the Anglicans siphoned off in the promotion of the Canterbury Colony in New Zealand. But his influence on Ludlow was bearing fruit in the activities of the Christian Socialists, and his associate James Silk Buckingham was to extend an even more powerful influence over a later figure in these pages: Ebenezer Howard.

5

❖◇❖

The Chartist Land Colonies

❖◇❖

(1)

AT the Hall of Science, Campfield, Manchester, a large 48-year-old Irishman with a rich baritone voice rose to his feet on 7 March 1842. 'I am going', he told his audience, 'to propound to you a subject which is somewhat novel.' There was no novelty in the title of the lectures: *The Land and its Capabilities* and *What is the remedy for our grievances?*[1] for considering the extensive propaganda which had been going forward during the previous decade his claim was, to say the least, presumptuous.[2]

Feargus O'Connor was an adept appropriator of ideas. With the help of workmen's pennies, he had sustained a newspaper, the *Northern Star*, for five years[3] and drummed up the Great Northern Union of Working Men, to which he acted as secretary. His leading disciples were either mystical Swedenborgians (like William Hill)[4] or the Old Testament prophets (like the

---

[1] An extant copy exists in the Foxwell Library of the University of London. Julius West, *History of Chartism* (London, 1920), could not find it and wrote (p. 202), 'This appears to be now lost, but Colonel Thompson's letters quote the most important passages.'

[2] For good recent accounts see A. R. Schoyen, *The Chartist Challenge* (1958) and Joy Askill, 'The Chartist Land Plan' in *Chartist Studies*, ed. A. Briggs (1959), 304–41.

[3] It first appeared in November 1837. For a lively retrospective account of this see William Hobson in the *Manchester Examiner* 12–16 November 1847.

[4] He subsequently became a Roman Catholic.

Rev. J. R. Stephens). Stephens wanted a Christian mass-movement moving 'as one united and indissoluble phalanx, God leading them by a pillar of fire . . . into the promised land'.[1]

The Owenite basis of O'Connor's ideas goes back even further. For in the *Northern Star* of 16 June 1838, he had endorsed Owen's idea of a communistic colony by calling on the depositors of the £207,170 in the Leeds Savings Banks to withdraw their money and 'invest' it in Owen. A spell in prison had sharpened his ideas, and between 10 July and 7 August 1841, he had published five *Letters to Irish Landlords*, advising them to allocate a proportion of their lands to peasant holdings to increase their rents and keep the manufacturers from spoiling Ireland. The application of this principle to England was but a short step. Twenty million small landowners, he told readers of the *Northern Star*, would keep the ironmasters and cotton spinners out of Parliament.

One might take O'Connor's ideas still further back. His father tried to prove that the pagan civilization of Ireland had been ruined by Christianity; his uncle had married the daughter of the French economist Condorcet. He himself had run away to England with his brother in 1817, but had been returned home by Sir Francis Burdett, another eccentric. By sheer personal charm he became the legatee of an estate at Fort Robert, and reappeared in London in 1833 as M.P. for Cork; it was an aptly named constituency, for it floated for a brief period through all the initial storms of English political life. In this two-year stint in Parliament he had tried to introduce a Bill to reform land tenures, but failed. Now, out of Parliament, he had taken himself to the north of England, where his birth and brassy eloquence won him numerous admirers in the dingy tenements of Manchester and Liverpool.

(2)

Whatever its origin, O'Connor was certainly convinced that his idea of a peasant proprietary class was right. In 1843 he had issued *A Practical Work on the Management of Small Farms*, containing instructions for the operation of smallholdings. In

[1] He was a Nonconformist minister at Ashton-under-Lyne where he later started the *Ashton Chronicle* (1848–9). J. T. Ward, 'Revolutionary Tory', in *Transactions of the Lancashire and Cheshire Antiquarian Society*, LXVIII (1958), 109.

the *Northern Star* of 15 May 1843 he argued that one such smallholder with four acres could, at a modest estimate, earn £100 a year. O'Connor wanted State sponsorship for his plan, and, to encourage Parliament to take it up, he wanted the Chartists to do so first. He said so at the Chartist Convention in 1843.[1] He repeated it at the Convention in 1844. And in April 1845 a convention of fourteen delegates at the Parthenium, St. Martin's Lane, agreed to support the purchase of large private estates for conversion to smallholdings. Money was raised by weekly subscription. All subscribers would ballot for holdings on which a house, ready-built, and a small loan of £7. 10s. would enable them to start life afresh. They would then pay rent equivalent to an interest of 5 per cent on the cost of the allotment, house and loan. This rent would enable more land to be bought for subsequent settlers. O'Connor calculated that, on the basis of three acres per family, he could place 24,000 families on the land in five years.

Of course, there were critics. O'Connor had overestimated the productivity of land. According to the *Leeds Mercury* of 27 May 1843 it was a South Sea bubble: 'but the South Sea bubble itself seems nothing to this Chartist bubble, which can be compared only to the dreams of the Alchemists in their search after the philosophers' stone'. O'Connor replied by publishing in the *Northern Star* of 9 September 1843 a report which Edward Baines editor of the *Leeds Mercury* had written in 1819 for the Leeds Overseers of the Poor, suggesting that settlement on the land was a desirable expedient.[2] The *Mercury* changed its tune and on 23 September expressed its pleasure that the Chartists were turning their attention to the cultivation of the land: 'It will give them an increased interest in the tranquillity and good

---

[1] J. H. Parry in *A Letter to Feargus O'Connor on the plan of organization issued by the Birmingham Conference*, September 1843, wrote: 'The plan is yours and yours alone, none other is responsible for it, and to saddle it upon the great body of the Chartists is a gross insult to their intelligence of which none but you and your tools would dare to be guilty.'

Parry was a Marylebone Chartist who declined nomination to conference saying: 'It was not a conference for the replies of the working classes, but a conference of Feargus O'Connor, with Feargus O'Connor, on the best means of vending a quack political medicine, opined by Feargus O'Connor to be a remedy for all our ills'.

[2] This was written as a report on a visit to New Lanark made by Baines and two others in 1819. See Podmore, *Life of Owen* (1923), 147, 262 and 263.

order of society, and make them anxious to preserve whatever is valuable in the government and institutions of the country.'

'The Land belongs to the people', he wrote early in 1845. 'It is the people's heritage. Kings, princes, lords and citizens have stolen it from the people. Usurpation is the work of the rich and powerful.'

Like Minter Morgan, he made a continental tour in 1845. In Brussels he talked with a group of exiled German communists, who presented him with an address of welcome, signed, amongst others, by Karl Marx and Friedrich Engels. (Readers of the *Northern Star* on 25 July 1847, were thus treated to the sight of a pair of names which probably meant nothing to them.) Engels, as a resident of Manchester during the previous three years, had made a detailed study of the English working classes now being published in Leipzig as *Die Lage der arbeitenden Klassen in England*. For O'Connor had already opened his columns to Engels' lively pen (on 9 October 1847 he was to open them to Marx too). He also held up the Flemish system of intensive farming as a model for his Land Scheme, and gave his opinion, in the *Northern Star* of 20 September 1845, that if England were organized on a basis of small peasant proprietors it would be able to maintain a population of 300 million people.

(3)

In March 1846 the Heronsgate estate, near Watford, comprising some 103 acres, and costing £2,344, including the valuations, was bought and named O'Connorville. Allotments were marked out, foundations dug, and general preparations for settlement put in train. A great ballot to select the first thirty-five settlers (thirteen got four acres, five three acres and seventeen two acres) was held in Manchester on 10 April. Subscriptions rose to £5,000 a week, and soon the land fund reached £50,000. Even O'Connor was surprised: 'When I first established it', he said, 'I had no more notion of receiving £5,000 than I had of flying in the air.'

To mark the high summer a cricket match took place at O'Connorville in July between the carpenters and the brick-layers. The bricklayers won by twenty-eight runs. Fortified by deep draughts of milk the high-spirited bricklayers christened the cow that supplied it Rebecca after the celebrated riots which had occurred in South Wales. Between the cabbage plots roads were laid and the winners of the ballot named them from the towns they had left: Stockport Road, Bradford Road, Nottingham Road and Halifax Road.

O'Connor himself, according to a witness, was 'never off the scaffold' whilst the colony was being built. Each house cost £100 and several of them can still be seen to this day. Ernest Jones[1] was moved to rhyme:–

> See there the cottage, labour's own abode,
> The pleasant doorway on the cheerful road,
> The airy floor, the roof from storms secure,
> The merry fireside and the shelter sure;
> And, dearest charm of all, the grateful soil,
> That bears its produce for the hands that toil.

Enough work was soon done to warrant holding an open day on 17 August 1846. From all over England visitors came: 12,000 according to the *Daily News*, 20,000 according to the *Northern Star*. O'Connor addressed them as an 'elevator', not a 'leveller'. 'I wish to see,' he cried, 'the cottage the castle of the freeman instead of the den of the slave.'

Two months later he bought a second estate in Worcestershire called Lowbands, for £8,560—four times the price of O'Connorville. The increasing size of his transactions obliged him to approach the Registrar of Friendly Societies for 'provisional' registration, and to convene a conference in December at Birmingham to found a Land and Labour Bank. The bank was duly established in January 1847, while the name of the enterprise was changed from 'The Chartist Land Company' to 'The National Land Company'. This new title became effective in March 1847.

He indignantly protested that his plan had 'no more to do with socialism', than it had 'to do with a comet'. But he professed to be 'a strong advocate of co-operation, which means legitimate exchange'.[2] His fellow Chartists did not agree.

---

[1] Ernest Jones entered the Chartist leadership with a great speech at the Chartist Convention at Leeds in 1846. His poem O'Connorville was published in the *Northern Star* for 22 August of that year and in January 1847 he became joint editor with O'Connor of *The Labourer*.

John Saville, *Ernest Jones: Chartist* (London, 1952), 22–28.

[2] *The Labourer*, II. 154.

Thomas Cooper, for trying to show that O'Connor was 'unworthy of the confidence of Chartists', was ejected from the Chartist Convention of 1846. James Bronterre O'Brien,[1] editor of a rival paper the *National Reformer*, warned the working man on 9 January 1847 that to join 'these land societies' was 'to enlist himself on the side of the Government against his own order'. 'His land scheme', he wrote five months later in another attack on O'Connor, 'is a government plot to stifle in embryo our movement for the nationalisation of land and property.' But O'Connor was by this time euphorically confident: his letters from O'Connorville were headed 'From Paradise'.[2]

(4)

Settlers formally arrived at O'Connorville in May 1847 in open carts to the sounds of music from a band. Crowds lined the streets to see his hegira from the north taking possession of their 'Promised Land'.[3] The fixing of the date of formal possession on 1 May enabled O'Connor to claim that it was *England's May Day*, and press ahead with the purchase of a third and fourth estate in the following month. William Howitt, the indefatigable chronicler of events, reported in his *Journal* on 12 June 1847.

> By far the most prominent and successful movement which the people are making at present, is amongst the Chartists. Many have set themselves earnestly since 1845 to accumulate savings and purchase lands, and settle themselves upon them, under the guidance of Mr. Feargus O'Connor. At present everything proceeds most prosperously. Within two years, they have collected a capital of upwards of 30,000, and purchased two estates, on one of which, this of O'Connorville, many families are located in their cottages. O'Connor is most indefatigable in his exertions, and the utmost confidence of ultimate success prevails amongst the Chartist body. May it be realised; for it is certainly a great experiment on the co-operative principle, and every attempt to incite the working class to accumulate and secure property, is deserving of the warmest commendation.

[1] For James Bronterre O'Brien see G. D. H. Cole (op. cit.).
[2] MacAskill (op. cit.).
[3] I am indebted to Mr. G. Cornwall of Rickmansworth for much help in this section.

A verse written for the official opening of the estate on the 17 August 1847 set the note :--

> Has freedom whispered in his wistful ear
> Courage poor slave! Deliverance is near
> Oh! She has breathed a summons sweeter still,
> Come, take your gurdon at O'Connorville.

Crowds assembled, all anxious to see how the experiment had succeeded. O'Connor on a public platform, waving a gigantic cabbage, seemed tangible proof that O'Connorville had taken root.

The third estate, Minster Lovell, 197 acres in Oxfordshire (manager, Christopher Boyle) and the fourth, Snig's End, 268 acres in Gloucestershire, cost £10,878 and £12,000 respectively. Preparations for their settlement went ahead vigorously. Minster Lovell was renamed Charterville and both the name and pattern of cottage and allotment can be seen surviving vividly to this day on the present-day Ordnance Survey Map.

Lowbands in Worcester, the second colony, was formally settled two months after O'Connorville—on 17 August 1847. O'Connor spoke to the settlers in a rainstorm. This impressed the *Economist*. 'It does seem to offer', wrote its correspondent of O'Connor's plan, 'a reasonable experiment, upon a small scale, of the establishment of a peasant proprietary in England.' Such praise of O'Connor's personal control seemed justified, for early in 1848, the third and fourth estates, Charterville and Snig's End, were settled, each with eighty-five houses and a school, and a fifth estate, Mathon in Worcestershire had been bought as well.[1]

There were still bitter attacks from the left. Joshua Hobson, the previous publisher of the *Northern Star*, attacked O'Connor in the *Manchester Examiner*. O'Connor replied by travelling up and offering to repay every shareholder in Manchester, and told his audience that he had brought money with him to do it. 'Nay, but we won't have it,' cried his audience. 'Well then,' boisterously replied O'Connor, 'I'll spend it all.' 'Do and welcome,' cried his enthusiastic listeners.

He found friends in the most unlikely quarters. The *Gardener*

---

[1] For the most detailed exposition of the story of the settlements see *Parliamentary Papers*, 1847–8, XIX.

and Florist ranged itself on his side. An artisan called William Robinson wrote a pamphlet saying that he was 'convinced that it was the only means by which the working class can eventually improve their condition'. A London stockbroker, Thomas Allsop, was so impressed by O'Connor's scheme that he accompanied him round the country and offered advice as to the investment of funds of the National Land and Labour Bank. He even divided some of his own property near Lincoln into allotments with cottages and sold them by auction in May 1848.

O'Connor went from strength to strength. In 1847 he had been elected to Parliament for Nottingham. He was flirting with the communists gathered in London in November 1847 for whom Marx and Engels were drawing up the *Communist Manifesto*. Marx himself said that if the Chartists carried the six points of their charter they would 'be hailed as the saviours of the whole human race'. This was heady praise, and when it was coupled with news of revolutions in Ireland and France, the two countries to which we have seen O'Connor was closely attached, he threw his weight behind the Charter. In the full flush of enthusiasm, in January 1848, he contracted for the sixth estate of 280 acres. This one, Dodford, near Bromsgrove cost £10,350. Mathon, the fifth and most expensive estate (it was contracted for £15,350) was still not paid for.

On 1 April 1848, he published an appeal. 'The time has now arrived', he wrote, 'when we are entitled to the reward of our labour . . . I would rather die than give up one particle of the Charter . . . I would not give a fig for the Charter if we were not prepared with a solid, social system to take the place of the artificial one we mean to destroy; and it was good that we did not succeed earlier with the Charter, before we were ready with the new social system. Look at France; the great trouble of the Provisional Government, is the organization of labour. And so will it be in Prussia . . . But in addition to the Charter we have land reform, which will give bread to the working men when the Charter is carried. The Charter and the Land! Protect us in our work, People of England! Sign the Petition!'

O'Connor, it was said, envisaged a peasant republic in Britain with himself as president. A Convention had been called at the Owenite Hall in John Street, Tottenham Court Road, to plan the presentation of the petition to Parliament similar to that of 1842.

This petition was housed in the offices of the National Land Company at 144 Holborn. With its alleged 5 million signatures, it was taken in three cabs to the House of Commons on 10 April. There upon examination it proved a farce.

(5)

In the neighbourhood of the five settlements in Gloucestershire and Oxfordshire local landowners and J.P.s were becoming very apprehensive. Stories of wild miners and textile operatives from the north thrashing their hungry pigs for squealing, aggravated their natural apprehensions that the settlers would ultimately need to be helped by the rates. So the Poor Law Commissioners sent John Revans to visit the five Chartist settlements.[1] The allotments at O'Connorville he found were 'quite inadequate' and their crops inferior to those on surrounding farms. The livestock on each plot—four cows and a few pigs—had no hay and straw and therefore no means of making manure. Even the farm work was being done by the local farm labour. There were no implements, ploughs being borrowed from neighbouring farmers to help the 'settlers'. Nine of the thirty-six original settlers he found had already left, as their wives were unused to dairy work and could not bake bread.

At Minster Lovell, Revans found settlers just arriving. At Lowbands (near Tewkesbury) the crops were better than at O'Connorville, but six of the original forty settlers had left. At Snig's End (near Gloucester) he found the houses as yet unoccupied. 'It seemed', he wrote, 'a large place, and there were as many allotments there, or more, than at Minster Lovell.' He did not go to Bromsgrove. He was favourably impressed by the houses. Those at O'Connorville, Lowbands and Snig's End were of brick, and those at Minster Lovell of sandstone. But his most damning observation was repeated before a Select Committee of Parliament investigating the affairs of the National Land Company, in the fourth of whose six reports it can be found: 'All those who occupy the Land Company's allotments with nothing more than the produce of their allotments to depend upon will fail to obtain a living . . . the operations of the Land Company are likely to lead to serious and sudden burthens upon the poor's rates in those parishes where they

[1] For his evidence see *Parliamentary Papers*, op. cit.

acquire land.' When he prophesied that their cows, fed on cabbages, would become diarrhoetic, and that the swedes offered them to eat would give the milk a 'nauseous flavour' he spoke to hearers who could understand him.

The Committee of Inquiry, set up by Parliament in 1848, exposed O'Connor's bad management rather than his bad faith. (Only three balance sheets, for 29 September, 25 December 1847 and 25 March 1848 were produced.) It found that the society, having no treasurer, no accounts, no trustees' control of banking and spending of money, could not and did not come within the scope of the Friendly Societies Act. It found irregularities in the purchase of the first estate: no trustee had countersigned the order, O'Connor purchased it, not in the name of the solicitor, Mr. W. P. Roberts, nor in that of the Chartist Land Co-operative Society, but in his own. Yet it found a discrepancy of £3,000 in O'Connor's favour. He promptly offered to transfer the management of properties to three trustees, and persuaded John Sillet, a holder of a two-acre independent allotment in Suffolk, to write *A New Practical System of Fork or Spade Husbandry*. He proposed to wind up the company and to exclude all those who had paid up two-thirds of their shares by 29 December 1849. The Land Company would then be 'the largest, the most remunerable, and best conducted benefit society in the world'. Meanwhile he prepared the fifth of the Chartist communities for settlement.

(6)

At this point the settlers themselves took a hand in events. Those at Snig's End (the fourth to be settled) had not taken up residence with the flourish and ceremonial accorded to their brethren at O'Connorville and Charterville. They felt as they told the *Leeds Mercury* of 7 October 1848, like horses turned into a field and told to stop there till the grass grew. This feeling was shared by settlers at Charterville. Both groups criticized O'Connor at the Land Conference which met at Birmingham on 30 October 1848. One old settler, James Beattie, loudly accused him of fraud. This, more than the failure of the petition or the proceedings of the Select Committee, led to a fall in receipts.

To restore confidence in the scheme O'Connor worked like a man demented. He left the Land Conference at Birmingham and spoke for three hours at Worcester, swearing great oaths that he would persevere in settling members on the land.

But settlers began to drift away from the estates. To arrest it O'Connor summoned the next Land Conference at Snig's End in August 1849, and to keep those at O'Connorville happy, he obligingly forgot to collect their rents. But when he asked all Chartist settlers for half a year's rent in November 1849, they refused to pay.

His constituents at Nottingham grew critical too. The *Nottingham Journal* attacked the 'provisional' nature of the Land Company's recognition and insisted that all the estates were being held in O'Connor's own name. It had already accused O'Connor of being 'the greatest swindler on a large scale that ever practised on the credulity of mankind' . . . 'an Irish pauper . . . amply provided for out of the funds and credulity of Englishmen'. It now accused him of playing off shareholders and settlers against each other. On 1 January 1850, he was accused of 'wheedling the people of England out of £100,000' and readers of the *Nottingham Journal* were invited to order future copies 'to witness the final overthrow of this great political impostor'.

So O'Connor sued the editor Bradshaw, for libel. But Bradshaw secured J. A. Roebuck, a vituperative and able lawyer later known as 'Old Tear 'em', as his counsel. O'Connor lost, and though his character was 'unanimously' opined by the jury to be 'unimpeached as regards his personal honesty', he had even more difficulty in raising money to meet the costs.

He was working hard to legalize the Land Company. In the Hilary Term of 1849 he applied to the Court of Queen's Bench for a writ of mandamus to the Registrar of Joint Stock Companies, Tidd Pratt, ordering him to register the Land Company. Tidd Pratt refused to register it and in 1850 the Court of Queen's Bench upheld his refusal. So on 9 July of that year, O'Connor, Doyle and M'Grath, Clark and Dixon, petitioned through Sharman Crawford for leave to present a Bill to dissolve the Land Company.

The settlers at Minster Lovell and Snig's End meanwhile had enlisted the assistance of Sir Benjamin Hall, M.P., against O'Connor, who had described them as 'located ruffians'. On 1 March 1850 they declared that they would even live on roots rather than be evicted. O'Connor therefore offered Minster Lovell with its eighty-two cottages for sale in August at Oxford. The colonists appealed for funds to contest his right to do this. Nobody was anxious to buy the plots and the auction fell flat. O'Connor, now desperate, sent bailiffs to collect the rents from the Snig's End colonists, but they sourly told the bailiffs that they would 'manure the land with their blood before it should be taken from them'. The bailiffs were more successful at Minster Lovell and actually ejected the colonists, leaving them to the mercy of the parish officers.[1]

The O'Connorville settlers were still loyal, and O'Connor and Wheeler hoped to save the scheme through them. So in May 1851, they started the National Loan Society. This was to buy up the Land Company's estates and operate like a building society. But in August an Act was passed, largely owing to O'Connor's petition the previous year for dissolution of the Land Company, allowing the scheme to be liquidated. All who had purchased their lands through the Land Company were confirmed in their possession; all portions not bought by others were to be sold. As he told the O'Connorville settlers on 19 July 1851: 'If the located members on Minster Lovell, Snigs End and Lowbands had been as honest and industrious as the located members at O'Connorville, then the company would not have been wound up and I would have had thousands of cottages built.'

In February 1852 O'Connor began to ramble about his 'unworthy settlers' and four months later was taken to Dr. Tuke's private asylum at Chiswick. He died three years later on 30 August 1855 at 18 Albert Terrace, Notting Hill Gate. When he was buried at Kensal Green Cemetery on 10 September over 50,000 people came to his funeral.

(7)

What did O'Connor accomplish? He certainly found 70,000 members to subscribe to his scheme, but it took £6,000 to put the names of all of them on the books. Finlason, the actuary of the National Debt, calculated for the Parliamentary Select Committee which investigated the scheme, that it would require

---

[1] *The Times* carried reports of the troubles.

£21 million to place all the 70,000 subscribers on the land and to do this would take 300 years.

His settlements continued. The largest of these, Charterville in Oxfordshire, consisted of eighty holdings varying from two to four acres with cottages and buildings, and a road between them. It can still be seen. Until 1887 most of these small cultivators did well, for Charterville was situated in a large corn-growing, stock-raising area; they grew potatoes and got a monopoly of the market. In 1914 the original eighty holdings were reduced to sixty-nine, of which twenty-five were dependent on the cultivation of the plots. The occupants of these, of whom eighteen were farm labourers, treated them as adjuncts to another source of income.

At O'Connorville, Feargus left two sons, born out of wedlock to a local girl. One, Rory, died young, the other, Feargus, lived to be an old man.[1] O'Connorville was auctioned at 'The Swan' in Rickmansworth in May 1857. At that time only three of the original settlers remained in possession of their plots. At Snig's End the inhabitants who had so courageously declared they would 'manure the land with their blood before it would be taken from them', failed miserably to earn a living by growing potatoes and started an experiment in glove-making, which also failed. Their school became a public house, 'The Prince of Wales', and exists as such to this day.[2] At Lowbands, by 1868, a visitor remarked :—

> The importation of the Chartist colony into this parish in the year 1847 . . . had a disastrous effect on the moral and social condition of the people and has nearly doubled the poor-rates. The Lowbands settlement is still occupied either by the deluded disciples of that visionary leader or their successors. At the death of O'Connor the Court of Chancery confirmed the right of ownership to each holder by granting them a title, and the estate has since generally fallen into the hands of a Manchester man, who is said to entertain similar views. A New Bible Christian Chapel[3] was established on behalf of these colonists a few years ago.

The scheme reverberated down the century, rousing interest in the most unlikely places. Thirty years later, in 1875, the

[1] Information from Mr. G. Cornwall of Rickmansworth.
[2] E. E. Kirby, 'Three Acres and a Spade', *Country Life*, 22 December 1955.
[3] J. Noake, *Guide to Worcestershire* (1868), 308.

Newcastle Daily Chronicle sent a special commissioner, Mr. Longstaff, to visit all the Chartist settlements. He wrote a stirring account, much appreciated in the radical north-east.

In 1902 the memory of the settler at Charterville who chastised his pig for noisiness was still alive. All but two of the settlers' families had 'drifted back' to the towns. Yet, as Mrs. Sturge Gretton remarked at the time, 'the holdings are now a success, being all occupied by agricultural labourers who pay rates and rents varying from eight pounds to fourteen pounds. Strawberries are grown for the Oxford market and good potatoes are sent to Bristol.'[1] By that time other schemes, showed that O'Connor's idea for rehabilitating a landed peasant proprietary class was not as Utopian as it seemed. It had become a hard and seasoned plank in the Liberal Party's political platform.

[1] M. Sturge Gretton, *Three Centuries in North Oxfordshire* (1902), 175.

6

From Toad Lane to Pottersville

CARBONATED black spots like Rochdale, Liverpool, Sheffield, Bradford and the Potteries harboured highly combustible material for the social pyrotechnics of the '40s especially when ignited by sparks from the previous experiments.

(1)

At Rochdale, for instance, the missionary for Manea Fen, S. Rowbotham, obtained, as we saw, a good response. There in 1844 some twenty-eight pioneers established a local co-operative which had personal links with other foregoing experiments too. The originator, Charles Howarth, had been a leader of the Owenites in the town. The president, Miles Ashworth and his son, Samuel Ashworth, a salesman, was to go to Minster Lovell, one of O'Connor's 'colonies' and return just as another Rochdale pioneer, William Cooper, was about to set out for O'Connorville. Another pioneer, John Scowcroft, was a local preacher for the Swedenborgians. Yet another, Thomas Swindelhurst, was a friend of John Finch, the Liverpool Owenite, of whom we shall have more to say later in the chapter.

These six, who with twenty-two others met together on 11 August 1844 to form a co-operative society, were passionate believers in the necessity of founding a community. Indeed they resolved:

> As soon as practicable, this society shall proceed to arrange the powers of production, distribution, education and government, or in other words to establish a self-supporting home colony of united interest, or assist other societies in establishing such colonies.[1]

They never got as far as a community, for their store, in Toad Lane, was to initiate such a surge of co-operative retail distribution that their attentions were absorbed full-time. For as G. J. Holyoake sagely observed, this fed the co-operative movement on the most valuable diet of all: profits.[2]

(2)

The Liverpool Co-operative Society, fifteen years older than Rochdale, stemmed from an even older resolution to form a community. John Finch, its founder, regarded Robert Owen as answering 'most exactly the description of the great person pointed out by the prophets as the honoured instrument in the hands of God for encompassing the moral revolution'. Having made a modest fortune as the Liverpool agent of the Low Moor Iron Company of Bradford (then exporting rails to America), he had founded *The Bee*, a short-lived Co-operative journal. His 'Dear Social Father' Owen (whom he addressed as 'your most sacred highness'), had convinced him that the day was at hand when 'the whole population of Great Britain, Ireland, and all other countries "would" unite in forming joint stock companies, with from 500 to 2,000 members, each having one common capital and one common interest, living together, working with and for each other, and thus supplying themselves and each other with all the necessities, comforts, conveniences and elegancies of life'. 'All these communities' he prophesied 'united together in a common brotherhood of interest and affection, till knowledge and virtue, peace and goodwill, shall cover the earth as the waters cover the sea.'[3]

Finch helped to choose the site for the Liverpool Hall of

---

[1] W. H. Brown, *The Rochdale Pioneers* (Rochdale, 1944), 20.

[2] G. J. Holyoake, *A History of Co-operation* (1906), i. 264.

[3] For a good study of Finch see R. B. Rose in *Transactions of the Lancashire and Cheshire Antiquarian Society*, CIX (1957), 159–84.

Science in 1840 in Lord Nelson Street. In the same year, his *Moral Code of the New Moral World, or Rational State of Society*, outlined his brief that 'man is made for society, and was as much intended by the Author of his being to live in a state of society, with united exertions and union of interests as the bee, the ant, or the beaver'.

No bee, ant, or beaver was more persistent than Finch. His dogmatism even annoyed his friends. Lloyd Jones remarked that Finch was

> a very excellent man, full of honest purpose, and good intention; but rather deficient in insight and tact. He was kindly in spirit, and prepared to do all in his power for the comfort and welfare of the people with whom he had to deal. He had however a half joking way of saying unpleasant things which made him unpopular.[1]

This 'half joking way of saying unpleasant things' was responsible for a schism in the Liverpool Hall of Science. As a trustee he wished to channel the energies of the Liverpool socialists towards making it a success. But this fatal habit of his, in May 1839, led to a group of Owenites breaking away and when Finch complained of the deviationists that 'the formation of their society has caused division and disharmony amongst us when we were all engaged in finishing our building' the rift did not heal, and it grew wider when Owen himself told them that they could not remain members of the Socialist movement. Encouraged by William Hodson's example at Manea Fen they defied Owen's warning that they would be isolated from, not integrated with, the movement, and early in 1840 they met at the house of William Westwick in Lord Nelson Street, Liverpool, to establish 'The Community of United Friends'. Their objects, which enabled them to register as a friendly society, were to provide all members with constant and suitable employment, with good and sufficient food, clothing and lodgings, in health, in sickness, and in old age; to maintain and educate their children, and to provide useful instruction for each, by the united labour of the whole. In a businesslike fashion, they elected a President, a Treasurer, and a Secretary, who, with eight directors were to form the governing body. Entrance fees to

---

[1] Lloyd Jones, *The Life, Times and Labours of Robert Owen* (1889), 11, 142. The *Working Bee*, 8 February 1840.

this community cost £12 for a man, £8 for a woman, £5 for an aged relative and nothing for children under 18 years of age, and after entrance each member paid a subscription of 6*d*. a week. The accounts of this body were to be audited on the first week of each month.

The moving spirit was John Moncas, who began as its secretary and rose to be its president in two months. He was responsible for the Community leasing a 1,000 acre estate in Merionethshire at Pant Glas, consisting of a farmhouse, out-buildings and cottages, where they would be able to establish a community in fact as well as name. The *New Moral World*, Robert Owen's own journal, looking with a favourable eye on this experiment in practical socialism, described the estate as 'exceedingly fertile, beautifully situated, and got upon very favourable terms. Its size and applicability to manufacturing purposes, by means of water power, make it appear a most valuable and suitable site for the agricultures and manufacturing operations of a community, and we hope that both will be taken advantage of to the uppermost'. But as the *New Moral World* pointed out on 14 March 1840, 'unless the society has large capitalists to back it, who will not require repayment of the capital advanced by them for a considerable number of years, the sums mentioned will be found far below what is required'.

Undeterred by their lack of capital, Moncas and the United Friends set about the establishment of their community. Encouraged by the constant demand for farm produce, it seemed a comparatively simple task to sustain the required rent of £140 a year. Indeed they looked forward fairly confidently to being able to take up the option of purchasing it for £4,000 at the end of two years' occupation. Moncas sagely observed: 'The funds now wasted in exciting and unsatisfactory Chartism, trades unionism, and clubism will find their way to social communities.' He wrote to the *New Moral World* on 4 April 1840:—

> It is to exhibit a practical example to the industrious, moral and intellectual working classes of this country, of the ease with which they may improve their condition, by establishing communities, founded on the principle of equality of rights and properties, in opposition to the system of individualised interests of competitive society, no palace-like buildings, terraces, libraries, cottages, or mechanisms for raising up children . . .

Leaving James Spurr of Great Cross Hall Street to forward articles from Liverpool, Moncas and a few followers, including Joseph Gregory of Harford Lane, set about raising their first crops in the Welsh hills. Describing their progress three weeks later he wrote to the *Working Bee* of 25 April 1840 :—

> A good many agriculturists have joined us, as well as carpenters, and others, but we are sadly in want of a good agricultural smith, a stone mason, shoe-maker, and tailor, and should be most materially served if you could mention this want of ours to some of the applicants for admission into your community, whose services you might not want, or for whose accommodation you are not prepared.
>
> With respect to accommodation, however, I must add that those who may feel desirous to join us must be very moderate in their expectations. If not they will be disappointed. We have only the *means of obtaining* comfortable accommodation. We have it not in possession . . . it can be obtained only by present self denial and by a patient, steady and well directed industry.

So optimistic was he that he expected the community to be able to set up its own printing press to report progress.

Three months later, trouble began to brew, for by this time money was needed, and arrangements were made to secure it. So that members of the Liverpool society (which now met every Sunday afternoon) might feel confident that their subscriptions were not being wasted, a deputation of members examined the Pant Glas estate. They reported in the *Working Bee* of 11 July 1840 :—

> Notwithstanding some disadvantages attached to Pant Glas, the estate possesses many valuable properties superior to others, and is calculated for the establishing upon it for a Social Community; and therefore strongly recommend the society to carry on with increased energy the operations necessary to realise the objects they propose in the formation of a community upon the estate.

One of the members, who had seen it, did however suggest that the society might transfer its efforts to Warburton Moss, but he was outvoted.

For four more months, the Pant Glas community struggled on. Then this same member, Joseph Gregory, burst into print in the *Working Bee* on 8 August 1840: 'I was the person who took the horses and cart there and have had the management of the farm, not by reading and theorising, but by being actively engaged, ploughing, sowing, and cultivating, as far as rocks and hills would permit.' He declared that there were only twenty acres under tillage and another twenty more of mowing grass; 'even this small quantity is interspersed with rocks and large heaps of stones', he complained, 'and the greater part of this is so steep that the horses can scarcely draw the empty plough up the hills'. He was so full of indignation that he begged his readers not to 'plunge themselves in the deepest poverty and misery' by believing John Moncas.

Others, notably James Stanley, replied in the *Working Bee* of the following week that the harvest was coming in well—two tons to the acre of corn with plenty of carrots and oats. So, too, did William Parkes. But Gregory, now back in Liverpool, at 3 Harford Lane, delivered the *coup de grâce* to any further support the project might have had. He pointed out in the *Working Bee*, 9 September 1840, that not one whole field could be ploughed or dug, that it was 2,600 ft. above sea level, that ten miles of fencing were needed, and that the roads were so impassable that the best horses could only drag 5 cwts at a time. He further revealed that in the previous sixteen years the farm had eight tenants, none of whom had made it pay.

What really seems to have riled Gregory was the hostility of the Welsh landowner, Sir Robert Vaughan, who owned a piece of common land called Mynydd Bach or Little Mountain, then in possession of Evan Roberts of Bryn Garth, and from which any cattle belonging to the society were ejected. Pant Glas, Gregory concluded, should not be further encouraged—it was a 'grazing farm in the clouds'. It died as quickly as it had begun, a fugitive venture.

Whilst Moncas and Gregory were quarrelling in their community in the Welsh mountains, Finch, with his 'half-joking way of saying unpleasant things' was busy at Tytherly. Neither failure seems to have disturbed him. Indeed a visit to America seems to have strengthened it, for in 1851 Finch secured the Windsor Foundry in Smithdown Lane, Liverpool, and made overtures to William Newton to convert it to a co-operative workshop.

The Windsor Foundry employed 500 workmen and in its

eight years' existence had built up a thriving trade in rails, at home and in America, and on the Continent. Finch offered it for £50,000, and Newton sounded the opinion of his newly formed Amalgamated Society of Engineers by a prospectus in *The Operative*. The Christian Socialists like Neale, Ludlow and Hughes took up the cause with characteristic enthusiasm. Unfortunately in January 1852 the Engineers became involved in a strike and this exhausted their funds. By the time they had recovered their members were more in favour of emigration than co-operation as a solution of their difficulties.

Finch's millenarian fervour is perhaps best expressed in his rearranged version of the Bible entitled *Seven Seals Broke Open, or the Bible of the Reformation Reformed*, which he published in 1853, four years before his death.

(3)

Equally capable of irritating a wide variety of people, Isaac Ironside was the Finch of Sheffield.[1] From being a stone grate fitter he had become a prosperous accountant, promoter of the Sheffield Mechanics' Institute, a Chartist member of the town council, and founder of the Sheffield Hall of Science. He had visited Manea Fen in 1839 and, as we have seen, persuaded the builder to migrate to Tytherly. After its collapse he took over the lease of one of the farms and offered to sink his personal fortune to make it work. He also considered establishing a community under his own direction in Sheffield.

'Land colonies' were popular in the Sheffield of 1843. The big local bank of Parker, Shore & Co. had collapsed and the trade unions convened a public meeting on 22 February of that year at a public house called 'The London Apprentice', which, amongst other things, formed a more comprehensive organization out of the twenty-seven separate trades in the town. They instituted an inquiry into the causes of the distress and on 22 April published their findings in the *Sheffield Iris*. After studying the 'various plans' suggested to them, they came to the conclusion that 'spade husbandry was of the greatest importance'. They hoped that by siphoning off surplus labour to the

---

[1] John Salt, 'Isaac Ironside and the Hollow Meadows Farm Experiment' in the *Yorkshire Bulletin of Economic and Social Research* (1960), XII. 45–51.

land they would save many thousands of pounds in unemployment relief. The report went on:—

> If, for instance, the table knife grinders, instead of spending £21,000 to keep their unemployed workmen in indolence had bought and expended it on land, which would have provided for them a comfortable subsistence, they might have been at this time in a flourishing condition, by being able to exercise an overwhelming influence on the demand and supply of their labour.

On 22 May one Ward (who had on 6 March proposed that the Guardians 'adopt the principles and plans of poor colonies which have been so successful in Holland') quoted the *Northern Star* to prove that putting money in banks would merely stimulate manufacturers to glut the markets. One of Ironside's supporters recommended that each trade union should contribute a sum towards the purchase of a farm where a practical farming man would superintend the cultivation. On 29 July the *Sheffield Iris* published the 'Second Address to the Workmen of Sheffield' emphasizing the idea.

O'Connor's enthusiasm galvanized the spade-salvationists over the next five years: O'Connor in fact gained 620 members in Sheffield, paying £839, and another 345, paying £557, in near-by Barnsley. Ironside took the chair for Thomas Briggs, at a Chartist meeting on 20 March 1848 where a scheme of allotments was proposed for keeping the price of food low. Briggs, the Sheffield delegate to the Chartist National Assembly, remarked 'with respect to those who spoke so loudly about guns and pikes and muskets, I think the best you can do is to take a spade and fall out with some common'. Briggs gave a rosy account of O'Connorville to a Sheffield meeting on 10 May and on 13 June O'Connor himself came to Sheffield, and was met by a brass band. His route from the station was lined with banners as he drove to address a large crowd:—

> 'Every little editor,' he cried, 'some of whom do not know whether potatoes are dug up ready roasted and buttered, or whether they grow upon trees, are all attacking my scheme. Mr. S. Crawford has seen the houses at Lowbands and was paralysed and astonished at not a weed to be seen on 150 acres of land . . . Lee, the manager, said he would not take £400 for his four acres . . . I have built 130 cottages in a ring fence and if Prince Albert had done the same he would have been lauded to the skies.'

On his right hand, as he spoke was Isaac Ironside, who urged the audience to cut up deer parks and race courses to provide employment for those displaced by the industrial change.

Feargus O'Connor had been preceded by Frances Wright, heroine of an experimental colony in Tennessee who gave a series of lectures in Sheffield in February 1848. The Sheffield unions took up land colonies with zest. Three separate schemes got under way. The Edge-Tool Grinders acquired a farm of sixty-eight acres at Wincobank 'with a view to employing their surplus hands', and the File Hardeners a similar one elsewhere. The Britannia Metal Smiths chose 1 April 1848 for the ceremonial cutting of the first sod on an eleven-acre farm at Gleadless Common Side, employing a manager and a dozen men, who supplied a shop which sold the produce at market prices. The employees were paid 14s. a week with 6d. a week for each dependent child. A fourth scheme involved the Board of Guardians and deserves larger treatment.

The appalling conditions of the workers in the hand flour mills owned by the Board of Guardians, where unemployed workers were made to work, stung seven of them to revolt. They appeared before the local magistrate on 28 January 1848 with Isaac Ironside as their spokesman, and were let off with a caution.

On 9 February, in the Town Council, Ironside demanded a full-scale inquiry into the employment of able-bodied paupers in the flour mills, where seventy men, 'wretched in appearance and the picture of ill-feeling and despair', were languishing. He was defeated, but on 10 March the Guardians decided that, in view of the severe and unhealthy conditions prevailing in the corn mills work was to be reduced to four hours a day. Rooms for oakum-picking were taken. By May 1848, a workhouse farm of forty-eight acres of moorland was decided upon. Moorland was chosen because land reclamation was regarded as the key factor of the scheme. A future profit was expected from the sub-letting of reclaimed land, although no hard and fast rules for this aspect of the scheme were laid down at the beginning. In any case, it would take several years to get the land into shape, although, in 1850, there were vague proposals for sub-letting the land in three-acre plots to small-scale cultivators.

A site was chosen at Hollow Meadows, at the head of the

Rivelin Valley, seven miles from the centre of town. A certain amount of land reclamation was already taking place, some three-quarters of a mile beyond the chosen spot and 1,100 ft. above sea level. This was the work of independent small-scale farmers, who since 1844 had leased land from the Duke of Norfolk and in some cases had built houses on the allotments brought into 'a good state of cultivation'.

To reclaim this land, it was argued, was a form of labour promising an economic return to the community without competing too obviously with free labour. The distance of the site from Sheffield was itself an advantage, since it permitted refractory elements in the pauper population to be removed from the influence of 'political agitators'.

Work on the site began in May 1848. On 10 July the foundation stone of the building was laid by Wilson Overend, J.P., the chairman of the Board of Guardians. In the remaining months of the year the building of a dining-hall and dormitories from local stone went ahead. The land was cleared of stones and underbrush, drains were laid and spade husbandry began. In the first year five acres were brought under crop, and in the second year nine.

Life on the farm was strenuous, but not unhealthy. A list of regulations for the management of the farm was issued stating that the men were to work 'in moderation, but with diligence'. There was to be 'no time allowed, either in the forenoon or afternoon, for general resting or smoking'. The men worked in groups of ten, each group headed by a pauper 'overseer' who was paid an extra shilling weekly. Refractory or lazy paupers were made to walk to and from the Sheffield Workhouse daily. Working hours were from 8.30 to 5 daily and the men were allowed one half day per week to visit their families.

By 1850 it was claimed that an average number of forty-five men had been employed at the farm and 'upwards of five hundred heads of families' accommodated there. By 1854, despite the marked fall in the numbers of able-bodied paupers after 1849, twenty-two acres had been reclaimed and planted under root crops. Moreover, it was claimed that in 1853 there was a clear surplus of £60, and the report declared that it was shown 'beyond dispute that pauper labour can be made productive'.

'New England', as it was sarcastically called, was constantly attacked by opponents who sought to emphasize the experimental nature of the scheme, the high initial outlay, the delay in the publication of accounts and the failure of the farm to show an immediate return.

Ironside defended it with vigour. In December 1849 he wrote a letter to the *Sheffield Times* against 'the Money Bags' who looked for 'direct pecuniary profit' from the experiment. He predicted it would ultimately show a profit to their 'low, grovelling minds'. In the meantime, he stressed, attention should be directed to the moral and economic advantages of the scheme. His opponents, he declared, had said 'not a word as to its indirect results in making better citizens in every respect of those who are submitted to its influence; not a word as to its preserving the lives of heads of families, thereby keeping the families from the parish; not a word as to its absorbing surplus labour in a manner that cannot injure a single ratepayer'. His vigorous championship led him to write a letter to the Poor Law Commissioner in September 1850 suggesting that the Poor Law Board should make and circulate an official report on the experiment. In August the *Athenaeum Magazine* had given an account of a paper read before the British Association by Dr. W. P. Alison, the Scots Poor Law Reformer, who had quoted the Sheffield scheme as a successful experiment. In the same year also *Chambers' Edinburgh Journal* reviewed a pamphlet by Alison and drew attention to 'the interesting character of the Sheffield experiment', noting 'a disposition to try similar experiments in other districts'.

Ironside insisted from the beginning that Hollow Meadows was a triumph for the community idea he had been championing since 1840. Within a week of the laying of the foundation stone he was claiming full credit for the scheme and sneering at the 'practical men', who, after so long a period, were at last coming round to his way of thinking. He looked further and saw it as a pilot experiment for other schemes of a more ambitious nature, and in a letter printed by the *Sheffield Times* on 15 December 1849 he pointed out that the original project might be improved on by the town acquiring freehold and more fertile land nearer its centre. All his speeches in support of the farm betrayed the fusion (or confusion) of Owenite and O'Connorite ideas that gave it birth.

Thornton Hunt, editor of the *Leader*, attended a public inspection of the farm in September 1850 and heard Ironside emphasizing, in true Owenite fashion, the changes in the character of the inmates produced even by such a limited experiment as Hollow Meadows. 'The moral effects', he said, 'are of the greatest importance . . . I know of some circumstances which have occurred at the farm—poor fellows who had constantly migrated from the workhouse to the house of correction and from the house of correction to the workhouse. But here is something humanizing and elevating—wholesome food, good air, good lodging, occupation and regularity, and it has been the making of them. This is the embodiment of the principle—"he that will work not neither shall he eat".' Two years later, in August 1852, at a meeting attended by Viscount Goderich of the Poor Law Association, Ironside, as an 'old radical, chartist and socialist', mentioned his association with Robert Owen on the central board of an agrarian community in Hampshire, and again he raised the question of the social and educational objects of land projects. Referring to an objection to the Hollow Meadows scheme as competing with free labour, he said: 'That's nothing to me . . . *Have we produced a better population?* . . . if we have . . . take your money bags argument and throw it to the devil if you like!'

In the early 1850s, however, improved economic conditions produced a weakening of interest in agrarian experiments, and the wider interest in the Hollow Meadows scheme tended rapidly to decline. Ironside himself became increasingly preoccupied with schemes, ultimately disastrous to his political fortunes, to adapt the medieval constitutional ideas of Toulmin Smith.

For a period Ironside sought to maintain an indirect influence on the farm scheme by protecting the position of Watkinson, the Union Clerk, whose views on the running of the farm to some extent coincided with his own. In 1851 the Sheffield democrat used his then not inconsiderable political power in an attempt to crush a group of Guardians, led by Philip Ashbury, who were conducting a bitter vendetta against Watkinson. But in spite of the individual election victories of what were termed 'his socialist and infidel friends', Watkinson, farm manager, failed to survive an inquiry by the Assistant Poor Law

Commissioner into alleged 'irregularity and laxity' in the management of Hollow Meadows, the results of which were made public in May 1851.

Watkinson's dismissal solved the problem as to whether pauper labour at Hollow Meadows was to be devoted to land reclamation (all the reclaimed land being sub-let to private farmers), or whether a certain amount of 'high farming' was to be taken up by the Union. The first would restrict the scope of the scheme, since it meant that only able-bodied paupers could be employed at the farm, land reclamation being very heavy work. The latter implied that the farm might become to some extent a self-supporting model community. Ironside clearly had this in mind when in 1853 he suggested that the whole workhouse should be transferred to the farm site. But the damage had already been done.

Final defeat came in 1854. In April of that year Watkinson was dismissed from his remaining offices, and on 16 August the Board of Guardians declared that they did not 'intend to further any plan of amateur farming, but strongly inclined to lease from time to time such portions of land as may be brought into a state fit for the energies of the private farmer'. In a last despairing effort Ironside had attempted at the July meeting of the Sheffield Town Council to persuade its members to request the Duke of Norfolk to refuse to consent to any large-scale lettings, which, in Ironside's opinion, violated 'the principles adopted in the leasing of the farm'. By 1861, however, over fifty acres had been reclaimed and let at 25s. per acre.

Ironside's failure to prevent the subletting of reclaimed land marked, to all intents and purposes, the end of his influence on the Hollow Meadow experiment. The very vigorous part he had played in the early years meant, it is true, that his name was popularly associated with that of the farm for the rest of his life. Indeed, as late as 1869 Ironside felt compelled to sue the *Sheffield Independent* for publishing a letter from 'A Sheffield Man', who jokingly suggested that the erstwhile Socialist wished to establish an 'Agapemone' at Hollow Meadows. But the original experiment was never developed, as Ironside would have wished, on a large-scale community basis. Nor does it appear to have stimulated any contemporary imitations. It ended a year later when the buildings were taken over by the newly created

Sheffield School Board as an industrial school for its problem pupils.

From now on Ironside fades protestingly into the interstices of community planning. He campaigned, with ever-decreasing effect, for administrative devolution as a protagonist of Toulmin Smith whose exhumation of the history of the medieval guilds was to arouse the interest of Kropotkin, the anarchist-philosopher. Later Isaac Ironside started a newspaper during the Crimean War to campaign against Palmerston. For this paper Karl Marx wrote. The unhappy Ironside found Marx's articles were too prolix and incomprehensible, and complained to the editor that they were 'entombing' the paper. Marx got to hear of this and replied 'I positively decline to make myself guilty of manslaughter by administering another "dose" to Mr. Isaac Ironside, and "entombing" him in the sheets of his own paper.' Ironside faded out of both local and national affairs and died forgotten in 1869.

(4)

In 1845 Titus Salt, Head Constable of Bradford, was responsible for convening and presiding over public meetings.[1] He may well have heard Minter Morgan, though as a Congregationalist he could not be expected either to swallow or follow his idea of building a 'self-supporting village' around the Church of England. Being a Yorkshire manufacturer, he was more likely to build it round his factory. In the following year, 1846, the Health of Towns Commission heard James Smith of Deanston describe Bradford as 'the most filthy town I visited'. Smith spoke of houses being put up regardless of any place for gardens or sport, crammed into as small a space as possible, and added 'if the lower orders have not places where they can engage in sports and keep their minds engaged in matters of that kind, it is the very thing to drive them to Chartism'.

Some of the Christian Socialists, who owed so much to Minter Morgan, thought the same. So did several manufacturers. After all, Disraeli had sketched the archetype in Mr. Trafford of *Sybil* and the Millbanks factory and village in *Coningsby*. So when in 1848 Titus Salt became mayor of Bradford and the town was gripped by both Chartism and cholera, he

[1] Robert Balgarnie, *Sir Titus Salt* (Scarborough, 1877).

began to consider the possibility of such a community for his own employees.[1] In 1850 he consulted the firm of Lockwood and Mason. In 1851 he went up to the Great Exhibition in London (where the Prince Consort's model houses for working men were being exhibited) and made an offer for the Crystal Palace itself, which he intended to use as a weaving shed. This idea had to be abandoned because of the vibration involved in the manufacturing process which would have broken the glass.

Such daring imagination and opportunism had been the key of Titus Salt's career. Born at Morley on 20 September 1803, he had attended the grammar school at Heath before following his father to Bradford as a wool-dealer. At that time, his father dealt in Donskoi wool: Titus, however, thought of making worsted out of it. And when he could find no one in Bradford who would listen to his suggestion, he decided to set up in the manufacturing business himself. He began in Silsbridge Lane and by the time he was 33 years old, he had four other mills hard at work.

That was in 1836. In that same year, he went to Liverpool on a visit. There, in the warehouse, he found 300 bags of llama or alpaca wool. Admiring its long staple and sheen, he was quick to appreciate the possibilities of this and bought the whole consignment at 8d. per lb., and began to make alpaca cloth.

In 1850 the chimneys of over 200 mills were polluting the air of Bradford. Titus Salt determined to emancipate his workers from the smoky canopy in which they lived, and made plans to transfer his factories to the valley of the Aire where the London–Glasgow Railway and the Leeds and Liverpool Canal joined each other. At the same time he proposed to build a complete community for the workers in the Salt factories. Thus Saltaire was conceived. Work began in the autumn of 1851, and within two years, the first part of the model town was finished: the factories and houses.

The great congregation which assembled on 20 September 1853 to see the opening of Saltaire was confronted with an amazing sight. Sprawling over ten acres was a huge works, shaped like the letter T. Built in the Italian style, the T was

---

[1] 'There is no doubt that the main concept of Saltaire came from Salt's reading of the novels of Disraeli.' R. K. Dewhurst, *Town Planning Review* (1960), XXXI. 135–44.

six storeys, or 72 ft., high. The façade of the building was the top of the T, and it contained on its top floor one of the longest and largest rooms in the world at that time. Great windows of plate-glass admitted light into the building, flues admitted fresh air, while noise was eliminated by placing all the machinery under the flooring. This last arrangement was a great novelty at the time, for it not only made for comparative quiet but enabled the weaving rooms to be kept free from dust.

The stem of the letter T was formed by the warehouses which ran down towards the canal some hundred yards or more away. Special conduits caught the rain-water and stored it in tanks, ready to be used by the factory. This great production unit was linked with the outside world by a number of roads. Perhaps the most striking object to those who were seeing it for the first time was the chimney—a huge 250-ft. shaft built in the style of an Italian bell-tower. Up it passed every day the smoke from fifty tons of coal, but little of it escaped at the top, for special smoke burning appliances consumed it. The engines, with a combined horse-power of 3,000, drove some three miles of shafting.

To build this mammoth works, twenty quarries worked full-time for two years, and its solidity, as late as 1876, was described by one proud native as 'having no equal in this or any other country'.

Around this great stone T rose houses of various sizes, also built of stone, each with a kitchen, living-room and scullery, a pantry, cellar and at least three bedrooms. In a few years, no less than 800 of these houses sprang up around the factory, covering a further twenty-six acres. Shops, too, lined the well-paved streets, and soon a church (finished in 1859) described as 'the most exquisite example of pure Italian architecture in the Kingdom', schools, a literary institute, and other social amenities all followed, and all provided by the generosity of Titus Salt.

In front of the schools and the institute were four carved lions; the story goes that they were designed by Thomas Milnes the sculptor for the base of Nelson's column in Trafalgar Square, but owing to some hitch, the commission was withdrawn and offered to Edwin Landseer, whose lions lie in Trafalgar Square today. Titus Salt saw the four lions made by Milnes, and had them moved to Saltaire.

Saltaire was an industrial Utopia—a man-planned frame, integrating industry, housing and, in time, parks, trout fishing and boating: indeed all the amenities which the mind of man could conceive, except one. For across the boundary of the town was written ALL BEER ABANDON YE THAT ENTER HERE. For to Titus Salt, as to Morgan and James Silk Buckingham, 'Drink and Lust' lay at the bottom of all social evils.

(5)

Others, besides Titus Salt, wished to escape from the pressures of urban life. In the Potteries, turners, handlers, hollow-ware-pressers, flat-pressers, overmen, slip-makers, throwers, lookers-to-ware, packers, printers, gilders and painters were threatened by a technological revolution. One machine they called 'the rolling monster', displaced printers by the score; another, 'the scourge', stamped out plates and, with them, the livelihood of men. As clay was in their hands, so they became in the hands of William Evans, a Welshman from Swansea, who established a newsagent's shop at Shelton where he sold the works of Mary Wollstonecraft, Rousseau, Mackintosh and Emerson. In 1843 he began to issue his own newspaper the *Potters' Examiner and Workman's Advocate*.[1]

In January 1844 he published letters from Six Mile Prairie, Illinois, following on 3 February with the suggestion that the potters should purchase land in America, where they could grow tobacco on land containing clay for making the pipes in which to smoke it. At sixty pence an acre freehold, as compared to £60 leasehold at home, this land, he argued was a bargain. Pots made from the clay wore as good as glaze, and were in greater demand than English ones. His jeremiad on 2 March 1844 was moving: 'England has had her day', he wrote,

> her sun is setting . . . How necessary then is it for us to awake from our lethargy, and, like intelligent men, to calmly consider the best means of escape. As a body of operatives, we stand unequalled for trades power and pecuniary means throughout the whole British public . . . The United States of America must and will become the most powerful nation of the globe . . . the great political leviathan that shall ultimately revolutionise the world.

[1] Harold Owen, *The Staffordshire Potter* (London, 1901); Grant Foreman, 'The Settlement of English Potters in Wisconsin', *Wisconsin Magazine of History*, XXI (1938).

To an audience nourished by the strong oratory of the Methodist New Connection he quoted Isaiah 35. 1–2 with particular reference to the western states of America: 'The wilderness, and the solitary place, shall be glad for them; and the desert shall rejoice, and blossom as the rose. It shall blossom abundantly, and rejoice even with joy and singing, the excellency of Carmel and Sharon; they shall see the glory of the Lord, and the excellency of our God.'

That Carmel and Sharon flourished in the Mid-West he brought eloquent witness, none more so than George Flower, whose Illinois community at New Albion he wished to imitate. To persuade the doubters and to strengthen the waverers, he reported every instance of a machine displacing human labour— as, for instance, in the issue of 6 April 1844: 'One of these machines with the assistance of two women or boys of fourteen years of age, will do as much work as six middling workmen. One woman for about *two shillings* will make 60 dozen cups, for which we should receive at most places, from fifteen to seventeen shillings.' For cautious, practical souls, Evans couched his arguments in hard economic terms. Surplus labour, he intoned, was 'the Pandora's Box of industry from which flow all the evils that afflict the sons of toil'. The only logical remedy was to create a scarcity of labour by emigration.

His campaign was successful. The newly formed Trades Union of Operative Potters decided to throw their financial resources into a Joint Stock Emigration Company. To supplement these funds, Evans urged that since there were 7,000 operative potters in the trade, it should be easy to persuade 5,000 of them to take out an individual £1 share, giving the the Joint Stock Emigration Company a working capital of £5,000. This could be raised, he went on, by each shareholder paying a shilling per week. To encourage them, he dangled a special report on the mineral wealth of Illinois before their eyes, written by David Dale Owen, son of the great Robert Owen.

The possibilities of a 12,000-acre settlement in the sun appeared most attractive to his Staffordshire audience working amongst the 'whirling dust and rattling engines' for sixteen hours a day. As Evans painted it 'Staffordshire offered infancy in rags, youth in decrepitude, manhood in graves, with the ever present prospect haunting the imagination like some frightful dream'. But the 'beautiful prairies of the West' offered the 'most liberal institutions of present man . . . untaxed plains, rivers and lakes of a free country' and 'an unfettered life of happiness and content amid the varied scenes of nature and the handiworks of God'.

The Potteries surrendered to him, as well they might, for they were paying some sixty or seventy pounds a week in unemployment benefits. This, as Evans pointed out 'might be dispensed with by the removal of its claimants to happy homes in the western world . . . where all the powers in their existence will be called into active operation'. Letters to George Flower and John Tyler were approved on the potters' behalf, and Evans busied himself with reprinting Flower's *Errors of Emigrants*, Cleave's *Immigrant's Handbook*, and Mann's *Emigrant's Complete Guide to the U.S.A.* On 25 August 1844 Evans was still plugging the urgency of the £5,000 capital. He asked intending shareholders to contribute 6d. a week for forty weeks, and urged each branch committee in the pottery towns to keep a book of all those members of the craft who had not paid, and to persuade them to do so. If local branch persuasion could not work, he urged them to send the names of unwilling members to the central committee who would 'appoint a special deputation to wait upon those parties to explain to such unwilling members . . . the objects of our society'. He concluded: 'Let your motto be *Five Thousand Shares.*'

George Flower from Illinois, in a letter dated 6 August 1844 which Evans printed on 5 October, suggested that two or three persons be sent as a committee, and offered 'to digest, or rather correct, the details of the plan'. Flower also warned the committee not 'to be in a hurry, but to take time'. By 12 October, all the potters' lodges had voted their confidence in Evans, whose success had brought down upon his head the attacks of the *North Staffordshire Mercury*.

So, for the next twelve months, subscriptions were collected and the estate committee, which was to travel out to the United States of America and survey the land, was appointed. In public houses all over Staffordshire, regular meetings were held, with the secretaries collecting sixpences of intending subscribers.

Early in 1846 the appointing committee in the person of Thomas Twiggs and two companions left Staffordshire to purchase land in America. Their plan was to buy as much as their capital would allow, and split it into twenty-acre tracts. Immigrants were to be chosen by ballot when subscriptions reached each successive £50 level. They would arrive to find a cabin built for them, five acres of land broken and sowed with wheat and corn, and the other fifteen awaiting cultivation. To repay the Emigration Society they would pay £5 a year for ten years, plus £10 expenses. These twenty-acre allotments were to alternate across the tract purchased by the Emigration Society, allowing the intervening spaces to be enclosed like squares on a crossword.

William Twiggs did his best. He and his companions rode out to Illinois, then on to Wisconsin. There they purchased land and called it Pottersville where in two years they settled 134 individuals on 1,600 acres. This cost money, and the original £5,000 was not forthcoming quickly enough while another £3,000 remained to be raised. What made matters worse, the former unity of the various pottery workers now began to be seriously threatened. The hollow-ware-pressers who managed to adapt themselves to the new Staffordshire technology, took a strong deviationist line, and set up a rival organization of their own. To counteract this, William Evans decided to broaden the basis of the Emigration Society by appealing to the distressed working men of other crafts and towns. With William Coates, he stumped parts of Lancashire appealing for further funds, claiming that 'emigration had stopped persecution of the working man in Staffordshire, and prevented the reduction of wages'. He also changed both the title and place of publication of his paper. From being the *Potters' Examiner and Workman's Advocate* published at Burslem, it now became the *Potters' Examiner and Emigrants' Advocate* published at Liverpool. He found many sympathetic hearers, and was well reported in the papers, but could not control new developments in Wisconsin.

Meanwhile in Pottersville, Wisconsin, a kind of constitutional crisis arose because of the arrival of an Estates Committee to secure equitable allotment of the lands which Twiggs and his two associates had purchased. Twiggs regarded them as unnecessary, and wrote bitterly: 'I am sorry to say that the generality of them are not the wise men of the East, but the foolish men of the West, and whatever unity there might have been amongst them prior to their leaving home, I can assure you that there has been very little since they came here.' This discord amongst such a community was doubly unfortunate, since it impeded the process of legalizing the potters' possession of the land they had bought (already a very difficult process), in addition to lowering the credit which such pioneer communities had to obtain if they were to purchase the very elementary necessities of life.

The immigrants complained of the heat, the water, the Indians, and the sandy soil. Twiggs returned home in 1849 a very sick man after three years, complaining that many of the immigrants cared for nothing but fishing and hunting and were not prepared to work. Evans redoubled his efforts. In January 1850 he was speaking as far afield as Hull in Yorkshire, claiming that a new plot of land on the Fox River in Wisconsin would prove even more successful than the old one at Pottersville, and would sell at $200 an acre. But however enthusiastic he might be, and however much he might prime the financial carburettor, the mechanism in far away Wisconsin just would not tick over. James Buck wrote back to the radical *Manchester Examiner and Times* that on his way out in that year, he met 'swarms' of emigrants returning from the settlement. The new land on Fox River he described as 'a succession of dry sandy ridges, and between most of these a bog where the soil is as black and deep as any bog in Ireland. The sandy ridges are covered with a stunted, poor timber, a sure indication of the properties of the soil.' The end came with an indignation meeting held on 3 June 1850 at Fort Winnebago. A grand indictment of the project was prepared, incorporating charges of misrepresentation, corruption, and incompetence. By January 1851 the Emigration Society was dead. Yet the census of 1860 showed that no less than 76 Staffordshire families were settled in Columbia and Marquette Counties, most of them 'prosperous farmers'.

Pottersville spelt the wreck of trade unionism in the Potteries for the next fifty years. It indicated, however, that Liverpool was becoming a gateway to a new freedom. And through that gateway was to stream, in the fifties, one of the biggest religious migrations yet: the Latter Day Saints, en route for Zion. But story of that migration is a chapter of itself.

7

Liverpool: Gateway to Zion

(1)

'ALL over this vast kingdom the laws of Zion are rolling onward with the most astonishing rapidity,' rhapsodized a Mormon apostle from London in April 1841. Euphoria, in this case, was based on evidence, for the Church of the Latter Day Saints had established a responsive and vibrating network in little over four years. In that very year it was dispatching over 1,000 converts to Nauvoo, Illinois, the City of Rest for the Saints.

In the previous year forty-one converts had sailed from Liverpool to join Joseph Smith, the founder of this new Church. Smith claimed to have been given, by an angel of God at Cumorah Hill, New York State, on 22 September 1827, a set of Golden Plates. Inscribed on these in mystic characters was the story of the Jaredites, Nephites and Lamanites. The first had come from the Tower of Babel to America in about 600 B.C., the other two coming after the birth of Christ. The Lamanites (or bad tribe) wiped out the Nephites (or good tribe) and were in possession of the entire American continent by A.D. 420. These Lamanites were, according to Smith, the ancestors of the North American Indians.

A pair of 'spiritual glasses', also thoughtfully provided by

This chapter is mainly based on the files of the *Millennial Star*, reinforced by W. A. Linn, *The Story of the Mormons* (London, 1923), M. H. Cannon, 'Migration of English Mormons to America', *American Historical Review*, LII (1946–7), 436–55, and 'The English Mormons in America', ibid., LVII (1951–2), 893–908.

the angel, enabled Smith to decipher the golden plates and write the story. His book took its title from Mormon, last chief of the Nephites who had engraved the plates but died, leaving it to his son, Moroni to finish. Mormon, said Smith, meant 'More Good'. In 1830 he founded the Church of the Latter Day Saints to redeem America, the promised land for the Nephites and sent into the mission field a band of evangelists to reap the most spectacular harvest of souls since Wesley's time.

They preached an attractive gospel. Man not being born in sin, was an immortal being with an eternal soul and a human body, and could become a god by living on earth according to the law. This earth was only one of many settlements in space. At first in Preston, then in Manchester, Southport, Bolton and Liverpool, audiences heard Heber C. Kimball boast that he would not suffer death before Christ's second coming, and prophesy that within ten or fifteen years the sea between Liverpool and America would dry up.

By tradition a hotbed of chiliastic hope, Lancashire audiences were used to this. Manchester had incubated the ecstasies of Mother Ann, foundress of the Shakers. Accrington kept the Swedenborgian metaphysic warm. Ashton had provided a temple for John Wroe. Salford had provided, with Rochdale, recruits for Manea Fen. Numerous Owenite cadets and cadres had flourished here. Now at Preston it was the turn of Heber C. Kimball and his fellow missionaries to harvest souls and bodies for their new revelation.[1] Goals like 'Zion', 'salvation', and 'social justice' reinforced with concrete examples, enabled them to reap abundantly.[2] Orson Hyde, another early Mormon missionary, actually read aloud a letter from America to a Preston audience claiming that a mile-long wagon caravan making its way to Missouri had heard from Canadian saints that the Lord had rained down manna in rich profusion over an area covering seven to ten miles. This manna, said Hyde, smacking his lips, tasted like wafers dipped in honey, and was relished by saints and sinners alike.

(2)

By calling themselves the Latter Day Saints, the Mormons were able to use the term sinners to anathematize all who did

[1] *Journal of Heber C. Kimball* (Nauvoo, 1840), 19.
[2] 1,500 converts 'in a few months', Cannon, op. cit., 438.

not join their church. One of the most effective exploiters of this technique was Brigham Young who arrived at Liverpool in April 1840 to inaugurate a new phase of recruiting. Promptly establishing an English newspaper there with the apt title of the *Millennial Star* (which under Parley P. Pratt reached a weekly circulation of 25,000), he promised Paradise, if his readers would only take the trouble to get there. A proclamation from Joseph Smith was published:–

> The spirit of emigration has actuated the children of men, from the time our first parents were expelled from the garden until now. It was this spirit that first peopled the plains of Shinar, and all other places; yes, it was emigration that first broke upon the death-like silence and loneliness of an empty earth, and caused the desolate land to teem with life and the desert to smile with joy.

The appeal was reinforced by Brigham Young's own talents for organizing the emigration of converted Saints. Four months after his arrival, the ship *North American* left Liverpool in charge of two elders with 200 emigrants on board, followed in February 1841 by the *Sheffield* from Bristol, with a second batch. Another five vessels sailed in 1841, making the total of 1,177 emigrants for that year alone. Eight vessels with 1,614 emigrants sailed in 1842, five with 749 in 1843, five with 644 in 1844 and three with 346 in 1845–6. The decline is significant: these were the years of Chartist activity, of Feargus O'Connor's schemes of home colonization and of rising prosperity after the slump of 1838–42. Yet these were the years in which the ground bait was laid. Some 8,000 converts were made as a result of meetings and a widespread distribution of the *Book of Mormon*. A copy was sent to Queen Victoria inviting her to take the trail to Nauvoo as 'Zion's nursing mother'. Though the Queen was not attracted, some of her subjects were and during the next thirty years 22,000 of them emigrated as Saints. As Lorenzo Snow, an apostle, remarked again 'Throughout all England, in almost every town and city of any considerable importance, we have chapels or public halls in which we meet for public worship.'

The class of these emigrants was steadily improving. In September 1842 the *Liverpool Albion* commented:–

> The emigration of the Mormons or Latter Day Saints is daily increasing . . . the class of persons thus emigrating are in

appearance and worldly circumstances above the ordinary men of steerage passengers. The bulk of them are from the Midland Counties—farmers and farmers' servants, with their wives and families. Upward of five thousand have already emigrated, and an equal number will probably leave before Christmas.

'These people', concluded the paper, 'possess at least an average share of intelligence.' At first this was not so. Indeed five years previously on 14 September 1837 Orson Hyde described those he had baptized as 'mainly manufacturers and other mechanics. They know how to do but little else than spin and weave cloth, and make cambric, mull and lace; and what they would do in Kirtland or the City of the Far West, I cannot say. They are extremely poor, most of them not having a change of clothes decent to be baptised in.'[1] Their departure disturbed many, like the Rev. Thomas Dent of Billington, near Whalley, who gave Henry Caswall material with which to publish *The Prophet of the Nineteenth Century, or, The Rise, Progress and Present State of the Mormons or Latter Day Saints* (1843).[2] Elder Amos Fielding's brother, a Nonconformist minister who had loaned his pulpit to the Mormons at Preston was typical of many of his kind who found that they were losing congregations to a church with a theology even more materialistic than theirs. Amos Fielding, with Reuben Hedlock, successfully managed the emigration until February 1846, dispatching 1,000 people to Zion.

Among the earliest English recruits to the Church of the Latter Day Saints was William Clayton, the personal secretary to Brigham Young.

(3)

After Joseph Smith was murdered in 1844, some of his followers expected him to rise from the dead and ride through the air on a white horse at the head of a heavenly host. Others, more practical, elected Brigham Young—now back in America —as his successor.

> Brigham Young, the Lord's anointed,
> Loved of Heav'n and fear'd of hell;
> Like Elijah's on Elisha,
> Joseph's mantle on him fell.

[1] Linn, op. cit., 256.
[2] Henry Caswall (1810–70), returned to England in 1842 and ultimately became a vicar in Wiltshire.

Secessions and quarrels within and without led Brigham Young to organize an exodus to the West. Like the Voortrekkers of South Africa, the Mormons struck out. The first long column of wagons crossed the Mississippi on 15 February 1846. Over prairies and mountains they went, travelling for seventeen months, till they found a new Jordan issuing from a mountain lake and losing itself in the salt waters of a Dead Sea. Brigham Young christened it Deseret, the land of the Honey Bee. In this tremendous operation the spirits of some 12,000 Saints were sustained by an English brass band, recruited by a missionary in England.

In less than a year after occupying Deseret, the Mormons built an adobe town of 5,000 inhabitants. Each communal holding was irrigated by canals and lakes. The town they called Salt Lake City and the surrounding desert of Deseret was formally renamed the State of Utah in 1850.

Others followed them, not for paradise but for gold. The 35,000 pilgrims on the Oregon trail in 1849, and the 55,000 who rushed to the goldfields in California in 1850 helped to build up Salt Lake City still further as a transport terminal. They also drew the eyes of Englishmen to the West.

In England, the news of the founding of Salt Lake City stimulated a fresh call for recruits. On 23 December 1847 a trumpet-tongued proclamation was issued 'To the Saints in England, Scotland, Ireland and Wales and adjacent islands and countries'. It ran :–

> Emigrate as speedily as possible to this vicinity, looking to and following the counsel of the Presidency at Liverpool; shipping to New Orleans, and from thence direct to Council Bluffs, which will save much expense. Those who have but little means and little or no labour, will soon exhaust that means if they remain where they are, therefore, it is wisdom that they remove without delay; for here is land on which, by their labour, they can speedily better their condition for their further journey.

It coincided with all the propaganda of Feargus O'Connor for Land Colonies, with the Chartist troubles, and the Utopist schemes outlined in the foregoing chapters. A writer in the *New York Tribune*, who dated his article 8 July 1849, observed, 'At first I thought it was an experimental order of things established purposely to carry out the principles of Socialism or Mormonism.'

To the bleakly comforted readers of the *Millennial Star* and the *Uidgorn Seion* [1] (its Welsh counterpart—published in Merthyr Tydfil) Elder Orson Spencer offered a tantalizing picture of 'The resting place of Israel for the last days . . . beautiful for situation and the ultimate joy of the whole earth is the state of Zion established in the mountains', all the more beautiful for being cheap. On 1 February 1848 he asked presidents of conferences to forward estimates of the number of people who would be ready to emigrate within eight to twenty-two days. For an advance of £1 and £6 on embarkation (children half price), the faithful could obtain passage to St. Louis, and for another £4 to Council Bluffs. Nearly 120 people hastened to answer, and in less than a fortnight the *Carnatic* carried with them the returning missionaries to St. Louis.

(4)

With his experience of England, Brigham Young realized that it was potentially his richest recruiting ground. The virtual collapse of Chartism in 1848 coincided with the dispatch of his right hand Elder Orson Pratt to England to organize the emigration. Pratt was one of the Twelve Apostles—the inner cabinet of Deseret. He too had been to England before and had stood close to Brigham Young in his hours of trial before he succeeded Joseph Smith, travelling with him on the great Hegira to Salt Lake City. Before Pratt's iron tongue, even the Gentiles quailed. 'He has', wrote one Englishman, 'thrust thought into a faith of ceremony which is supposed to dispense with the trouble of thinking, and has intruded human learning into a scheme whose essence is the utter abrogation of the individual will.' [2] This was the man who now preached the new Zion of the West to disillusioned Chartists. Little wonder he was able to dispatch 5,369 converts in little over two and a half years. True, he was helped by the Perpetual Emigration Fund to which all Saints contributed.

For as little as £10, emigrants could go to Council Bluffs. From there they could work their way across country. But he did not throw money away: 'Let the Saints', he wrote, 'go with expectation of helping themselves, without throwing a heavier

---

[1] 'Mormonism in Wales', *The Spectator*, XXXVI (1863), 2142.
[2] M. R. Werner, *Brigham Young* (1925).

burden upon the American brethren. After arriving at the Bluffs, diligence and patience will, within a few years, enable you to perform the balance of the journey.' And at Council Bluffs there were three more of the twelve apostles O. Hyde, G. A. Smith and E. T. Benson, to help them do so.

This Smilesean project was abandoned by Pratt's successor, Elder Franklin D. Richards, for more ingenious schemes via Panama or around Cape Horn. This was as expensive as the Council Bluffs project had been cheap. So in 1852 only 251 emigrants got away, and then only to Council Bluffs, with the help of £1,000 given by the Perpetual Emigration Fund. But the numbers of would-be emigrants continued to beseige the Saints at Liverpool: 'Elder Richards was frequently asked to organize companies who would walk the entire overland journey, and assist to haul the provisions and luggage also'; whilst Brigham Young was constrained to issue a seventh general epistle to console them: 'Doubt no longer, but come next year to the place of gathering, even in flocks as doves fly to their windows before a storm.'

A steady homing call was intoned by the *Millennial Star*: 'Every particle of our means which we use in Babylon is a loss to ourselves . . . Every Saint who does not come *home* will be afflicted by the Devil.' And so 2,312 British subjects left Liverpool in 1853 helped by the Emigration Fund. Even the Irvingites were impressed.[1] To help subsequent emigrants a magnificent folio was published in England in 1855 entitled *The Route from Liverpool to Salt Lake City*, with engravings and a fine text. This, the pamphlet literature, numerous meetings, and a constant exhortation of missioners, kept the human tide flowing through the Mersey.[2]

This tide was clean and sweet, unlike other privately organized emigrations of the day. This the House of Commons acknowledged.[3] Charles Dickens himself sketched a picture of it in Chapter 12 of *The Uncommercial Traveller*. Unfortunately, once it reached America it mixed with the great swell of the

[1] *Millennial Star*, XIV (1852), 20; 201, 210; XV (1853), 260, and 439 for figures of the P.E.F.

[2] F. Piercy and James Linforth, *Route from Liverpool to Great Salt Lake Valley* (Liverpool, 1855), subsequently withdrawn from circulation.

[3] *Second Report from the Select Committee on Emigrant Ships*, XIII (1854), 109.

gold rush. This created a problem, for wagons became so costly as to be virtually unobtainable. Even the Perpetual Emigration Fund broke down under the bad harvests of 1855 when the Church was short of money.

So began the epic utilization of handcarts—pushed from Council Bluffs to Salt Lake City. It took some justifying, to English ears, and Brigham Young tried to do so: 'The money usually spent in England for extra clothing and unnecessary "fiddle-faddles"—for extra freight on the same, and for hauling this across the plains, can all be saved', he wrote to Liverpool, 'and most assuredly may be more profitably used on the arrival of the Saints here.' A song was composed for the occasion:

> Hurrah for the Camp of Israel!
> Hurrah for the hand-cart scheme!
> Hurrah! Hurrah! 'tis better far
> Than the wagon and ox-team.

1,300 men, women, and children left Liverpool in the summer of 1856 for winter quarters at Council Bluffs. There they split into five companies. The first travelled safely to Utah, but the last did not. Winter caught them in the mountains. Sixty-seven of one group of 400 died and survivors took a long time to recover. Most of the cattle were lost. Such appalling loss of life led to the scheme being called off and 'prairie schooners' obtained once more.

The high-water-mark of the Saints' influence in England was the great conference of Elders held in London on 1 September 1857. And though they continued these demonstrations up to the end of the century, the first flush of their success faded. The Civil War of 1861–5 and the subsequent alarm occasioned by controversy over polygamy, together with the increasing 'establishment-mindedness' of the Mormon Church was to change its appeal. By 1879 thirteen of the twenty-one Mormon Bishops in Salt Lake itself were British born.[1]

(5)

These pilgrims to paradise came from areas where Owenism and Chartism had made great strides. John Finch, from Liverpool, had visited the Saints in 1847 to lecture on 'English

[1] Cannon, op. cit., 908.

Socialism'. Five years later one of the Saints in England remarked that they had accomplished what the French communists had aimed at but failed to do.[1] Their organization was, as another Englishman remarked, 'Owenism Personified',[2] and the community aspect of this was later to be embodied at Orderville in Utah.[3] Nonconformists thundered against them. Their impact on the Potteries was deplored. Jabez Bunting condemned them as 'from first to last, a singular scheme of social life, originating in imposture, managed by the cunning of politicians pretending to be priests, and carried on by a plan of proselytism to a professedly religious system'. W.B.F., initials covering 'a clergyman', lamented that by harping on the joys of Zion the Mormons induced a 'longing' in hearers 'to leave their English homes'.[4]

Other Englishmen experienced Zion and recanted. Henry Caswall was told that Joseph Smith was the Joseph raised up to deliver Englishmen from bondage. According to Caswall, the first missionaries had 500 converts at Preston in 1837, and in villages on the Ribble had converted 'several Methodist and Baptist preachers'. Caswall returned to England in 1842, and became a Wiltshire vicar, writing other denunciations of 'The Light that Failed' in the manner of a twentieth-century convert from communism.[5] John Hyde, unconvinced by or ignorant of Caswall's work, joined the Mormon Church in 1849 and went to Salt Lake City. He, too, returned disillusioned, to lecture and preach against them, and ended up by joining the Swedenborgian Church of whose Conference he three times became President.[6]

Watching the Mormon ferries lying at anchor in the Mersey, Dr. Conybeare, the perceptive intelligent Principal of the newly founded Liverpool Collegiate School, sadly agreed that the

---

[1] *Millennial Star*, XV (1853), 389.

[2] Anon, *The Mormons or Latter Day Saints* (London, 1851), 251.

[3] L. J. Arrington, *Orderville, Utah: A Pioneer Mormon Experiment in Economic Organization* (Utah, 1954).

[4] Jabez Bunting, *Mormonism: its origin and character* (1853). W. B. F., *The Mormons, The Dream and the Reality*, ed. by a clergyman (1857).

[5] Henry Caswall, *The Prophet of the Nineteenth Century, or, the Rise, Progress and Present State of the Mormons or Latter Day Saints* (London, 1843).

[6] John Hyde published *Mormonism, its Leaders and Designs* (1857), and *Swedenborg, the Man of the Age* (1859).

See for instance John Lyon, *The Harp of Zion* (Liverpool, 1853).

Eliza R. Snow, *Poems* (Liverpool, 1856).

materialist theology of 'the extreme section of popular protestantism', the confusion of Mosaic ordinances with Christian
Laws and the meaningless repetition of verbal shibboleths from
the Old Testament had done the Mormon's work for them
before they actually came. Not even more education would
protect them from Mormon evangelists, he mused, for 'two-
thirds of the converts' had 'gained all they could by that'.
Conybeare also pointed to the Mormon insistence on 'the
speedy coming of the Saviour, and his personal millennial reign,
and the attractiveness to many minds of the idea of an infallible
church, relying for its evidences and its guidance upon revelations made perpetually to its rulers'. Millenarianism was, in his
words, one reason why the Saints had obtained 'a position and
importance with the working classes, which, perhaps, should
draw to it much more than it has yet received of the attention of
our public teachers'.[1]

William Hepworth Dixon, a traveller and historian of distinction, agreed: 'These notes of the faith as it is held in Salt
Lake City—as it is taught in our own midst—in the Welsh
mountains, in the Midland Shires, among the Mersey dockmen,
in the Whitechapel slums—mystical though they read in the
main, exert a mighty spell over the imagination and almighty
power upon the actual life of their people.'[2]

Of the 76,335 Saints in Utah in 1861 (a generous figure it
must be admitted, since it came from their own census) by far
the largest proportion were English, and the second Scottish,
with Canadians, Danes, Swedes, Norwegians, Germans, Swiss,
Poles, Russians, Italians and French following behind.[3] By 1887
out of the 82,220 European migrants to the Mormon settlements, 43,356 were from Britain.[4]

What did these Englishmen give to Utah beyond the sweat of
their brows? They gave Brigham Young his secretary, William
Clayton, as well as his 'best' wife. They provided the Saints
with their greatest hymn writer, Adam Craik Smith, author of
'Jesus Bids me Shine', 'Beautiful Mountain Homes', 'Hail
Bright Millennial Day', 'Zion Stands with Hills Surrounded'.
G. D. Pyker has computed that a third of the Mormon com-

[1] *Edinburgh Review*, CCII (April 1854), 110.
[2] W. H. Dixon, *New America* (8th edition, 1868), 163.
[3] Jules Rémy, *A Journey to Great Salt Lake City* (London, 1861), 223.
[4] M. H. Cannon, *American Historical Review*, LVII (1951–2), 893.

posers were British. The ecstasy of Zion stimulated many of them to compositions which have made the Mormons one of the great singing sects of the world. To this very day the Mormon choirs can recapture the massed thrills of the great Exodus and the glory of the sight of Zion. English converts gave the Saints what they could because the Saints gave them, whoever they were, an office in the Church. One in every five participated in their form of government. For, as that shrewd Liverpool head-master, Dr. Conybeare observed:

> It is humiliating to confess that this fanatical superstition has made more converts in England than in all the world beside; yet the instrumentality by which they have been gained also contained matter of encouragement. The principle of organisation which has been so powerful a course of error might do good service to the cause of truth.

That 'principle of organisation' was full participation in a community life. That is why one of their most popular hymns 'Come, Come, ye Saints', was composed by an Englishman—William Clayton.

(6)

The Mormons had baptized nearly 100,000 people in Britain by 1870.[1] Though growing perceptively fainter, apocalyptic noises other than theirs were still heard in Britain in the '70s and '80s. One of them, at least, had Owenite links. A great recruiting campaign for the American Shaker Settlements, so attractive to early Owenites, was inaugurated on Sunday evening, 6 August 1871, at St. George's Hall, London. In the chair was William Hepworth Dixon, an avid reporter of community experiments, who claimed to be 'perhaps the only Englishman in the assembly who had actually slept under a Shaker roof and seen with his own eyes that beautiful Eden which the order had created'.

The leading speaker at this meeting was also an Englishman, F. W. Evans. Born in Worcester of army stock, his formal education had ended at the age of 8. Sailing to the United States at an early age he had settled in New York (where two of his uncles already lived) and was apprenticed to a hatter. There he

---

[1] M. H. Cannon gives 96,214 baptisms up to 1869 and 126,593 up to 1937. He disagrees with figures given by R. L. Evans, *A Century of 'Mormonism' in Great Britain* (Salt Lake City, 1937), as being too optimistic.

became an Owenite and walked 800 miles to Massillon, Ohio, to join a community. He stayed till it broke up, then returned in 1829 to England. But soon he was in America again, with a group of freethinkers associated with Frances Wright, Robert Dale Owen and Robert L. Jennings. He also helped his brother, George Henry Evans, to edit and publish successively the *Working Man's Advocate*, the *Daily Sentinel* and *Young America*. Amongst other radical publications they published the *Bible of Reason*. And in the course of this he visited the Shaker community at Mount Lebanon, New York. Here to the amazement of his radical friends he was converted, and remained there for the next sixty-three years of his life, for fifty-seven years of which he was an elder.

Evans, in a vigorous apostolate, stumped Britain. The Spiritualists had had him to themselves on 23 July, and in the weeks following he toured the north. He spoke at Bradford on 13 August and Bishop Auckland the day after. On 15 August he was at Worcester, going on to Birmingham, Manchester and Liverpool. He set sail to America on 24 August 1871 with I. M. Peebles and a party of converts.

Behind him in England he left a recruiting agency: the Progressive Literary and Spiritual Institution, 15 Southampton Road, London, W.C., together with the opinion that 'there are many people in England prepared to enter the Order, and a revival of spiritual life is all that is necessary to inaugurate Shaker Communism on British soil. From the great number of inquiries being made, and the tone of the audiences addressed, it would appear that the time has already arrived.'[1] He returned again seventeen years later for a fresh draft. The Shaker system, which had so intrigued the socialists at the beginning of the century, continued to interest them at its close, and in 1898 the *Labour Annual*, published at Manchester, could report 'several from England have joined the Shakers at Mount Lebanon'.

(7)

Matthew Arnold was once moved to exclaim 'To popular religion the real Kingdom of God is the New Jerusalem with its jaspers and emeralds; righteousness and peace and joy are only

---

[1] *Report of a meeting at St. George's Hall, London* . . . (1871); *Labour Annual* (1898).

the Kingdom of God figuratively.'[1] Even as he wrote an American commercial traveller, C. T. Russell, became convinced that Jesus would return in invisible form in the autumn of 1874. Russell's pamphlet, *The Object and Manner of Our Lord's Return*, sparked off a millenarian movement that lasts to this day: Jehovah's Witnesses.[2] In 1879, as pastor of an independent church in Pittsburg, Russell issued a magazine called *The Watchtower and Herald of Christ's Presence*.

A year later, in 1880, he sent J. C. Sunderlin to England to organize the Watchtower movement. Sunderlin taught that Russell's followers were the nucleus of the Kingdom that would be established after the second advent. The Kingdom would be announced by the return of the prophets and its imminence was expected daily. As 'witness' to God's imminent return, they took the name of 'Jehovah's Witnesses' and, acting on Exodus xx, 4–5, refused to salute the flag or undertake political duties. From being the fag-end of the nineteenth-century sects they have become one of the better known of the proletarian millennial movements of the twentieth. But compared to others they are a passive, if hopeful group, epitomized in the words of the *Watchtower*—the semi-monthly they issue throughout the world—for September 1896: 'The strongest of all ideas is the idea that it is in the hands of men to accelerate or retard the accomplishment of God's great and glorious designs. To hurry God's movements; what comment is adequate to such towering pride.'[3] Like the Mormons they exist to this day.

---

[1] *St. Paul and Protestantism* (1875), 90.

[2] Millennial Dawnism was the name by which his creed was known to W. G. Moorhead of New York, James Grey of Chicago and B. H. Shadduck of Philadelphia, who published studies of it in 1891, 1920 and 1928 respectively.

[3] H. H. Stroup, *The Jehovah's Witnesses* (New York, 1945).

8

❖◇❖◇❖◇❖◇❖◇❖◇❖◇❖◇❖◇❖◇❖◇❖◇❖◇❖◇❖◇❖◇❖◇❖◇❖◇❖

Esoteric Communities in
Victorian England

❖◇❖◇❖◇❖◇❖◇❖◇❖◇❖◇❖◇❖◇❖◇❖◇❖◇❖◇❖◇❖◇❖◇❖◇❖◇❖

As the Mormons reaped their harvests of souls, some glean-
ings were being made by native charismatics in London,
Somerset and Yorkshire. As their argosies of converts left for
Utah, Robert Owen organized a public meeting for 14 May
1855 to celebrate the commencement of the millennium. Two
months later he published the *Millennium in Practice, being the
Report of the Adjourned Public Meeting of the World's Convention,
July 30, 1855.* On 14 May 1856 he held a congress 'of the
reformers of the world', and in the same year he began to publish the last of his many newspapers, entitled *Millennial
Gazette: Explanatory of the Principles and Practices by which, in
Peace, with Truth, Honesty and Simplicity, the New Existence of
Man upon the Earth may be easily and speedily commenced.* In 1858,
the year of his death, yet another meeting was convened 'to
consider the best means immediately to commence practical
measures to New Form Man and New Form Society'.[1]

(1)

But to the new generation the challenge to 'New Form Man'
and to 'New Form Society' had more exotic overtures. Owen's
own language indeed might have been used by another pro-
claimer of a new dispensation: Henry Prince.

[1] F. Podmore, *Life of Robert Owen* (1905).

To adherents of the old dispensation, Prince said, salvation of the soul alone was possible, but to adherents of the new, salvation of the body could be enjoyed as well. He had founded a community whose members on entering could sin no more, since their flesh was no longer mortal or sinful.

The 'Beloved', as Prince had called himself, celebrated 'the marriage supper of the Lamb'. On milk, honey and fruit, bread and wine, he and his followers lived 'like the angels in heaven, neither marrying nor giving in marriage'. No 'devil's love' defiled them. In 1849 under his direction sixty persons had gathered at Spaxton, five miles west of Bridgwater, to found the Agapemone, or the Abode of Love. Two years later the general public were regaled by Prince's visit to the Great Exhibition in a carriage with postillions in scarlet coats and outriders. Other demonstrations were the publication of *The Little Book Open* (1856–9)—his 'Testimony concerning what Jesus Christ has done by His Spirit to Redeem the Earth', *The Testimony of the Two Anointed Ones that stand by the Lord of the Whole Earth* (1856–9), and *Brother Prince's Journal, or An Account of the destruction of the works of the Devil in the Human Soul* (1859).

Before his days as a community founder, Prince had been a medical student. Deprived by illness from continuing his studies, he came under the influence of a middle-aged spinster of Catholic views. He trained for the ministry at St. David's, Lampeter, where, amongst some fellow students known as the Lampeter Brethren, he read the Song of Solomon, fasted and prayed. Increasingly preoccupied by the importance of redemption and grace, he married his elderly Catholic spinster friend, and in 1840 went out to minister at the parish church of Charlinch in Somerset. His wife died not long after.

At Charlinch Prince electrified his rustic congregations. Services were extended from Sundays to weekdays. The absentee vicar whom he had served as a curate, the Rev. Samuel Starky, was moved to return and assist him. The Bishop intervened. Prince was deprived in 1842 and replaced by one of his Lampeter friends, George Thomas. Thomas proving no milder, he too was deprived, this time with the vicar. Luckily, however, Thomas got a wealthy civil engineer, William Cobbe, to endow him an independent chapel at Spaxton. Prince having meanwhile migrated to a curacy at Halstead, Essex, married the sister of his former vicar Samuel Starky, had again been deprived, this time by the Bishop of Ely, and again been succeeded by a friend from Lampeter—this time Lewis Price. Prince then went to Brighton, where he began to minister in the 'Adullam Chapel' in Windsor Street. This time three of his Suffolk congregation followed him: Harriet, Agnes and Clara Nottidge, daughters of a wealthy paper manufacturer. He moved again, this time to Belfield Terrace, Weymouth, in 1845, where he was joined by his brother-in-law, the Rev. Samuel Starky. They preached on the coming of the Holy Ghost, and established an Abode of Love. It was aptly named, for Harriet Nottidge married Lewis Price, Agnes Nottidge married George Thomas, whilst the third, Clara, married the wealthy civil engineer, William Cobbe. With the resources of the Nottidges (some £6,000 each) and Cobbe (who had already built the church at Spaxton), land was purchased at Spaxton and buildings erected. So was established in 1849 'the Community of the Son of Man', or, as it was known generally, the Agapemone.[1]

(2)

While the Agapemone flourished in Somerset, another millenarian community was taking root in Wakefield. It was inaugurated on Whit Sunday, 1857, when 200 people, clothed in white robes, marched in procession to dedicate a home for Shiloh—the messiah. They marched in the grounds of a newly-built house three miles outside Wakefield. At their head was their 75-year-old leader dressed in a long brown coat, with a long beard, a thick thatch of hair, on which was a low-crowned hat. His name was John Wroe.

A lot of the money for this house came from the accumulated funds of the followers of Joanna Southcott: collected especially for the purpose of publishing the eternal gospel forty years after Joanna's death. And, since Joanna had died in 1814, Wroe did not have much difficulty in persuading her followers in 1854

---

[1] W. H. Dixon, *Spiritual Wives* (1868), *Newbury House Magazine*, November 1891; E. Miller, *History of Irvingism*; *Reports of Cases*, iii. 758–81; *Illustrated London News*, 29 March 1851; 'View of Agapemone', 28 July 1860, 81; 28 August 1866, 173; *Daily Telegraph*, 10 January 1899, 7; A recent fictional account has been given by Aubrey Menen in *The Abode of Love* (1957).

(forty years later) that this was the time to invest their capital. So they invested some £2,000 in the Melbourne House funds, hoping that it would house the Shiloh. Their faith was reinforced by the examples of many followers up and down the country. They sent so many postal orders to John Wroe in the subsequent two years that it was said at the time that Wroe did more business with the post office than all the tradesmen of Wakefield put together.

The building was the result of a dream which Wroe had had in 1853. In this dream, Wroe said, the Lord had commanded him to build a mansion. So he had bought 100 acres of high ground outside Wakefield on the Bradford Road, and begun to build a house dedicated to the Lord: one which was to belong to all members of the House of Israel, representatives of whom were among the 200 white-robed persons. The house was built as the Spirit directed, and no architect was at first employed. And a very good house it proved to be too. It was a large square stone structure with a fine staircase made of wood specially imported from Australia, reception rooms hung with tapestries, walled grounds and a lodge at the entrance. In the stables rested a fine four-wheeled carriage with silver-plated harness to take John Wroe when he wanted to ride abroad.

Wroe, as opposed to Prince, was a near illiterate. He had joined the Southcottians at Leeds in 1820. He delivered a message to the Queen Caroline in London on 30 August of the same year, and two years later claimed the succession as their Leader. As such he had settled in Ashton, where he was publicly circumcized on 17 April 1824. He let his beard grow (his followers were known as 'the beardies') and began to travel (Gibraltar, Spain, France, Germany and Italy in 1823, Scotland in 1827 and Wales in 1828), using Ashton as a home base. There a sanctuary was opened in Church Street on Christmas Day 1825. There was a vigorous reaction against him, which expressed itself in accusations of sexual misconduct, and in 1830 he left.

Evicted by his scandalized Ashton followers on 27 February 1831, he began a life of energetic travel and propaganda. He had covered America in 1840, 1848 and 1853, and Australia in 1850 and 1854. In Australia he won such success that his followers were recognized, and nicknamed 'beardies'. They called themselves Israelites, or Christian Israelites. Australian support, in fact, had made it possible for Wroe to build his great house near Wakefield. In recognition of that support, Wroe modelled it on the Melbourne Town Hall and called it 'Melbourne House'. When Wroe saw how the money was pouring in from the rest of his followers (some £9,000 in all), he had the north-east wing taken down and enlarged the building.

The hopes of the Southcottites, and the 'Christian Israelites' (as Wroe's followers were called), were not fulfilled. For Wroe, instead of making the Melbourne House estate over to the society, as he promised to do, left it all, when he died in 1864, to his grandson. And when he died, aptly enough, at Fitzroy in Australia, his Australian followers were most angry, for he had promised them he would never die. They asked for their subscriptions back, and manhandled Benjamin Eddow (Wroe's secretary) so severely that he was forced to hide until he could get a ship back to England. Eddow returned a further £700 to keep a room in Melbourne House, Wakefield, warmed and prepared in case John Wroe should come as the Shiloh.

He never did. But it is not without interest that an American called Daniel Milton did—claiming he was the rightful Shiloh. And it took James Wroe, the grandson, all his time to get this particular impostor convicted of trespass.[1]

(3)

Minter Morgan's old ally W. F. Cowper, patronized an even more exotic group formed by an American, Thomas Lake Harris. 'No one I think ever attracted William more', said Mrs. Cowper. 'He particularly interested us by his belief that the Kingdom of Christ was soon to be set up on the earth, and that we might all help in its unfolding.'[2] After Cowper inherited Broadlands from his stepfather, Lord Palmerston, and became W. F. Cowper-Temple, he and his wife began to hold meetings there, where 'something akin to the spirit of the meeting on the day of Pentecost' was experienced by those present. The Broad-

[1] *An Abridgment of John Wroe's Life and Travels* (Gravesend, 1859–61); *The Life and Journal of John Wroe* (Gravesend, 1859–61); Davis, *The Wroeites' Faith* (1850); Glover & Andrews, *History of Ashton-under-Lyne* (1886); S. Baring-Gould, *Yorkshire Oddities* (1874), i. 23–25; Lupton, *Wakefield Worthies* (1864), 219–25, 255.

[2] Cowper-Temple, *Memorials of Wm. Cowper-Temple* (printed for Private Circulation, 1890), 108.

lands conferences attracted such figures as James Hinton, George Body, Lord Radstock, Boyd Carpenter, Lord Chichester and Pearsall Smith.

Harris also attracted those who had once trod the path to Salt Lake City, then recanted and returned to England, like John Hyde. When Harris arrived in England, Hyde had become a Swedenborgian and published a book entitled *Swedenborg, The Man and the Age*. Another of Harris's converts once interested in Mormonism was E. Brotherton, a silk merchant of Manchester. The latter, with James Garth Wilkinson issued a periodical called *The Dawn*. All three rallied to support Harris on his arrival in England in 1859.

He was no novice in matters concerning revelation, for previously, in the Mohawk Valley and New York City, he had drifted into spiritualism under the influence of Andrew Jackson Davis. He had been a member of a psychical community at Mountain Cove, Virginia, and when this broke up in 1853 he had organized a congregation in New York City known as the First Independent Christian Society. His belief in Christian Spiritualism and the doctrines of Swedenborg are explicable, for Swedenborgism was the gospel for American social reformers of every colour, from the anti-slavery crusaders to the German communitarians of Ohio and Iowa: colonies like Yellow Springs and Cincinatti in Ohio, and Jasper in Iowa were virtually communistic settlements.

In Manchester Harris drew audiences of from 400–500 over the twelve weeks. Beginning in October 1859 he gave three lectures a week in the evenings at the Athenaeum and spoke every Sunday at the Mechanics' Institute. Success enhanced his vision of apocalypse. 'England', he wrote back to the *Herald of Light*, the American Swedenborgian journal (IV. 117–18), 'requires truth stripped bare, requires God's word unfolded, not alone in its mere moralism, but in its spiritual sciences and social truths. England requires to be convinced that no legal precedent, though of a thousand years' standing, can convert a wrong into a right.' He converted J. C. Walters, later editor of the *Manchester City News* and went to London. Here, at the Marylebone Institute, he delivered twelve lectures during February and March 1860. These were subsequently published as *The Millennial Age*: a striking castigation of the divorce of the intellect from the heart. 'Its splendid rewards', he wrote, 'practically demonstrate that greatness, in its popular acceptation, may be won without goodness, and that the understanding towers up towards the Heavens while the feet take hold on Hell.'

Harris then gathered up a group of followers in Scotland, which he called the Brotherhood of the New Life. Shocked by the economic problems in England, he turned from the idea of founding a new church (as a 'pivotal man') and began to think of founding a community. As he wrote, 'A solemn conviction rests upon us, that the Lord has forever removed us from any special relation to the Swedenborgian sect. For three years, incessantly, we have laboured to promote, by personal appeals to its members, evangelical holiness. Our special work in this direction is done. Henceforth we turn to the Gentiles'; and again, 'The Archetypal American Commonwealth is placed in the centre of the new Heaven, because it is the will of Almighty God that the pivotal power of the earth shall descend through it. There will arrive on earth a Society called the Brotherhood of the New Life . . . in Christian and pagan nations, among Jews and Gentiles, both bond and free.'

Through Cowper-Temple, Harris made his most spectacular convert: Laurence Oliphant,[1] a wealthy intelligent member of the House of Commons, who abandoned his career to put his fortune at the absolute disposal of Harris. And Harris showed how absolute this disposal was by establishing a community at Brocton, on the shores of Lake Erie, where amongst the seventy-five members, Oliphant was set to work on the farm. He drove horses, laboured, and 'cadged strawberries by the railway'. To discipline him, Harris made him draw water at night 'till his fingers were almost frost bitten'. And when his mother had joined him, he was forbidden to communicate with her.

Still under Harris's orders, Oliphant returned to Europe in 1870 to resume his former occupation as a *Times* correspondent in the Franco-Prussian war; but a bullet, grazing the hair of his head, sent him back to Harris. Harris ordered him to return to Paris, which he did in 1871, where his mother joined him. There

---

[1] H. L. Schneider and George Lawton, *A Prophet and a Pilgrim* (Columbia, 1942).

he met Alice le Strange, a girl of property and charm. He was married from the Cowper-Temples' house in Curzon Street. But because of Harris it is doubtful whether the marriage was ever consummated.

Again on Harris's instructions, Oliphant, his wife and mother returned to Brocton in 1873. This time the wife and mother were employed in menial tasks and Oliphant was ordered to become the bread-winner of the community. He went to England, Canada and New York. He joined the Board of the 'Direct United States Cable Company' and obtained such insights into the world of high finance as practised in his day that he published an article in *Blackwood's Magazine* for 1876 called 'The auto-biography of a Joint-Stock Company'.

In 1875, the community was moved to the other end of the country—to Santa Rosa, California. Harris began with four disciples and called the rest over in 1881. Santa Rosa became the settlement for those who had been purified and who had obtained the power of breathing in Divine commands. Here a most pleasant prospect awaited them. Seven hundred acres (later expanded to 1,700) were given over to dairy farming and later to vineyards, communal crafts, a communal hotel and coffee shop—everything that would conduce to unselfish work was practised. There was a press, run by Arai, a Japanese whom Harris brought over from Brocton.

'Aestivossa', his own house, with stained-glass windows and equipped with every luxury, housed him, his wife, Oliphant's wife and some others. The rest of the community lived in two other houses on the other side of the wood. The farm stood a quarter of a mile away. This opulence was financed, not only by Laurence Oliphant, but also by sympathizers like the Cowper-Temple and Ruxton families in England. Set amongst the lawns and ponds was a communal dining-room where in the evening the community would gather, in the light of gas pumped from gasoline.

Here they heard light verse by Harris, danced quadrilles, and sang—usually hymns of Harris's own composition, like :–

> If you would stay the Social Snake,
> That brings the bosom grief and ache,
> Dance while you may, dance while you may,
> For Heaven comes forth in social play.

Here he evoked 'electro-vital form' on his piano, for early in his apostolate an angel had commanded him: 'Sing of love, dear brother . . . sing of conjugial love . . . Be the poet of Maidens and Lovers and the Conjugial consorts. Make thy poetic house a garden of Eden.' 'Conjugial love' to Harris (who lost his first wife in 1850 and had married again five years later) was only to be attained through the Divine Breath with a 'counterpart' (which existed in heaven) enabled to inhabit earthly forms. Counterparts would not necessarily be the earthly partner, but this union of counterparts was a mystical experience. So he refused Oliphant permission to see his wife. This was a great blow to Oliphant when he came to San Francisco in 1878. As a result Mrs. Oliphant left Fountain Grove and began to teach in Vallego and the Benicia. Oliphant took up the colonization of Palestine by Jews and tried unsuccessfully to obtain concessions from the Turkish government. He bought out Harris from Brocton and left his mother to look after his interests.

In 1881 his wife joined him and they returned to Brocton, where his mother was ill and troubled. Oliphant went to Fountain Grove where he saw a ring of his mother's on the hand of one of the inmates. Astonished, he returned to Brocton and removed his mother (who died soon after). For the rest of his days he spent his time promoting the colonization of Palestine, and collecting a kind of community at Haifa on the Brocton model. Indeed a number of visitors from Brocton, as well as some native Jewish immigrants, regarded him as their head. As if to show his real dedication to the communitarian tradition, Oliphant, after the death of his wife returned to America where he married Rosamond Dale Owen, the granddaughter of the great Robert Owen. Could a circle close more fittingly?

The millenarian expectations kindled by Harris in England survived his jettisoning of Swedenborgian orthodoxy. The Cowper-Temples (as they were now called) still kept in touch with the Oliphants, and an English family called Ruxton helped finance the community. Another member, A. A. Cuthbert, who returned from Fountain Grove in 1885, organized a 'Department of Great Britain of the Brotherhood of the New Life'. Its members included Dr. C. M. Berridge, a Theosophist; C. W. Pearce of Glasgow; William Robson of Manchester and T. W.

Swainson. Cuthbert was to republish Harris's books to prepare Britons for the 'vortex' into which their country was destined to fall, and assiduously circulated the 'hymns to divine Socialism'. Sending a copy to Frank Smith of the Salvation Army and later founder of the Labour Army on 21 October 1891, he hoped 'that you will endeavour to prevail upon the circles of workers who are especially influenced by you to adopt them for singing at their gatherings'. T. W. Swainson later joined the Brotherhood Church and tried to persuade them that Harris was a pioneer Theosocialist.[1]

Though Harris approved of the efforts of Utopian Socialists to reconstruct society, he claimed that he alone could give the new religion needed by a new social system. To that new religion he gave the name Theo-Socialism, insisting that it was not a new cult, nor an endorsement of any existing creed. It grew from his experiences as a young Swedenborgian minister in Glasgow, later in London and Manchester, and he was well aware of its implications. It was not communistic, nor was it materialistic. For Owenism, Harris wrote:

> Notwithstanding the merits of its distinguished founder, I also entertain only a partial sympathy . . . I recognise an immense truth and good in many of the features of these working communities . . . (but) as the world goes, we are not communists; we follow neither the celibate idea, nor the perfectionist ideal, nor the red republic banner. I recognise no right in the natural man to share my goods . . . and by the natural man I mean any man whose natural passion is the rule of self.[2]

(4)

A Maecenas of millenarians, Cowper-Temple sustained an interest in community experiments. Two years after he made the historic amendment to the 1870 Education Act, that no denominational religious instruction was to be given in the new board schools established by that Act, he was extending a

---

[1] *The Labour Annual* (1897), 100, indicates that he was still secretary of the Brotherhood of the New Life by then.

[2] T. L. Harris, *The New Republic* (1891). His busy pen also produced *Hymns of Spiritual Devotion* (1861), *The Arcana of Christianity* (1858–78), *The Lord Two-in-one, Declared, Manifested, and Glorified* (1876), *The Wisdom of the Adepts* (1884) and *Star-Flowers* (1887).

protective hand over Mary Ann Girling, a 45-year-old charismatic.

Born as Miss Cloutery, she had married an ironfounder and machine fitter in Ipswich and had two children. One Christmas time she was alleged to have received the stigmata in the hands, feet, and side, and experienced the divine call. Subsequently she had travelled the eastern counties proclaiming the New Revelation and speaking, as with absolute knowledge, of hidden mysteries. Her following grew, and she was invited to London to conduct a revival. Here she preached the brotherhood of man and proclaimed a New Dispensation. When chapel doors were shut against her, she started an independent mission at Battersea at 107 Bridge Road, based on a community of her followers. It was because this community suffered a good deal from rowdy characters that Miss Julia Wood, a supporter, bought New Forest Lodge, Hordle, for them to settle, where they did on 2 January 1872.

The New Forest community numbered thirteen in all—three married couples, three girls, three elderly men and Mrs. Girling. The price of the property was £2,250, but Miss Wood only paid £1,250, leaving the rest on mortgage. As soon as they moved in, the community grew to 160 persons, nearly a third of whom were children. Each member had to live on the resources of the community. Mrs. Girling managed the financial affairs, accepting money from farmers for help with the harvest. Clothes and shoes were made in the community, as well as farming and building. A special bloomer costume was worn by women when working on the farm, but a uniform white dress on Sundays. They earned the nickname of 'Shakers' because of their habits of dancing when moved by the spirit of God in their services.

Naturally enough they soon caused comment in Hampshire. A. T. T. Peterson, a wealthy retired Indian judge who was then living near by, was sure that Mrs. Girling's influence was mesmeric. With the co-operation of the Vicar of Yeatton, he brought over a mesmerist to prove his point. But Mrs. Girling was unshaken. So someone else had her apprehended as a lunatic and taken before the Lymington magistrates, but Mrs. Girling convinced them she was sane. Much of this ill-feeling was undoubtedly due to her sheltering of a large number of unemployed.

The real blow, however, was the confining of her benefactress, Miss Wood, in an asylum.

Mrs. Girling's administration of the common fund was complicated by the fact that she kept no accounts. All the money from the sale of her followers' property or their produce had not only to sustain them, but pay rates, taxes and interest on the mortgage. This latter requirement became particularly onerous, even though the amount involved was a mere £25. This provided the pretext all were looking for and the whole community—140 of them—were ejected by the Sheriff's officer in 1875. Two or three pianos, seventy-seven beds and bedding, farm implements worth about £1,000 were all 'placed on the high road'. There was a fierce east wind blowing with heavy rain and sleet and snow, which penetrated the thin dresses of the women and children. The furniture was soaked and spoiled. Hay, straw and beans were strewn about the road and the scene said a reporter 'was one of terrible privation and desolation'. The evicted community prayed until nine o'clock that night when they obtained the shelter of a barn.

W. F. Cowper-Temple leaped to their defence. In letters to the Press he protested against the harsh treatment they had received. His friend Auberon Herbert allowed them to use a barn on the Ashley Arnewood Farm. From there they moved to a field which Mrs. Girling had leased, but were again turned adrift and lived on the road for several weeks.

Eventually they succeeded in renting a small farm in Tiptoe, where they erected huts and tents including a large wooden building as a place of worship. They remained here until 1886, when Mrs. Girling died. One tangible result of her activities can be seen at Arnewood—a lone tower built by A. T. T. Peterson, the wealthy Indian judge who originally thought she was a mesmerist, for, as a result of investigating the secret of Mrs. Girling's powers, he became a spiritualist and he claimed in 1878 to have received directions to build the tower—largely to provide work for the forty or so men whom he was employing to relieve distress in the district. It was built in concrete as scientifically as was possible at the time, and no outside scaffolding was used. Instead wooden frames were fitted from the inside. All the moulds, woodwork and iron, together with the concrete work, were made by this group of men under Peterson's direction. His intention was to equip it with electric light, but that was refused by Trinity House in case it should be mistaken for a lighthouse. So he decided to use it as a mausoleum, but his wife refused to agree. His ashes lie buried in the basement, where they were placed in 1906. Mrs. Girling's mortal remains lie, with those of the rest of her community, in Hordle Parish Church.[1]

(5)

Another woman community founder, more apocalyptic than Mrs. Girling, was Clarissa Rogers of New Brompton, Kent, the daughter of a sawyer. She made preaching tours of America in 1877 and 1878, and in 1879 married James White, a private in the 16th Regiment. White had joined the army on 15 October 1875 and soon afterwards was posted to India, where he changed his name, returning under that of James Jersham Jezreel. This change was due, he claimed, to a revelation which he had received, the contents of which were embodied in the *Flying Roll*. After her preaching tours of America she had taken the name Esther Jezreel. She was the prime mover in erecting on Chatham Hill, in her home town of New Brompton, a large tower, to be paid for by the common fund raised by their numerous followers, with the help of *Extracts from the Flying Roll*, published between 1879 and 1881.

White's death on 1 March 1885 at Gillingham in no way abated her zeal. She promptly took the title of Queen Ezreel, the mother of Ezreel, and commissioned the construction of the tower, laying the foundation stone in the September following her husband's death. The tower cost £30,000. It contained shops for a butcher, a baker, and a grocer, a restaurant, and a row of houses. But before it was finished she herself died, also at Gillingham, on 30 June 1888, a year after publishing *The Messenger of Wisdom and Israel's Guide*. Her successor, Michael Keyfor Mills, came from Detroit to complete the tower. The Jezreelites left it in 1905.[2]

---

[1] T. A. Wylie, 'The New Forest Shakers', *Milford-on-Sea Record Society*, June 1927; *Lymington Chronicle*, 23 and 30 September 1886; *Irish Monthly*, October 1878, pp. 555–64; *Co-operative News*, VII. 261; XIV. 620, 736.

In Laurence Housman's novel *The Sheepfold*, she appears as the Shepherdess.

[2] *Pall Mall Gazette*, 6 March 1885, 12; 2 July 1888, 10; *Strand Magazine*, 1907; B. Jones, *Follies and Grottoes* (1953), 144; *Notes and Queries*, 29 January 1887, 98.

(6)

A curious link between the charismatic and community experiments at this time was provided by Auberon Herbert. He married Cowper-Temple's niece, and also sheltered the disciples of Mrs. Girling when they had been evicted from their community in 1878. Herbert himself was to be responsible for an experiment in land settlement. In a series of articles in the *Newcastle Weekly Chronicle* later republished as *The Right and Wrong of Compulsion by the State* (1885) and dedicated to 'the workmen of Tyneside', he urged the organization of voluntary land companies, and linked the companies together by a newspaper. 'Let us try', he exhorted his readers, and try he did.

Convening a meeting in London in April 1885 to consider 'the multiplication of landowners and those living on the land', he secured the formation of a company to purchase land and (here the project had a characteristic flavour) resold it as smallholdings—on the instalment plan. Ten per cent of the purchase price was to be paid as a deposit, followed by instalments spread over twenty years, on which 5 per cent interest was to be charged. Experiments were made at Lambourne, Cottenham (in Cambridgeshire), Foxham (in Wiltshire) and Hay Farm (in Essex), till in 1901 the company was wound up and the estates put up for sale. Herbert himself was occupied after 1890 in editing a monthly *Organ of Voluntary Taxation* and grew steadily more interested in psychic research.[1]

His daughter, the Hon. Nan Ino Herbert, became a Theosophist, and, in 1907, gave the Old House, in the New Forest, to Katherine Tingley as the English counterpart of the 'White City', or ideal community of Point Loma, established by Theosophists in California.[2] Unfortunately its site proved unsuitable. Annie Besant wrote :–

After a second visit to the Old House property, I found that although it was splendidly located, and had a historical name, it was unhealthy. But I never told that to Nan for she would not have it. The area was very small; and it was built right in a basin, in the

---

[1] L. Jebb, *Small Holdings* (London, 1907), 144 ff. for a full description.
[2] E. A. Greenwalt, *The Point Loma Community in California 1897–1942* (University of California, 1955).

midst of the forest; and the trees were so heavy that rarely could the sun get in through them to the ground, and there was mould and dampness all the year round.[1]

It became a summer vacation spot for poor children; by now a characteristic way for the Utopian to become practical.

[1] Theodore Besterman, *Mrs. Annie Besant: A Modern Prophet* (1934), *Daily Mirror*, 19 August 1907; *Daily Telegraph*, 22 August 1907; *I.L.N.*, 31 August 1907; *Theosophical Path*, V (October 1913), 291–92.

The Labour Year Book of 1901 (p. 47) refers to the Universal Brotherhood Organization of Katherine Tingley as aiming 'to make Brotherhood a living power in the life of human society'.

PHASE IV

The Rustic Vision

1

◇◇◇

The St. George's Guild

◇◇◇

(1)

Oғ all those entertained by the Cowper-Temples at Broadlands, one stood out. They called him Chrysostom; St. John the golden mouthed; John Ruskin. He, in return, called them φιλον and φιλη. Mrs. Cowper-Temple, nursing him through a serious illness at Matlock in 1871, became his 'tutelary power', 'Egeria', 'Grannie', 'Isola'. She in her turn found he gave 'a halo to life', and 'set us all to manual work'.[1]

'Manual work' had been the therapy advocated by many Utopian associates of the Cowper-Temples from Minter Morgan to Laurence Oliphant. But Ruskin's advocacy was stronger. It began at Oxford when, as a professor, he gathered about him several earnest young undergraduates to build a road at Hinksey. One was Arnold Toynbee, who rose to the rank of foreman. Another was W. H. Mallock, who later described the professor in the *New Republic* (the only portrait in that book which is not a caricature) as a 'disconsolate spirit, hovering over the waters of Babylon and remembering Sion'. The professor's lectures were even more wayward than his roads, for his friends came to him 'with grave faces, to remonstrate against irrelevant and Utopian topics being introduced'.[2] These 'Utopian topics'

---

[1] *The Works of John Ruskin*, ed. E. T. Cook and Alexander Wedderburn (London, 1905) (henceforth called *Works*, XXXVI. xcvii–cix; XXV. 503.

[2] E. T. Cook, *Studies in Ruskin* (1890), 26, 47.

coalesced into a comprehensive social creed, affirmed throughout the country. Like most prophets, the professor sought his desert places, in his case Brantwood on Coniston Lake. From here he issued *Fors Clavigera*, a monthly letter 'to the workmen and labourers of Great Britain'. Here too he founded in 1871 the Guild of St. George to show that 'the highest wisdom and the highest treasure need not be costly or exclusive'. And so Cowper-Temple became one of the first two trustees of the St. George's Guild. The other was a sturdy Devonshire squire, Sir Thomas Acland.

Ruskin would urge Mrs. Cowper-Temple to 'take an acre of ground, make it lovely, give what food comes of it to people who need it, and take no rent of it yourself'. There was a hint of apocalypse as he warned her that 'the Foundations of Society are rotten with every imaginable plague, and must be struck at and swept away, and others built in Christ, instead of on the back of the Leviathan of the Northern Foam'.[1]

Unlike other Utopian friends, John Ruskin gnawed at the consciences of the Cowper-Temples. Mrs. Cowper-Temple received a letter from him in 1874, written before breakfast, in the Sacristan's cell at Assisi.

'I have been thinking', he wrote, 'as I walked down the hillside to the church, why you couldn't believe in Utopia; and whether you really, since you don't *see Him either*, believe in Christ?'[2]

On another occasion he asked her to imagine Christ coming to dinner. 'Consider how you will array your guests—who is to sit next Christ on the other side—who opposite, and so on; finally consider a little what you will talk about, supposing, which is just possible, that Christ should tell you to go on talking as if He were not there.'[3]

Utopianism, said Ruskin, was the devil's pet word. 'Modern Utopianism', he wrote, 'imagines that the world is to be stubbed by steam, and human arms and legs to be eternally idle; not perceiving that thus it would reduce man to the level of his cattle indeed, who can only graze and gore, but not dig! It is indeed certain that advancing knowledge will guide us to less painful methods of human toil; but in the true Utopia, man will

[1] *Works*, XXVIII. 180.
[2] *Works*, XXXVII. 110.
[3] *Works*, XXVIII. 180.

rather harness himself, with his oxen, to his plough, than leave the devil to drive it.'[1] Though Ruskin disclaimed any idea of personally directing a Utopia[2] he hoped that Cowper-Temples and the Aclands would help him to show 'how much food-producing land might be recovered by well-applied labour from the barren or neglected districts of normally cultivated countries'. Land was to be purchased for labourers who would work 'under the carefullest supervision and with every proper means of mental instruction'. Agriculture would be revived. Land would be managed, if not owned, by 'Companions' of the Guild, which as the Society of Mount Rose, would number its members (ultimately by myriad) all over Europe.[3] A hierarchy ranging from the supreme 'Master' through provincial 'Marshals', 'Landlords', and 'Labourers', was drawn up, with provisions for 'Companions' who would give tenths of their income to the Guild but not live according to its laws. Wealth was to be personally carried by Guildsmen in ornaments. Schools and museums were to be developed on every 'estate' and a special currency would circulate amongst its members as a medium of exchange.

His first essay in translating these principles into practice was to be at Sheffield. There, in his words 'the devil had to be got under foot'.[4] He visited it in 1875 and *Fors Clavigera*, letter 56, published in August of that year, announced: 'I have become responsible, as the Master of the Company, for rent or purchase of a room in Sheffield, in which I propose to place some books and minerals, as the germ of a museum arranged first for workers in iron, and extended into illustration of the natural history of the neighbourhood of Sheffield, and more especially of the geology and flora of Derbyshire'.[5] This purpose, however, was not carried out. When Councillor Bragge of Sheffield wrote offering Ruskin space in the existing Sheffield Museum for whatever he wished to put there, Ruskin declined as it might possibly be filled with 'an accumulation of uselessly multiplied ugliness'. To Ruskin's annoyance his letter was made public by

[1] *Works*, XXVIII. 180.
[2] *Works*, XII. 56; XXIX. 498–9; XXVIII. 236; XXVII. 296; XXIX, 32.
[3] M. E. Spence, 'The Guild of St. George: Ruskin's attempt to translate his ideas into practice.' *Bulletin of the John Rylands Library*, XL (1957), 147–201.
[4] *Works*, XXIX. 44.
[5] *Works*, XXVIII. 395.

Bragge, who further interpreted it as 'setting up an opposition museum'. The place Ruskin chose was the 'top of a high and steep hill' at Walkley so that 'the approach to it may be at once symbolically instructive and practically sanitary'.[1] By February 1876 Ruskin was able to pay, out of the annual income of the Guild (some £240 a year) one of his old pupils from the Working Men's College, Henry Swan, £40 a year to act as curator, with rooms in a little house earmarked for the museum.

In a special carriage (for he had no great love for the railway), Ruskin made a posting tour to the north of England in April 1876, visiting Sheffield on the way. There, on the 27th he met a few friends of the museum—secularists, Unitarians, and Quakers—mostly gathered by Henry Swan. As the *Sheffield Telegraph* reported on the following day, 'The proceedings were chiefly of a conversational nature and no set speech on any one of these several subjects dealt with was given. Primarily, the subject of communism came up and its most extreme principles were freely and enthusiastically advocated by one or two of those present.' Ruskin was in high spirits, dilating on the broad principles of communism and pointing to his sustained advocacy of it. He also attacked machinery—from sewing machines (which would not be used by members of the Guild) to the gigantic steam devices of his day. He argued that steam should only be used for cutting icebergs in the frigid zones and for blasting rocks to provide more land on which people could live.

At this meeting one of the audience suggested that a community should be established in Sheffield where members could live together in furnished apartments and establish some system of co-operative manufacture—like making boots. Having a government of their own they would inspire similar communities, gradually to grow up stronger and more powerful than the government of the country.

In the same month Ruskin wrote: 'A few of the Sheffield working-men who admit the possibility of St. George's notions being just, have asked me to let them rent some ground from the Company, whereupon to spend what spare hours they have, of morning or evening, in useful labour. I have accordingly authorized the sale of £2,200 worth of our stock, to be re-

---

[1] *Works*, XXVIII. 449–51. This letter was printed in the *Sheffield Daily Telegraph* and the *Sheffield Independent* on 7 September 1875.

invested on a little estate, near Sheffield, of thirteen acres, with good water supply. The workmen undertake to St. George for his three per cent; and if they get tired of the bargain, the land will always be worth our stock. I have no knowledge yet of the men's plans in detail, nor . . . shall I much interfere with them, until I see how they develop themselves. But here is at last a little piece of England given into the English workman's hand, and heaven's.'[1] His action precipitated the resignation of both Cowper-Temple and Acland, and from now on, Ruskin was solely responsible for the Guild's actions.[2]

(2)

'I have determined to make the first essay of St. George's work at Sheffield, because I have seen you, the Sheffield working man to be capable of co-operation, and to have conceived among yourselves the necessity of severe laws for its better inforcement', he wrote. Sheffield workmen were to be, as he said, 'Life Guards of a New Life . . . more in the spirit of a body of monks gathered for missionary service, than of a body of tradesmen gathered for the promotion even of the honestest and usefullest trade.'[3]

So was born the experiment which has, to this day, kept the name of St. George's Farm.[4] The shoemakers who mainly composed it were to raise their standard of craftsmanship, as well as experiment with a suitable form of self-government, 'Life Guards of a New Life', Ruskin christened them in *Fors Clavigera*. 'You are called', he went on, 'into a Christian ship of war; not hiring a corsair's hull, to go forth and rob on the high seas. And you will find the engagements you have made only tenable by a continual reference to the cause for which you are contending, not to the advantage you hope to reap.'[5] It was to be 'the first essay of St. George's work'.

'You must get your simple and orderly tyrant, or Cyrus, to begin with,' he advised them in May 1877. 'Cyrus, first suppose,

[1] *Works*, XXIX. 98.
[2] Ruskin lamented that their resignation convinced him that the hope of 'mastership and captaincy in the sacred war' was 'in vain'. *Works*, XXIX, 137.
[3] *Works*, XXIX. 147–8.
[4] See Ordnance Survey Map of Derbyshire 1/20,500 Sheet, 43–47. MR. 317796.
[5] *Works*, XXIX. 148.

only over green grocers . . . in these gardens of yours.' As to
their shoemaking enterprise he commanded:–

> You are to make shoes with extremest care to please your customers
> in all matters which they ought to ask; by fineness of fit, excellence
> of work, and exactitude of compliance with special orders; but you
> are not to please them in things which they ought not to ask. It is
> *your* business to know how to protect, and adorn' the human foot.
> When a customer wishes you really to protect his or her foot, you
> are to do it with finest care; but if a customer wishes you to injure
> their foot, or disfigure it, you are to refuse their pleasure in these
> particulars, and bid them, if they insist on such *dis*-service, to go
> elsewhere.[1]

Their accounts were to be open to the public so that their profits
might be known.

The tenants were not chosen immediately. 'I do not care to
be hasty in statement of so important matters', he wrote in the
following month, but added, 'I have pleasant intelligence'.[2]
Perhaps the reason was that he was experiencing difficulty in
transferring the property at once to the society as a body, for as
it stood, it was in his own name.[3] He realized he 'ought to be in
Abbeydale' (as he called the property) but being 'wholly
occupied in examining the growth of *Anagallis tenella* and
completing some notes on St. George's Chapel at Venice . . .
the Dalesmen must take care of themselves for the present'.[4]

So it was little wonder that, with the Master out of the way,
the men in his absence 'tried at first to get on by vote of
majority'. 'But', added Ruskin, 'they have entirely convinced
themselves of the impossibility of getting on in that manner.'[5]

(3)

The 'simple and orderly tyrant' whom the shoemakers chose
as their head—William Harrison Riley—was a Republican,
temperance enthusiast, a socialist, and much-travelled. The son
of a Manchester local preacher, he had learned the art of engraving, and later emigrated to America where he worked for

---

[1] *Works*, XXIX. 112.

[2] *Works*, XXIX. 140.

[3] *Works*, XXIX. 206.

[4] But he did say (*Works*, XXIX. 248), that he would not fall from St. George's
work as long as he had strength for any work at all.

[5] *Works*, XXIX. 272.

three years. Returning to England, he became a commercial traveller for his father who was connected with a cloth printing factory, and in doing so became interested in socialist thought. Soon he was in America again, this time associated with the jewellery trade, varied by journalism. He met Walt Whitman and in 1870 decided to return to England again.

In London Riley published his *Yankee Letters to British Workmen*. Joining the International Working Men's Association, he began on 2 March 1872 to produce the *International Herald*, which soon became the voice of the English section of the International. After eighty-two numbers the title was changed to the *Republican Herald* and in April 1874 it was changed again to the *Herald and Helpmate*. The last number appeared in April 1875 from Bristol where Riley had moved: he and his wife were managing a Mutual Help Club, in Redcliffe, on the bend of the road facing the statue of Chatterton. The object of this club was co-operative distribution, as well as educational work. Riley objected to the sale of intoxicants on its premises, and this provoked a quarrel with the members, so he moved, with some members, to form a Social Improvement Institute at 6 Brunswick Square, on 4 December 1875. This was wholly a temperance society. Unfortunately, this too had to close its doors after eighteen months for lack of financial support. He then left Bristol for Sheffield.

In Sheffield, Riley edited and published the *Socialist*, a monthly which ran from July to December 1877. He proclaimed himself a Christian Socialist. 'During the time of Jesus and his Apostles, no person was accepted as a Christian who was not a socialist. If the "Christianity" of these times is identical with the Christianity of Christ's time, then you are Socialists or you are not Christians, but followers and imitators of Ananias and Saphira.' Somebody sent Ruskin the fourth number and Ruskin replied on 10 October with a letter in which he remarked, 'I am thankful to be able to concur without qualification: but let me earnestly beg of you not to confuse the discussion of the principles of Property in Earth, Air, or Water, with the discussion of principles of Property in general . . . Any attempts to communize (our neighbour's property) have always ended, and will always end, in ruin and shame.'[1]

[1] *Works*, XXXIV. 533.

Riley's own particular brand of Utopianism can be seen from his twenty-two clause 'Draft of a British Constitution', printed in the final copy of the *Socialist* in December 1877. Five of these clauses are worth quoting :–

Article 1. The association of the people as a Commonwealth is for the purpose of increasing the happiness of the people. . .

Article 2. As the maintenance of human life is, inevitably, at the cost of human labour, it is the duty of all able-bodied persons to earn their own living by their own labour . . .

Article 5. The land of Great Britain is the national inheritance of the Commonwealth, and all buildings on the land of Great Britain, and all the crops or produce of the land and the water of Great Britain are the property of the Commonwealth, to be used for the good of the Commonwealth.

Article 6. Food, fuel, clothing, and all other portable materials necessary for maintenance and protection of human life shall be distributed to all citizens according to their needs from the public stores . . .

Article 19. All citizens have a right to do as they please, providing they do not threaten or interfere with the rights of other people.

As Riley confessed to himself :–

I am glad to know that I am, to some extent, a visionary—a seer. I know that the blind—the non-seers—will grin and chuckle at this thankful confession and will continue to lead other blind men into every orthodox ditch. I will continue to respect the faculty of sight —insight and foresight—and will continue with other and greater seers to endeavour to enlarge and improve the sight of mankind, and to oppose the champions of darkness—the revilers and destroyers of sight.[1]

(4)

Now the installation of Riley as custodian or Master of the Totley communitarian experiment was in accordance with the principles of the St. George's Guild. The Sheffielders, however, had other ideas. They had existed as a group since 1874, originally meeting as members of a Mutual Improvement

---

[1] Samson Bryher, *An Account of the Labour and Socialist Movement in Bristol* (Bristol, 1929), 13–15.

Society that met at the Hall of Science in Rockingham Street, Sheffield, an institution founded by Isaac Ironside under Owenite auspices. Their contact with Ruskin had been arranged, as we have seen, by the curator of the Ruskin Museum at Walkley, and he had proposed that Ruskin should really lend the Sheffielders the money with which to buy the Totley Farm, leaving them the responsibility of managing it and paying him back within seven years. This the Sheffielders had agreed to do.

So they engaged a man to work on the farm, then another. Visitors flocked to see them, so many that a profitable side industry grew up supplying them with tea. The fruit, eggs and vegetables were brought back by the members and sold in Sheffield. Everything pointed to the fact that, at no distant time, the participants would become full dwellers in community rather than daily travellers to it; communitarians rather than commuters.

The original reader of the paper on 'Communism' in July of 1875 was anxious to accelerate this movement, and wrote to Ruskin. Ruskin sent him a cheque for £100, which he cashed, and brought the money to the Committee of Management. The committee, however, passed a vote of censure on him, and returned the £100 to Ruskin. Ruskin did not reply. The enthusiastic communist then came forward with another proposal, namely, that he should lease his cobblers' shop to the committee and take up full-time residence at Totley. The committee, however, turned this proposal down too. He was so disappointed that he consulted William Harrison Riley. Riley immediately communicated with Ruskin.

The dénouement was startling. In the words of one of the original committee :—

Riley . . . went to the farm and took absolute possession of everything, telling our manager that *he* was *master*. The poor man came to our meeting looking not too delighted at the change and gave us the information. Now, considering that the society had agreed to pay Ruskin back on his own terms this thing seemed impossible, and a chosen number of the committee went to the farm to seek an explanation. . . . Mr. Riley coolly informed them that he was master there, and that they had no power. He met their remonstrances with sneers, and in one case with threats of personal violence. Two letters were written to Mr. Ruskin seeking *his* explanation, but no answer was returned to either. Then the committee caused another letter to be written declining all further responsibility or connection with the farm. The story is finished as far as we were practically concerned.[1]

By this time, Riley seems to have exhausted his own and Ruskin's patience, so he emigrated with his wife and child to the United States of America. Ruskin's disappointment with him was heartfelt. 'Mr. Riley was no friend of *mine*. I tried as an exponent of modern liberalism, and was as little pleased with the result as your members were.'[2] So the St. George's Guild turned Totley to another purpose.

(5)

This new purpose was announced in the *Report of the St. George's Guild* for 1879. It was to be cultivated 'with the object of showing the best methods of managing fruit trees in the climate of northern England; with attached greenhouses and botanical garden for the orderly display of all interesting European plants'. It was to be 'connective with the work of the Museum of Sheffield', and to be placed under the superintendence of David Downs, Ruskin's own head gardener, 'on whose zeal and honesty' Ruskin said he could rely, 'this superintendence being given at present without expense to the guild'.[3]

Ruskin hoped that the gardens would soon become important enough to require the establishment of a curatorship in connexion with them. On 29 August 1878, he wrote to a friend: 'I have just given orders that Abbeydale shall be made a vegetable and Botanic garden, giving employment to any workmen or workmen's children who like to come so far—for an hour's exercise—and furnishing model types of vegetable produce to the Sheffield markets; while I am going to build good greenhouses for keeping out frost, but not unhealthy hot houses, needing watching all night.'[4]

The visit of Prince Leopold to Ruskin's Walkley Museum in October 1879 undoubtedly stimulated civic interest in this as

[1] For this account of the settlement see M. A. Maloy's letter in *The Commonweal*, V, 25 May 1889, pp. 164–5, and 15 June 1889.
[2] *Works*, XXIV. 620.
[3] *Works*, XXX. 21.
[4] *Works*, XXX. 303.

opposed to any other of his projects. The Clerk to the Sheffield School Board, J. F. Moss, commenced correspondence with Ruskin on the subject, and a public subscription was opened to provide a building fund for it. This was duly accomplished and the Ruskin Museum was opened at Meersbrook Park on 15 April 1890.

St. George's Farm, on the other hand, languished, and in spite of the efforts to produce strawberries, currants and gooseberries on it, Ruskin was writing to Down on 24 April 1881: 'Suppose we sell all that good-for-nothing land at Totley and take somebody else in, for once—if we can—instead of always taken in ourselves, for a change.'[1] Three years later, he spoke of it in his *Report* for 1884, as 'thirteen acres of very poor land'.[2] Luckily, a tenant was found for it, through the agency of Edward Carpenter, a friend of Riley's and a pioneer of socialism in Sheffield. Carpenter introduced one of his young friends, George Pearson, to Ruskin, and as a result Pearson leased it from the Guild until 1929, when he bought it outright.[3]

(6)

The Totley experiment was not without significance. Young Edward Carpenter, then a young university extension lecturer, confessed that, 'The year 1879 was in many ways the dim dawn or beginning of a new life to me', and began to 'knit up alliances more satisfactory to me than I had known before'. He visited Bradway and Totley—indeed he lived in Totley for a few months in 1880—before going to Millthorpe. He was certainly a friend of the Rileys, whom he visited in 1884 whilst on a visit to the United States, staying with them for three weeks at their farm near Townsend Centre, Massachusetts.[4]

Carpenter's own enthusiasm for sandal-making, stemming as it did from his Indian friends, was undoubtedly encouraged by the very cobbling communitarians who had originally enthused over the St. George's project.

---

[1] *Works*, XXX. xxvii.
[2] *Works*, XXX. 71.
[3] *Sheffield Daily Independent*, 17 January 1938. *Works*, XXX. 303. Information gleaned from Mr. Fred Pearson in 1955.
[4] *My Days and Dreams* (London, 1917), 117–18. He was particularly friendly with George Riley, the son.

Carpenter has, in fact, left us a history of the project which has been overlooked by the editors and biographers of Ruskin. It can be found in the newspaper published by William Morris, *The Commonweal*, for 9 March 1889. There, in an article entitled 'A Minstrel Communist', Carpenter wrote an obituary of Joseph Sharpe, one of the original dozen of the group for whom Ruskin bought the land. In telling the story, however, Carpenter referred to Riley as 'one of the most active' members of this group. Riley was quick to reply, and on 20 April his letter from America was published in *The Commonweal*, stating categorically that he was employed by the Guild of St. George to check the workings of the group.

As a result of this, another Ruskinian disciple, George Sturt, of Farnham, Surrey, wrote a long disquisition on the significance of the Totley experiment and asked 'for more light on these experiments at Totley, as perhaps the nucleus of contemporary tendencies in the evolution of Socialism'.[1] As a result, Carpenter replied :–

> I think one reason why all these little communal schemes fail is their narrowness—and it is a good thing they do fail, though it is also a good thing (and a very good thing) that they are started and succeed for a time. I think they all help the Cause on, and break in one direction or another; but you come to have a score or fifty, even a hundred people penned together in a little community, they are bound either to chafe and gall each other into a state of exasperation and explosion, or else if they *are* so like-minded as to have no serious differences it can only be by reason of their exceeding narrowness and sectarian character (as of some of the communities in the United States), which of itself condemns them beforehand to failure. Personally, I would not like to belong to a community of under a million people! I think with that number one might feel safe, but with less there would be a great danger of being *watched*. If one used the common funds, for instance, to have a glass of beer on the sly, and the majority were blue ribbonites; or to have a good dinner, and they were vegetarians; or if one wanted to use bad language, and the rest of the community was highly aesthetic; how one would be made to feel it! But in a large body an immense

---

[1] *The Commonweal*, 20 April 1889. This strange figure was later to make his pseudonym George Bourne famous as the author of *The Wheelwright's Shop* (1923). In turn he influenced Dr. F. R. Leavis and Denis Thompson, the 'Scrutiny' critics, who in turn have influenced a generation of teachers.

variety of opinion and practice (though there would have to be limits even here) would be represented and allowed for; and under those circumstances Communism would be splendid. However, all success to these small ventures, all the same. Some of them may grow to become large ones, and may rise as it were from below to meet the great general movement towards Communism, which owing to economic conditions is taking place from above. And all honour to those who have fought to establish these little communities. They have kept the sacred fire alight through a long and dark night.[1]

(7)

In spite of Totley, Ruskin continued to toy with community experiments. 'The notices which I see,' he wrote in January 1886, 'in the leading journals, of efforts now making for the establishment of industrial villages, induce me to place before the members of the St. George's Guild the reasons for their association, in a form which may usefully be commended to the attention of the public.'

As early as 1876 Ruskin had recorded the sending of a cheque to a Mr. Rydings, a Companion of the Guild, to encourage the older and feebler workers at his manufactory of home-spun wool on the Isle of Man at Laxey. By 1881 he was referring to it as 'the most important step hitherto taken in furtherance of our objects'. This was followed in 1884 by a grant to Albert Fleming, another Companion of the order, for the revival of the Langdale Linen Industry in Westmorland. This hand-spinning spread to Coniston, Keswick and other places. A third experiment was led by a trustee of the Guild, Mr. George Thomson, who began a co-operative mill and whose story is adequately told elsewhere.[2]

(8)

Ruskinism provided an enriching nutriment to the Utopian tradition. Octavia, daughter of Robert Owen's friend, James Hill of Wisbech, persuaded Ruskin in 1864 to buy three houses in a court near Marylebone and allow her to run them. And, as the daughter of a man who had once thought of initiating an Owenite community on his estate at Wretton, she ran the three

[1] *The Commonweal*, 4 May 1889.
[2] *Works*, XXX. 330–5.

houses on community lines. Rules for the payment of rents were supplemented by a club and a recreation ground, lessons on the rates and the kindling of a real civic sense. So successful was she in this that her efforts ranged beyond the Thames to Lambeth, Southwark and Deptford, and her influence extended beyond the Channel and across the Atlantic. Women from Europe came to her for training. Convinced that the green windows of the countryside should be brought into the crowded smoky tenements of the big cities, she successfully worked to secure 'small, open-air sitting-rooms' (as she called her open spaces) wherever she went. 'You cannot deal with people and their houses separately' she insisted, and the climax of her work was the formation, with Canon Rawnsley, of the National Trust in 1895.[1]

By 1884 Patrick Geddes, a young disciple of Huxley, was convinced that Ruskin brought 'tidings of the establishment for the hundredth time of a new Utopia'. That year he wrote:–

A modern city, however stupendous its wealth—on paper—has, after all, hardly any ultimate products to show save a sorry aggregate of ill-constructed houses, mean without and unhealthy within, and containing but little of permanent value . . . men are everywhere awakening to see that this is no longer to be endured, and it is the central merit of our author to have at once inaugurated that criticism of production, and that practical action for its improvement which has been setting in so hopefully of recent years.[2]

As another modern critic has pointed out, Ruskin was also anticipating the programme of the Guild Socialists.[3]

Equally active were Ruskinians in the northern towns. His friend T. C. Horsfall established an Art Museum and University Settlement at Manchester in 1877, and with T. R. Marr, formed a pressure group for housing reform known as the Citizens Association.[4] At Liverpool, the Ruskin Society was toying with the idea of establishing an 'industrial colony' in 1881. One of its members, J. C. Kenworthy, writing in *St. George* lamented 'no movement came, except in the cases of one or two individuals,

---

[1] E. Moberly Bell, *Octavia Hill* (London, 1942), also P. H. Mann in *Town Planning Review*, XXIII (1952), 223–7.　　[2] *John Ruskin, Economist* (1884), 36.
[3] J. T. Fain, *Ruskin and The Economists* (Nashville, 1956), 120.
[4] Shena D. Simon, *A Century of City Government* (London, 1938), 278, 295.

who left the city to become peasant cultivators. There was not sufficient power of conviction or clearness of perception; something was wanting in our moral, or spiritual constitution. This I felt, and set out to seek the something wanted.' That something was, in Kenworthy's case, to be supplied by Tolstoy.[1]

A college which still bears Ruskin's name was founded at Oxford. This aimed at exposing its students to

> 'the daily discipline of social life'; as its council opined, 'this learning to live with men in a common social life is one of the best things the college does for the students . . . Most of the domestic work of the college is in the hands of the students. . . Each student passes in turn through the posts of official life. There are no servants except a cook, so that each student by washing up or scrubbing floors learns how exacting are the claims of household drudgery unless relieved by a simple life.'[2]

The Trade Unions, Co-operative Societies and the University continued to help the College, which in the first six years of existence sustained 232 students, on the penny levies of the Amalgamated Societies of Engineers and Railway Servants, the Northern Counties Weavers, the London Compositors and other workingmen's associations. These students were among the first Labour intellectuals, as Max Beer has shown, to respond to the syndicalist teachings which originated in America (Industrial Workers of the World) and in France (the Confédération Générale du Travail).[3]

The Ruskinian creed was taken up by D. H. Lawrence, then a young pupil teacher at Ilkeston, who was also turning over this idea of a community.[4]

By 1900 a 'Ruskin Movement' was under way. Launched in St. Martin's Town Hall on 8 February, it comprised twenty-three affiliated societies and 200 members.

[1] *St. George* (Birmingham), 204–7.

[2] *The Story of Ruskin College, Oxford* (Oxford, 1955), 5.

M. Sadler, *Continuation Schools in England and Elsewhere* (Manchester 1907), 49.

Max Beer, *A History of British Socialism* (London, 1929), 11, 352.

[3] Richard Aldington, *Portrait of a Genius But . . . The Life of D. H. Lawrence 1885–1930* (London, 1950), 33.

A. Huxley, ed., *The Letters of D. H. Lawrence*, 215, 221.

[4] For his influence on America see W. A. Hinds, *American Communities* (Chicago, 1902), 400–2.

(9)

But the most immediate influence of Ruskin's work can be seen in the life of William Morris, who, raised in 'rich establishmentarian puritanism', found Ruskin's books 'a sort of revelation . . . one of the few necessary and inevitable utterances of the century'. 'It seemed to point out', he wrote of one, 'a new road on which the world should travel'.[1]

This new road was that the social format of society should be changed in order to change its art. 'I don't touch on matters theological' wrote Morris 'which I never could understand, except to say that a God who stood in the way of man making himself comfortable on earth would be no God for me.' Christianity too, for Morris was an historical phase through which the world of civilization has passed or is passing. He told Bruce Glasier that God was 'a big-hearted, jolly chap' and that if there was an after-life 'we shan't be any less fit for its fellowship by having made ourselves good fellows in this'.[2]

Morris saw that the 'aim of socialists should be the founding of a religion' and wrote in *The Commonweal* in 1887 that 'Christianity will be absorbed in Socialism, for no separate system of ethics will then be needed'. Morris in other words gave the Ruskinian vision a sharp focus and brilliantly projected it for those in the following pages to make of it what they did. The rustic vision had become the religion of fellowship. 'Fellowship is heaven', says the priest in the *Dream of John Ball*, 'and lack of fellowship is hell: fellowship is life, and lack of fellowship is death.'

[1] C. H. Kegel, 'William Morris and the Religion of Fellowship', *Western Humanities Review* (Salt Lake City, 1958), 233 ff.

[2] J. Bruce Glasier, *William Morris and the Early Days of the Socialist Movement* (1921).

2

Anarchist Colonies

(1)

The corrosive law of natural selection, enunciated by Charles Darwin in 1859 and endorsed by Marx, tested rather than weakened the tradition of social experiment now so firmly established. That jungle-law was now challenged by the Anarchists, and it is thanks to them that it did not command as large a measure of agreement as it might well have done.

Amongst these, Kropotkin was a leader.[1] His appearance in England, first in 1876, then in 1881–2, and finally from 1886 onwards, gave force and direction to constructive thought about the free village community. For he not only took issue with Darwin in the more reputable journals to show that co-operation was a vital stage in the evolution of the species, but he also took up the thinking of such earlier apostles as Toulmin Smith to present a coherent dynamic programme based on a belief that human nature was basically good, and that this goodness could be discovered and fostered by scientific experimentation. In this he preached no more than a nineteenth century version of the free spirit, leavened by the teaching of Godwin, Proudhon and Bakunin amongst others. From Godwin he imbibed the notion that property was 'a mouldy patent', from Proudhon, that it was 'theft', and from Bakunin, that the free co-operation of individual groups should supplant the State.

[1] G. Woodcock and D. Ivakumovic, *The Anarchist Prince* (London, 1950).

'We must not forget', he wrote, 'that perhaps in a year or two we shall be called upon to decide all questions of the organisation of society.'[1] Kropotkin's 'intense perturbations'[2] had a chiliastic warmth: 'There is need', he wrote again, 'of a frightful storm to sweep away all this rottenness, to vivify torpid souls with its breath, and to restore self-sacrifice, self-denial, and heroism to our senile, decrepit, crumbling society.'[3] The 'restoration' would be effected by establishing free village communities. This, he proclaimed was the 'task which history sets for us'. Whilst softening the sharp contours of Social Darwinism and the 'scientific' sociology of Herbert Spencer, he and the Anarchists were also confronted by the Fabians (an offshoot of a group we shall meet in the next chapter) who deployed Bernard Shaw against him.

But Anarchism grew on opposition. When T. H. Huxley's *Struggle for Existence* with its insistence on the survival of the fittest was published in 1888, Kropotkin, to refute it, published a series of articles with such significant titles as 'The Breakdown of our Industrial System', 'The Coming Reign of Plenty' and 'The Industrial Village of the Future', showing how the guilds and free communes of medieval Europe afforded examples of non-political institutions freely co-operating. Oscar Wilde regarded Kropotkin as one of the two really happy men he had ever met, and put forward in *The Soul of Man under Socialism* Kropotkin's doctrine of individuality based on voluntary co-operation in production and distribution.

By also writing for the scientific journal *Nature*, Kropotkin captured the sympathies of Ruskinians like Patrick Geddes and the Syndicalist Education League of Tom Mann. Kropotkin's enthusiasm for Fourier (expressed in *Modern Science and Anarchism*) and aversion to St. Simon and Cabet, gave a new dimension to Utopist thinking and planning. There were many of his disciples who believed with him that the commune of the twentieth century would not only be communalist, but communist: a federation of free communes in which the small group would be autonomous. As Kropotkin said 'We are Utopians . . . So Utopian . . . we go to the length of believing that the

[1] *Studies*, 26.
[2] *L'Anarchie dans l'evolution socialiste*, 13.
[3] *Paroles d'un croyant*, 280. See also C. M. Wilson, Fabian Tract No. 4, and Bernard Shaw, Fabian Tract No. 45.

Revolution can and ought to assure shelter, food and clothes to all . . . It is certain that the coming Revolution . . . will burst upon us in the middle of a great industrial crisis. Things have been seething for more than a dozen years now and can only go from bad to worse.'[1]

(2)

'The anarchist element in us', wrote William Morris, 'seems determined to drive things to extremity and break us up if we do not declare for Anarchy—which I for one, will not do. The only thing to do is to go on strengthening local bodies.'[2]

Morris was as fervent an opponent of Social Darwinism as Kropotkin, certainly a more imaginative one. He was perhaps more preoccupied with the destructive power of time than any other English writer, except perhaps Sir Thomas Browne.

> Though the days of the spring tide are waxing, the hours of our lives are waning; nor may we abide unless thou canst truly tell us that this is the Land of the Glittering Plain. . . . Is this the Land? Is this the Land?

His work was irradiated by the passion of catching something from its ever-rolling stream. *The Earthly Paradise* (1868–70) and *News from Nowhere* (1891) were protests against the Victorian spirit. The endless struggle to snatch the Earthly Paradise was his favourite theme :–

> And to me, the least and the youngest, what gift for the slaying of ease?
> Save the grief that remembers the past, and the fear that the future sees;
> And the hammer and the fashioning iron, and the living coal of fire;
> And the craft that createth a semblance, and fails of the heart's desire;
> And the toil that each dawning quickens and the task that is never done;
> And the heart that longeth ever, nor will look to the dead that is won.

He could not bear to think that work should be a drudgery and founded a pioneer firm engaged in decorative design and a

---

[1] Tom Bell in *Centennial Expressions on Peter Kropotkin* (New York, 1942), and see *Freedom*, January–February 1894.

[2] Philip Henderson, ed., *The Letters of William Morris* (1950), 230.

pioneer printing press. Liking his own work, he could not see why other people should not like theirs. He looked to the guild movement to alleviate the soullessness of industrial society and founded three guilds—The Century Guild (1882), the Art Workers' Guild (1884) and the Arts and Crafts Exhibition Society (1888) to crystallize his hopes.

His own Socialist League (a group which seceded in 1884 from Hyndman's Social Democratic Federation) established branches all over the country. Through *Commonweal*, its journal, these branches were informed and nourished as the skeleton of a new society, and the fleshly lineaments Morris sketched for them in his great Utopian romance, *A Dream of John Ball* (1888).

To prevent Englishmen becoming passive industrial cogs in a hideously complicated industrial society, Morris hoped to establish small semi-agricultural communities. That veteran Utopian E. T. Craig of Ralahine took the Chair for him at a public meeting in February 1885. 'Old Craig in great force now,' Morris remarked. Though embarrassed by Anarchist support he agreed with them that State-Socialism was 'rather a dull goal', so when Edward Bellamy outlined a system of State-Communism in his Utopian *Looking Backward* (1888), Morris first attacked it in the *Commonweal* of 22 January 1889, and then put forward his ideas of what the future could and would be. These ideas emerged as *News from Nowhere* in 1891.

(3)

A number of new movements or enterprises animating mystical ideas and working for a new social order arose in 1881. There was Hyndman's Social Democratic Federation, Edmund Gurney's Society for Psychical Research and Madame Blavatsky's Theosophical Society and the Hermetic Society. Hyndman, according to Carpenter, 'was confident that the Millennium was at hand—that the S.D.F. would resolve itself into a Committee of Public Safety, and that it would be for him as Chairman of that body to "guide the ship of the State into the calm haven of Socialism"!'[1] Edmund Gurney worked with Frank Podmore, Robert Owen's biographer and a member of the Fellowship of the New Life. Madame Blavatsky, the gross blue-eyed carnivore among the vegetarian lambs of early socialism, attracted Alfred

[1] E. Carpenter, *My Days and Dreams* (1915), 240.

Russell Wallace, at the same time a Theosophist and a land reformer, an admirer of the Ralahine experiment and a prime mover in the Land Nationalization Society. Other Theosophists like A. P. Sinnett and Anna Kingsford founded the London Lodge. They issued a journal called *The Vegetarian*. It was for this journal that Jack Yeats worked.

Jack Yeats' brother, William Butler Yeats, was profoundly moved by reading Thoreau's *Walden*. It was whilst walking through Fleet Street and thinking of *Walden* that he wrote 'The Lake Isle of Innisfree'. The desire in the 'deep heart's core' for peace in a small cabin of clay and wattles, in a bee-loud glade, led Yeats to the house of William Morris, where he met Kropotkin and Ernest Rhys. He intended with them 'to lie on his back and kick' and 'only gradually gave up thinking of and planning some change for the better'. Yeats' mystical urges concentrated round the notion of planning an order whose members could retire to an Irish castle for contemplation. One of his enthusiasms, the Society of the Golden Dawn, had as its leader McGregor Mather, brother-in-law of Henri Bergson. Yeats complained of being 'deprived by Huxley and Tyndall, whom I detested, of the simple-minded religion of my childhood; I made a new religion, almost an infallible church of poetic tradition'.[1] He read the *Upanishads*, Jacob Boehme, the works of Madame Blavatsky and Blake. '*The Morning Redness* by Jacob Boehme', he wrote, 'is a great book beautifully named.' And again, 'Jacob Boehme is certainly the greatest Christian mystic since the Middle Ages.' Yeats also confessed to having been a student of Valentin Andreae since 1887.[2]

It was Yeats who introduced G. W. Russell to the Irish Agricultural Organization Society in 1897. Russell was then a thirty-year-old theosophist draper's clerk who had published some verse under the pseudonym 'AE', which led to his followers being nicknamed 'Aetheists'. Nine years later Russell became editor of the society's newspaper *The Irish Homestead*.[3]

[1] W. B. Yeats, *Autobiographies* (1955), 149–53. See also Joseph Hove, *W. B. Yeats, 1865–1939* (1942).

[2] A. Wade, *The Letters of W. B. Yeats* (New York, 1955), 234, 262, 592.

[3] The Irish Agricultural Organization Society was established by Horace Plunkett, an Englishman, who had made a fortune by ranching in Wyoming and had returned to Ireland, where he organized co-operative creameries, out of which the Society emerged in 1894. Ireland was, for Plunkett, to be a co-operative laboratory.

(4)

A friend of Kropotkin, Morris and Yeats, and a luminary in his own right was Edward Carpenter. In 1878 at the age of 33 he had settled near the St. George's experiment at Totley. Carpenter was well-primed as a detonator of current assumptions about social life, for he had been a curate of F. D. Maurice, and was a friend of Walt Whitman. His withdrawal from the world enabled him not only to contribute to the great debate sustained by Kropotkin and Morris on the virtues of the village community but to inspire an experiment.

Like Yates, Carpenter was influenced by the *Bhagavat Gita*. He read it in 1881 at the same time as his mother died. 'All at once', he wrote, 'I found myself in touch with a mood of exaltation and inspiration—a kind of super-consciousness— which passed all that I had experienced before.'[1] It gave a cue to, and precipitated the crystallization of, *Towards Democracy* (1881). This was reinforced by a visit to India where his friend Harold Cox (who had previously run a community farm at Tilford in Surrey) had gone to teach; and by his reading of William Morris.

Kropotkin, lecturing in Sheffield at his invitation, convinced him of the desirability of individual liberty in free association, and he worked 'definitely along the socialist line: with a drift, as was natural, towards anarchism'. He made sandals and grew vegetables in the Cordwell Valley to sell at a stall in the Sheffield market. This was in the spirit of Thoreau, whose *Walden*, Carpenter regarded as 'the most vital and pithy book ever written'. He also wrote for the Anarchist journal *Freedom* urging his readers to desert the cities for a more natural life on the land.

His teaching bore fruit in 1896 when Hugh Mapleton, then the 30-year-old manager of the Home and Colonial Stores, and Herbert Stansfield, a 20-year-old art student, joined together to form the nucleus of a colony in the grounds of Norton Hall, then owned by a retired lace manufacturer from Nottingham. They lived in an unfurnished gardener's cottage and were joined by 21-year-old Frank Johnson in May 1897 and by John Murray, a 30-year-old file cutter. By 1898 the group increased to seven. They grew cos lettuce, manufactured sandals, and maintained a

[1] Carpenter, op. cit., 246.

strict internal regimen, being vegetarian, teetotal and non-smoking. The fruit and footwear were hawked from door to door.

The Norton Colony, as it was called, attracted keen attention in Sheffield. Sympathizers, many of whom had met in *Clarion* glee clubs, came at week-ends, dined at tables under the trees and slept in a tent on the lawn. That pioneer Socialist paper the *Clarion* sent its van to Norton and published an account on 25 June 1898 :–

> The van reached Norton about noon on Wednesday, the 15th. The first thing that struck me was the colonists singing at their work in the garden. Working under capitalism, whether in the mill, factory, or mine, one seldom hears the worker singing at his task.
>
> Shortly before the meeting time the local policeman came and advised us not to hold the meeting. The law and the agitator met, and after listening to the policeman I told him firmly that the meeting would be held.
>
> He suggested some persons might object. When cross-examined he admitted someone had objected.
>
> We were not to be gain-said. The van was 'manned' to the village green on which had been erected a stone monument to Chantrey, the sculptor. A good audience assembled; Mapleton, of the colony, presided.
>
> Stansfield and two other comrades addressed the meeting and were interrupted several times by a by-stander. Before speaking, I offered to allow questions from the interruptors but they sneaked away. It was virgin soil, but a good meeting was held.
>
> The members of the colony are vegetarians, teetotallers, non-smokers. After the meeting the friends assembled in the colony establishment, about sixty persons, for supper. 'England Arise' was sung; a vote of thanks to the van and its promoters was given and acknowledged and we dispersed.

Thirty-year-old Hugh Mapleton, its leading spirit, was a strict principled leader: 'communities need to be careful about taking invertebrate people as members because they can disgrace the name of communism', he wrote. Mapleton was a strong personality, and reporting in the *New Order* in January 1899 on the colony, wrote :–

> All original members are in the colony and several new faces are among us. Although the colony has been self-supporting from the first we have never been sufficiently financed so that we cannot fully

use our opportunities; a little additional capital would be of the greatest advantage either introduced by a new member or advanced for a time from outside.

Our group had made arrangements to amalgamate with other groups to develop the Starnthwaite property, but after 4 members had spent 2 or 3 months there it was thought advisable to continue our effort at Norton as a separate colony. Differences of aims, methods, and ideals seemed to render this imperative, and we strongly felt that several smaller groups gradually increasing will do better work at present than one large community. *Sandal Dept.* We intend to give this work a large share of our attention and intend to experiment with non-animal material.

This experiment only ceased when the lease ran out and could not be renewed. Two or three of the colonists, including Hugh Mapleton and his brother Henry, joined up with Herbert Mills at Starnthwaite.

Hugh Mapleton then joined Albert Broadbent, Secretary of the Manchester Vegetarian Society, and began to manufacture vegetarian foods. With Henry Mapleton they set up a factory and a large house was taken over at 3, Dolphin Street, Manchester. These premises were eventually extended to embrace two more houses. In 1907 a Public Limited Company was formed with a capital subscribed by an enthusiastic body of Food Reform pioneers. A larger factory was taken at Wardle, Lancashire, and since the business still continued to develop a larger factory was chosen at Garston. This is now one of the largest vegetarian food manufacturing firms in the country. Stansfield later became a Professor of Industrial Design at Toronto; Murray a manager of a steelworks, and Johnson ended his professional career as chief food and drugs inspector for the Sheffield Corporation.[1]

(5)

Perhaps the best known anarchist experiment was at Clousden Hill, Forest Hall, near Newcastle. There a Czech tailor named Kapper in 1893 had built a colony. Described four years later by the *Labour Annual* (p. 107) as a 'Free Communist and Co-operative colony' it comprised Doctor Complevitz (Swiss), Harry Rasmuson (Danish), Peter Yonson (Danish), Rolf

[1] Mr. Frank Johnson, interview in *Sheffield Telegraph*, 30 September 1957.

Wondestick (German), Dick Gunderson (British), James Shearman (British), Charles Davis (British), J. Boomstead (British), John Shirt (British), Jerry Dennilee (Belgian), and one or two others numbering about twenty-four. They built three greenhouses and used to sell their produce to the Sunderland and Newcastle Co-operatives. The Home Colonization Society of Glasgow affiliated with them. A letter written by Mr. Glover, one of the few survivors who remembered the colony, tells its history more vividly than any newspaper:–

All these men who started the Colony were true Labour men.

Tho. Mann used to come and stay there a few days also Harry Snell, whom I can remember when he had hardly a pair of boots on his feet and he became Lord Snell.

It started the year 1893 and continued for seven years. The pioneers, Mr. Kapir, Mr. Rasmuson, Mr. J. Shearman, Mr. Wondestick and Mr. and Mrs. Boomstead, Mr. P. Jonson they each put so much money into one common fund. They had no wages but each got paid pocket money according to how the fund stood. Yes they all got their food together, but the married had a house rent paid out of funds.

The local Co-ops gave their support; Sunderland and Newcastle Co-operatives took a large quantity of tomatoes, cucumbers, and vegetables, flowers, etc. Also Bradnums of Newcastle Green Market took a lot of vegetables, flowers, etc., in fact they had good markets. Also local people used to come to the colony and purchase tomatoes, etc. They got them about 2d per pound cheaper than they could buy them in the shops. And I had all the dances to supply them with their buttonholes which brought good prices, 1/6 for ladies and 1/- for gentlemen.

The *Clarion* very often gave reports of their doings and Mr. and Mrs. Bruce Glasier were visitors to the colony. The local people were very friendly and the members of the colony made some very good friends. When it first started my father Walter Glover was the first they made contact with. As at that time my father was one of the very first that was a member of the I.L.P. and he was many times boycotted for his views but he always in them far off days said he would live to see a labour government with a labour Prime Minister and he did.

Mr. Starr was a Londoner and was a compositor; they had a daughter but they were not at the colony at its start. There was also a Mr. Harry Lawson who was also a Scotchman but had been in U.S.A. as a Professional golfer and teacher of golf. He was the first one I ever saw play golf and as a lad I and Stanley Bumstead used often to knock golf clubs up and down the grass field that was before any golf clubs in Newcastle.

They had their own cow for milk also kept a lot of poultry and ducks also Belgian hares and bees that were Mr. Kapir's job. Their own horse and cart also a flat. They used to grind their own wholemeal and I can tell you that their brown bread was a treat. I wish we could get the same quality today it was as sweet as a nut. They fed well and as regards entertainment they used to have some very jolly evenings Rolf Wondestick with his mandolin, Charles Davis recitations and others singing a song or two. My father was a good baritone and used to sing a few songs for them. It was a great pity that some of the men who came into the colony had not ideas for horticulture as they were a drag on the others who were expert men at the way of running a market garden.

It broke up and Rolf Wondestick and Harry Rasmuson took it over but they did not agree and the place was sold. Rolf then went to be gardener to Mr. Montaldi, Italian Consul for Newcastle and later he went to Seattle, U.S.A. He married a girl called Slater of Forest Hall but she died during the time he was with Mr. Montaldi. Rolf died at Seattle and Harry Rasmuson at Santa Monica, California. He was a very clever man and invented a new idea in raising from seed new fruits.[1]

The Labour Annual gave a directory of these community experiments and Evacustes A. Phipson urged its readers: 'Let one single community acquire a tract of land, however small . . . let them organize themselves in miniature as a real Socialist State . . . in short, allowing the utmost possible degree of individual freedom compatible with social justice—and its speedy and brilliant success is certain.'[2] To the charge that attempting the 'vain task of artificially manufacturing little heavens in impossible surroundings' withdrew men from helping the evolution of socialism another *Labour Annual* contributor replied:—

'The reformers' army can well spare a few sappers and miners for this arduous work. At the worst, the development of character and

---

[1] Private letters to the author from Mr. Ben Glover, who remembered the Community. *The Labour Annual* (1896), described it as 'a free communist and co-operative colony to demonstrate the superiority of free communist association, over the competitive production of today'.

[2] *Labour Annual: A Year Book of Social, Economic and Political Reform* (for) 1896, ed., Joseph Edwards (London, 1895), 58.

deepening of experience which must always result to those who thus boldly take their welfare in their hands, and go out to seek new forms of life under the sun and stars, is a gain. To us who do not follow their path, their example may be a stimulus in the work we have chosen. And when they succeed they atone for many failures. The fortresses of injustice, inequality, and all evil, are very many and very strong; they must be assailed from many sides. We cannot prevent each other from choosing our own methods of attack; and we can learn to sympathise with each other's efforts, and to note and understand the comparative value of the breaches they make, so that from our failures and successes future reformers may choose the best means for bringing the 'age-long war' to a close.[1]

Carpenter himself, in *Forecasts of the Coming Century* (1897) agreed: 'From Solomon to Dr. Watt,' he wrote, 'we have been advised to go to the Ant and Bee for instruction—and lo! they are unpractical and Utopian too.' He closed with the prophecy 'We can see plainly enough the communistic direction in which society is trending'.[2]

[1] op. cit. (London, 1900), 117.
[2] *Forecasts of the Coming Century* (1897), 183. Other contributors to this symposium were A. R. Wallace, Margaret MacMillan, Tom Mann, Bernard Shaw and Grant Allen.

3

Evangelism and Economics

(1)

'HOLY writ wells up from him unbidden, like petroleum in Oil City.' *Justice* on 11 January 1884 was not unfair to the prophet of San Francisco: Henry George. His meetings were little Bethels and his *Progress and Poverty* (1879) was received in England (as William Morris said) 'as a new gospel'. Over a hundred thousand copies were sold in the first decade of publication. When George came to England in 1881, he converted masters at Eton as well as unemployed in Manchester to his idea that the social value of the land should be restored to the people by a land tax. Societies were formed to promote his ideas. One of them, the English Land Restoration League, had H. H. Champion as its secretary.[1] Evacustes Phipson used a legacy of £16,000 to establish a single tax colony in Australia in 1881. It failed, so he joined another in Mexico called Topolobampo and then returned to England, still anxious to found a colony.[2]

[1] E. P. Lawrence, *Henry George in the British Isles* (East Lansing, 1957), and P. Henderson, ed., *The Letters of William Morris* (1950). H. M. Hyndman described Henry George's 'bump of reverence' as 'of cathedral proportions' (*Records of an Adventurous Life* (1911), 291).

[2] Phipson was a zealous correspondent of John Samuel, the Welsh-born (1831) secretary of the National Co-operative Union of America, and told him in 1894 'I am still anxious to see a . . . colony started by real solid and true Rochdale co-operators' (Clifton K. Yearley, Jnr., *Britons in American Labour* (Baltimore, 1957), 298).

But there were others who detested Henry George; Arnold Toynbee especially. This brilliant young historian who had explored the dimensions and concept of the Industrial Revolution felt that the single tax nostrum of the American economic evangelist was so wrong that he shortened his life by his exertions to prove George wrong. His sacrifice was keenly felt by his friends, among them the Rev. S. A. Barnett, then vicar of St. Jude's, Whitechapel. Meeting together on 17 November 1883 eight months after his death, they established a 'Settlement' in his honour. Toynbee Hall, as it was called, opened in Whitechapel on Christmas Eve 1884, as a centre of reconciliation between young university graduates and the working classes. It was to span the gulf which separated class from class and encourage new forms of social responsibility. The Settlement movement provided a training in social work that put those who worked for it into the front rank of social reformers: Toynbee Hall itself became the post-graduate nursery of, amongst others, W. H. Beveridge and C. R. Attlee.[1] One of its promoters, E. T. Cook, was later to edit the monumental edition of the works of John Ruskin.

Barnett proposed to the Whitechapel Guardians that a Land Colony to help the unemployed should be established and his suggestion was considered by the Mansion House Conference on the Unemployed, in 1888. They agreed that 'any experimental scheme of agricultural colonies should be worked by private charity, in co-operation, as far as possible, with the Poor Law, rather than as part of the Poor Law System'.

(2)

One of those who read *Progress and Poverty* was Frank Smith, who had joined the Salvation Army in 1879 and was on his way to America to take charge of Army affairs there. He read it during the voyage and it was, as he said later 'a revelation to him'. On his return to England, General Booth asked him to take charge of the Army's social wing, and Smith urged that this should be greatly developed, with a separate department and staff. Booth and his son Bramwell disagreed.

But the challenge of the submerged tenth of London was

[1] H. Barnett, *Canon Barnett: His Life, Work and Friends* (1921), 307.

calling for a major salvage operation. The respondent was sixty-one-year-old General Booth himself:—

'I say nothing against any short cut to the millennium that is compatible with the Ten Commandments', he wrote. 'I intensely sympathise with aspirations that lie behind all these Socialist dreams. But whether it is Henry George's Single Tax on Land Values, or Edward Bellamy's Nationalism or the more elaborate schemes of the Collectivists, my attitude towards them is all the same . . . I keep my mind open on all these subjects; and am quite willing to hail with open arms any Utopia that is offered me. But it must be within range of my finger-tips. It is of no use to me if it is in the clouds.'

Just as Stanley had torn through the apparently impenetrable tropical forests of Africa to the sunlight and peaceful meadows beyond, so Booth hoped to burst through the gloomy jungle of what he called 'Darkest England'. Like Stanley in Darkest Africa, Booth saw in 'Darkest England' a light beyond. It was to reach to that light that he published his famous *In Darkest England and the Way Out*. In the preparation of this, Smith had no inconsiderable hand.

Booth acknowledged that the scheme was not original: 'I have discovered', he wrote, 'that some [of the plans] have been already tried.' He had spent his adolescence in Nottingham, the constituency of Feargus O'Connor, and he had studied, amongst others, the Ralahine experiment, an account of which he included in an appendix. His own scheme was not, he claimed, perfect: 'If you wait until you get an ideally perfect plan you will have to wait until the Millennium, and then you will not need it.' But he was confident that it would do something and declared that with God's blessing he would raise at least £100,000, raise the submerged tenth who lived, as he put it, 'at the level of a London cabhorse'. The instrument of this regeneration (or refabrication) was to be the farm colony. The 'open secret' of the social problem, as he saw it was to form 'self-helping and self-sustaining communities, each being a kind of co-operative society, or patriarchal family'. These communities, or colonies as he called them later, were to consist of three kinds: a City Colony, a Farm Colony and an Overseas Colony. The City Colony was to recruit, the Farm Colony was to enable the recruits to train themselves, and the Overseas Colony, a settlement in the Commonwealth, would enable them to preserve their manhood and self respect. The three together would be a 'great machine' for rehabilitating the outcast poor. Booth knew quite well what he was up against. But he was even surer of the tradition he was appropriating: 'I have read,' he wrote,

> the history of the many attempts at co-operation that have been made to form communistic settlements in the United States, and am perfectly familiar with the sorrowful fate with which nearly all have been overtaken; but the story of their failures does not deter me in the least. . . . Broadly speaking your experimental communities fail because your Utopias all start upon the system of equality and government by vote of the majority, and, as a necessary and unavoidable consequence, your Utopias get to loggerheads, and Utopia goes smash. I shall avoid that rock.[1]

The pitfalls of voluntaryism at one end, and the co-operative communities at the other were to be avoided by what he called 'the directing brain', not 'the principle of counting noses'. 'Universal and unquestioning obedience from those at the bottom' was to be the rule, and those unwilling to be directed would leave. Booth pointed out that the instinct to obey was so universal that 'there cannot be a greater mistake in this world than to imagine that men object to be governed'. He also insisted on having enough money to launch the scheme. Booth asked for £100,000 in October 1890, and within four months he got £108,000.[2]

But 'universal and unquestioning obedience from those at the bottom' was strange language, even for late Victorian England.

---

[1] *In Darkest England and the Way Out* (1890), 79, 133–231.

[2] R. Sandall, *History of the Salvation Army* (1955). E. I. Champness, *Frank Smith*. For detailed accounts see the *Annual Reports of the Salvation Army*, supplemented by B. Bosanquet, *In Darkest England. On the Wrong Track* (1891); G. W. Foote, *Salvation Syrup or Light on Darkest England* (1891); C. S. Loch, *Examination of General Booth's Social Scheme* (1890); W. J. Ashley, 'General Booth's Panacea', *Political Science Quarterly*, September 1891; L. R. Phelps, 'In Darkest England', *Economic Review*, January 1891; W. Hazlitt Roberts, *General Booth's Scheme and the Municipal Alternatives* (1891); *The Darkest England Social Scheme; Hadleigh The Story of a Great Endeavour* (Salvation Army, 1891); W. Booth, *Light in Darkest England* (1895; F. de L. Booth Tucker, 'The Farm Colonies of the Salvation Army', *Forum* (1897); W. Booth, 'What has come of the Darkest England Scheme', *Sunday Strand*, January 1900; W. H. Hunt, 'General Booth's Darkest England Scheme: an interesting Industrial Experiment', *Westminster Review*, 1900; Catherine Carson, *Hadleigh Labour Colony: How the Salvation Army raises the Fallen* (1901); Herman Ausubel, 'General Booth's Scheme of Social Salvation', *American Historical Review*, LVI (1950), 519–25. C. L. Mowat, *The Charity Organisation Society* (1961), 136.

Frank Smith, one of the Army's ablest officers, resigned two months after it was published to become the close friend and associate of Kier Hardie, who was elected the first chairman of the newly formed Independent Labour Party in 1893. He later became one of the first two candidates put forward by the Party for Parliament.[1]

T. H. Huxley, scenting 'socialist autocracy' warned the public against this Boothian variant of 'despotic socialism'. *The Times* took up the cry. But the public warmed to Booth's appeal and provided £129,288. 12s. 6d. for Booth's son, Bramwell, to begin organizing depots, rescue homes and labour bureaux in the industrial towns and purchasing a farm at Hadleigh in Essex. This money, raised in two years, was the subject of sly innuendo, so Booth invited the great Liberal lawyer Sir Henry James to Chair a committee of inquiry to examine the application of the funds. He was completely vindicated.

The Farm Colony, an estate of from 500–1,000 acres, lay away from the public houses. With its living-quarters and workshops on the estate for making glass-houses, bricks, cottages, furniture and clothing it was to offer a haven for the destitute. To gather its strawberries, Booth was confident that girls would desert the pavements of Piccadilly. Boys and men would be at 'a great school of technical agricultural education, a Working Men's Agricultural University', in training for life in the new countries they would go forth to colonize and possess. It was as Booth wrote, 'a co-operative farm on the principles of Ralahine'.

Just such a property was bought on 2 May 1891 between Leigh, Rayleigh and South Benfleet, in Essex. A notice was put up, reading:

THE SALVATION ARMY

DARKEST ENGLAND

The Castle and Park Farms with other
properties have been purchased by
General Booth for the establishment
of the first Farm Colony and the
Elimination of the Submerged Tenth.

[1] He later returned to the Salvation Army in November 1901, resigning his seat on the London County Council. He left the Army again and ultimately became M.P. for Nuneaton. He was a great organizer, as his record in the U.S.A. showed. See St. John Ervine, *God's Soldier: General William Booth* (London, 1934).

Five miles from Southend, the Farm Colony comprised 1,052 acres, of which 630 was in grass and 370 arable, and the remainder were saltings or land periodically covered by high tides. Buildings included the ruin of an old castle and two farmhouses. To this was added a fifth and smaller farm to give them easier access to the station.

Within three months over two hundred 'colonists' were installed, and by June 1892 there were 325. Large capital sums were spent and by 1894 the balance sheet estimated the assets as worth £94,473. 4s. 7d. Attempts to found industries were 'entirely unsuccessful', and after 1893 the Army concentrated on agricultural work.

The President of the Board of Agriculture, Mr. Henry Chaplin, accompanied by his permanent secretary, visited the colony in 1895 and declared he 'had never seen anything like it'. W. T. Stead, the editor, was 'completely captured' and enthusiastically offered to obtain the help of the Prince of Wales. Cecil Rhodes and Lord Lock were 'entranced' when they visited the colony in May 1898. Social theorists like Francis Peek detected a plan for the erection of 'modern suburban villages . . . grand in its conceptions and practicable in its proposals'.[1] And Bernard Bosanquet, though he professed to find it 'a huge and fatal blunder', which would only be used in winter and would disappear during the summer, yet reluctantly agreed that an experimental farm would be 'well worthy trying'.[2] Such was its success that *Reynolds News* saw it as the herald of a Socialist Revolution :–

> The fantastic religious side of Salvationism will disappear in the course of time and what will be left? A large number of men and women who have been organised, disciplined, and taught to look for something better than their present condition, and who have become public speakers and are not afraid of ridicule. There you have the raw materials for a Socialist Army.[3]

(3)

Just such a Socialist Salvation Army was actually being formed. It took shape on 26 April 1891 under John Trevor,

---

[1] *Contemporary Review*, December 1890; *Fortnightly Review*, February 1895.
[2] B. Bosanquet, *In Darkest England. On the Wrong Track* (1891), 65.
[3] *Reynolds News*, 21 December 1890.

minister at the Upper Brook Street Church, Manchester. He was 'inspired' to do it he said by the aversion to 'enthusiasm' which his fellow delegates exhibited at a conference of the United Free Churches. On the doctrine that 'Man must become the Human Providence of the world as God is the Divine Providence', Trevor called his group the Labour Church. 'The Salvationist', wrote Trevor, 'in a rough way is true to the facts about the relations between God and the human soul.'[1] The Labour Church opened on 4 October 1891, and from the pulpit John Trevor took as his text 'Seek ye first the Kingdom of God and all these things will be added unto you.'

Like General Booth, John Trevor's life registered the impact of the Utopian tradition. He was at first articled in 1871 to an architect in Norwich at the age of 15. Going to Liverpool to practise he found 'the influence of Ruskin was overwhelming'. Repelled by this, and the general 'tendency to look backwards', he had emigrated to Australia. From there he re-emigrated to attend a college at Meadville, U.S.A., for Unitarian ministers, where he wallowed in Emersonian transcendentalism. He also visited the Oneida Community and was as repelled by it as he had previously been by Ruskinism in Liverpool.

'The problem of a community', he wrote, 'is not the problem of the world. The problem that the community solves, when it does solve it, is purely personal—how a small number of people, of like ideas and sympathies, with a very narrow range of life, or a very definite purpose in view, can organize their industry and their intercourse to their liking.'[1] Renouncing the Unitarian ministry and America he returned to England in 1880 and practised as an architect in Folkestone. Not even marriage helped him to send down roots and he confessed to a greater sense of loneliness than ever before. He read Clough, Kropotkin and Mrs. Besant, and found himself drawn once more to the Ministry, this time to a more ethical type of religion as represented by Felix Adler. After attending Manchester New College, he served in 1888 as an assistant to P. H. Wicksteed at the Little Portland Street Chapel in London and in 1890 joined Upper Brook Street Chapel, Manchester, where the veteran co-operator E. V. Neale was in his congregation. There he came across 'a small group of Anarchists', and used to attend their

[1] John Trevor, *My Quest for God* (1908), 238.

meetings after preaching his own sermons in church. As a result Brook Street Chapel appeared 'a prison to his soul', especially after he had attended a conference of the various Free Churches in 1891. More and more he wanted a 'gospel'. More and more he lamented that even the Free Churches were afraid of 'enthusiasm'. And the only religious leader with whom he found himself in sympathy was General Booth. So, after a meeting convened in the Charlton Town Hall on 4 October, the Labour Church was founded. It grew rapidly. James Keir Hardie, Robert Blatchford, Ben Tillett, and above all, the Rev. Philip Wicksteed rallied round him. A full-time secretary was appointed and by January 1892 the *Labour Prophet* was issued. Within four years twenty-two churches were founded and eighteen more were contemplated. As Trevor wrote:

> The Labour Church was founded for the distinct purpose of declaring that God is at work, here and now, in the heart of the Labour movement; and that the religion of today consists in co-operating with the divine energy which is still operating on our planet.

In July 1893 the first conference of Labour Churches was held at Manchester and at a second conference in November 1893 an organizer, Fred Brocklehurst, was appointed. Trevor himself had a breakdown and went to Macclesfield where he planned a Labour Brotherhood, to be launched in 1894. He wrote an account of his spiritual Odyssey in which he confessed that at this time 'I felt I was in Heaven—an inward state of peace and joy and assurance indescribably intense, accompanied by a sense of being bathed in a warm glow of light, as though this external condition had brought about the internal effect'.[1] His lively pen and earnest manner, deployed in the various northern groups, attracted a number of sympathizers including Raymond Unwin, another architect, whom we shall meet in a later chapter.

(4)

The importance of General Booth's scheme lay, not in its working out, but in its impact. Stanton Coit, 'minister' to the Ethical Movement in England (whose motto, taken from its American founder, Felix Adler, was 'deed not creed') admitted

---

[1] Trevor, op. cit., p. 146; K. S. Inglis, 'The Labour Church Movement', *International Review of Social History*, III (1958), 445–60.

that 'No one has yet accepted, in the full sense in which he meant it, General Booth's challenge to bring forward a better scheme than his for lifting the fallen classes of society into independence and prosperity'.

Fresh from Adler's pioneering of co-operative shops, settlements, good government clubs and working-men's schools in America, Coit saw reasons for questioning whether even Toynbee Hall could be 'a permanent force on the side of culture and character unless it unified its activities'.[1] Booth's challenge led him to propose a scheme for 'neighbourhood guilds' co-operating one with another to keep a home in the country, for training workers and providing relief. Coit insisted that his guilds should be 'neutral' in religious outlook, by which he really meant that they should 'transcend' creeds.

(5)

Colonies sprang up everywhere. The Church Army, founded four years after the Salvation Army in 1882, now started a colony at Thelnetham in Suffolk. Walter Hazell, the printer, set up in 1891 a training farm of twenty-eight acres at Longley, Essex, which he subsequently transferred to Chesham in Beccles, writing an account of it as *A Social Experiment* (1896). Major Poore bought in 1892 the 195-acre Cooper's Farm at Winterslow near Salisbury and sold it in lots of varying sizes either for cash or by instalments. From the forty-nine smallholdings so created, a landholders' court (registered as a limited company) was set up to collect rents. This court had £1,500 at its disposal to advance as working capital on an interest of 3 per cent. Some of the small plots were used as building sites, and thirty-three out of the forty-nine holders had built houses, whilst a Rechabite Hall and a Mission Hall were built on land belonging to the land court. This more nearly approached the system advocated by the English Land Colonization Society: a body founded by that eminent Congregational divine and philanthropist, John Brown Paton, in 1892. Paton projected many schemes for social regeneration, and in this same year launched the Bible Reading and Prayer Union. His major contribution to evangelism and economics appeared in 1910, a year before his death: *Christ and Civilization*. Paton's Land Colonization Society took over an

---

[1] Stanton Coit, *Neighbourhood Guilds: an instrument of Social Reform* (1891).

experimental colony at Starnthwaite in 1900, which under H. V. Mills, had been one of the pioneer groups in this field.[1]

Land colonies seemed such an alleviation of civic distress that in 1893 the Whitechapel Guardians set up a committee consisting of Captain Gretton of the East End Emigration Society, Walter Hazell, F. C. Mills, and Bolton Smart, of the Stepney Union, to sound farmers on the feasibility of a scheme. In 1894 Bolton King, secretary of the Mansion House Committee on the unemployed, who had already conducted an experiment in co-operative agriculture at Radbourne, declared himself for an experiment.

The temptation to follow the efflorescence of this settlement work, to relate it to the great political drive of the Liberal group under Jesse Collings and to resurrect the various pressure groups like the Allotments Extension Association and the Rural League, must be resisted. It is sufficient to say that the agrarian evangel was still at white heat when the Salvation Army took another step to community founding by purchasing a 400-acre estate at Boxted near Colchester in October 1906. This was the very year in which Collings published *Land Reform*. Divided into eighty plots, varying from three and a half to six acres each, the land was staked out for a house on each plot to make it self-contained. A working stock of manure and seeds, together with capital to help the settlers over the first years, was supplied. Three-quarters of an acre of each plot was planted with mixed fruit trees and bushes, and another quarter of an acre with strawberries. Two roads were built to add to the convenience of the estate. Tenants were to go on probation for the first three years. Then, if they proved satisfactory, they were to be granted a 999-year lease, and allowed to purchase their plots over a period of thirty years, paying 6 per cent interest together with the capital repayment. This capital repayment, on a five-acre holding, amounted to some £500. An expert adviser was available, together with a successful grower from the Evesham area who came as a settler. Co-operative distribution of the produce was organized and a central grading store for the colony established. When L. Jebb visited Boxted forty-four cottages were being erected in pairs. A large number of applications were received of which 40 per cent were from towns, and so successful did the

[1] J. A. Hobson, ed., *Co-operative Labour upon the Land* (London, 1895).

scheme appear that the Army decided to form a company called
'Land for the People Ltd.'[1]

(6)

By now a steady head of pressure had been building up
against the modern Moses, especially when he talked of settling
workers in Canada and Rhodesia on large tracts of land. The
more General Booth's schemes were endorsed by leading
politicians like Rosebery, or popular writers like Rider Haggard,
so the more did those for whom the schemes were intended protest.
In 1905 the London Trades Council erupted with a strong protest, and were reported in *The Times* of 2 October as resolving :-

> That this conference of organised London workers emphatically
> denounces the proposals of Messrs Booth and Carlile to transport
> for life thousands of the flower of the working classes as a pretended
> relief for the unemployment difficulty, believing that such methods
> would be suicidal from the national point of view . . . and would
> stave off the growing demand on the part of the workers for urgent
> social and economic changes which would effect a solution of the
> problem at the present time and in this country.[2]

Their sentiments were endorsed from a most unlikely
quarter: the very conservative *Quarterly Review*. Commenting
on Rider Haggard's favourable report on the Salvation Army
experiments for establishing a peasant proprietary class it
observed 'we are not likely to find them among the failures of
urban life'.[3] John Burns, the Liberal politician was more succinct:
to him such labour colonies were 'merely doss houses'.[4]

It was obviously time to raise the people's eyes to a higher
level. Efforts to do that had been made and these were much
more successful. The vision of a new Utopia was flickering on
the wall, projected by a young enthusiast, H. G. Wells, who
observed through one of his characters: 'The Anarchist world, I
admit, is our dream; . . . but the way to that is through education,
discipline and law. Socialism is the preparation for that higher
anarchism. Socialism is the schoolroom of true and noble Anarchism, wherein by training and restraint we shall make men free.'[5]

[1] L. Jebb, *Small Holdings* (1907).

[2] *The Times*, 2 October 1905.

[3] *Quarterly Review* (1905), 244. See also Morton Cohen, *Rider Haggard: His Life and Works* (1960).

[4] *Morning Post*, 27 November 1905.

[5] H. G. Wells, *New Worlds for Old* (1908), 257.

4

The Fellowship of the New Life

(1)

THE trends which society was taking also preoccupied Thomas Davidson. 'Kant and Comte have done their work, taken the sun out of life, and left men groping in darkness', he wrote. 'Without metaphysics even physics is meaningless; that which *appears* also *is*; that beneath all seeming is that which seems.'[1] Davidson, a graduate of the University of Aberdeen, became after a brief period of teaching in England, Rector of Aberdeen Grammar School and sessions clerk of Old Machar Parish. In his Don Street lodgings he would give suppers on Sunday evenings to which would come not only his brother, John Morrison Davidson, but William Wallace and the two Macdonnells, John and James. Food for thought was provided, and Thomas tasted the heady delights of the philosophical discussion group. After three years (1860–3) he moved to England, again teaching in several schools before emigrating to Canada, where he taught at the Collegiate Institute, London, Ontario for a year (1866–7). He seemed to be seeking a receptive environment and, by crossing the border, he found the very stimulus he needed in St. Louis.

Here, he taught as a classical master under William T. Harris, five years older than himself and one of the most notable city superintendents of schools that America has produced.

---

[1] *Memorials of Thomas Davidson*, ed. William Knight (Boston, 1907).

Harris was a student of Hegel, and infected Davidson who then returned to his Aristotle. This as he said 'threw me back into the great clear current of the world's natural thought (out of which modern Europe was thrown by Descartes and Locke; thrown into muddy pools on the banks—pools ever becoming earthier and drier)'. He also became much preoccupied by the pastoral responsibility of a teacher. He began to edit the *Western Educational Review*, stressing the solidarity of the individual with society in true Hegelian fashion. The first of the nine articles he wrote for it between February 1870 and November 1871 was called 'Self government in the classroom'. The eighth of his articles on 'Pedagogical Bibliography—its possessions and wants' was a plea for the widening of the concept of education as embracing the history of science and philosophy. Only by giving the very widest interpretation to the meaning of the word education could clear conception of its nature and aim be obtained. As an essential preliminary to this, he pleaded for a full scholarly history of education from the earliest times to the present.

Four years later, he took a step which would enable him to forward such a project. He left St. Louis for Boston, where he became a neighbour of Longfellow. Here, in his rooms at Temple Street, the discussion group of Don Street was repeated, this time with G. H. Howison, Eliot Cabot, C. C. Everett and William James. James wanted him to join the Harvard Faculty, but Davidson's attack on Departments of Greek in the *Atlantic Monthly* put him outside the academic pale. William's brother, Henry the novelist, met his wife through Davidson's introduction, and has left us a picture of him in *The Knight Errant of the Intellectual Life*.

In the summer, Davidson would take private pupils to Europe. There, he met Schliemann, who gave him a piece of pottery found in Agamemnon's tomb at Mycenae ('Clytemnestra's teapot', Davidson used to joke); the Pope, who accorded him an hour's interview (conducted in Latin to Davidson's satisfaction); and, most important of all, the Rosminian monks at Domodossola. It was here that Davidson would spend much of his time, alternating between Rome, Paris, Berlin, and London. From his study of Aristotle, Davidson rekindled his religious convictions, which the Presbyterianism of his youth had extinguished. He determined to investigate both the Greek and the Roman Churches. A year in Greece convinced him that the Greek Church at least was not an organ of the divine, but a further period in Rome convinced him, after six years, that in the Rosminian community at Domodossola some answer was to be obtained. It was in these *wanderjahre* that he fulfilled his role as a carrier and disseminator of ideas. He lectured with Emerson at Bronson Alcott's summer school, moving Alcott to write, 'our rooms are too small to seat our visitors', and 'he brings a wealth of illustrations hardly surpassed by that of any other persons'.[1]

Rosmini, to Davidson, was the evangelist of the future and he advised Havelock Ellis to read him so as 'to be able to free' himself 'from the last remnant of that terrible monism from which hardly any English thinker escapes'. He even meditated joining the editorial staff of the Vatican edition of *St. Thomas*, but contented himself with publishing an English version of Rosmini's *Anthropology* in 1882 and his *Psychology* in 1883. He spent the winter of 1882 in a villa above Domodossola with Wyndham R. Dunstan, near to the Rosminian monastery, and they both went constantly to the monastery to discuss philosophic questions. Davidson's lectures and articles on Rosmini brought both of them to the attention of the English-speaking world. The Domodossola community provided him with a model. 'After all', he wrote, 'our work must result in *our doing*. We must not only know the truth, we must also live it. And we can only live it by establishing noble and wise social relations.' 'Jesus', he wrote, 'undertook to establish a kingdom of heaven upon earth, and, if there had been more like him, would, no doubt have succeeded, but there were not, so his efforts ended in a—church.'[2]

'The thought of a church was maturing in my mind,' said Davidson in an autobiographical sketch; 'while still at Domodossola, I was visited by two young Englishmen of deep spiritual natures, with whom I discussed this question in all its bearings. At that time we came to no definite conclusion; but the matter

[1] Wm. A. Knight, *Some Nineteenth-Century Scotsmen: Brief Personal Recollections and Memorials of Thomas Davidson* (1907); Joseph L. Blau, 'Rosmini, Domodossola and Thomas Davidson', and Albert Lataner, 'Introduction to Davidson's *Autobiographical Sketch*', *Journal of the History of Ideas*, XVIII (1957), 523–8, 529–36.

[2] Blau, op. cit., 5, 26–27.

remained before our minds and when in the autumn of 1883 I paid a brief visit to England my friends and I undertook to lay the basis of the scheme. We were very awkward about it, and hardly knew where to begin.'[1]

'He was alive, intensely and warmly alive, as even his complexion and colouring seemed to show; here was the perfervid emotional Scottish temperament carried almost or quite to the point of genius . . . I came away feeling that this was the most remarkable man, the most intensely alive man I had ever met; I am not at all sure I should not say so still.'[2] So Havelock Ellis described Thomas Davidson in Chelsea. Havelock Ellis had met him in the rooms of Percival Chubb, a clerk in the local Government board. Davidson was apostolizing for a community where 'each and all' could cultivate 'a perfect character'.

During the summer of 1883 another disciple was drawn within Davidson's orbit, this time Frank Podmore, a clerk in the G.P.O. and later the biographer of Robert Owen. Podmore invited a few friends to his rooms to hear Davidson's idea of a community. As a result of this meeting, Davidson proposed that they should form a Fellowship of the New Life.

(2)

From Podmore's room, the Fellowship continued in the rooms of E. R. Pease at 170 Osnaburgh Street, Regent's Park, on 24 October 1883. This time sixteen people assembled, including Maurice Adams,[3] H. H. Champion,[4] Havelock Ellis,[5] J. L. Joynes,[6] Percival Chubb,[7] James Hinton's widow and her sister

[1] Lataner, op. cit., 535.

[2] Havelock Ellis, *My Life* (London, 1940), 159–61.

[3] Maurice Adams was the author of *Ethics of Social Reform* (1887), an edition of More's *Utopia* (1890), an exposé of *The Sweating System* (1896), and a biography of *Giordiano Bruno* (1905).

[4] Then the secretary of the Social Democratic Federation of which William Morris was treasurer and H. M. Hyndman, chairman. It had just issued a manifesto reviving the old Chartist demands.

[5] A. Calder Marshall, *Havelock Ellis: A Biography* (1959).

[6] J. L. Joynes was, with Champion, a member of the S.D.F. He was a schoolmaster at Eton who had travelled in Ireland with Henry George in the previous year and had been arrested. Forced to resign from Eton he became editor of *To-Day* and died in 1893.

[7] Percival Chubb was then a clerk in the Local Government Board and seems to have acted as secretary to the group. For a biographical notice see *The Guardian*, 31 March 1960.

were also present,[1] and Frank Podmore, the biographer-to-be of Robert Owen.

Davidson elaborated his proposal for 'a new communistic society whose members should lead a higher life'. As Pease reports it, 'the idea of founding a community abroad was generally discredited, and it was generally recognized that it would not be possible to establish here in England any independent community'. To Pease, Davidson seemed in retrospect as 'spiritually descendant of the Utopians of Brook Farm and the Phalanstery, and what he yearned for was something in the nature of a community of superior people withdrawn from the world because of its wickedness, and showing by example how a higher life might be led'.[2] Ernest Rhys, also introduced to Davidson by Chubb, thought the same. Though he confessed 'his great debt to Davidson', yet he admitted that 'The Fellowship of the New Life aimed, like Hawthorne's Brook Farm, at setting up a colony of workers and craftsmen, with no underground railways and rich parasites to suck up the air and life-blood of the commonalty.'[3]

Community was the sole topic of discussion a fortnight later, when Miss Owen (granddaughter of Robert Owen) was asked to give her experiences of New Harmony. Though Miss Owen could not come, a proposal was made to constitute the group as an association 'whose ultimate aim' was to be 'the reconstruction of society in accordance with the highest moral principles'. This was agreed and a committee appointed to draft proposals.

Miss Owen did attend a third meeting held on 23 November to discuss the proposals. After a lively discussion another committee was appointed which, at the fourth meeting on 7 December, constituted the Fellowship of the New Life.

The Fellowship was based on the subordination of material things to spiritual and aimed at 'the cultivation of a perfect character in each and all'. The community idea was again

---

[1] E. R. Pease, *History of the Fabian Society* (1925).

[2] James Hinton, 1822–75, was a doctor much attracted by Jacob Boehme. 'Why does not someone, enlightened by Boehme, give us a new translation of one of his works, with a general account of them, so that we might know?' he asked in 1874. 'The few things I have made out of Boehme's quite charmed me.' Ellice Hopkins, *Life and Letters of James Hinton* (1878), 116.

[3] Ernest Rhys, *Everyman Remembers* (1931), 132 ff.

discussed, stress was laid on education, simple living, manual labour and religious communion. Unfortunately no agreement could be recorded and at a subsequent meeting Frank Podmore moved resolutions constituting the Fabian Society, so-called because it intended to move with calculated caution as an intellectual pressure group rather than a communitarian experiment.

From now on the two groups—the Fellowship of the New Life and the Fabian Society—went their separate ways. As Bernard Shaw who joined the Fabian Society in May 1884 put it, 'one to sit among the dandelions, the other to organize the docks'.[1] And Shaw later brought along his friend Sidney Webb, then a clerk in the Colonial Office, who read the members of the Fabian Society a paper on 'The Way Out'. That way was not the community way.

(3)

Davidson returned to New York, and was soon followed by Percival Chubb, who joined the Ethical Church. A branch of the Fellowship was founded in New York in 1884. Too much a philosopher to be pinned down; too much a peripatetic to hold a pulpit; too humble and altruistic to assume the leadership of a crusade; he devoted his time to writing. He told William Knight (who later wrote his biography) that he intended to make his work on medieval philosophy the great work of his life and that the English Fellowship was not what he had hoped for. 'He could never', said William Knight, 'sympathise with the socialistic views of many of the English members', since he cherished the idea that it was possible to remove social injustice by individual remedies alone.[2]

Yet by his nature he was intensely gregarious. The resolution of this paradox in his nature was resolved by his establishment of an educational community at Glemore in the Adirondac Mountains in 1888. Here W. T. Harris of St. Louis came from his exalted post as U.S. Commissioner of Education to teach, and Percival Chubb of London left his post with the local

---

[1] H. Winsten, *Henry Salt and His Circle* (London, 1951). St. John Ervine, *Bernard Shaw, His Life, Work and Friends* (1956), 124, says that they split over a proposal to emigrate to Brazil.
[2] *Some Nineteenth-Century Scotsmen* (1903), 351–67.

government board to join him. Here too he secured Stephen Weston and John Dewey to reinforce them. Though the idea of this Farmington community stemmed from Bronson Alcott's summer school (where he had lectured ten years earlier) its materialization was different. A number of small cabins were built on Davidson's 166-acre estate, the farm buildings were converted into a lecture hall and refectory, and in the centre of a grove of silver beeches his own cottage was built. William James came over from Harvard to open it. In the ten summers of its existence it was a collegiate holiday camp and retreat. The prospectus defined the 'culture' sought by those who attended it as 'Man's spiritual nature, his intelligence, his affections, his will, and the modes in which they express themselves. This culture includes a history, a theory and a practice, a certain familiarity with which must be acquired by every person who seriously desires to know his relations with the world and to perform his part worthily in these relations.'

(4)

The English branch of the Fellowship was left in the hands and hearts of Maurice Adams and J. F. Oakeshott. They carried on the work privately, but in July 1889 came to the conclusion that the time had come to make the principles and aims of the fellowship known to a wider circle. This quarterly, originally called *The Sower*, was later renamed *Seed Time*. Apart from articles, it served as a medium for advertising lectures on various themes ranging from Adams himself on 'Utopia, or Socialism in the Sixteenth Century' to Henry Demarest Lloyd on 'The New Conscience or the Religion of Labour'. This idea of 'the religion of Labour' was very much in Davidson's mind, since he was to go on and organize what he called 'a society of the nature of the Church' on the Lower East Side of New York City, known to us as 'the Breadwinners' College'. It was a variant of the Settlement movement.[1]

Other recruits to the English branch of the Fellowship were Cecil Reddie and Edward Carpenter who in *Seed Time* gave notice of a 'Fellowship School' to be founded at Abbotsholme, Staffordshire. This enterprise, like the 'neighbourhood guild and free kindergarten' at White Hart Street, Drury Lane, was

[1] Blau, op. cit., 527–8.

to make manifest the need for Brotherhood. 'All schools', insisted *Seed Time* 'ought to be communities, miniature commonwealths or states, as they were in the Middle Ages. How otherwise can they impart the preparation necessary for adult life.' 'Seek ye first the Kingdom of God, and his righteousness, and all these things shall be added unto you.' Seizing this text, *Seed Time* dilated on the need for a 'new transmissable consecration' to remedy the 'ethical and economic confusion of society'. That new gospel was to be Tolstoyan, based on daily contact with nature, physical labour, affectionate family relationships and a dissolution of class barriers.[1] Havelock Ellis insisted on the need (as he said) to 'socialise what we call our physical life, in order that we may attain greater freedom for what we call our spiritual life'.[2] 'The name of Tolstoy', wrote another contributor three months later, 'has become of late a household word in England, and especially among those who are interested in the Social Revolution.'[3] The Secretary of the New Fellowship, Edith Rees (who later married Havelock Ellis), rhapsodized, 'This is Utopia . . . for God's sake let us try it, for this other thing is Hell.'[4] To Edward Carpenter, Edith Rees was 'one of the most active and vigorous' and helped 'to organise and to carry on for some time a joint dwelling or co-operative boarding-house near Mecklenburg Square, where eight or ten members of the fellowship dwelt in a kind of communist Utopia'. The use of the word Utopia is significant, for at this time Maurice Adams published an edition of More's famous classic.

(5)

The 'Utopia' was established at 29 Doughty Street in the shape of 'a Fellowship House'.[5] J. Ramsay MacDonald, who succeeded Edith Rees as secretary, lived there, and other members of the Fellowship were invited to take up residence. Pease described the venture as 'a mild attempt to carry out the com-

---

[1] *Seed Time*, April 1890.

[2] Rix lectured to the Fellowship on 11 March 1890, and Havelock Ellis wrote on 'The New Spirit' in *Seed Time* in July 1890, and in January 1893 Rix wrote on 'The Later Works of Count Leo Tolstoy'.

[3] *Seed Time*, October 1890.

[4] Ibid., January 1891.

[5] Announced in *Seed Time*, October 1891. E. Carpenter, *My Days and Dreams* (1915), 225. Edith Lees wrote a fictionalized account of her experiences in *Attainment*.

munity idea by means of associated colonies. Members lived near each other at a co-operative house which was established at 49 Doughty Street, Bloomsbury.'[1]

But the real centre of the movement lay in Croydon. There the printing was carried on, and there the Fellowship (always willing to listen) was now distracted by three singular and forceful preachers. The first, W. J. Jupp, had established 'a free religious movement' at Croydon late in 1890, and was lecturing to members on 'The Sources of Moral Enthusiasm'. His creed, based on Emerson and Thoreau, was that fellowship was 'an anticipation of the communal order'.[2] An even more forceful advocate of the Fatherhood of God and Brotherhood of Man was John Page Hopps. Hopps had established a new church at Lee Hurst, Leicester, and came down to Croydon to urge, amongst other things, 'the establishment of the Kingdom of Heaven everywhere upon the earth'.[3] Jupp and Hopps both wrote for *Seed Time*. The third, J. Bruce Wallace, moved to Croydon from Limavady and brought with him his journal *Brotherhood*, formerly called the *Christian Socialist*.

There was a distraction of purpose too, which showed itself by an almost indiscriminate enthusiasm for Utopist projects of every kind. In 1892 there was a long article on Theodore Hertzka's *Freeland*. Arthur Ransom, the translator advocate of the English Committee for initiating an African Colony on Hertzkan lines, received warm support,[4] as he expounded the scheme to members of the Fellowship, initiating 'a lively discussion' in which Dr. Gümpel, the chief organizer of the movement in London, joined. The Charity Organization Society, the Land Nationalization Society, John Trevor's Labour Church, H. V. Mills' scheme for English Industrial Villages for the Able-bodied Poor, and the Mexican experiment of Owen at Topolobampo, all claimed the sympathetic attention of the Brotherhood.

---

[1] The conflict of numbers can be resolved by taking the *Seed Time* number 29.

[2] The actual title of his address in *Seed Time*, April 1893. On 24 July 1894 he was taking the chair at meetings of the New Fellowship.

[3] In January 1891 he started a journal called *The Coming Day*, fifteen volumes of which are in the British Museum. In *Seed Time*, July 1892, J. Page Hopps wrote the main article, with Ramsay MacDonald writing on 'Municipal Workshops' and Maurice Adams on 'The New Reformation'.

[4] His translation appeared in 1891.

The excitements at Croydon were probably one reason why Ramsay MacDonald relinquished the secretaryship late in 1892 to J. F. Oakeshott, and the experiment in communal living at Doughty Square came to an end. With falling receipts, and a programme which consisted mainly of intellectual discussions, in the rooms of Herbert Rix at Burlington House, or the rooms of the treasurer, Commander Carpenter, the Fellowship's following dwindled to a remnant.

(6)

At this point a brisk and imaginative member of the committee (first elected in July 1894), J. C. Kenworthy, leapt into prominence. Kenworthy, who had worked in the Mansfield House settlement and had visited America, turned their eyes to present realities in his *Anatomy of Misery*, which was reviewed in *Seed Time* in January 1894. In the same year he told readers: 'In our bitterness of heart we have listened to the negations of Karl Marx and shut our ears to the words of the true prophets of the Reconstruction (Carlyle and Ruskin). The healing of society must come from within, through individuals and communities, who by living and extending the new life, will at last cast off from Society the slough of the old.' His enthusiasm was shared by Henry Binns (later to achieve distinction by his work with Rowntree) who wrote, 'Former failures and "Brook Farms" are no deterrent. They but whet the appetite with pretastes of experience.' Ripples even reached William Harrison Riley in Townend Centre, Massachusetts, who wrote back to *Seed Time* urging that 'workers should be employed by the Commonwealth for the Commonwealth'.

Kenworthy was particularly active in the work of the English Land Colonization Society,[1] which had been formed to establish a residential colony near London 'for middle and lower-middle class people who were anxious to escape from the conditions of city life'. After 1893, under the inspiration of Dr. J. B. Paton and Harold Moore,[2] it was directing attention to the unemployed. In November 1893 it had published a brochure to guide Poor Law Guardians as to the possibility of founding farm

---

[1] See its leaflets *Management of a Hand-Husbandry Farm, Farm Labour Colonies, A Farm Colony of Small Holders*.

[2] Whose *Home Colonies: The Need and Opportunity of our time* occasioned some comment at the time.

colonies under the Poor Law, and began to organize lectures and propaganda for that end. To accomplish what Paton wished, the re-establishment of the 'yeoman' class, Kenworthy saw but one means, communal tenure and co-operative cultivation, and he was trying to persuade Richard Stapley (who had a projected colony of smallholders at Hareham Road, Sussex) to join with him at Croydon. He also supported very vigorously the work of the Agricultural Banks Association.

Thanks to the generosity of J. Passmore Edwards, the English Land Colonization Society was able to organize a conference at the Holborn Town Hall in October, 1894, at which a Central Council of Home Colonies and Rural Industries was formed,[1] to supply a bond of union and to issue a quarterly journal. R. A. Yerburgh, became the President and T. Locke Worthington, Secretary.

It was but natural that, as a committee member of the Fellowship, Kenworthy should try and swing it in this direction. He had already (in June 1894) opened a Brotherhood Church at Croydon 'for people to *think* rather than follow preachers', where five o'clock Sunday tea parties were found to be 'of more spiritual profit than sacraments'. This late nineteenth century *agape* resulted in a resolution that they would look for a 'Brotherhood Camp' where they might dig on summer evenings.

Kenworthy was much affected by Emerson, Ruskin, Henry George, the Home Colonization Movement and the Industrial Village established by Herbert Mills at Starnthwaite near Lake Windermere, which since its foundation in 1892 had cleared 130 acres for fruit growing. These and other experiments, like that of Goodrich at Methwold, were publicized in *Seed Time*. In October 1894, soon after Kenworthy's *Anatomy of Misery* was reviewed in *Seed Time*, he was invited to explain his purpose to the Fellowship of the New Life and other sympathizers :–

It seems to me we may now, after the Socialist agitation and discussion of the last twelve years, gather together sufficient evidence

[1] The proceedings were published as *Co-operative Labour upon the Land* (ed. J. A. Hobson), in 1895. Members included the Agricultural Banks Association (London), the Allotments and Small Holdings Association (Birmingham), the Association for Improving the Conditions of the People (Glasgow), the Christian Union of Social Service (London), the Home Colonization Society (Kendal), the Mansion House Unemployed Committee and the Rural Industries Co-operative Society.

to enable us to formulate plans for the realisation of a right social order, which shall receive those who are willing and fit to enter, and to convince us that the horrors our ignorance forecasts, need by no means come upon us. To begin with we can only emancipate ourselves by the power of association.[1]

This was the first of several such exhortations which Kenworthy addressed to readers of *Seed Time*. The second—six months later—was more emphatic :–

Our times impose upon us a necessity which was never before so extreme. We must *organise*, and that on a great scale; we must confront capitalist organisation by fraternal organisation. The healing of society must come about from within; through individuals and communities, who by living and extending the new life will at least cast off from Society the slough of the old.[2]

Kenworthy's plan was that each neighbourhood—of twenty-five families or so—should save and use their savings to establish self-supporting industrial communities. Land in the country was to be acquired, and, as opportunity arose, members of the Fellowship were to be drafted off to the colonies. He was sanguine : 'The policy and methods of these operators', he wrote, 'are no more difficult than those involved in the Co-operative, Insurance, Friendly, or Building Societies which people carry on.' In April 1895 he wrote in *Seed Time* :–

In economics we are Socialists; in our ideal we are Communists, in politics we are, some of us, Anarchists of Peace . . .

The part of our 'programme' which differentiates us from others who seek after the ideal society, is the determination that, let the world go in such way as it pleases, we, each one for his own part, for 'the salvation of his own soul' must live *honestly* and *fraternally* towards all men. That principle of conduct, seemingly so individualistic, is really the basic principle of their Kingdom of Heaven which Jesus and all prophets have foreseen.

A monthly *Croydon Brotherhood Intelligence* was started to spread the gospel further.

Kenworthy had allies. His creed was helped by the accession to the committee of Gilbert Slater, then winning fame as an agricultural historian. Moreover, Henry Binns lamented the

[1] *Seed Time*, October 1894.
[2] *Seed Time*, April 1895 and January 1896.

blurring of the real purpose of the Fellowship as categorically stated in the original manifesto of 1882. 'Lastly, it will work towards the establishment, through its members, of a residential industrial settlement, on co-operative lines, by way of illustrating its ideal.'

Ideals of the earthly paradise, insisted Binns, were not sufficient, and he called for a collectivist church in London (on the lines of the Croydon Fellowship, the Croydon Brotherhood Church and the Labour Church) and a network of Rural Fellowship Settlements to 'wake up' the villages.[1] Richard Heath contributed his share by publishing the story of the *Anabaptism: From its rise at Zwickau to its fall at Munster 1521–1536*,[2] whilst John Trevor on 29 November added his voice to urge the fellowship to think communally.

Kenworthy had become in fact the heir of such of the Fellowship's following as existed, and Croydon, the centre of his operations, soon assimilated them. In a retrospect the editor of *Seed Time* remarked, somewhat ruefully, that once the new Fellowship had 'stood alone' as a mouthpiece of the ideal of a perfect individual in a perfect society, and that *Seed Time* had had 'no rivals' as an expositor of its outlook. 'But now', he continued 'the *Daily Chronicle*, the *Commonwealth* and the *New Age*, three out of many journals now abroad, cast among tens of thousands the ideas that fourteen years ago were, with difficulty, brought to the attention of a mere handful.' The *New Age* was Kenworthy's paper. Kenworthy was still talking to the Fellowship on 'Religion and Myth', and by February 1898 Maurice Adams closed the Fellowship (and *Seed Time*) for good, with the valediction that, 'It is not to its meetings that the Fellowship must look for the spread of its teaching, but to the lives of those who have received the Fellowship ideal.'

(7)

Tracer elements of 'Fellowship ideals' can be seen in the work of J. F. Oakeshott, the poor law reformer; Corrie Grant the champion of smallholders in Parliament; H. S. Salt, of the Humanitarian League (whose autobiography, *Seventy years*

---

[1] *Seed Time*, April 1895.
[2] He had published an article on 'The Anabaptists and their English Descendants' in the *Contemporary Review* for March 1891.

Among the Savages, published in 1921, showed by its title that the author was full of kindly humour); Herbert Rix, the assistant secretary of the Royal Society, who wrote on the world as a spiritual organism, anticipating the holism of Jan Smuts, and Edward Carpenter and his brother, at odds with their times, and anxious to read the signs aright.

Of these, perhaps Henry Salt was its most typical member. Brother-in-law of J. L. Joynes, and a great friend of Edward Carpenter, he published a *Life of H. D. Thoreau* in 1890 and was accredited by Bernard Shaw with a project for 'setting up land colonies'. Shaw claimed that when Salt and Carpenter were contemplating this, he told them 'that the socialist colonies in America failed except when they were monastically celibate . . . Any colony however is better than the damned Bohemian anarchism which never succeeds anywhere.' But Salt's latest biographer finds no evidence of this, though he agrees that Salt and Carpenter 'might well have discussed such a scheme in the intervals of Wagner-shrieking'.[1]

Salt's great friend Edward Carpenter had, as we have seen, helped Cecil Reddie to found a new type of school, Abbotsholme in Derbyshire. To Reddie, Davidson's gospel of enabling the human unit to reconstruct society had a powerful appeal and he could only reconcile it with the environmentalist doctrine of character he had imbibed from socialist teaching at Göttingen by founding 'a school state' which would achieve the emancipation of the boy. The *Pall Mall Gazette*, always anxious to keep its readers abreast of the newest ideas, devoted an article to it six weeks before the school opened, and commented on the timetable as 'somewhat of a curiosity in the educational line'. The article was supplemented by an interview with Edward Carpenter who was pictured as 'an exponent of what may be called the Gospel of Potato-digging'.

To Reddie Abbotsholme was a Kosmos.[2] In one of his reports he wrote: 'To us, personally, the English towns, the English houses, railway stations etc. seemed most inadequate. All were the outcome of English fog and insularity, want of ideas and social co-operation. All bore the stamp of selfish individualism, and all preached mental and social chaos to the wearied be-

[1] H. Winsten, *Henry Salt and His Circle* (London, 1951), 14.
[2] B. M. Ward, *Reddie of Abbotsholme* (London, 1934), 52.

holder.' Hence his school was to be a community and in time send off 'colonies which would furnish the legitimate outlet to masters of ability who had perfected themselves in the methods of Abbotsholme'. One of his 'colonists', J. H. Badley, left Abbotsholme after three years to found Bedales, at Hayward's Heath.[1]

(8)

But of all those over whom Davidson exercised an influence, none worked more effectively to establish a heaven on earth than Ebenezer Howard. When Davidson was first promoting the Fellowship, Howard was 33 years old, a friend of Bernard Shaw and Sidney Webb. As a shorthand writer in the Law Courts, he was not without experience of listening to advocates of a cause. He had been to America as a farmer, and had returned to work on a shorthand machine. (He is generally credited with improvements to the Remington typewriter.) C. B. Purdom remarks that his 'enthusiastic but puritanical and moralistic nature' was influenced by the Fellowship of the New Life. 'We can have little doubt', says Purdom, 'that Howard was influenced by the project made in the late eighties of the last century for a co-operative, industrial, educational and residential settlement in the neighbourhood of London under the auspices of Davidson's New Fellowship. He must have known about the project, but Howard was always very reticent about anything connected with the inception of his ideas.'[2]

Perhaps the strongest endorsement of this suggestion is that, when in 1902 Letchworth Garden City was established as a result of Howard's book *Tomorrow: A Peaceful Path to Real Reform* (1898), one of the architects was Raymond Unwin, a friend of Edward Carpenter, and that other members of the English Fellowship like J. Bruce Wallace, W. J. Jupp and H. B. Binns should take up residence there.

It is to Bruce Wallace that we should now turn.

---

[1] 'To the farm manager [of Abbotsholme] the main attraction of the venture had been to make of it an experiment in practical socialism. He looked upon the school as an agricultural community whose object was training for work on the land'. J. H. Badley, *Memories and Reflections* (1955), 107.

[2] C. B. Purdom, *The Building of Satellite Towns* (London, 1949), 27–39.

5

◇◇◇

The Tolstoyan Communities

◇◇◇

(1)

TREVOR was not the only church founder of this decade: another was J. Bruce Wallace. Bruce Wallace was a social mystic.[1] Born at Gujerat in India and educated at Dublin and Belfast for the ministry, he was so influenced by Henry George that on settling in Limavady in Northern Ireland, he began to issue, in 1889, a weekly known as *Brotherhood*. Originally a Presbyterian, he found it impossible to conform to the Westminster Confession and became a Congregationalist. He held pastorates at Dublin and Belfast. At Belfast *Brotherhood*, now a monthly, carried pointed comments on social conditions, which Wallace underlined by open-air campaigns. It carried Edward Bellamy's *Looking Backward* as a serial. And when, in 1889–90 Wallace visited America, Canada and Mexico, it also carried accounts of Topolobampo, A. K. Owen's famous community experiment. When Wallace came to north London in 1891 and took over an almost derelict church in Southgate Road, *Brotherhood* became the magazine of a church: the Brotherhood Church. This was founded as a result of a social questions conference which he held in 1892.

[1] W. R. Hughes, 'A Modern Franciscan', *Christian World*, 25 May 1939.
'Bruce Wallace and Brotherhood', *Congregational Quarterly*, October 1947. Wallace died in 1939 at the age of 85. The *Labour Annual* (Manchester, 1898), 198, gives a portrait of him. W. P. D. Bliss, *A Handbook of Socialism* (1907), 261.

J. Bruce Wallace now joined forces with J. C. Kenworthy.[1] Long before Kenworthy had been a member of the Ruskin Society in Liverpool (his birthplace), which was toying with the idea of establishing an 'industrial colony'. But, as he confessed, 'there was not sufficient power of conviction or clearness of perception; something was wanting in our moral, our spiritual constitution. This I felt, and set out to seek the something wanted.' That 'something wanted' led Kenworthy first to the Fellowship of the New Life. Then he found it in Tolstoy.

Tolstoy rejected the modern State and all efforts to organize the external condition of men's lives. He held that such efforts diverted attention from men's inner needs, and to countenance them was a sin. These efforts, usually based in his view on violence, were the social counterpart of the individual ego, and he would have none of them, advocating a clean-cut break with the predatory state. He looked forward to a new Christian order, an organic society based on self-government and brotherly co-operation of free men working in federated groups. These groups were to be small communities, with as close a connexion with nature as was possible, and animated by a new religion, intimations of which assailed Tolstoy in his thirties.[2] 'A conversation about divinity has suggested to me', he wrote in his diary during the Crimean Campaign,

> a stupendous idea, to the realisation of which I feel myself capable of devoting my life. This idea is the founding of a new religion corresponding to the present state of mankind: the religion of Christianity but purged of dogmas and mysticisms; a practical religion not promising future bliss, but giving bliss on earth. I understand that to accomplish this, the conscious labour of generations will be needed. One generation will bequeath the idea to the next and some day fanaticism or reason will accomplish it. Deliberately to promote the union of mankind by religion.[3]

[1] For biographical details see *Labour Annual* (1896), 177. For his Ruskinian experiences see *St. George* (Birmingham). Kenworthy's articles and poems can be found in I. 204–7; II. 42–43, 167, 190; III. 80, 138, 191–3.

[2] S. S. Koteliansky and L. Woolf, *Reminiscences of Leo Tolstoy* (London, 1920). 'The thought which beyond others most often and conspicuously gnaws at him is the thought of God.'

G. B. Shaw, *The Intelligent Woman's Guide to Socialism and Capitalism* (1929), 468.

[3] Janko Lavrin, *Tolstoy* (New York, 1946), 93.

In *The Kingdom of God is within You* Tolstoy developed the theme that the Nicene Creed must lose all value for a man who accepted the principle of the Sermon on the Mount. Like J. K. Vanderveer in Holland, who edited a Tolstoyan paper *Vreda*, and like Eugen Schmidt in Austria-Hungary who edited *Ohne Staat*, Kenworthy became his disciple. It was, as Tolstoy's most distinguished English translator put it, 'as though an unseen brotherhood, reaching round the world, had suddenly made itself manifest'.[1]

While Kenworthy was on his way to America with his family in 1890 Tolstoy's works first came into his hands. He had intended to settle there but returned to England after eighteen months to live in Canning Town, where he lived among the poor for two years, dreaming of establishing co-operative societies in connexion with Mansfield House University Settlement. His experiences stimulated him to write *The Anatomy of Misery* (1893) and join forces with Bruce Wallace.

(2)

Both Kenworthy and Wallace were convinced that a frontal attack on property, involving conversion of a political party or the passage of an Act of Parliament, should not distract from attempts being made to establish a voluntary co-operative system in England. So Wallace took the initiative in establishing the Brotherhood Trust on 19 January 1894, as the centre of an effort to discover, enrol and thoroughly organize a million altruists within four years into 'a voluntary Co-operative Commonwealth'; it was to interpenetrate the capitalist system and shame it to decay.

Organized in groups of ten, each under an elected decanus, each member was to co-opt out of separate profit-making business or industry and give custom and service to the organizing of 'fraternal industry and commerce'. Each was also to do his utmost to find, every quarter, one other person. Every quarter they were to attend quarterly meetings or report to their dean, and they were to persevere in this until 'the new century' began.

---

[1] Aylmer Maude, *Life of Tolstoy* (1911), 549. For a good brief account of Tolstoy's religious teachings see Julius F. Hecker, *Religion and Communism: A Study of Religion and Atheism in Soviet Russia* (London, 1933), 155–73.

Every ten deans were to meet together to elect a centurion, and every ten centurions were to elect a chiliarch.

To show their faith in this great scheme, a grocery and vegetable co-operative was opened on 20 January 1894 in North London at 1 and 5 Downham Road, Kingsland. They aimed to pay trade union wages and to provide old age pensions and sickness benefits to members from profits. They were also going to buy land. This land was to be the site of settlements, and herein lay the differences between them and contemporary co-operators, in that the capital subscribed by the Brotherhood for the store earned no interest and that the customers' net profit was never payable to them but was saved for the purchase of land for communities.

(3)

Not only Tolstoyans, but others like William Swainson[1] (a follower of Thomas Lake Harris) and Mary Grover (a Theosophist and Fabian) joined them. With David Frazer and his wife (both Spiritualists), G. D. Blogg, Frank and James Henderson and Fred Muggeridge (Socialists), they formed the committee. The first secretary was William Gilruth, who died in December 1894. He was succeeded by Fred Muggeridge, who resigned in 1895 and was in turn succeeded by H. P. Archer.

Other supporters were Mary Boole, widow of the famous mathematical professor; Miss S. A. Miller, then principal of the Diocesan Training College at Oxford, R. S. Gillard of Bristol, and Arthur St. John. St. John had been a captain and adjutant in the Royal Irish Fusiliers in Burma, after passing through the United Services College at Westward Ho. On a voyage home from Burma he read *The Kingdom of Heaven is Within You* and resigned his commission to join Kenworthy and Bruce Wallace. For them he managed the store, and taught children Swedish drill. His conversion was not as quick and dramatic as this bald narrative would imply: for on his own confession he had read Matthew Arnold and 'believed with him that the Kingdom of Heaven was to be realized here on earth'.[2]

---

[1] Swainson's paper, *Thomas Lake Harris, Mad or Inspired?* was read before the Brotherhood Church Social Conference on 28 February 1895. In it Swainson concluded that Harris was 'a truly inspired prophet' of Theosocialism.

[2] Arthur St. John, biographical memoir prefaced to his book *Why not Now?* (London, 1939).

To further the interests of the Trust, Kenworthy and Wallace founded the Brotherhood Publishing Company. In the winter of 1895–6 Kenworthy visited Moscow. His reward was a letter from Tolstoy giving him full rights over English versions of his work. 'My dear Friend', Tolstoy wrote, 'I intend to put at your disposition the first translation of all my writings as yet unpublished as well as forthcoming . . . should any pecuniary profit therefrom ensue, I would desire it to be devoted to the work of your Brotherhood Publishing Company.'[1] To devote his full time to this, Kenworthy relinquished his pastorate in the Brotherhood Church, which was taken over by Arthur Church, a mathematician and author of *A Plea for Communism, Shakers and Shakerism* and *The Brook Farm Experiment*.

The Brotherhood Churches began to multiply. To that run by Bruce Wallace at Southgate Road, Hackney, others were added. A Conservative club was taken over in Harrow Road, another began in the house of Sidney Goode in Leighton Road, London, and a third at 43 Monkhouse Road, Walthamstow. To encourage them Kenworthy began a journal called the *New Order*, which gave reports on current communitarian experiments: Topolobampo, Kaweah, the Dunkards in Indiana, the Fairhope Community in Mexico, and the Brotherhood of the Co-operative Commonwealth at Ruskin, Tennessee.

Kenworthy, by 1896, was wallowing in anarchist activity. He participated in the conference held on 28 July to welcome the International Socialist Workers' Congress. His fellow speakers, Tom Mann, Elie Réclus, Kropotkin, Malatesta and Louise Michel, listened to him proclaim that 'the English nation is ready to give up politics as a weapon and turn to industrial co-operation on free Anarchist Communist principles'. He wrote articles for the anarchist journal *Freedom*.[2] He was also one of the signatories of *The New Charter*, a humanitarian manifesto issued by a group which included Frederic Harrison, the positivist; A. L. Lilley; G. W. Foote and C. W. Leadbeater. After quoting the Sermon on the Mount, the manifesto continued: 'We are in the last stages of a corrupt civilization. A wrong conception of life, a belief that selfishness is the necessary

[1] A. Maude, *Life of Tolstoy* (1911), 515.
[2] *Freedom*, July, August, October 1896 on 'Charity True and False'. He also wrote, with Walter Crane and Kropotkin, an obituary of William Morris.

law of conduct, had ended for us any wide perception of spiritual truth, and surrendered us to the grossest errors of materialism'.

It was to redeem that 'corrupt civilization' that a colony was established at Purleigh on the free anarchist-communist principles Kenworthy was so enthusiastically endorsing.

(4)

Begun in February 1897 with five earnest souls, a house, two small cottages, workshops and an incubator, Purleigh was greatly stimulated in the ensuing months by the arrival of Tolstoy's confidant and friend, Vladimir Tchertkoff[1] in March 1897, to appeal for funds for the Dukhobors. The Dukhobors seemed to offer an example of a community based on Tolstoyan principles which was prepared to suffer for them and not disintegrate.

After Tchertkoff came Aylmer Maude, who had in the previous year begun translating Tolstoy. Maude had lived in Russia for twenty-three years, and Tolstoy's influence hastened his retirement from business, for, as he said, 'Tolstoy's indictment of the industrial system is so scathing, that, as it were, it wiped out the discrimination between better and worse businesses and sets one comparing things as they are with things as they should be'. At Tolstoy's recommendation he joined with Kenworthy.

A pantechnicon, which had to be manhandled for the last stages of its journey, arrived in April with the Hone family. They were followed by Arnold Eiloart, a young medium-built man of 35 who had studied both at the Royal College of Science and at Cornell University. He was living in Croydon in 1894, but when Purleigh was founded he bought two fields for the colony together with land and cottages at Wickford. Though awkward with his hands, he helped to build a greenhouse, a brickmaking plant and two cottages. Purleigh was now large enough to provide a holiday for visitors willing to pay for board and lodging.

And visitors came. They listened to Labour Church hymns and concerts. Kenworthy himself began to build a house there, and in February 1898 handed over the editorship of the *New Order* to F. R. Henderson. The colonists, now numbering

---

[1] A description of Tchertkoff can be found in Salome Hocking, *Belinda the Backward*, and a portrait in the *Reformers' Year Book* (Manchester, 1905), 185.

sixty-five—of whom fifteen were on the colony and fifty scattered around the district—held weekly meetings to discuss their plans. The publicity which the persecution of the Dukhobors attracted led Canon Scott Holland to write in the *Commonweal* in July 1898 on Tolstoy, and when Aylmer Maude left with the Dukhobors for Canada he was reinforced by over £1,000 collected by the Purleigh Colonists.

In August 1898 the *Daily News*, the *Manchester Guardian* and the *Essex County Chronicle* sent reporters to Purleigh. The *Clarion* was, in fact, rather tart, describing it on 20 August 1898 as 'an attempt to cut a Suez Canal to the Kingdom of Heaven'. 'They have jumped', it continued, 'the chasm from competition to Co-operation without waiting for the plank of social democracy and have arrived on the shores of anarchism.' It was regarded with horror by the respectable. The parents of one 'colonist' offered him £1,000 a year if he would leave. Yet the *Clarion* bore witness to the 'siege of applications'. But Kenworthy was undisturbed: he saw it as 'a community visibly ordered by the principles Ruskin had taught'. 'Last year', he wrote on 18 July 1898 'it was not much changed from the surrounding half-desolate fields of the country where agricultural ruin has gone so far; but now, you could not well miss it, because of four acres of market garden, a hundred feet of greenhouse, some finished new buildings, including a new brick house, and buildings going up.'

In addition to the colony there was a contingent of Russian exiles on the twenty-three-acre estate. All met together at dinner-time in a large marquee.[1]

Kenworthy wanted to establish a printing press at Purleigh, and got his way. By May 1899, the *New Order* was being printed there.

As a colony it began to thrive. Two hundred apple trees, 250 gooseberry bushes, a kitchen garden with celery and potatoes, cows and hens, ensured that the inhabitants had enough to eat. Its sole source of agricultural power was a horse—Johnny— which used to pull a London bus, and much time was spent breaking it from the habit of pulling a plough at the same speed. Coal was sent from the Swadlincote Co-operative Colliery. Cottages began to rise. William Hare proudly reported in the

[1] *St. George* (Birmingham, 1898), 202–7.

New Order of May 1899: 'We are a small group in the midst of a world wide movement towards a better and truer life for humanity. We think it is a step worth taking, though our ideal is beyond it all. Not beyond the necessary productive labour, but beyond some present aspects of it'. All had different ideas, and as Hare said, 'some have decided not to hold legal titles in property, others endeavour not to use money, others not to use stamps, others protest against railways'.

(5)

Other colonies were not long in forming. Arnold Eiloart had, as we have seen, purchased some land at Wickford, and one group, led by Henry Power, announced that it was 'useless waiting for the millennium, but hoped to get a little closer to it by endeavouring to act on brotherly principles'. As Henry Power put it in the *New Order* of February 1899 :—

> It will not be on the same lines as the Purleigh Colony, for the members of this new group are not able to shake themselves so free from their commercial fetters, and to this extent fall short of the examples set by the more fearless brothers. It is proposed that each member shall work and cultivate his land on the lines he may think best. Co-operation will spring up naturally when people of similar aims and ideas get together; the land will be conveyed to each member separately, and in fact perfect freedom is the watchword of the colony.

Essex became a virtual nursery of communities. In addition to Purleigh, the *Labour Annual*, for 1897 listed three more ventures. The first was Althorne, a place 'where socialist settlers would find skilled advice and like-minded comrades' from 'Comrade Edwards'. The second, Assingdon (near Hockley) had a small anarchist group under James Evans; whilst the Forest Gate Christian Socialist League under E. W. Wooley announced their intention of making preparations for a land settlement there.

Further attempts to form Tolstoyan groups were made at Leeds, Blackburn and Leicester. At Leeds, Albert Gibson, formerly the owner of a workshop, had been so influenced by the teaching of J. C. Kenworthy that he joined in April 1897 with T. H. Ferris, Eliza Pickard and Jackson Ferris to immediately apply the principles of the Sermon on the Mount at 6

Victoria Street. In December 1898, one of them wrote in the *New Order* :–

> Here around us are Socialists, Anarchists, and members of Christian Churches watching with curiosity and interest the success or otherwise of the small beginning on the lines of industrial communism at 6 Victoria Street, while in its members is awakening a social conscience such as will enable them to work effectively and with increase of joy for the common good.

Blackburn was an offshoot of the Leeds group. There the Christian Communist friends at 35 Victoria Street, under William Murray, began to think of a community. This was in April 1899. On 15 July the *Blackburn Times* reported their activity and in August the *New Order* published their creed: 'We circulate Tolstoy because his conception of the ideal life is nearest to ours.

'We in Blackburn are like a city set on a hill. The utter futility of any attempt to live by external rules is only equalled by the utter fatality of the smallest conscious departure from principle.'

Leicester started last of all in January 1899 with five members. All were vegetarians and they acquired half an acre of land at Braunstone and formed a land society to acquire another. They hoped, so they told the *Labour Annual* of 1900, eventually to live 'a communal life on the land'.

(6)

These northern experiments stimulated the publication of *The Free Commune*, a new monthly. *The Free Commune* was published by W. MacQueen[1] from 21 Mellor Road, Slade Lane, Longsight, Manchester, and was 'not only edited, but printed on the lines of free initiative'. The first number had appeared in April 1898 at Manchester. It explained that the needs of the group included those of some who were 'producing electrical apparatus and bicycles'. It reported that some of the Clousden Hill colonists had spoken at a conference of Northern Co-operative Societies at Sunderland. The second number, which appeared in

---

[1] William MacQueen subsequently emigrated to New York in 1902 and was soon in jail 'nominally for inciting Italian and Hungarian weavers of Paterson to violence'. R. T. Berthoff, *British Immigrants in Industrial America* (Cambridge, Mass., 1953), 104.

June 1898, carried not only a description of the Leeds Co-operative Workshop by MacQueen and the Norton Colony of Hugh Mapleton, but advertisements of 'anarchist groups' at Manchester, Liverpool, and Derby and a 'Socialist League' at Leicester. MacQueen's article on Co-operation stressed that all comrades should group together to acquire land and set up colonies adjacent to towns on the model of Clousden Hill. These colonies would 'help to form the nucleus of a better society and act as havens of the victimized'.

MacQueen himself seems to have removed to 79 Markham Avenue, Leeds, by the time the third number (dated October 1898) was issued.

In November 1898 Kenworthy's house at Purleigh was finished and he decided to make a missionary tour link the scattered groups. He came to Leeds to confer with the Tolstoyans and the Free Communist group and discuss the People's Church. He also went to Bolton, Nottingham and other places trying to generate enthusiasm.

By January 1899 *The Free Commune* was being issued quarterly from Leeds by the Free Communist group as a 'magazine of libertarian thought'. MacQueen was still working for it, together with A. Barton of 2 Watts Street, Levenshulme, Manchester. 'We do not believe in schemes' was the burden of his writings. But they were evidently in touch with two anarchist groups in America; one in San Francisco (which published the *American Anarchist*) and the other in New York (publishing *Solidarity*). They rejected political action in a strike and displayed the purest Tolstoyan stigmata.

(7)

If the cause was prospering elsewhere, it was foundering at Purleigh. Samuel Veale Bracher, a young journalist from Gloucester who had joined in 1898 intending to stay for a year, quarrelled with Kenworthy. According to one report, Purleigh was admitting tramps and Bracher objected violently. He was supported by Arnold Eiloart, who had subscribed generously to the Dukhobor migration; Miss Dunn, a member of Maude's household and friend of Havelock Ellis; Miss Nellie Shaw and Joseph Burtt (who had left the comfortable precincts of a bank at Cheltenham to join the colonists). Together they decided to move away and found a colony of their own. They discovered a fine stone-built house at Whiteway near Stroud in Gloucestershire with forty acres of land which they bought for £450, Bracher supplying £405 and Burtt £45. Bracher also bought farm implements and spent £1,200 on improvements.

Another journalist at Purleigh, Aylmer Maude, was even more disturbed than Bracher. Maude had handed over his translation of Tolstoy's *What is Art?* to the Brotherhood Publishing Company. When it appeared a reviewer commented that 'Mr. Maude was evidently too anxious to keep himself unspotted from the (commercial) world in the cloistered seclusion of . . . Wickham's Farm, near Danbury, Essex', and added 'Mr. Maude wants the equivalent of a piano—some form of inviting advertisement, something to make Tolstoy go down'. Maude was evidently piqued by the lack of business sense displayed by the Brotherhood Company and wrote: 'The rejection of ordinary ways of carrying on industry and business did not conduce to efficient or harmonious activity; while the more zealous partisans of the movement, reluctant to admit that there was a flaw somewhere in the teaching, preferred to lay the blame on one another. Quarrels were therefore frequent, and Kenworthy's eccentricities . . . helped to involve and embitter these disputes.'

Even greater tensions arose from the Dukhobor migration. Maude was helping to arrange the migration of the Dukhobors to Canada with Vladimir Tchertkoff, Prince D. A. Hilkoff (who had given away his estates), Ivan Ivin and Peter Mahortof—all at Purleigh. The first idea was to transport the Dukhobors to Cyprus. Ivin and Mahortof had visited the island in July 1898 but found it unsuitable—too late, however, to prevent the temporary migration of 1,126 Dukhobors.

Tchertkoff, Tolstoy's nominee, as superintendent of the emigration quarrelled with Hilkoff: one had the subscriptions, the other the ability to organize the migration. As Maude lamented, 'Their relations became in fact so strained that all direct intercourse between them had to cease. A similar misfortune befell several other people who tried to co-operate with Vladimir Tchertkoff or to work under his command'.

Hilkoff and Maude left Purleigh for Canada with an advance party of the Dukhobors in September 1898. Tchertkoff (who sentimentalized the Dukhobors as Christian Martyrs, and did not realize that many of them believed that their leader, Peter Verigin, was a messiah)[1] stayed at Purleigh superintending, in a singularly inept way, the financing of the movement. H. P. Archer left Purleigh to act as a schoolmaster to the Dukhobors in Canada, and whilst there received a peremptory letter from Tchertkoff demanding that Maude should apologize for 'errors' made. Tchertkoff announced that unless apologies were forthcoming, all further communication between him and Maude would cease. 'So', wrote Maude, 'I asked to be permitted to state my case. This request Tchertkoff refused to entertain, and though, in deference to Tolstoy's wish, I subsequently repeatedly expressed my readiness to make any apology, and do anything in my power to heal the breach . . . Tchertkoff and I have never met since that day.'[2]

(8)

The loss of Arnold Eiloart, S. V. Bracher, Joseph Burtt, Nellie Shaw and Miss Dunn deprived Purleigh of its hands. The loss of H. P. Archer to Canada as a Dukhobor schoolmaster deprived it of a steady head. All that was now left to Kenworthy was the Brotherhood Publishing Company, on which he relied as a source of income, since Tolstoy had promised him the royalties accruing from the 'first publication' of any of his works. As Maude said, 'probably much that was eccentric in his (Kenworthy's) conduct can be traced to the hopes aroused by this curiously indefinite promise, and by his subsequent disappointment over it'.[3] These eccentricities now revealed themselves as the group disintegrated. In the summer of 1899 it was obvious that Purleigh was breaking up, and Maude wrote to tell Tolstoy so. Tolstoy replied on 15 December 1899 :—

The failure of life in the Colony, about which you wrote, is only an indication that the form of life which was chosen by the Colonists for the realization of their spiritual needs was not adequate. When a definite inner content exists in man, it finds for itself a corresponding

---

[1] Contrast V. Tchertkoff, *Christian Martyrdom in Russia*, with a preface by J. C. Kenworthy and a concluding chapter by Leo Tolstoy published by the Brotherhood Publishing Co., and Aylmer Maude, *A Peculiar People: The Dukhobors* (London, 1905).

[2] *The Life of Tolstoy: Later Years*, 554.

[3] *Life of Tolstoy*, 516.

form—generally unconsciously, i.e. when one is not thinking about the form, and when the form is not defined in words.[1]

Maude's comment was astringent:–

Partly owing to the strain it put upon men's minds, and partly because every strenuous movement attracts some ill-balanced people, there was much insanity at Purleigh. At least five who lived and stayed at the Colony while I was there, were subsequently put under mental supervision on account of their mental condition. Even those of us who kept our sanity did not always keep our tempers.[2]

Poor Kenworthy, the unhappy artificer of disaster thought it was

not want of means, not want of recruits, but want of *character* brought the crash. And not merely from Tolstoy's warning, but from prior experience, I knew what to expect, and was prepared, as well as one can be, for a certain kind of ruin. When that came, despite Mr. Tchertkoff's pressure to the contrary, I determined to again visit the one friend who understood.[3]

So he went to Russia, and on his return devoted his time to spiritualism and interpreting Tolstoy, publishing *Tolstoy: His Teaching and Influence in England* (1901), and *Tolstoy, His Life and Works* (1902). He was later confined in a lunatic asylum. Aylmer Maude, reflecting on the adventure, mused:–

To hold a commune together requires either a great identity and immutability of life-habits, or a stereotyped religious tradition: so that the members, from force of habit or from religious hypnotism, may not wish to do anything that runs counter to the communal customs. The only other thing, apparently, that renders communism possible is a very strong leadership dominating the entire group. In the case last mentioned, rapid collective material progress is quite possible, so long as the strong and capable leader is there to sanction changes and decide what changes shall be tolerated, and when they shall be introduced.[4]

(9)

Yet the impetus of the movement continued. S. V. Bracher, the journalist who bought the forty-acre estate at Stroud, near

[1] ibid., 598.
[2] ibid., 547.
[3] J. C. Kenworthy, *Tolstoy, His Life and Work* (London, 1902), 16.
[4] A. Maude, *A Peculiar People: The Dukhobors* (London, 1905), 261.

Whiteway, and settled there with colonists from Purleigh, now had to face the very problems which had broken Kenworthy. He began with a colony of nine men, four women, and two children. A quarrel began almost immediately over the ownership of the land. Bracher had put up most of the money for its purchase, but neither he nor anyone else wished to have their names entered as legal owners. One suggestion was that the land should be reconveyed to the Real and Eternal Owner, but this did not meet the requirements of the law, so eventually three of the group, Joseph Burtt, William Sinclair and Sudbury Protheroe, agreed to have the conveyance drawn up in their names. Having done so, the parchment was handed over to the group, and promptly but ceremoniously burnt. 'We had a very merry time', wrote one of them, 'burning the deeds. The tax man wanted to know if they were destroyed so we thought it simpler to destroy them and have done with it.' This was to emphasize the fact that their land was not held as the private property of any individual. Since they had left Purleigh on the issue of admissions, they now made plans to work the land and erect the necessary buildings, and to receive settlers without any distinction of race or creed. Half an acre of land was put under spade cultivation. After being thoroughly cleaned and double-dug, it was planted out with fruit trees—apples, pears and plums. In the spring additional land was under cultivation, sown and planted with various kinds of vegetables.

Meanwhile Bracher had married, and his outlook on life altered considerably. He demanded half the income for the exclusive use of himself and his wife. They occupied a separate house in a village nearby, and took less and less part in the communal work. Sufficient funds were, however, left to enable two cows to be bought and a dairy and store to be built. The sympathizers and visitors who had thronged to Purleigh now came to Whiteway. Journalists and photographers gave publicity to the so-called 'new movement' in the summer of 1899. With a new century, new settlers arrived. A sailor with a tent; two Quakers (Edward Tregellis and Edward Rickard) with a printing press and the manuscript of a book they were bringing out; a compositor in the last stage of consumption; a farmer who had been dispossessed of his farm through the action of the War Office; an ex-Congregational minister who had taken to wearing sandals and preaching at street corners; a trained boxer, 'strong as an ox but simple as a child', and several others of various trades, occupations and nationalities, increased the numbers of the colony.

But before that summer ended a young married couple in the colony decided to separate, the husband going back to the city while his wife and two children remained at Whiteway. A few months later the wife formed a 'free union' with another colonist. The first husband returned. There was a row. Bracher and his wife wrote to the local papers dissociating themselves from the group. The suspicion of polygamy quickly dispersed sympathizers and visitors jealous of their reputations. Some of the prospective settlers also moved off.

The *Labour Annual* of 1900 reported the colony (p. 115) as having eighteen men and six women, who occupied forty-one acres, arable and pasture. 'Does not barter, but gives and takes freely, recognizes no laws or external rules beyond those of the conscience, and has burnt its title deeds, not believing in property owning. . . . At present the group have no prospects and desire none.'

Whiteway's grim future in the last winter of the nineteenth century was obvious. Their cows had been driven away and sold by Bracher. Their hay was pounced upon and carted off by a young farmer, to test the communism of the group: he afterwards absconded. Their goods were recklessly given away by one member of the group, formerly a commercial traveller. William Sinclair lost a watch, a pair of winter boots and leggings, and sundry articles of clothing after some visitors had been.

Normal communal obligations of working the land virtually collapsed. Some of the colonists had drifted into it hoping to throw off all external restraint. One colonist absconded to enlist in the Navy. Another disappeared when crops required to be harvested. Yet another refused on principle to arrange for the next day's work; he later ended his days in a lunatic asylum.

Finally, it was decided that it would be better if each took up and cultivated his own plot of land—co-operating with others when necessary. During the years that followed, new settlers came in; all the available land was taken up; several dwelling-

houses and other buildings were erected, the land under cultivation was got into much better condition, with corresponding
better results for labour expended; a good bakery for the production of wholesome bread was put in operation; and hand-
loom weaving was introduced. When the colonists wished to
meet they did so with a freshness and interest that was getting
to be unknown in the days when there was too much crowding.[1]

(10)

The remainder of the original Brotherhood group split into
factions. The Brotherhood Publishing Company was captured
by Tchertkoff, with the help of A. C. Fifield, and renamed the
Free Age Press. They took a building at Christchurch, near
Bournemouth, and one correspondent recollects that 'anyone
approaching was questioned through loopholes of a barricade
before being admitted'. Aylmer Maude pointed out that the
secrecy was due to the fact that Tolstoy's publications had to be
smuggled into Russia.[2]

The second factor was the Brotherhood Trust, which remained as a propaganda organization registered to issue barter
notes on the actual production of goods. In 1920 it merged with
the London Co-operative Society, but its successor, the Brotherhood Extension Society (with its currency) continued to help
community experiments in general, whilst J. T. Harris, its
moving spirit, also organized the Production for Use League
with Edward Unwin.

The third group was the Brotherhood Church. This continued to exhibit half Christian, half Marxist leanings with
readings from the Bible alternating with hymns from the *Labour
Song Book*. It became a centre, if not a cell, of early revolutionary activity. Perhaps the strangest meeting that ever took place
within its walls was that of the Fifth Congress of the Russian
Social Democratic Party. Four of the major Russian revolutionaries were there, Stalin, Gorki, Lenin, and Zinoviev. It was
from there that Stalin hastened to take part in 'the expropriation

---

[1] Nellie Shaw, *Whiteway: a Colony on the Cotswolds* (1935), and private letters
to the author from Mr. G. Marin, 4 December 1955. *Manchester Guardian*, 23
and 24 November 1955.

[2] Eugene Schuyler, 'A Secret Press in England'. *The Bookman's Journal* (1928),
XV. 217, XVI. 278.

of Tiflis' and Lenin sat on the platform listening to arguments for the revision of the Party programme.[1]

During the First World War it witnessed a violent scene in support of the Kerensky revolution in Russia. Someone had distributed pamphlets in the nearby public houses accusing them of being in league with the Germans, and signalling to their aeroplanes where to drop bombs. A mob, including women armed with boards studded with nails, attacked the church, and amongst those besieged were Bertrand Russell and Francis Meynell. On a subsequent occasion Russell was to address the Brotherhood Church, only to discover that a mob had set fire to the pulpit. Characteristically he remarked 'These were the only occasions when I came across personal violence.'[2]

One of its branches in Pontefract, under A. G. Higgins, started a land colony based on knitting and bee-keeping in 1921. This lasted until just before the Second World War. The Southgate Road Church was pulled down on 12 April 1924.

Independently of these three groups the Tolstoyan mystique expanded. Two affected most powerfully were H. W. Massingham, who wrote on Tolstoy's ideas under the title of 'The Philosophy of a Saint' in the *Contemporary Review* of 1900, and W. T. Stead. Curiously enough, Stead, like Kenworthy, took up psychical research. Massingham went on to a distinguished career in journalism as editor of the *Daily Chronicle* and later of the *New Statesman*, where his ascendancy amongst the literary columnists of his day gave 'non-conformist' journalism a new dimension.

The rump, under J. Bruce Wallace and W. J. Jupp, joined forces under the inspiration of Ebenezer Howard, to promote Letchworth Garden City. Before exploring that particular trial, we might glance for a moment at another Utopian scheme that excited interest just before Howard issued his manifesto.

[1] A. P. Dudden and T. H. von Laue, 'The R.S.D.L.P. and Joseph Fels', *American Historical Review*, 61 (1955), 26.

[2] Bertrand Russell, *Portraits from Memory* (London, 1956), 31–32.

6

Cosme Colony 1893—98

---

(1)

Hot apocalyptic denunciations of city life were contributed by John Miller to *Seed Time*. He wrote from Cosme, an experimental settlement in Paraguay, describing modern cities in July 1895 as 'Rosewatering their leprousness with modern buildings, and lighting their darkness through the dungeon windows of public parks'. 'Do we not all know', he asked, 'that the modern city is unnatural, and that street and road and lane and alley have not been twisted further from their original significance than man has in them from his normal life.' 'Socialism or no Socialism', Miller declared, 'reform or no reform, the city must go.' Other accounts of the Cosme Colony were published by *Seed Time* in January, April and October 1896. It was listed in the *Labour Annual* for 1896, and extracts from its reports were published in the *Clarion*. So when William Lane came to England in July 1897, readers of *Seed Time*, on reading the announcement that inquiries to him should be addressed to the Paraguayan Consulate, were well appraised of the reasons for his visit and the significance of his experiment.

Lame, small-sized and short-sighted, William Lane, the 'onlie begetter' of Cosme was 35 years of age when he appeared in England to recruit followers for his experiment. Born in Bristol in 1861, and educated at its grammar school, he had emigrated to the United States with his parents just when Ruskin was founding the Guild of St. George. He took to journalism and, following his profession, migrated first to Canada, then to Australia and six years after leaving England found himself editor of the *Brisbane Courier and Observer*. He was then 22.

Brisbane was Lane's road to Damascus. He founded there a Brisbane Trades and Labour Council on the model of a similar organization at Bristol, and in 1887 started another newspaper called *Boomerang*. Reading Henry George converted him to Socialism and he started to edit in 1890 a third paper called the *Worker*.

Lane was also much influenced by Bellamy's *Looking Backward* which he published as a serial in the *Worker*. When Hertzka's *Freeland—A Social Anticipation*, appeared, Lane was convinced that it was possible to go forward and establish A Working Man's Paradise. He published a novel with that title in 1892 as a manifesto, following up by founding the New Australia Co-operative Settlement Association, with a subscribed capital of £30,000.

When Lane first laid his plans before one of his followers he was urged to keep within the boundaries of Australia. He himself applied for land in western New South Wales and waited on the Minister, who was quite willing for a Co-operative Colony to be established there, but the Minister was overruled on a technical point. So Lane came to the conclusion that the old ties needed breaking and sent three agents to South America to prospect for a suitable site. They found that in Argentine the land was not suitable, but in Paraguay they found a hospitable and co-operative government which agreed to give them free entrance and transport and promised to exempt them from taxes. In return Lane agreed to settle 800 families in a Paraguayan colony in four years.

Like a modern prophet Lane won the support of skilled workers and intellectuals, as well as sheep shearers. He bought, for £1,200, a sailing ship of 600 tons called the *Royal Tar*. Like Hetzka's ideal colonists, he planned to sail it away to Paradise. Unfortunately there was a two-months delay whilst a new mainmast, new cable and anchor and three large new boats were fitted. Then the government insisted that adequate provisions be taken for 130 days—so his followers camped in the open for weeks, amassing what they thought would be needed, including a steamhammer. The carpenters amongst them converted the holds into berths and dining-tables, but their efforts only provoked the *Sydney Bulletin* of 22 July 1893 to describe the ship as 'a wilderness of bare boards with no entrance for the sun's rays except what may be afforded by the deadlights'.

(2)

The *Royal Tar* sailed to Paraguay on 17 July 1893 from Sydney with 250 'colonists' on board. Lane occupied one of the smallest cabins on the boat. He also took his turn in the galley peeling potatoes. Everyone was so keen to undertake menial tasks that there were not enough for them to do. Lane's particular problem was that sixty of the complement were bachelors, who slept above boards. He had planned that the women should go below at nightfall. But the women objected to staying in the stuffy atmosphere of the holds, below the waterline, from sunset to sunrise, in atmosphere illuminated by a smoky hurricane lamp. So they flocked above-decks to the bachelors, and Lane was forced to issue an edict that all women were forbidden to appear on deck after sunset. The women were furious, all the more so when they discovered that Lane had consulted only the married women of the party and not the spinsters. The spinsters stormed the hatchway to remind him that they were also members of the community, and had as much right to order Lane to his cabin as he had to order them to theirs. One of the outraged spinsters tore down Lane's edict from the notice board and trampled it underfoot and others stayed on deck half the night merely to assert their freedom to do so.

At this point Lane fell ill and a general meeting was convened to discuss the matter. They decided that Lane was not to be obeyed. So Lane resigned. A second general meeting was held asking him to reconsider his decision. Lane recovered and summoned a third general meeting which, like a flock of sheep, responded to his bark and passed a unanimous vote of confidence in him as leader.

From now on, Lane was supreme.

The remainder of the voyage was spent in organizing each department of activity. Foremen were approved for each group.

Lane also held a collection to supplement the bare £25 with which he had embarked, in order to cover their expenses in Montevideo.

They arrived at Montevideo, and embarked for a further 1,300 miles trip up the river to Asuncion.

The Paraguayan government lent the Opera House as a temporary home for Lane's party. A British observer was much impressed by them and reported: 'Everybody who saw them had been struck by their manners, their appearance, and their intelligence . . . they appeared to be, in fact, the very men . . . to help Paraguay on the road to recovery.'

In the hot sunshine they travelled on the railway to Caballero through magnificent forests and grazing grounds. At Caballero they transferred their possessions to bullock-carts and set off through fruit-laden trees, in which gaudy parrots and butterflies flew, to their concession. They negotiated rivers by floating the bullock-carts slung between canoes as floats. They chopped down trees. They made simple clearances in the forests. And, when they reached their destination, they set to work immediately building houses.

Since no stone was available, wood supports were used with walls of clay baked on to a wickerwork skeleton, and roofs of shingle or thatch. A large hall 144 ft. by 20 ft. was made at the centre of the colony to house twelve families, whilst the remainder was laid out in allotments of a quarter of an acre each. They worked with such a will that an official opening date was fixed for the colony on 11 October 1893. To the open day came the Minister for Foreign Affairs, the President's Secretary and a military escort. The hall, partly finished, served as a reception centre. Lane, with the Minister ceremonially hoisted the Paraguayan flag, inscribed Pas Y Justicia, to the accompaniment of cheers and rifle fire. A great cattle ring was made to receive 2,500 head of cattle. They formed a brass band of thirty-six instruments, costing £250. A teacher, Murdoch, joined the colony to organize the education of the children.

(3)

But, as the colony moved from sheer expediency to comparative stability, troubles arose. The first cause of trouble was Lane's ban on the use of alcohol, for on 15 December 1893, two months after the opening, Lane expelled two members for wilful and persistent violation of the clause . . . relating to liquor drinking. Uproar followed, and when the expelled members refused to leave he invoked his powers as an executive officer of the Paraguayan government to summon soldiers to drive them out. One of the expelled had given the cause £1,000, but it availed him little. Lane's revolver and the Paraguayan soldiers were stronger than words.

The second cause of trouble was that Lane had, without consulting the members, registered the Association as a limited liability company. This gave him even more power than he had previously possessed and eighty-five members decided to secede, taking with them an average of £3. 2s. 6d. This comprised about a third of the colonies' strength. The seceders approached the British Consul at Asuncion, and the second secretary of the Legation at Buenos Aires, M. de C. Findlay, was sent to patch up a truce. Unfortunately he found it impossible to do so, and wrote:–

> The colonists have started with everything in their favour—free land, immunity from taxation, a good climate, and a certain amount of capital. They are a fine class of men, and if they were less disposed to stand on the letter of their rights and took a more reasonable view of the failings of their fellows they would be sure to succeed. As it is, they came to found Utopia, and before I visited the colony had succeeded in creating (as they said) 'a hell upon earth'.

Rather than endure this hell, the eighty-five seceders threw themselves on the generosity of the Paraguayan Government which fed and housed them for three weeks at Villa Rica and then offered them a grant of land at the Gonzalez Colony near the railway line.

The Gonzalez Colony had been established two years before Lane's by the President for Frenchmen, Germans and Poles. Endowed with a family land grant of thirty acres, tax exemption for ten years, the necessary implements and seeds and a six months' sustenation allowance, the seceders from Lane's colony came to join them. They stayed till July 1894, when, after a revolution which drove Gonzalez from office, the generous endowment ceased. In September, therefore, twenty-five of the eighty-five seceders sold up and took a boat to Buenos Aires where further charity enabled them, and one or two others, to return to Australia.

Lane's wife had, just after the secession, returned with her children by the *Royal Tar* with instructions to organize a party of single women.

(4)

Meanwhile, in Australia, the *Royal Tar*'s first return on 7 December 1893 stimulated further recruiting. The second contingent of Utopists were camped awaiting its arrival and there was a rush amongst members of the Association in Adelaide to sell up and sail too. The Association was said to be negotiating for the sale of three more ships.

Just as the *Royal Tar* was about to sail on 28 December 1893, the Governor at Adelaide received a telegram informing him of the secession. The telegram gave the number of the seceders as 'eight', not 'eighty', and the news was communicated to the passengers on the *Royal Tar*. A meeting was summoned but, since the number of seceders given was eight, the emigrants passed a unanimous vote of confidence in William Lane and sailed away without delay.

They arrived at Asuncion on 7 March 1894 to be met by William Lane. Apart from a few defections, 190 people proceeded to 'New Australia'—as Lane's colony was called, where they were placed in a new site, Loma Rougua, about ten miles distant from Las Ovejas, the original settlement. His purpose was obviously to isolate them.

The newcomers, especially in view of the rumours they had heard, had no wish to be isolated. And, having made their individual ways to the original settlement, they came to the conclusion that the constitution of the colony should be enforced, and that Lane should resign. Permission was obtained from the Board in Australia and a new chairman was appointed.

Lane asked to be allowed to found a settlement at Codas, which was refused. So with forty-five adult followers and a dozen children, some implements and cattle, he left New Australia. Leaving them encamped outside the New Australia territory he went to Asuncion to obtain a further grant of land. This he received in the Mate country, some eighteen miles from where his party had encamped. It was a wild country tract on sandy soil, near the mountains of central Paraguay, and Lane shrank from planting his little settlement here. So, helped by some money from his followers, plus a further substantial sum from New South Wales he bought for £400 five and a half acres of good land only thirteen miles from a railway station, in the fork of the Pirapo and Tebicuari rivers. He paid £100 down and agreed to pay the remainder in annual instalments of £100.

(5)

In July 1894 this third colony was set up and christened Cosme. Amongst the waist-high grass the tents were pitched, and to symbolize the birth of a new world, two babies were delivered. One was Lane's niece, promptly christened Cosma. The Cosmeans worked with grim determination. Forests were felled, roots lifted, and soil hoed with desperate intensity. The only relaxation they allowed themselves was to compile a magazine, *Cosme Evening Notes*, to serve as a living memorial of their joys and sorrows.

The first six months were hard. Women washed without soap, food was cooked without fat, clothes were darned without material. Anything that could be bartered for kerosene, beans, salt and maize, was collected. Even when the harvest came in meat, flour and butter were still unobtainable.

Yet they kept together and William Lane occupied himself with another constitution. This deprived married women of the suffrage and made provision for dividing Cosme into villages under a central authority. The villages were to elect three committee-men, the committee was to elect one executive officer and an executive officer was to be eligible after his service for the chairmanship of the village. The central authority was to be composed of a general chairman, each village chairman and one committee man from each village. It was to maintain Cosme principles and the establishment of new villages, and to hold the funds. These funds were to be built from the value of one day's work per week from each village and were to be allotted for loans (3/5ths), emergencies (1/5th) and enlargement (1/5th).

No dividend was to be made until maintenance, education, sanitation and other expenses had been provided for. Any withdrawing member could claim from the village as much as a share (1/10th for each year he had been a householder). This withdrawal share was to be arranged at the general village meeting with the consent of the local authority. An eight hour day and a four-and-a-half day week was instituted as the irreducible weekly minimum.

Lane also introduced a theoretic element into Cosme. 'It is clear', he told his community, 'that Jesus, like Tolstoy, never understood the healthy physical life, and so expounded an unbalanced philosophy.' He, like other Utopists, now produced his own religion, Communism, 'the brotherliness in society of man'. There was an initiation ceremony for new members, and readings were given on Socialism.

It was to win more recruits for Cosme that Lane decided to come to England in 1897.

(6)

The English recruits set sail for Cosme straight away. Arriving with civilized clothes and habits, expecting to share in the increments of three years' work by the colonists, these recruits had little experience of the chores necessary in such a community, and were tenderfeet in every sense of the term. In all, five British parties arrived, the first on 25 May 1897, the fifth on 8 April 1898. Some of them left again because of the climate, others because of the hostility they met. From the *Cosme Monthly* their professions and home towns can be discovered.

> MARCH 1897. *Arrival:* Alf. Bray, the first member from England, arrived on the 24th.
> *Departure:* A.Mc.C.——, who was accepted as a member in January, resigned membership on March 18th, the reason assigned being that climate of Paraguay did not agree with his health.
> *Present Population:* Fifty-three men (including two absent on leave, and two in England on Cosme business), twenty women, thirty-one children. Total 104.

> APRIL, 1897. *Arrivals:* The first of the monthly parties from England arrived on the 16th. The party consisted of: Arthur Lewis, a mason from Stockport; Mrs. Lewis and one child; George Pridmore, a carpenter from Leicestershire; James Ricketts a carpenter from London.
> *Present Population:* Total 109.

MAY, 1897. *Arrivals:* On the 25th, the second party from England arrived. They consisted of: Cyril Allen, gardener from Nottingham; Harry Buckley, ex-soldier from Macclesfield; Sidney Cash, deal-worker from Birmingham; John M. Parish, wood-carver from Bradford; Robert Rayner, warehouseman from Huddersfield; Nicholas Vallance, postman from York.

On the 22nd Thomas and Mrs. Burgum and three children arrived from Queensland.

Departures: On the 25th, G.W.P.——and J.R.——, both newly arrived from England, resigned membership.

Present Population: Total 118.

JUNE, 1897. *Withdrawal:* On the 25th R.W.R.——, a new English member, resigned.

Present Population: Total 118.

JULY, 1897. *Withdrawal:* Writing from South Australia, H.S.T.——, a foundation member absent on leave, notified that he will be unable to return to Cosme on account of domestic reasons.

Present Population: Total 118.

AUGUST, 1897. *Withdrawals:* On August 6th, J.A.——, W.M.—— and Mrs. M.——, left Cosme. (All old members. Ill-health given as reason for leaving.) To. Burgum and Mrs. Burgum and family left the colony on August 11th.

Present Population: Total 110.

SEPTEMBER, 1897. *Arrivals;* On the 4th September, from Edinburgh, William and Mrs. Titilah, and five children. W. Titilah is a bootmaker. Alice Clark (age 15) from London. *Membership was refused to two arrivals from Scotland.*

Present Population: Total 119.

OCTOBER, 1897. *Arrivals:* On October 6th, the fourth British party arrived at Cosme. The new members are: George Gumm from Somerset, Georgina and Annin Noon from Hawick.

Present Population: Total 122.

DECEMBER, 1897. *Withdrawals:* On December 21st, E.T. —— and his nephew, N.V.—— left Cosme (E.T.—— was a pioneer member). He gave as his reason for going that he found that he was not a Communist. His nephew, who only arrived from England in May, left to keep him company.

Present Population: Total 129.

JANUARY, 1898. *Arrivals:* On January 31st, William and Mrs. Bennett arrived from Australia.

Withdrawals: On January 8th, S.C.—— and G.C.—— and on the 20th, A.W.L.—— with wife and child, left Cosme. All were English recruits and found Cosme life unsuited to them.
Present Population: Total 127.

FEBRUARY, 1898. *Withdrawals:* On February 10th, A.B.—— a young English member, left on account of his unsuitableness for Cosme life. On the 12th, C.B.——, a junior, preparatory to his parents withdrawing. The Miss T.——'s, who arrived from England on February 5th, left for Buenos Aires on the 10th, they not being satisfied enough with the place to apply for membership.
Present Population; Total 125.

APRIL, 1898. *Arrivals:* On April 8th, Robert Ogilvie, wife and two children; George Holland, Annie Ashton, from England.
Present Population: 53 men (including five absent on leave), 27 women, 46 children. Total 126.

MAY, 1898. *Departures:* At beginning of month J.B.—— and wife, R.O.——, wife and two children, recently arrived from Scotland. Towards end of month. *H.B.——, wife and one child; J.P.——, wife and three children; *J.A.S.——, wife and two children; F.B.——, G.B.——, *C.B.——, G.C.——, G.H.——, L.P.——, *P.P.——, *H.S.——, *J.W.——. Those marked (*) were with the pioneers. Early in the month J.T.W.—— left on leave of absence.
Present Population: 39 men (including six absent on leave), 22 women, 38 children. Total 99.

(7)

Lane returned to Cosme to hold a committee meeting on 9 May 1898. In his absence the committee had allowed a number of deviations from the creed. Now, orthodoxy was imposed with all Lane's customary energy. This meant further disaster, for amongst the new exodus was his lieutenant and co-recruiter, Arthur Tozer. By July 1898 there were only thirty men, twenty women and thirty-six children left at Cosme. And to keep these alive, every shift was resorted to: mortgages, rationing, and hard work. The task of recruiting single women and married couples proved impossible, since the Paraguayan government grew tired of the derelicts who crowded their doors seeking relief.

Lane began to feel the strain of his six years' campaign and at the ensuing election, indicated that he did not intend to stand as chairman. In his place the colony chose his brother, John. William went back to Australia where he assumed the editorship of the *Sydney Worker*, and sent a loan of £211. 4s. to the struggling community to tide it over difficulties.

His brother, John, introduced the principle of employing native labour—which William would never have tolerated. This too led to resignations. But the change led to an increase in sales from $2,366 in 1899 to $20,658 in 1904. And so good an investment did it appear to the Paraguayan government that they financed a round the world recruiting tour by John Lane in 1901. It proved as great a failure as his brother's and in May 1904 he too was replaced by a new chairman.

The admission of native labour not only offended those who objected to wage slavery, it horrified those who saw miscegenation as an inevitable consequence. Ultimately, both in New Australia and Cosme, the Paraguayan government stepped in, divided the colonists' lands into individual holdings, and assimilated them into the general framework of Paraguayan life.

By 1908, when the British Consul was reporting on its progress, there were eighty-six adults and seventy-five minors; all British, Australian, English, Irish and Scottish. They were growing tobacco, had a steam sawmill, a small distillery and two stills. There were ardent spirits certainly in the settlement but not ones of which William Lane would have approved.[1]

[1] Apart from the *Cosme Monthly, Seed Time, The Times*, 14 April 1896, the *Labour Annual* (1896), 21, and the journals mentioned in the text, the Diplomatic and Consular Reports for 1895 (358), 1901 (2610), 1909 (4362) give objective descriptions of the experiment. This should be supplemented by A. Rogers, '*New Australia*': *A Report presented to the British Board of the New Australia Association* (London, 1896). The best synoptic account is by Stewart Grahame, *Where Socialism Failed* (London, 1913).

7

From Rurisville to Garden City
1898—1918

◇◇

(1)

THE cult of the country as the regenerative bed of society had become a very fissiparous social fad in the closing years of the century. Its addicts needed an authoritative revised version of the old gospel. This was provided by Ebenezer Howard, in *Tomorrow: A Peaceful Plan to Real Reform* (1898) which offered 'the Master Key' to contemporary problems: a Garden City of 30,000 people on a 6,000-acre estate of six wards, combining the benefits of both town and country life. A cluster of such cities separated by belts of open country, 3,000 yds. wide would, Howard prophesied, shrink the existing cities to some 58,000 inhabitants apiece. Howard believed that the 'new sense of freedom and joy pervading the hearts of the people', would result in a 'just system of land tenure for one representing the selfishness which we hope is passing away'. Like most enthusiasts, he believed that his plan would 'silence the harsh voice of anger, and . . . awaken the soft notes of brotherliness and goodwill'.[1] It would also, he added, show the 'true limits of Government interference, ay, and even the relations of man to the Supreme Power'. 'In the search for truth', Howard wrote in

[1] W. A. Eden, 'Studies in Urban Theory', *The Town Planning Review*, XIX (1947), 123–43.

370

a footnote outlining his intellectual debts, 'men's minds run in the same channels.' These channels were Herbert Spencer's land scheme (itself a mutation of the Spencean plan), Buckingham's model city, as well as numerous others.

This astonishing manifesto was issued by a man who began working as a stockbroker's clerk at the age of 15, who had served as an amanuensis to a Nonconformist preacher, had visited America before he was 26, served as a shorthand writer in the House of Commons, and made some improvements to the Remington typewriter. Above all, he was a good listener. He heard Henry George lecture on the land tax and read his book. He knew, and was influenced by, the Fellowship of the New Life. He quoted Nathaniel Hawthorne, whose *Blithedale Romance* was written about experiences at Brook Farm. Viewing parliament as a kind of recording angel must have quickened his interest in the associative side of politics.[1] But 'the decisive influence', according to C. B. Purdom, was Bellamy's *Looking Backward*, which 'gave Howard the idea of a town built as a whole on scientific principles',[2] which would restore people to the land, and unlock the doors obscuring the illumination of many social problems. Howard himself later said :—

> The phrase 'Rural City' is, I think, even a better, a truer, and a more descriptive title of what a Garden City should be than the title 'Garden City' itself, which I then chose as the name of a then purely imaginary town about ten years ago. Indeed, . . . I discarded the name 'Rurisville' which I had at first chosen, in favour of the title 'Garden City,' only because I did not like the mixture of Latin and French in one word.' [3]

Tomorrow had a mixed reception. *The Times* was patronizing : 'It is quite evident that if Mr. Howard could be made Town Clerk of such a city, he would carry it on to everybody's satisfaction. The only difficulty is to create it, but that is a small matter to Utopians.' The Fabians were positively hostile : 'The author has read many learned and interesting writers, and the extracts he made from their books are like plums in the unpalatable dough of his Utopian schemes. We have got to make the best of our existing cities, and proposals for building new ones

[1] For biography see *Garden City and Town Planning*, (Letchworth, September 1908).

[2] C. B. Purdom, *The Building of Satellite Towns* (London, 1949), 26.

[3] *Garden City and Town Planning*, September 1909.

are about as useful as would be arrangements for protection against visits from Mr. Wells' Martians.' But others wrote for further information and to satisfy their requests, Howard enlisted Rev. J. Bruce Wallace, whom he later described as 'one of the most devoted servants of humanity living on our estate'.[1] Thomas Adams, later to become secretary of the Garden City Association, the First Garden City Company, and editor of its first journal *The Garden City*; and Ralph Neville, a Judge and Q.C., who became chairman of the Garden City Association.

Neville wrote the opening article in *Garden City* and sounded a note of urgency:—

> Sociologists are aware that in this country human development has reached a point at which the efficiency of existing social conventions has been determined; they are neither adequate nor appropriate to social requirements . . . The outlook is a serious one . . . the advancing position which our development has thrust upon us nevertheless demands that we shall do this or perish.[2]

This Garden City Association was formed on 10 June 1899 with T. W. H. Idris, a mineral water manufacturer, as chairman. Some supporters admired the Lever settlement at Port Sunlight, others the Cadbury experiment at Bourneville. By June 1902 a meeting was held to form the Garden City Pioneer Company Limited. A number of sites were inspected. One, some eight miles north of Stafford, was nearly chosen when Letchworth came into view. In September 1903 the First Garden City Ltd. was incorporated. The city itself was 'opened' on the ninth of the following month on some 3,822 acres, costing £160,378. As one of the architects the company obtained Raymond Unwin, a friend of Carpenter and a former member of the Ancoats Labour Brotherhood.[3] In the month of its foundation, A. R. Sennett, a civil engineer, delivered a rhapsodic address to Section F of the British Association, on 'The Potentialities of Applied Science in a Garden City', proposing that the consumption of solid fuel should be strictly prohibited; that city-owned gas and electricity should provide heat and power; that all services should be carried in subterranean tunnels to render

---

[1] *Garden City and Town Planning*, September 1908.
[2] *Garden City and Town Planning*, January 1904.
[3] Raymond Unwin designed at this time a labour hall for the Attercliffe L.P. in Sheffield. The plans are in the Sheffield Central Reference Library.

access easier; and that the roads should slope towards the centre where grid drainage would carry away the water. So intoxicated was he by the possibilities of his idea that he immediately expanded his paper to two volumes of some 1,404 pages, which were published two years later.[1]

Ruskinians rallied to support Howard too. From Manchester T. C. Horsfall published in 1904 *The Example of Germany*, showing that others were practising what Howard was preaching. From Bourneville another old Ruskinian, J. H. Whitehouse, then editing *St. George*, published one of Ebenezer Howard's articles on Letchworth, which significantly enough, began with quotations from Kingsley's *Yeast*, and the phrase that has haunted (or inspired) all the Christian Socialists since his time: 'Seek first the Kingdom of God and his righteousness'. Amongst other supporters of the first garden city Ernest Rhys, a director of Dents the publishers, gave practical support by building a printing works there. Rhys had been a great admirer of Thomas Davidson and on the fringes the Fellowship of the New Life.[2] Even the Land Nationalization Society, founded in 1888, lined up behind Howard. Its secretary Joseph Hyder was an enthusiastic disciple of Henry George and his yellow and red lecture carts had been active for a decade up and down the country. He spoke also for A. R. Wallace, the admirer of Ralahine. 'Letchworth Garden City', wrote Joseph Hyder, 'is an example of the policy we stand for. Its founder was a land nationaliser, and most of the pioneers who supported him in the early days of the scheme, as well as some who are still very prominently connected with its management, are members of the Land Nationalisation Society'.[3]

But above all, Letchworth attracted the community enthusiasts of the time, as the symbol of the new century. Evacustes Phipson regarded it as the English Fairhope.[4] Tolstoyans of the previous decade, like J. Bruce Wallace and W. J. Jupp, migrated from Croydon to Letchworth immediately, Wallace establishing there his journal *Brotherhood* to focus attention on the other community experiments of the new century. With the support

[1] A. R. Sennett, *Garden Cities in Theory and Practice* (1905), 2 vols.
[2] E. Rhys, *Everyman Remembers* (1931), 132 ff.
[3] *Garden City*, April 1908. It is also worth mentioning that W. E. Swinton, who founded the Land Nationalization League in 1881, left the money to found the Alpha Union.
[4] *Garden City*, February 1907.

from W. R. Hughes (who had worked in a London Settlement),
James Henderson (another ex-Tolstoyan) and H. B. Binns (a
former member of the Fellowship of the New Life) a lively
group was formed. Binns also edited a monthly called the *City*.
'Have you heard of Garden City?' says a character in Bernard
Shaw's *John Bull's Other Island*, 'D'ye mane Heav'n?' 'No: it's
near Hitchin.' There was Joseph Wicksteed, the authority on
Blake, George Bates, P. J. Ellis and S. G. Hobson, all members
of the I.L.P. There was W. F. Kensett, the trade unionist, W. J.
Brooks, the socialist, T. G. Rogers and W. H. Burrow, both
Ruskinians.

Attracted, as an early industrialist remarked, by the idea that
the town was to be 'a Utopia of clean, pure air, flowers and
perpetual sunshine',[1] enthusiasts for the simple life flocked to
Letchworth. In a diary of events, there is a sketch of 'a typical
Garden citizen' clad in knickerbockers and, of course, sandals, a
vegetarian and member of the Theosophical Society, who kept
two tortoises 'which he polishes periodically with the best
Lucca oil'. Over his mantelpiece was a large photo of Madame
Blavatsky and on his library shelves were *Isis Unveiled* and the
works of William Morris, H. G. Wells and Tolstoy.[2]

(2)

The Tolstoyans realized the potentialities of Letchworth as
'a huge experiment where minor experiments can be carried
out'.[3] Two such 'minor experiments' were associated with Bruce
Wallace. The first was the Alpha Union, which took its name
from a book by E. N. Dennys entitled *The Alpha: or First Mental
Principle and Truth-guide to General Well-being and Progress—
a Revelation but no Mystery*. This appealed for a Man-Redeeming
Confederation, a Holy League, a World Brotherhood to help the
poor and friendless to obtain, not religious faith but 'education
in the reality of an infinitely beneficent God over all, through all
and in all, and the reality of the Spiritual nature in himself and
his fellow-men'. Dennys stirred W. E. Swinton, who founded
the Land Nationalization League, to bequeath £3,000 to

---

[1] Lewis Falk, *Town and Country Planning*, XXV (1957), 476.

[2] Charles Lee, 'From a Letchworth Diary', *Town and Country Planning*, XXI (1953), 435–6.

[3] John Julian, *An Introduction to Town Planning* (1914).

J. Bruce Wallace to 'lift people to an adequate conception of what they essentially are'. By 1908 the money was available and Wallace associated with himself as Trustee Dr. Winslow Hall, M.D. of Kilburn, and W. R. Hughes, a Fellow of Jesus College Cambridge and Sub-Warden of Mansfield House Settlement. A circulating library was formed, lists of sympathizers were drawn up, and the trustees determined 'to help people to clearer thought on both spiritual and social questions' by conferences up and down the country.

A second gift, this time of a new building called 'The Cloisters', was made by Miss A. J. Lawrence (the sister of Lord Pethick-Lawrence), as a centre of education for those who wished to live a fresh air life. They were optimists who believed in a coming religious revival led by minorities, for as they said: 'Through a determined minority's persistence in a policy of this kind, the way might be prepared for a federation or alliance, industrial or commercial, which would be at length practically irresistible for fraternal purposes, as a well organised American trust is for increasing capitalists' profits.'[1] So, every August a summer school was organized to bring this programme into practice and train 'missionaries' for Social Christianity and Land Work. A school, St. Christopher, was also founded, which under its headmaster Lyn Harris (and his son and successor) became nationally famous. Like Abbotsholme (which stemmed from the Fellowship and 'threw off' Bedales) St. Christopher 'threw off, Frensham Heights School, at Farnham.[2]

Both these schools aimed at affording fullest possible community life of work and play. There was no distinction between the location of boarders' rooms and the family rooms of the headmaster and staff. The school diet was based on plenty of butter, milk, eggs and fresh fruit and vegetables. The school elected the officials, frequent staff meetings were held, and the morning assemblies were deliberative rather than devotional.

One outpost of the Alpha Union was the Mansfield House Settlement in London, where Hughes' sister Mrs. McKenzie initiated a training college for women teachers. One of those

---

[1] *The Alpha Union* (Letchworth, n.d.), and conversations with W. R. Hughes 8 January 1958.
[2] Trevor Blewitt ed, *The Modern Schools Handbook* (1934), 71–81 (Frensham Heights) and 96–112 (St. Christopher School).

who helped was Edmond Holmes, whose book *What Is and What Might Be* (1911) was one of the best Utopist works of the time. Indeed the second part of his book, 'What Might Be' began with a chapter entitled 'A School in Utopia'. In this, Holmes set the fashion for 'progressive education' for the decades that followed.[1] Holmes was in the true tradition of the Alpha Union. To him the idea of 'secular education' was uncongenial. He held indeed that 'it cannot be too religious'. But to Holmes, as to the Alpha Unionists, 'the path of self-realization was the path of salvation, and "knowledge of God" had as its necessary counterpart "a right attitude towards the surrounding world and its inhabitants".' This movement came full circle in 1919 when there was founded yet another progressive school—Bembridge, in the Isle of Wight. In view of what has already been said about the Ruskinians, it is, therefore, not surprising that its creator and first Warden was J. Howard Whitehouse.

(3)

It is tempting to think that Bob Hope, the American radio comedian, had his early experience of fantasy from the family firm which built some of the early houses at Letchworth. A local need for stomach powders (for psychosomatic disorders?), stimulated one of the early inhabitants, A. G. Maclean, to found in the garage of his house the famous pharmaceutical firm.

But perhaps V. I. Lenin, who found refuge there for a short time, needs extended mention. Lenin visited England in May 1907 (when he behaved 'as if he were Marx incarnate'), and went to the Tolstoyan Brotherhood Church in Southgate Road, for the conference of the Russian Social Democratic Party.[2] H. N. Brailsford, who reported the congress for the *Daily News*, said 'there can have been nothing quite like it since stealthy gatherings of primitive Christians under the early emperors'. For three weeks their marathon debates continued, lubricated by beer supplied by Gorki's wife from a barrel in the hall. It was a momentous occasion, for as it had been said 'the future of R.S.D.L.P. was at stake, and in retrospect the fate of the entire

[1] E. Holmes, *What Is and What Might Be* (1911), 157, 174, 180, 184.

[2] James Maxton, *Lenin* (1932), 65, said Lenin 'liked to go to the Socialist churches then in existence' where 'socialist meetings were conducted with all the usual forms of a church service, sermon, reading of lesson, singing of hymns and sometimes even prayer. Such a thing was a new phenomenon to him.'

revolutionary movement and of all Russia as well'. The galaxy of names included Plekhanov, Axelrod, Deutsch and Zazulich; Martov, Alexinsky, Tseretelli, Gorki and Stalin. It is worth recording that the conference had friends in England: Prince Kropotkin, H. N. Brailsford, H. M. Hyndman, the Fisher Unwins, Cunningham Grahame and Constance Garnett and her son David. But its greatest friend, indeed its 'angel', was Joseph Fels, who, when the delegates ran short of money and it looked as if they would have to go home, put up the money for them to stay.[1] And Joseph Fels brought another thread into the Garden City.

(4)

Joseph Fels was a small dynamic American who had made a fortune out of naphtha soap. Like Howard, he had been influenced by Henry George and the idea of salvation through the land. But he was not allowed to pursue his land projects unmolested. The Fabians in particular disliked him. 'It is always the same,' lamented Bernard Shaw, 'the lunacy of country life always attacks the manufacturer first.' Beatrice Webb regarded him as 'a decidedly vulgar little Jew, with much push and little else on the surface'.[2]

This push, coupled to the social conscience of George Lansbury led to three land colony projects, taking shape. On 4 March 1904 Fels handed over to the Poplar Guardians a 100-acre farm called Sumpners at Laindon in Essex, to be worked by the able-bodied unemployed under their charge. For three years the Board were to have free use of the land, and the right, at any time during that period, to buy it from him at £2,175—the cost price.

A hundred men volunteered to go there from the workhouse and live in corrugated iron buildings on the estate. They were so enthusiastic that a special correspondent of the *Illustrated London News* described the settlement nine months later in glowing terms: 'Everything goes at the colony with almost Kitchener-like precision, from the constructing of a reservoir to the building of chicken houses.'[3]

---

[1] *Joseph Fels, His Life Work,* by his wife (1916).
[2] A. P. Dudden and T. H. von Laue, 'The R.S.D.L.P. and Joseph Fels', *American Historical Review* (1956), LXI. 39.
[3] *Illustrated London News*, 24 December 1904.

Credit for this was given to the superintendent, John Clarke, who made up the 'little gangs' to carry out the varied kinds of work, choosing the men most carefully. He was also careful to vary the work as much as possible 'so that a man may not be sickened with the monotony that would arise from sticking an eight-inch fork into a hard clayey soil week after week'. The use of a military metaphor by the correspondent was appropriate, since most of the colonists were young ex-soldiers. A Conservative Cabinet Minister, was 'surprised and distressed' to notice this.[1]

Laindon was followed up on 14 October 1904 by a second larger project: Hollesley Bay. Here Joseph Fels acquired a large set of buildings (once used as an Agricultural Training College) for the Central Unemployment Committee, lending some £40,000 for three or four years free of interest. The colony was not far from Felixstowe, and consisted of 1,300 acres of varied types of land. The former college had accommodation for 335 men, together with residences for farmers. There were thirty cottages, four sets of farm buildings and an open-air swimming bath. It had workshops, a wharf, a warehouse on the river front, and a light tramway connecting the wharf to the farmers' gardens. There were eight glasshouses and 200 acres of gardens. George Lansbury, together with C. H. Grinling (one of the first 'settlers' at Toynbee Hall) and others used to come down every week-end to organize classes and recreation. Hollesley Bay got a cold scrutiny from another visitor in the New Year of 1908 who came to 'ascertain the possibilities of the working colony as an element in any scheme for dealing with unemployment', for Beatrice Webb was not impressed by the 300 men she saw there, and wrote in her diary :—

> The atmosphere—the impression of the place was mournfully tragic—half-educated half-disciplined humans, who felt themselves to have been trampled on by their kind, were sore and angry, every man of them in favour of every kind of protection, protection against machinery, protection against female, boy and foreign labour, protection against Irish, Scotch and Country men, protection against foreign commodities, protection against all or anything that had succeeded whilst they had failed. There was a growing assumption in their minds that they had the *right* to 30s. a week . . .

[1] Raymond Postgate, *The Life of George Lansbury* (1951), 71.

they were a faint-hearted, nerveless set of men, their manner sometimes servile, sometimes sullen, never easy and independent.[1]

Nor were Laindon or Hollesley Bay popular with the permanent officials of the Local Government Board. They recon-
verted the latter into a deterrent workhouse, but the first was a
more difficult case, being under the Poplar Board of Guardians.
So they initiated an inquiry in 1906, which, thanks to Corrie
Grant appearing for the Poplar Guardians, did not rake up as
much sensational evidence as was hoped. By 1911 Canon
Barnett was lamenting the refusal of the Central Board to imple-
ment the original decision to establish co-operative smallholdings or to give effect to the training scheme. 'The present
position', he wrote in the *Westminster Gazette* in 1911, 'consti-
tutes almost a tragedy.'[2]

The third land project in which Fels interested himself was
launched in Toynbee Hall in 1907: the London Vacant Land
Cultivation Society. He was persuaded by J. H. Whitehouse and
W. H. Beveridge (then editing *St. George*) to give an account
of it, and he pointed out that there were 10,000 acres within tram
journey distance of the Bank of England which could be utilized
for smallholdings.[3]

(5)

Thomas Adams, the first secretary of Letchworth, agreed
with Fels' and Lansbury's original ideas and took the opportunity in 1904 to promote a conference on 'The Garden
City in its relation to Agriculture'. As a speaker he invited
H. Rider Haggard, who had reported on General Booth's
schemes. Adams was worried about rural depopulation which
he had seen at first hand in Scotland, and his conference surveyed
the four remedies hitherto tried (smallholdings, co-operation,
people's banks and an agricultural parcel post), only to conclude
that the Garden City offered as good a remedy as any. Indeed
Adams' enthusiasm led him to write in the *Garden City* an
account of the various model towns and communities that preceded Letchworth. In doing so he quoted Emerson's verdict that

[1] *Our Partnership* (ed. B. Drake and M. I. Cole, 1948), 291.
[2] H. Barnet, *Canon Barnet* (1921), 643.
[3] *St. George* (Birmingham, 1908), XI. 230–7.

'the value of communities is not what they have done but the revolution which they indicate is on the way'.[1]

Letchworth, Hadleigh and Hollesley Bay had, to one acute contemporary observer, one thing in common: they were all centres for therapeutic manual work for the unemployed.[2] This observer, W. H. Beveridge, joined J. H. Whitehouse as an editor of *St. George*, which now became far more sociological in tone, publishing in 1909 a number of 'Utopian Papers' inspired by Patrick Geddes, who more than anyone at this time saw the way out of the impasse. Not for him the 'phantom sunsets' of agrarian colonies, or the equally 'phantom dawns' of anarchist communities. He proclaimed, in ringing tones, the gospel of the twentieth century. 'As the community in its religious aspect was the church, as the community in its political aspect was the state, so also the community in its cultural aspect is the university'. Here he put forward his own scheme—based on Zinzendorf's of 150 years before—of a great community in Chelsea.

Geddes was also an intimate friend of Joseph Fels, sending his son Alasdair down to Fel's 'colony' in Essex. Fels wished to adopt Alasdair as heir to his vast soap fortune.[3] This was not to be. Geddes himself plunged ever more deeply into the problem of community planning. Soon he was writing:–

> It will be said that this is Utopia. It is, and should be, beyond the dreams of the historic Utopists, right though they also were in their day . . . The material alternatives of real economics are broadly two, and each is towards realising an ideal, a Utopia. These are the paleotechnic and the eotechnic—Kakotopia and Eutopia respectively. The first has hitherto been predominant, the second . . . happily has now its material beginnings everywhere.[4]

(6)

Though at Letchworth the managing agent 'made it clear', as Purdom so delightfully puts it, 'that he was going to stand no nonsense from the idealists, and that the company was a business concern intending to make its business pay',[5] the revolution

---

[1] T. Adams, *How to solve the Problem of Rural Depopulation* (1905).

[2] *Garden City*, May, July 1906.

[3] P. Mairet, *Pioneer of Sociology. The Life and Letters of Patrick Geddes* (1957), 128–9.

[4] *Town and Planning Review*, III (Liverpool, 1913), 176 ff.

[5] C. B. Purdom, op. cit., 487.

indicated, if not initiated, by these enthusiasts was under way by the middle of the decade. The green banner of the garden city became respectable and the sharp Utopian outlines of Howard's sketches softened and blurred. In such warm approval, garden suburbs sprouted like mushrooms.

Joseph Rowntree, appalled by his brother Seebohm's revelations of housing conditions in York, bought in 1901 123 acres outside the city and established the New Earswick village. Three years later it became a Trust. Its link with the Garden City Movement is shown by the selection of Raymond Unwin as architect. Here the concept of the 'neighbourhood unit' was really explored.[1]

When the extension of the tube railway to Hampstead threatened the Heath with rape by the speculative builder, Mrs. Barnett leaped to its defence. In an article in the *Contemporary Review* she proposed a garden suburb at Hampstead to give working people an opportunity to 'develop a sense of home life and an interest in nature which form the best security against temptation', to bridge the gap between the classes, and to preserve the natural beauty of the Heath. The idea took shape in 1907 as Hampstead Garden Suburb.

Thomas Adams yearned to join the movement, so in October 1906 he resigned the secretaryship of the Garden City Company to Harold Craske in order to join Sir Richard Paget in developing a Garden City at Fallings Park near Wolverhampton. This was followed by others at Warrington, Hull, Newport (Mon.), Bristol, Cardiff, Manchester, Hyde, Penkhull (Staffs.), Sealand (Winchester), Rosyth, Liverpool, Ruislip Manor, Bolton and Rochdale. Perhaps the most interesting of them all, from the Garden City point of view, was Woodlands—a community planned with the help of the Garden City Association for the employees of the Brodsworth Colliery near Doncaster.

Old industrial towns like Manchester, itself an incubator of social reform, were galvanized into fresh action. There the 'Unhealthy Dwellings Committee' of Manchester City Council, formed in 1885, had already been tackling the problem of the cul-de-sacs, the courts and the narrow streets. Now, in 1906, Councillor T. R. Marr became chairman of the Housing Committee and, in the words of one of his successors, 'under his

[1] Anne Vernon, *A Quaker Business Man* (London, 1959).

leadership the reconditioning campaign was pursued with much greater vigour than before'. Marr's book *Housing Conditions in Manchester and Salford* (1904) pointed out that the reconditioning programme had merely scratched the surface, and quoted a case where one water closet was shared by eight houses and a water tap by forty. Marr made the committee adopt a new policy and as a result the annual number of houses reconditioned quadrupled from the figure of 500 (which was the average between 1885 to 1906) to 2,000. By 1914 he had virtually reconditioned all the bad houses.[1]

(7)

Raymond Unwin might say that Howard was 'too theoretical and experimental to appeal very widely to the English public', and Geddes' 'helpful and stimulating essays were not always practicable',[2] but it looked as if he was, for once, unduly disparaging, for by the second decade of the century Town Planning had become an accepted part of the established thinking about society.

The tentative provisions of the first Town Planning Act of 1909 for securing that, in limited parcels of land, development should only take place in a certain way, were passed at a significant time. For, at a conference organized by the Royal Institute of British Architects from 10–15 October the following year, John Burns, the President of the Local Government Board, and the Minister responsible for the Act, spoke in the tradition of the foregoing pages.

'I conceive the city of the future as Ruskin, Morris, Wren and Professor Geddes wished a city to be—that is an enlarged hamlet of attractive healthy homes, with development proper and adaptable for its growing needs and trade and transit, harmonizing so far as may be possible with the life and characteristics of the people.'[3] Geddes' gospel of the twentieth century was also on the march, linking up with the advance of town planning. And to provide personnel for the operation there was

---

[1] E. D. Simon and J. Inman, *The Rebuilding of Manchester* (1935), 17. See also the story of the 16 Co-partnership Housing Associations as told in *Sociological Review*, III (1910), 42.

[2] R. Unwin, *Town Planning in Practice* (1913), 3, 141.

[3] *Report of the Town Planning Conference . . . held in 1910.*

established also in 1909 through the generosity of W. H. Lever[1] of Port Sunlight the Department of Civic Design in the Liverpool School of Architecture. To disseminate the ideas generated there first appeared in 1910 also through the generosity of W. H. Lever, the first English journal to be devoted to the subject: *The Town Planning Review*. Its first editor, Patrick Abercrombie, played a large part in the Council for the Preservation of Rural England. He swelled the voices of the Liverpool School of Architecture (under C. H. Reilly) and the Department of Civic Design (under S. D. Adshead) and was to become in his own right one of the foremost planners of the new cities of twentieth-century Britain. Could Geddes' conception of the university be described as 'not always practicable'?

By the time Howard had obtained a Civil List pension in 1913, the movement was bearing all the signs of the 'tiredness of spirit' and 'lack of historic sense'. It had become an 'establishment': a movement without opposition. 'There is a great sloppiness in the conception of the garden city,' A. Trystan Edwards insisted. 'It has served its purpose. It was from the beginning a sectarian movement, which originated in a protest against overcrowding in our towns.'[2] Edwards turned the attention of critics to the results of the low density policy in the suburban aborts known as the garden suburbs.

Since all sects lose something when they become churches, the Garden City movement lost something when the Town Planning Institute was formed in the year in which Edwards wrote these words. Luckily the evangel was kept alive by the Town and Country Planning Association, which was to gain in vitality after the First World War. The Utopian flavour of the Garden City is well illustrated in John Buchan's *Mr. Standfast* (1918), a spy story about the war. In this, the villain masquerades as Ivery, an intellectual leader of the Garden City of Biggleswick. Some of Buchan's descriptions of 'the modest folk who sought for a coloured background to their prosaic city lives

---

[1] Like Fels, a soap magnate. Towards the end of the First World War he bought the islands of Lewis and Harris. Lewis was to be the Port Sunlight of fishing, and, to market their catches, he bought over 350 fish shops in the main streets of British towns. The Lewis project foundered, but the fish distribution side of it developed into MacFisheries, now part of Unilever. For the story see Nigel Nicolson, *Lord of the Isles* (1960).

[2] *Town Planning Review*, III (Liverpool, 1913), 150 ff., 312 ff.

and found it in this odd settlement', if they did not mirror, certainly helped to project, the image of a group animated by 'a lot of ignorance, a large slice of vanity, and a pinch or two of wrong-headed anarchy'.[1] Yet even Buchan's patronizing picture pays indirect tribute to the feelings which animated them. 'It is glorious to feel', says one of the characters, 'that you are living among the eager vital people who are at the head of all the newest movements, and that the intellectual history of England is being made in our studies and gardens.'

[1] John Buchan, *Mr. Standfast* (1918), 40–41.

8

From Rananim to Thelnetham

(1)

ONE contributor to *Garden City* was Philip Morrell, then M.P.
for Oxfordshire and after 1910 M.P. for Burnley.[1] He and his
wife Lady Ottoline were an advanced pair who at Garsington
Manor, Oxfordshire, entertained or employed most of the
intellectuals of their day—Clive Bell, Edward Garnett, W. B.
Yeats and D. H. Lawrence. Lawrence regarded her almost as a
St. Simonian *femme libre*, and in February 1915 told her:—

> I want you to form the nucleus of a new community which shall
> start a new life amongst us—a life in which the only riches is
> integrity of character . . . And the new community shall be
> established upon the known, eternal good part in us. This present
> community consists, as far as it is a framed thing, in a myriad
> contrivances for preventing us from being let down by the meanness
> in ourselves or in our neighbours. But it is like a motor car that is so
> encumbered with non-skid, non-puncture, non-burst, non-this and
> non-that contrivances, that it simply can't go any more . . . The
> ideal, the religion, must now be *lived*, *practised*. We will have no

---

[1] *Garden City*, August 1907. He died in February 1943.

In *The Flowers of the Forest* (London, 1955), 37, David Garnett describes
Lady Ottoline as 'an original character who had managed by strength of will to
escape from the conventionality of her upbringing without losing her position in
Society. Physically she was extremely handsome: tall and lean, with a large head,
masses of dark venetian red hair, which, when I first knew her, she had rashly
begun to dye, glacier blue-green eyes, a long straight nose, a proud mouth and
long jutting out chin made up her lovely, haggard face.'

more churches. We will bring church and house and shop together. I do believe that there are enough decent people to make a start with. Let us get the people. Curse the Strachey who asks for a new religion—the greedy dog. He wants another juicy bone for his soul, does he? Let him start to fulfil what religion we have.[1]

This was no sudden impulsive letter of a provincial climbing boy to a patroness, but the expression of a conviction that had been growing for over five years. Whilst a teacher at Croydon in 1910, Lawrence had been talking on Thursday evenings on social problems, 'with a view', he wrote, 'to advancing a more perfect social state and to our fitting ourselves to be perfect citizens—communists—what not'.[2] He had something of the Messiah in him too: Middleton Murry, four years younger, felt himself 'in the presence of a man of destiny, a prophet, a Messiah', one in whom, 'life itself was making an experiment towards a new kind of man, and . . . the experiment was crucial. Everything he did and was, was therefore significant; it had a meaning transcending Lawrence's own personality.'[3]

One day in August 1914, Lawrence went walking in the Lakes with a Russian friend of his, S. S. Koteliansky or 'Kot', a short, broad-shouldered man with black hair brushed up straight, whose dark eyes, shrouded by a pair of gold eyeglasses pinched on the end of an arched nose, gave him, 'an air of distinction, of power, and also a tremendous capacity for fun and enjoyment'.[4]

[1] A. Huxley, ed., *The Letters of D. H. Lawrence* (1932), 220. Hereafter cited as *Letters*. Lawrence was first thinking about his 'colony' in 1902 when he was 17. Richard Aldington, *Portrait of a Genius, But . . .* (London, 1950), p. 33, calls attention to his desire to 'have a big house' and 'gather all the people we like together'. 'He knew Ruskin through and through', adds Aldington (p. 7), and again (p. 38), 'both in temperament and opinions he had much in common with Ruskin even down to his inveterate habit of wrangling about abstract ideas in terms of a personal symbolism'. Lawrence could also have met Edward Carpenter and Ramsay MacDonald at Alice Dax's home at Eastwood: K. and M. Allott, 'D. H. Lawrence and Blanche Jennings', *A Review of English Literature*, I (1960), 58.

[2] H. T. Moore, *The Life and Works of D. H. Lawrence* (1951), 80–81. Ernest Rhys (see *ante*, 309, 331, 372) was a friend of Lawrence at this time.

[3] John Middleton Murry, *Reminiscences of D. H. Lawrence* (1933), 61, 63. Hugh Kingsmill said that 'reading Murry is like listening to an auctioneer . . . The impulse to attach his feelings to something outside himself is probably one of the causes of the strange assertions which stud his writing that . . . D. H. Lawrence was a man of the same order as Christ.'

[4] K. W. Gransden, 'Rananim: D. H. Lawrence's Letters to S. S. Koteliansky', *Twentieth Century*, CLIX (1956), 22–32, and *Encounter*, December 1953. Koteliansky was very interested in Tolstoy. *New Statesman and Nation*, 5 February 1955.

One is irresistibly reminded of Coleridge and Southey walking in the west, talking Pantisocracy. But Lawrence was preaching revolt, a revolt against 'the rule and measure mathematical folk'. Koteliansky gave him the title for his Utopia of revolt—Rananim. As they sang together at the parties Lawrence and his wife Frieda held at their cottage in Cholesbury, Koteliansky hummed *Rananim Sadikhim Badanoi*—the first verse of Psalm 33. 'Kot's' peculiar intonation had an effect on Lawrence, who promptly assumed the name Rananim for his dream of a community of such friends. Lawrence believed that Law and Love were the two dominant forces in human life. Rananim would balance them.

He began to talk of a rebirth, a phoenix-like regeneration from the ashes of old England that was dissolving. These beliefs he conveyed to his friends, who seemed always to eat their suppers with him. These suppers, he thought, could be used as a basis of a community for social regeneration, just as its symbol was the phoenix. Lawrence, according to Murry, was 'violently' occupied by it.

As Lawrence was about to move to Pulborough, Sussex, where he and Frieda his wife had borrowed a house he wrote to his old friend, W. E. Hopkin, whose daughter Enid was a great friend of Kot's, in Nottinghamshire, asking him to come and stay and 'talk of my pet scheme'. 'To gather together about twenty souls and sail away from this world of war and squalor and found a little colony where there shall be no money but a sort of communism as far as necessaries of life go, and some real decency. It is to be a colony built up on the real decency which is in each member of the community. A community which is established upon the assumption of goodness in the members, instead of the assumption of badness. What do you think of it? I think it should be quite feasible. We keep brooking the idea— I and some friends.'[1] This was on 18 January 1915.

(2)

Another young man of letters, then, on his own admission, 'intellectually cautious' and 'not at all inclined to enthusiasm', met Lawrence and was 'startled and embarrassed' by him. So much so that he said he would join the scheme.[2] This was Aldous

[1] *Letters*, 215.
[2] ibid., p. xxix; and *Times Literary Supplement*, 6, 27 January, 3 February, 1956.

Huxley, who, incidentally, found at Lady Ottoline's house at Garsington, his wife Maria Nys, just as Julian, his brother, first met his wife Juliet there.

Rananim, as Lawrence saw it, involved the 'washing off' of the 'oldness and grubbiness and despair' of England. It also involved casting off the 'bit and bridle' of the intellect. 'My great religion', wrote Lawrence, 'is a belief in the blood, the flesh, as being wiser than the intellect. We can go wrong in our minds. But what our blood feels and believes and says, is always true.' It was this mystical belief which at times passed the comprehension of his friends.

Five months later Lawrence had attracted another recruit: Bertrand Russell. Together they planned to hire a lecture hall. Lawrence told Lady Ottoline Morrell that they would give lectures, 'he on Ethics, I on Immortality: also have meetings, to establish a little society or body around a *religious belief, which leads to action*. We must centre in the knowledge of the Infinite, of God. Then from this centre each one of us must work.'[1] Lady Ottoline was to be president, 'the centre pin' that held them all together, 'the needle' which kept their directions constant.

There was method in this, for Lawrence envisaged her Oxfordshire home, Garsington, as the place of retreat, 'where we come and knit ourselves together . . . like the Boccaccio place where they told all the Decamerone'. He told the Murrys, 'We must draw together.' By 9 July he was feeling, as he prepared to move from Pulborough, 'there is the entry on a new epoch'.[2]

But Bertrand Russell was cold. Lawrence burst out, 'Are we never going to unite in one idea and one purpose? Is it to be a case of each one of us having his own personal or private fling? If we are going to remain a group of separate entities separately engaged, then there is no reason why we should be a group at all.'

Frieda, too, was not enthusiastic, and this weighed more with Lawrence than any other factor. He believed, as Middleton Murry said, that he was conscious of her 'participation in his

[1] ibid., 239. It is worth noting that Russell lectured in the Brotherhood Church at this time.
[2] ibid., 240

work to such an extent that it almost depended on her active goodwill'.[1] And that goodwill was not now forthcoming. Frieda was, at heart, jealous of Lady Ottoline's influence over him and herself said she wondered whether she ought not to abandon Lawrence to Lady Ottoline altogether. 'What might they not do together for England?' she asked. 'I am powerless, and a Hun, and a nobody.'[2] Who could blame her for so feeling, in war-time?

So Lawrence started on another tack, and by 16 August was reflecting, 'I had hoped and tried to get a little nucleus of living people together. But it was no good. One must start direct with the open public without associates.'[3]

So for the open public Lawrence started a little fortnightly, *Signature*, scheduled to begin publication in October. 'The paper is really *something*,' he told Lady Cynthia Asquith: 'the seed, I hope, of a great change in life: the beginning of a new religious era from my point.'[4] Koteliansky found a Jewish printer in the Mile End Road who agreed to print it for £5 an issue. The paper seemed so likely to succeed that Lawrence began to talk of taking rooms at 12 Fisher Street where 'club' meetings could be held.

But this too failed. Lady Cynthia was nervous of its attitude to the war. There was a violent row with Russell. So *Signature* stopped after Number 3. The war pressed on Lawrence more hardly than ever, and by 26 October of that year he was exclaiming, 'I must see America—here the Autumn of all life has set in—the Fall. We are hardly more than ghosts in the haze, we who stand apart from the flux of death.' 'I cannot bear it—this England, this past, this great wave of civilisation 2,000 years, which is now collapsing, ours is the age only of Decline and Fall.'

(3)

Lawrence now began to concentrate on America. He told Lady Cynthia Asquith, 'I want to transplant my life. I think there is hope of a future in America. I want if possible to grow towards that future! There is no future here, only decomposition.'

[1] *Reminiscences* (London, 1931), 45.
[2] H. T. Moore, *The Life and Works of D. H. Lawrence* (1951), 133.
[3] *Letters*, 250.
[4] ibid., 258.

Here he would start a new school, 'a germ of a new creation'. Fort Myers was his goal. And, as he waited for the necessary permits to go, he told Katharine Mansfield: 'I want it now that we live together. Let us all live together and create a new world. It is too difficult in England because here all is destruction and dying and corruption. Let us go away to Florida soon. But let us go *together*, and keep together, several of us, as being of one spirit.'

'We want', he told Lady Cynthia Asquith, 'to make a new life in common, a new birth in a new spirit, together. We shall do it and we shall bring it off, and it will be good.'[1] Philip Heseltine, a young musician, and Robert Nichols, the poet, were also considered likely recruits.

'This is the first move to Florida', he wrote on 30 December 1915 as he and Frieda borrowed J. D. Beresford's house in Cornwall. 'We begin the new life in Cornwall,' he wrote, 'some members of the Florida Expedition are coming down too.' Here in Cornwall life was to grow from the deepest underground roots, from the unconscious. 'This', he wrote to Kot, 'is the first move to Florida. Here already one feels a good peace and a good silence and a freedom to love and to create a new life. We must begin afresh—we must begin to create a new life altogether—unanimous. Then we shall be happy. But we shall only be happy if we are creating a life together. We must cease this analysis and introspection and individualism—begin to be free and happy with each other.'

His own experiences at Ripley in Derbyshire (where he spent Christmas with his sister) led him to react even more violently away from the industrial world. As he told Lady Morrell, 'These men . . . they *understand* mentally so horribly: only industrialism, only wages and money and machinery. They can't *think* anything else . . . That is why we are *bound* to get something like Guild-Socialism in the long run, which is a reduction to the lowest terms.'[2]

(4)

At the beginning of March 1916, Lawrence and Frieda got a cottage at Zennor, near St. Ives, for £5 a year. 'When I looked down at Zennor, I knew it was the Promised Land, and that a

[1] ibid., 295.   [2] ibid., 306.

new heaven and a new earth would take place.'[1] Even his gathering mistrust of Middleton Murry evaporated. Heseltine came down to stay and so did Kouzoumdjian (who later changed his name to Michael Arlen). Lawrence described the cottage under the moors on the edge of a few rough, stony fields that go to the sea. 'It is quite alone, as a little colony', he told Murry, after he had been there a week. Extending his anticipations, he urged Murry to come down and take another cottage, that Heseltine would join him and that they would become 'like a little monastery'. 'It would be *splendid* if it could come off,' he went on: '*such* a lovely place: our Rananim . . . It seems to me we *must* strike some sort of a root, soon: because we must buckle to work. This is the best place to live in which we shall find in England, I firmly believe. But we mustn't go in for any more *follies* and removals and uneasiness.'

The Murrys duly arrived on 6 April. Lady Ottoline offered money. Lawrence was at a peak of feeling as he refused it. 'I hate the "public", the "people", "society" so much that a madness possesses me when I think of them. I hate democracy so much. It almost kills me. But then, I think that "aristocracy" is just as pernicious, only it is much more dead. They are both evil.'[2]

But the Murrys didn't like the country. It was too rocky and bleak. Nor could Murry understand Lawrence. They moved thirty miles away.

Here a new disciple appeared to rally round Lawrence now that the Murrys were tacitly dropped, Catherine Carswell, who also regarded Lawrence as a Messiah. She wrote, 'I believe that there not only may be, but must be, a new way of life, and that Lawrence was on the track of it.'[3]

And Lawrence was also writing Lady Ottoline Morrell out of his system in *Women in Love*. Here Lady Hermione Roddice at her home Breadalby (a literary analogue for Lady Ottoline's home at Garsington) entertains Birkin (Lawrence) but makes him ignominious in the eyes of everybody, including her husband (a tall and jaunty M.P., obviously Philip Morrell) and Joshua Matheson (Bertrand Russell). So much did Lady Hermione hate all that Birkin said that she tried to brain him with

[1] ibid., 332. [2] ibid., 344.
[3] Catherine Carswell, *The Savage Pilgrimage* (1932), IX.

a paperweight but he interposed a volume of Thucydides between the weight and his head. Birkin was ridiculed in a restaurant by the Bohemians of Bloomsbury. His prophecies 'almost supersede the Bible' one says of Birkin: 'He makes me perfectly sick. He is as bad as Jesus. Lord, *what* must I do to be saved.'

But Catherine Carswell was pregnant and too fond of her husband to take Lady Ottoline's place. That, for the time being, was occupied by Esther Andrews. She came down to see him in 1916, and helped Lawrence surmount the indignity of the military medical examination on 30 June 1916. Esther Andrews helped to sustain the dream too, described by Lawrence in January 1917: 'the only way is the way of my far off wilderness place which shall become a school and a monastery and an Eden and a Hesperides—a seed of a new heaven and a new earth'. Esther Andrews now appeared as a desirable associate; 'we want her to go with us to America', wrote Lawrence, 'and to the ultimate place we call Typee or Rananim. There is indeed such an ultimate place.'[1]

He wrote to Pinker, his literary agent, for passports in order to leave in March. Since Frieda had colitis and Lawrence himself was laid up, plans were changed. To prepare for the exodus Lawrence 'thought of doing a set of essays on the Transcendental Element in American Literature'. In his *Studies in Modern American Literature* he discussed Pantisocracy: an interesting link with his own predicament. Then he and Frieda went to London, first to Hampstead then to Hilda Aldington's (the wife of Richard) at 44 Mecklenburg Square. Here in November 1917, Rananim seemed to get under way at last.

(5)

Now its venue changed to the east slopes of the Andes. He told Catherine Carswell: 'We have got a much more definite plan of going away. There will be Frieda and I, and Eder and Mrs. Eder, and William Henry and Gray, and probably Hilda Aldington, and maybe Kot and Dorothy York. We shall go to the east slope of the Andes . . . Paraguay or Columbia. Eder knows the country *well*. Gray can find £1,000 . . . what about you coming with Don? This plan at last *will come off*. We shall go and we shall be happy.'[2]

[1] *Letters*, 391. [2] ibid., 420. Dr. David Eder (1866?–1936) was a pioneer psychiatrist and a Zionist.

The buoyant emphasis of Lawrence's conviction in this November was occasioned by the recruitment of Dr. Eder, who had relatives with big estates in Columbia in the Cauca Valley. Lawrence hoped to get as far as these and then move off to find his own place. A definite sailing date was fixed—the spring of 1918. 'It has become so concrete and real, the Andes plan, it seems to occupy my heart', he told its benefactor, Cecil Gray, who was gently railing him on his 'disciples', and 'women'. For Gray, like Murry before him, detected the Messianic role which Lawrence was destined to play.

But at this very moment detectives from the C.I.D. were chasing him, primed by stories of Lawrence singing German songs in Cornwall. Poor Lawrence was forced to appeal to Lady Cynthia Asquith for help in calling them off. 'Just write a letter to your man at Scotland Yard, will you?' he asked her. 'At least this last vileness against me I ought to be able to quash.'

He also began to rope in Gertler, a vivacious, amusing artist with thick, dark, curly hair and large, grey eyes, urging him that 'we have got to get some foothold on some new world of our own'.[1] 'We need to go away', he told him on 21 February 1918, 'as soon as we can, right to a new scene, and at least for a bit, live a new life—you and Campbell and Kot and Shearman and Frieda and me—and whosoever else you want—and in some queer way, by *forgetting* everything, to start afresh'.[2]

(6)

The venue was always changing. When the war ended Lawrence did leave the country. He went to Ceylon. And from Ceylon the trail led to Australia, and then to New Mexico. There he stayed, and his hostess, Mabel Luhan, has left us an account of him. There was, of course, Lawrence's usual intractability: quarrels with Frieda, with guests, with Mabel Luhan herself. But Mabel had bound him to her by the gift of land containing three or four other ranch houses—and about 170 acres. This the Lawrences called Kiowa.

Kiowa was, for Lawrence, 'the end of the lost trail'. He returned to England with hopes of reviving Rananim. Frieda had arrived before him and was living in a flat above the Carswells. Murry had made overtures for peace and Frieda was prepared

[1] ibid., 426. [2] ibid., 431.

to support him in a peace move with Lawrence. Indeed Murry accompanied Koteliansky to the station to meet him.

Lawrence immediately sized up the situation. On the way back to the Hampstead flat he suggested that Murry should give up the *Adelphi* and return with him to Mexico to 'begin the nucleus of a new society'. He was most emphatic to Catherine Carswell: 'The English are no longer flowering . . . we are the seed . . . we should be scattered. We are the best-bred people on earth.'[1]

At this time he attracted yet another disciple, the Hon. Dorothy Brett, a daughter of Viscount Esher, a painter. 'Bret', as she called herself, 'The Brett', as Lawrence called her, added a touch of Debrett to the group with her ear trumpet (for she was deaf). She now danced attendance on him, teaching him to model figurines and flowers.

Catherine Carswell, under whose roof no less than five of the protagonists were living, said, 'It had to come to this, that Lawrence's only purpose for staying a day longer in England was to discover if all of us, or some of us, or even one of us, would feel the compulsion to go with him and Frieda to a freer and richer air, where things "could happen" as they could not happen in England.'[2]

(7)

Koteliansky, as Lawrence's major disciple at the beginning, now played a major role at the end of the enterprise. With Lawrence he organized a dinner in a private room at the Café Royal. To it came Murry, the Carswells, Mark Gertler, Mary Cannan, and Dorothy Brett with her ear trumpet. No function could have emphasized more tragically the unstable, deliquescent structure of the group. Gertler was not at all communicative, Koteliansky was. Indeed he made a most dithyrambic speech on Lawrence, smashing wine glasses to emphasize his point. Lawrence then spoke. He asked the audience to go to New Mexico with him, to channel their separate strengths into his way of life. It was a pathetic appeal for them to support him.

Mary Cannan was the first to break the silence; 'No,' she said, 'I like you, Lawrence, but not as much as all that, and I think you are asking what no human being has the right to ask

[1] Carswell, op. cit., 207.   [2] ibid., 208.

of another.' Gertler temporized, Koteliansky and Carswell both said that they would go but did not mean it. Only the deaf Dorothy Brett really heard the appeal. Murry went up to Lawrence and embraced him, promising never to betray him and, at that point, Lawrence fell forward with his head on the table and vomited.

The action was symbolic. Lawrence had had his last supper, and in March 1924 he sailed for Taos with Frieda and Dorothy Brett. Rananim, like Pantisocracy, was dead.

(8)

In his *Collected Poems* Lawrence imagines he is a Samson pulling down the corrupt world upon himself. He was encouraged in this by his disciples. Mabel Luhan saw him as Jesus. The Hon. Dorothy Brett painted a crucifix in which the suffering figure on the cross bears the face of Lawrence. Lawrence's final statement of Rananim is in the *Plumed Serpent*.[1] Quetzalcoatl was his Utopia made literate, the idea allegorized.[1]

The allegory, with its Blavatskyan overtures, has not been lost on posterity. For in 1938, eight years after Lawrence had died, J. P. Cooney founded a journal called *The Phoenix*, published at Woodstock (New York), and Paris. This stressed the messianic character of Lawrence's teaching, and insisted that it outlined a path which fallen men should follow. In its intellectual Luddism and its cult of the spade it proposed to establish an agrarian community as a way of pioneering into a new order of world society. A site in South Georgia was selected and, as Cooney wrote, 'If the War Department and Government officials allow us to work there in peace, we are confident that we shall succeed in restoring the law and opening the way to others who wish to join us'.

The Phoenix did not command much sympathy in England. The *Criterion* (then edited by T. S. Eliot) called Cooney's project 'a bromide view of the Noble Savage' and accused its editor of 'stumbling about in an old pair of Lawrence's shoes which are evidently much too big for him'. Cooney was not abashed and wrote: 'While the mass of humanity is thus terribly

---

[1] For a fuller interpretation of this see W. Y. Tindall, *D. H. Lawrence and Susan His Cow* (New York, 1929), and N. A. Scott, *Rehearsals of Discomposure* (London, 1952).

engaged in liquidating the death within itself, there must be some of us . . . those who possess the seeds of a new civilization . . . to extricate ourselves from the general disintegration and to go off and find a propitious place for our sowing.' Cooney and his friends were 'determined to serve no longer under any industrialist state, but to be sufficient unto ourselves in a commune through tilling the earth, hunting, fishing, and the handicrafts, it seems most wise to us to seek our place in those parts of the earth which are least dominated by industrialism . . . and it seems to us that certain parts of South America would be the best favourable of any such place'.

(9)

Like Cooney, Murry sought a Messiah. In 1924 he wrote *To the Unknown God: Essays towards a Religion*. Not till Lawrence died in 1930 did Murry read Marx and come through to the belief that

> ultimately the dynamic of a victorious political revolution must be sought in religious conviction. Economic causes do, and can do, no more than afford the opportunity for creative revolution. They so dispose the forces within society at a given historical moment that there is the opportunity of creative advance. But the power of actually seizing upon that opportunity comes from another source altogether—from something that can only be called religious faith.

Community among socialists, he decided, was itself a religion, for: 'The fight against the *Ego* could be carried on only in a real community: for that was the only medium in which the ramifications of the Ego became visible. It was also the only place where the finer order of life, for which the Ego must be sacrificed, could be actually manifested'.[1]

Yet Murry went further than Lawrence; indeed he talked of 'fulfilling' him. 'The man who intuits the necessity of a "new community" must needs demand that its nucleus shall actually exist', he wrote in 1933. He realized that 'Utopian impatience' was not enough, action towards the new order had to be 'continually re-inspired and purified by its own part realization'. So to create the nucleus as the 'sole guarantee of the integrity and vitality of the politics that is aimed at the creation of the new

[1] T. Dent, ed., *Community in England* (1938), 116.

community itself' Murry put forward the idea of the Adelphi Centre.

He secured The Oaks, Langham near Colchester as a place where socialists 'could keep fit for the battle of life against death by constantly renewing their morale'. It was a return (as he realized) to monasticism and retreat. So three years after Lawrence had died, Middleton Murry set up his 'socialist centre' there, and wrote :—

> The Adelphi centre will be a training centre for making socialists— but real socialists not socialist 'politicians'. We believe that the essential element in making socialists is almost wholly neglected. The essential element is 'education into community'. This education cannot in the nature of things, be theoretical merely. It is, we think, self-evident that it can be accomplished, only by actual co-operation in ordinary human work. No such socialist centre can be really living until each member, or guest, takes as an obvious duty his full share, according to his capacity, of the actual work of the place; not can it be truly healthy until it becomes largely self supporting in the simple necessities of life.[1]

A year later he resigned from the I.L.P. and organized a summer school at Glossop, 'one of the crucial experiences of his life'. At the third of these summer schools, which lasted through August 1936, he came to the conclusion that a social community and a Christian community should go hand in hand, for the effort to restore a community 'culminates', he wrote, 'in the effort to restore the vital meaning of the sacrament of communion'.

The *Adelphi* now took as its motto Blake's proverb 'Religion is Politics and Politics is Brotherhood'. At the summer school George Orwell and Herbert Read (among others) spoke to audiences numbering several hundreds. Murry felt justified in writing in the October *Adelphi*, 'an attempt at Socialist living is a necessary basis for Socialist thinking', and publishing testimonies by the participants.

Unfortunately the Centre came to an end in 1937 when Murry joined the Peace Pledge Union.

(10)

The Peace Pledge Union owed much to Mark (or as he preferred to be called, Max) Plowman, who had taken over the

[1] ibid.

editorship of the *Adelphi* from Murry in 1930 and was a really strong character. He fed and wrote on William Blake, and was a friend and correspondent of Joseph Wicksteed, another Blakeian, of Letchworth Garden City and a master of St. Christopher's School there. Plowman was no Laurentian: 'I think D. H. Lawrence *is* my opposite', he wrote. 'I feel we've the same object but approach it from opposite directions. He's of the lineage of Hardy and Keats, whereas the only way I ever hope to go is that of Blake and Shelley.'[1] And again: 'It is the prophets who have failed—the peace and plenty prophets of the nineteenth century. They have spread a disease that has covered the earth, though one word of true religion can dispel it . . . I had hopes of him (Lawrence) but they seem to be rather in abeyance. He has served his day and generation but not much more I think.'[2] Nor did Plowman love the I.L.P., for he described them as 'only the struts of a tumbledown pigsty', and their socialism as 'mainly confined to the heroism of turning themselves into human gramophones for the reiteration of other people's opinions'. He spoke of them 'wearing the air of disaffection as if it were a natural grimace'.[3]

When a second world war threatened to break, Plowman converted the Adelphi Centre into a home for Basque children. When war began he got ready for aged evacuees and then switched to land cultivation. With Murry he bought twenty-two acres (which was later increased to seventy).

Also with Murry, Plowman set himself to marry up the pacifist movement and the pacifist land communities. These began to develop with great rapidity all over the country. For thanks to the integrity of many of the conscientious objectors' tribunals no less than 60,000 men of military age chose the land as a protest against the destruction involved in war. Some of them saw the possibility of establishing cells of integrity, in the interstices of a decadent and collapsing social order, communities based on free association and common labour, seed beds of a new and co-operative order. Some regarded themselves as lay members, keeping the good life alive for man in a dark age. Many of them had met or had read the accounts of the Kibbutzim

[1] D. L. Plowman, *Bridge with the Future* (1944), 140.
[2] ibid., 264.
[3] ibid., 417.

in Palestine, a country then struggling for its integrity in the face of persecution on all sides.[1] There were several hundred of these pacifist communities, varying from small family groups to over a thousand members, ranging occupationally from farming units to living communities in towns and from free schools to theatre groups. The majority were obviously agricultural groups because of the conscientious objectors' tribunals.[2]

One by one they ran into difficulties. Sometimes they ran out of money. Sometimes they inadvertently contained people 'on the run'. At others, domestic difficulties like overcrowding, food, isolation, and personal incompatibilities combined to wreck them.[3] Plowman and Murry regarded them as nuclei from which a communal structure could spread, not based on the acquisitive motive.

To prevent more breaking down Plowman pressed forward with the Community Land Training Association in March 1941. This was to train younger men as farmers and makers of agricultural goods. He bought a farm at Holton Beckering in Lincolnshire; but only with difficulty, for as he lamented, 'The land-racket has already begun. Interest-bearing capital is looking for a funk-hole and finding it on the land.' Those words were written on 7 February 1941. Less than three months later Plowman was dead.

Murry now fell back on the help of F. A. Lea, assistant editor of the *Adelphi*, a former member of Plowman's group at Langham, a biographer of Shelley and Chesterton and later of Plowman himself. Lea cited Lawrence, especially his letter to Lady Ottoline Morrell, as the expression of the need which the wartime communities were trying to satisfy, and dissenting from Plowman (who regarded modern communities as analogous to

[1] George Woodcock, *Anarchy or Chaos* (1944). This was issued by the Freedom Press. It is interesting, not so much for its brief account of the community farms, but for the references to Lao Tse and the Tao way of life. See *The Community Broadsheet* (issued from Chancton, Dartnell Park, West Byfleet, Surrey, at the time.)

[2] Lewis Maclachlan, *C.P.F.L.U. A History of the Christian Forestry and Land Units* (1952), gives some details and the *Community Broadsheets* give more.

[3] 'The pattern of community life imposed a strain that many were untrained to bear; the fundamental need was for self-discipline, and though the "communiteers" had often seen the Promised Land from afar, their provision for the journey was often sketchy in the extreme.' Denis Hayes, *Challenge of Conscience, The Story of the Conscientious Objectors* (1949), 216–19.

medieval monasteries) insisted they were reconstitutions 'at a new level of technical achievement and social awareness' of the village community of the Middle Ages. Lea also reveals a latent sense of apocalypse: 'It has happened seldom in this epoch, whose death-throes we are witnessing today, that the true leaven, the prophet, has been recognised and given his rightful place in society. That has been the tragedy of the West, and one indication among others of its spiritual deathliness, its dearth of humility.'[1]

(11)

When the Air Ministry requisitioned Murry's land, Murry decided to establish his own community. 'We can easily conceive', he wrote, 'a multitude of comely village communities animating a country that is beautiful—though differently beautiful—as the nineteenth-century recreation of the upper class.'[2] But, as he confessed, 'I am constrained to cry like Blake in *Jerusalem* "Awake, Albion, Awake".' He was determined to conduct an experiment. So, after the requisition, he looked for a farm of 200 acres on which a community could take shape. He found one of 183 acres at Thelnetham on the border of Norfolk and Suffolk, occupying it on 5 October 1941. Profits were to be shared and applied to the purchase of the farm from him together with an interest of 4½ per cent. Stock was bought from the Adelphi Centre, and Murry found himself at the age of 52 investing £3,325 (all his savings) in land so poor that even the mangel-wurzels grew no bigger than oranges. An even poorer harvest of personalities appeared to disillusion Murry, who soon discovered that in war-time a vocation for co-operative agriculture was more often than not an alibi for some other more pressing duty. 'A chapter of cranks', 'sexually unfulfilled or

---

[1] *Community in a Changing World* (1942), 29–32; F. A. Lea, *The Life of John Middleton Murry* (1959), 306, calls attention to Murry's dislike of all preconceived ideas of community. 'I am quite certain' Lea quotes him as saying 'that community, if it is to have any practical validity for ordinary people and any real appeal to them, is a form of living which has yet to be discovered and manifested in the concrete.'

Or again, 307, 'Community is, essentially, a new form of social organism that is capable of welcoming and digesting its own experience, without being disintegrated, and growing thereby.'

[2] J. M. Murry, *Christocracy* (1944), 127.

For his address to the trainees at Holton Beckering, see *Community in a Changing World* (1942), 131–5.

frustrated' were some of the phrases that in retrospect occurred to him by way of description. Bitterly he commented: 'Instead of being a social relation which requires more than the ordinary sense of responsibility "community" is for them a relation which absolves them from all responsibility.'[1]

Murry's community at Thelnetham survived till 1948. It is tempting to speculate whether George Orwell, who joined the original Adelphi summer school and who knew him well, found, in the very shape of Murry's agrarian community, a hint for casting his own anti-Utopian *1984* as a farmyard story. For a farmyard story—minus Napoleon—was what Thelnetham seems to have been.[2]

[1] J. M. Murry, *Community Farm* (1952), 25. He went on 'George Fox calls them "notionists . . . who are not in possession of the thing they talk of".' Murry himself later refers to them as 'communiteers'.

[2] Murry himself wrote in *Community Farm* (1952), 24, 'I think now that it was a Utopian idea, and I have learned that "community" is a dangerous word to use among young people of a certain type.'

9

◇◆

Expedients and Experiments
1919-60

◇◆

(1)

WHILE Patrick Geddes was replanning Jerusalem (where the Jews were gathering once more) the Sociological Society in England were exploring, with sophisticated secularity, the third alternative to capitalism and communism. Its special Cities Committee, in a report entitled *Earth, Hell, and the Third Alternative* looked for a rebirth of the mystique of the city:[1] the establishment of a truly co-operative state where the school would be vitally and systematically connected with the social unit which it served.[2] Geddes' successor as Jerusalem's planner, C. R. Ashbee, even more eschatologically insisted that industrialism had collapsed, and that only a 'unified city' could foster a 'new ethic of human relationships'.[3]

---

[1] *Sociological Review*, XXIV (1921).

[2] *Sociological Review*, XXII (1919), 16.

[3] From 1892 to 1896 Ashbee had built a group of houses on the Chelsea Embankment. He had also worked with G. F. Bodley and, as a disciple of Morris and Ruskin, had settled in East London, where he founded the Guild of Handicrafts, an association of men and boys united in the joy of making. In 1902 he had moved to Chipping Campden with 150 of them to found an art and craft colony, but the scheme failed though many of the East-Enders settled permanently there. In 1917 he left Campden and took up planning work in Cairo, subsequently becoming 'Civic Advisor' to the City of Jerusalem, writing 'I have become the residuary legatee of the work P.G. has been doing here. He too has had a hand in the shaping

(2)

Such a 'new ethic' for post-war Britain preoccupied the London Yearly Meeting of the Society of Friends, which set up a special committee to explore ways of fostering it. The report written by Philip Burtt insisted that

> 'The City of God' and 'The New Jerusalem', are not mere figures of speech. They have to be realised amongst men here on earth and the past way of life will not build these. Henceforth the Society of Friends should definitely dedicate itself to the vast communal uplift which is so pitifully needed today. A new community ought to be started to embody the new vision of life.

Reviewing nineteenth-century experiments in community founding, Philip Burtt, was 'full of hope'.

> 'They show us', he wrote, 'that the fundamental dynamic must be a spiritual yearning towards human association in the Spirit of Christ. The fact that persons with a religious bond of fellowship, living communistic lives, have been the most successful pioneers in the problems of human association, excites the hope that the Society of Friends will one day add their quota to this work.'[1]

This appeal for action stimulated Percy Alden, M.P., who had 'little doubt' that there was 'room for such an experiment among the 16 million inhabitants of the big industrial towns'. Only an experiment, not an Act of Parliament, could offer an ideal to which people could approximate. Alden did not want 'to create another communistic colony which stands outside in isolation, and has no influence on the existing ones, but rather to prove that the housing question must be regarded as only one part of the whole problem'.[2]

Before the war ended, the Society of Friends launched on 28 February 1918 the Pioneer Trust with Harrison Barrow, Ralph Crowley, J. T. Eliot, Mary O'Brien Harris, T. Alwyn Lloyd, Harris Smith and Henry Lloyd Wilson as directors. The trust was

[1] *War and the Social Order* (London, 1916).
[2] Percy Alden, 'Wanted: A New England', *The Friend*, 22 February 1918.

---

of Civitas Dei: and for all his failures his work has ever a touch of prophecy. We have worked together now for many years and shall never fall out.'

See his *An Endeavour Towards the Teaching of John Ruskin and William Morris* (1901), *Echoes from the City of the Sun* (1905), *The Hamptonshire Experiment in Education* (1914), *A Palestine Notebook 1918–1923* (1927) and his obituary in *Journal of the Royal Institute of British Architects*, June 1942.

to raise £50,000 and prospect for a site, on which a 'Holy Experiment' in the tradition of William Penn could be undertaken. 'If it shortens in the least degree the road to the millennium, it will not have been in vain', they said with the quiet confidence that bespoke conviction.[1]

Helped by the Brotherhood Trust and the Alpha Union, the Pioneer Trust now promoted a New Town Conference at Oxford in 1920, at which a new co-operative town based primarily on agriculture was canvassed. W. R. Hughes urged members 'to study and profit by the experience of the Utopian Socialists'.

> The causes of their failure are not difficult to detect. Often they had not enough respect for the varying needs of human personalities and asked too much of the individual. There was too much in common, too little private life in the group. Their scale was too small, their programme too limited to give the necessary freedom and variety to different individuals. Their promoters did not recognise the unity and complexity of the social life in which we are all bound up together, nor how much was yet to be learned of the arts of social life and self-government.

The 'New Town Movement', launched by this meeting, appealed for £75,000 to launch an experiment on 3,000 acres. They believed that it was 'necessary and possible

> . . . for a body of people to come together, in the spirit of Owen's movement but with the benefit of all the subsequent experience and with no hopes of an immediate Utopia, in order to work out on a moderate scale an attempt to integrate in a social community all the separate movements to which we have referred. It is not our purpose to separate ourselves from the national life in a group apart, but we want to make a fresh start in a fresh place with all these things at the same time.'[2]

Like Geddes, Hughes wanted the school to be the living core of the new town.

From these deliberations crystallized the New Town Trust, mainly of Quakers and residents in Letchworth.

[1] Howard Hodgkin, 'A Proposed New Town', *Friends Quarterly Examiner*, October 1918.
    The presence of T. Alwyn Lloyd shows how the National Housing and Town Planning Council was influential in this group. See *Jubilee Book of the National Housing and Town Planning Council* (1950).
[2] Author's correspondence with W. R. Hughes, and Hughes' book *The New Town Committee*.

(3)

The persuasive founder of Letchworth, Ebenezer Howard, with his chief lieutenants F. J. Osborn, C. B. Purdom, and W. G. Taylor had meanwhile formed a 'New Towns Group' to see that 'new towns' should be a public responsibility. They tried to persuade Dr. Christopher Addison, the Minister of Health from 1919–21, that this was a sound policy. But Addison's Housing and Town Planning Act of 1919 was mainly concerned with subsidizing council houses, not with planning new towns. So, on his own initiative, Ebenezer Howard bought at an auction a large area of land for a second garden city. To develop this his loyal associates then formed the Welwyn Garden City Ltd., with a capital of a quarter of a million pounds.[1] Their intention, announced in a prospectus of 4 May 1920, was to cater for forty or fifty thousand people.

At Welwyn, Hughes and his associates leased 500 acres from the Garden City Company to form an agricultural guild. This was to supply the inhabitants of Welwyn with milk and vegetables, integrate agriculture with the life of the town, and raise the status of agricultural workers. Indeed, its only relationship with that body was that it paid rent for the 500, and later the 1,650 acres of land it leased from the Garden City Company and it sold its products, like any other retail company, to the inhabitants. The Guild kept 244 pedigree dairy shorthorns, 500 pigs, 47 horses and 2,000 hens; which employed first 29 then 72 people. It even managed to sell 'certified' milk when others could not. But its land was neither fertile nor held on a permanent lease. Pieces and parcels were constantly liable to be taken up as sites for houses by the Garden City Company. The separation from the Garden City Company was fatal. For faced with the agricultural depression in the late '20s it had nothing to fall back on. So it was wound up and the land re-let to tenant farmers.[2]

(4)

The Welwyn agricultural guild was not the only experiment of its kind.[3] There were other rebels against the collectivist

---

[1] F. J. Osborn, *New Towns after the War* (1918). See new edition of 1944 with historical preface.

[2] C. B. Purdom, *The Building of the Satellite Towns* (London, 1949).

[3] Witness for example, the work of John Hargrave and the Kindred of Kibbo Kift.

state like A. R. Orage and A. J. Penty. Through the *New Age*
they enlisted the support of G. D. H. Cole to explore the
possibilities of a series of functional bodies working in conjunction with, but not under the authority of, the Leviathan State
through 'communes' functioning at local, regional and national
levels. Each commune was to have the same general representation from industrial guilds, civic guilds, co-operative guilds,
collective utilities guilds, health councils, and cultural councils.
All were to send representatives to the local commune, which
would in turn send representatives, supplemented by representatives of agricultural guilds, to regional communes, and
they would, in turn, send representatives to the commune of the
nation.

A practical trial of the guild idea at local levels was initiated
by S. G. Hobson, when the Building Trades Union of Manchester
decided to bid for contracts. The response was immediate. The
Manchester Building Guild proposed to work without the
intervention of 'capitalist employers,' and to pay standard rates
when their fellows were laid off by bad weather.

A second experiment was tried in London, mainly organized
by A. J. Penty. Money was borrowed from the C.W.S. on
interest, and some local authorities advanced payments on a
week-to-week basis. A. J. Penty also helped to establish a
National Guild of Builders to supply the local guilds with
materials and undertake architectural work.

Other local authorities warmed to the project, largely because
of the elimination of profits, and by December 1920 guilds had
secured twenty-four contracts for 2,605 houses. In July 1921
one local authority joined the Guild in celebrating the completion
of the contract at a special ceremony on the site. By December
1921 they were strong enough to establish a periodical, *The
Building Guildsman*.[1]

Other industries followed suit. A House Furnishing Guild, a
Guild of Clothiers, an Engineering Guild were organized and a
Tailor's Guild was conceived. All these guilds came together in
May 1922 at a special conference—a forerunner of the 'Guild
Congress' of the grand scheme. A hundred delegates attended.
But A. R. Orage, editor of the *New Age*, was a wayward and
inconstant leader. For, after a brief flirtation with the social

[1] Niles Carpenter, *The Guild Socialist Movement* (1922).

credit scheme of Major Douglas, he resigned the editorship of the *New Age* to go to Paris in 1922, where he joined the community of the Russian mystic Gurdjieff at La Prieure at Fontainebleau,[1] where, incidentally, Middleton Murry's first wife, Katherine Mansfield, also died.

(5)

Several of the Guild Socialists now moved over to join the ebullient G. K. Chesterton who was insisting that 'mankind has as much right to scrap its machinery and live on the land, if it really likes it better, as any man has to sell his old bicycle and go for a walk if he likes it better'. In the *Outline of Sanity* (1926), Chesterton pointed out that society as a human construction could be refashioned upon any plan that ever existed. 'If we make men happier,' he wrote, 'it does not matter if we make them poorer: it does not matter if we make them less productive: it does not matter if we make them less progressive.' 'The point about communism', he went on, 'is that it only reforms the pick-pocket by forbidding pockets.' His cure for the centralization of his day was decentralization. 'We are not choosing between model villages as part of a safe system of town planning,' he went on, 'we are making a sortie from a besieged city, sword in hand.' Chesterton was, in his way, a believer in catastrophe, and thought 'it not unlikely that in any case a simpler social life will return; even if it return by the road of ruin'. 'We are threatened,' he wrote, 'not with a long decline, but rather with an unpleasantly rapid collapse.'[2]

Following on *The Utopia of Usurers* (1917) and *The New Jerusalem* (1920) he took over his brother's paper as an instrument for spreading distributist ideas and called it *G.K.'s Weekly*. 'To choose between socialism and capitalism', he wrote, 'is like saying we must choose between all men going into monasteries and a few men having harems.' 'Distribution may be a dream; three acres and a cow may be a joke. We are indeed Utopian; in the sense that our task is possibly more distant and certainly more difficult. Utopia has done its worst.

---

[1] For Gurdjieff see books by his disciples P. D. Ouspensky and Kenneth Walker.

[2] Maisie Ward, *Gilbert Keith Chesterton* (1944), 415–48, for a good account of the movement.

Capitalism has done all that socialism threatened to do. The clerk has exactly the sort of functions and permissive pleasures that he would have in the most monstrous model village.'

Outdoor meetings were held in all the large towns and a number of vigorous speakers like Father Vincent McNab, W. J. Blyton, and Hilaire Belloc became apostles of the Distributist League, of which M. B. Reckitt, a former Guild Socialist became the treasurer. Eric Gill, devoted his artistic talents to the cause: 'A Revolution is coming' he wrote after the First World War. 'I try to meet it (1), by living or learning to as much as possible upon my own resources as a small landed live proprietor and (2), by doing what I can to propagate the faith so that the Revolution may be guided in a direction consonant with the fundamental facts of human nature and man's essential perfection.' He practised what he preached, establishing at Ditchling up to 1924, then at Capel-y-ffin near Abergavenny to 1928, then at Pigotts, High Wycombe, a kind of community to fulfil his ideals. In 1940 he was 'perfectly clear' in his mind 'that communities of lay folk religiously cutting themselves off from the money economy are an absolute necessity if Christianity is not to go down either to the dust or the catacombs'. 'I am sure', he wrote, 'that all attempts to create cells of the good life in the form of small communities are not only much to be encouraged but are the only life.'[1] By sheer artistic genius, Eric Gill undoubtedly influenced many people up to and during the Second World War.

A more specifically distributist experiment was initiated by John Hawkswell at Langenhoe, in Essex, when an estate of 1,500 acres was purchased by Mrs. Judges. Thirty people formed the nucleus of the group and some others worked on the estate. Langenhoe came to an end in 1935, when John Hawkswell and his family left to found another community at Laxton. In a letter to the author he wrote :–

> It would be true to say we were very much influenced by Chesterton and Belloc, especially in their insistence on Distributism. The whole Catholic land movement of those days took Distributism for granted as the basis of healthy social life.

[1] Walter Shewing, *The Letters of Eric Gill* (1947), 133, 458. See also Stephen Hobhouse, *Forty Years and an Epilogue* (1951). Hobhouse worked at Ditchling and subsequently made a name as an interpreter of Jacob Boehme.

Langenhoe was wound up about the end of 1935, it certainly failed in its object, and looking back one can see many reasons why it failed simply on the plain of failure in Prudence, and even more in the want of Patience. It should have been developed much more slowly, and added to bit by bit, on more sure foundations. For example too much financial responsibility was heaped on Mrs. Judges, whereas the estate could have, and should have been got on to a paying basis first. I was myself far too casual in committing Mrs. Judges to too heavy burdens. This I regret.

But apart from failures of this kind, I doubt if the time was ripe for the venture, or even if it ever will be ripe, because there was a sufficient 'Idée générale' for such a bold attempt to sweep back the Atlantic.

Nevertheless, there is more to be said for the Distributist ideal than even Chesterton or Belloc ever asserted, and I should not accept responsibility for abandoning hope in the possibility of some day a Saint arising and doing in Prudence and Patience, what we tried to do, in quite alarming deficit of those two useful virtues. But 'Man proposes, God disposes', and though we Humans don't deserve the best (and the modern Cornucopea of endless Trash can hardly be the best), a reaction may come.[1]

(6)

Publicized and influenced by the Distributists was the scheme of Professor J. W. Scott of University College, Cardiff. Having seen in 1921–2 the working-class housing communities established by George H. Maxwell in California he was anxious to try a similar experiment in England. As his book *Syndicalism and Philosophical Realism* (1919) shows, he was much interested in the economics of the smaller group, and in 1924 published another plea for self-sustenance.[2] With the help of the *Spectator*, he founded the National Homecroft Association, a public utility company registered at Cardiff in 1926. This dangled a vision of each man entrenched behind his own food supply. A beginning was made at Cheltenham by building houses for ten families with sufficient ground to enable them to raise their own poultry,

[1] Letter to the author.
[2] *Unemployment: A Suggested Policy* (1925), had on its cover 'The Policy here suggested amounts to A NEW KIND OF TOWN PLANNING'. Scott acknowledged that Kropotkin had 'first awakened the World of Labour to the interest that it has in the whole matter of Homecrofting'.

pigs, potatoes and fruit. As the scheme developed, the N.H.A. hoped to replace individual by group homecrofts.

When even greater numbers of men were thrown on their own resources by the depression, the Cheltenham experiment was used to teach groups of unemployed how to grow food. A miniature market on the croft, run with a paper currency of half-penny units was set up, so that each producer could sell his product and buy from his fellows. Students of University College, Cardiff (where Scott was professor of philosophy) co-operated in preparing the land and teaching the unemployed the rudiments of toolmaking. The N.H.A. got no financial help from any charity.[1] By 6 March 1934, when *The Times* published an article on the scheme, light hand-looms were being operated on the site. *G.K's Weekly* pushed the scheme very strongly between 26 December 1936 and 8 July 1937.

(7)

Another expedient which became an experiment was launched by Peter Scott (no relation to the Professor) at Brynmawr, South Wales, in 1929, based on the principle that control of the work must be in the hands of those engaged in it. Peter Scott felt the need for radical change in the existing economic and social system, and decided to make an experiment with a derelict township: in this case Brynmawr. Here, by means of a community council, a survey was made (which was published in 1934), a swimming bath, paddling pool and gardens were built, and clubs were started, assisted by leaders from the community house. Two new industries, Brynmawr Bootmakers Ltd., and Brynmawr Furniture Makers Ltd., began production. In addition the Brynmawr Subsistence Production Society (for older men) worked in close relationship with it.[2]

Brynmawr in turn inspired John Hoyland, a firm believer that 'the time was ripe for a new proletarianizing of Christianity' to establish a Land Settlement Association, for settling co-operative groups of thirty men on contiguous five-acre plots: a pilot scheme being started at Burnley. With the help of the

---

[1] The Land Settlement Association, formed in 1934 to acquire estates and split them into 5- or 10-acre holdings settled 440 families on the land with Ministry help.

[2] *Men without Work. A Report made to the Pilgrim Trust* (Cambridge, 1938), 355–70.

International Union of Students, Hoyland also organized a work camp.[1]

Brynmawr itself, a co-operative production experiment, was, under Scott's guidance repeated in Lancashire, where at Up-holland near Wigan in March 1934 eleven men and two women began to build a greenhouse, dairy, cobbler's shop, tailor's room and common-rooms. With a cow, ten pigs and a hundred poultry they produced 200 lb. of bacon, ham and pork, 400 lb. of tomatoes, and raised their standard of living by ten shillings a week. There was no sale outside the group. Members were credited with the number of hours worked and the commodities they sold were priced in those terms. Labour was paid for by labour. *The Times*, reviewing the first year of the experiment, remarked 'as a laboratory experiment it has succeeded admir-ably'.[2] The Nuffield Trust gave £30,000, which enabled the scope of the experiment to be considerably extended. The original Upholland site was supplemented by four others all west of Wigan: Parbold Hall, Billinge, Pemberton and Ashfield House, Standish. A visit by the Duke of York on 9 July 1935 gave the experiment a national significance.

Brynmawr itself, as the original exemplar, forged ahead. A central workshop had been developed in an old brewery at Cwmavon. It fed seven 'colonies' at Llandegveth, Beili Glas, Trevithin, Ponstymoile, Griffithstown, Pontrewydd and Cwm-bray. Help from the Commissioner of Special Areas and a loan from the Prudential Assurance Company enabled the projects to go forward.

In autumn 1937, the Order of Friends (as Peter Scott's group was called) began to issue a quarterly journal, *Towards the New Community*. The very first number contained an 'Outline for a New Community', for unemployed men of 45 years and over. It was to consist of homes for 250 families, surrounded by open

---

[1] John Hoyland, *Digging for a New England* (1936).

A number of service units had sprung up to cater for the unemployed. The Rev. Conrad Noel at Thaxted promoted 'The Order of the Church Militant', Vernon Herford 'The Order of the Christian Faith', and the Rev. C. C. Stimson 'The Brotherhood of the Way'. In addition there were service units proper like Leslie West's Grith Pioneers near Derby, the International Voluntary Service for Peace (in which Jean Inebnit was prominent), there was also the Peace Army led by Maude Royden and Joyce Pollard, and the Scottish Work Camps. All these were based on the idea of community service.

[2] *The Times*, 6 November 1934.

gardens and lawns; a food factory containing a community
kitchen and dining-rooms, bakery, butchery and cold store,
laundry and boilerhouse; and a community house to contain
library, common-room, and workshops for repairs. A health
centre, a school and village green were also envisaged. Brynmawr was not only rehabilitating unemployed miners; but
reinvigorating the tradition of social experiment when more
deterministic philosophies were sapping its vitality. Hilda Jennings, who wrote an account of it, also remarked 'The non-
aggressive community on the national or supernational scale is
in its birth throes, and it may become the most fatal of tyrranies,
or it may be worth the toil and struggle of a century's idealists.'[1]

(8)

Rehabilitation, of which Brynmawr was such an exemplar in
South Wales, was, in a different context, the purpose of
Dartington Hall in Devonshire. This was a New Harmony in
reverse: a scientific centre on the Dart, as New Harmony had
been a scientific centre on the Wabash. Founded a century later,
it had many points of similarity with the American scheme. Two
people were concerned: Leonard Elmhirst and his wife,
Dorothy Whitney Straight. Elmhirst had served during and
after the war with Lionel Curtis, founder of the *Round Table* and
a promoter of the concept of Commonwealth as opposed to Empire, and with Rabindranath Tagore, the promoter of agrarian
reconstruction at his International University at Santiniketan.
Dorothy Whitney Straight, whom he married after leaving
India in 1924, was the widow of Willard Straight, the wealthy
founder of that most liberal American weekly, the *New Republic*.
After their marriage in the following year, they bought an estate
near Totnes in September 1925 known as Dartington Hall.

With this as a base, operated as an economic unit, they built
up a lively centre of agricultural, forestry, and artistic life as an
example to the area. Though the whole venture was educational,
there was also a school, which, under W. B. Curry, became one
of the foremost of its kind in the country. Both estate and school
sought for the best people to help them in discharging their
ideas, and in this way a number of distinguished scientists and
artists were enlisted.

[1] Hilda Jennings, *The New Community* (1934), and *Brynmawr* (1934).

Suspected of being 'a nest of communists', 'a free love colony', and 'a heaven on earth', it left in a myriad ways its imprint on the West Country. Perhaps the most visible are the lovely houses built by what is now one of the largest construction companies in that part of England: The Staverton Builders, founded by Leonard Elmhirst, from the original works department of the estate in 1930. The anastomosing threads linking it to that other great experiment of this generation are perhaps symbolized by the appointment of A. E. Malbon as director from Welwyn Builders. And Malbon was responsible for securing the designs for his houses from Louis de Soissons, also a veteran of Welwyn.[1]

(9)

Yet another group were quietly working to reanimate community work. Inspired by the efforts of Job Harriman, an American lawyer who had founded the co-operative colony of Llano first near Los Angeles, then in Louisiana, Arthur St. John founded the British Llano Circle. With the help of Ernest Bairstow of Guildford Road, Farnham, Surrey, a *British Llano Circle Bulletin* advocated an experiment on the Llano model. Arthur St. John was a veteran of Purleigh, who had travelled for Tchertkoff, met Tolstoy in Russia and suffered imprisonment for helping in the great emigration of the Dukhobors. When Purleigh broke up, St. John settled at Bilston in Staffordshire, where after establishing the *Midland Herald* he helped Mrs. Cobden Sanderson to found the Penal Reform League. His community interests were not forgotten. He issued a short-lived journal called *Crank*—'a little thing that makes revolutions'— and had served in the First World War as an ambulance driver.

Ernest Bairstow wanted to form a federation of communal settlements, and enlisted J. Humphrey, T. Dent (author of *Voluntary Socialism*) and Sisley Tanner. His federation seemed possible by 1938, because a number of experimental communities now existed. So Sisley Tanner and Herbert Shipley, acting for the Community Service Committee, convened conferences at Bath in April 1937 and Kingsley Hall, Bow, in December 1937, to illustrate what experiments were afoot and how they were

[1] Victor Bonham-Carter, *Dartington Hall, The History of An Experiment* (1958).

run. The conveners outlined the convictions of those who attended that 'governments cannot do everything for us, but that a
new approach must be found by the people themselves and that
those who really mean their socialism can live it here and now'.[1]

J. Howard Whitehouse, the old Ruskinian, put it more vividly
when he said 'Really what we are all scheming for is Utopia.
We shall not build it suddenly. Perhaps gradually we can lay a
few foundation stones.' Whitehouse talked of redeeming English
agriculture and the English village.[2] But the really stirring note
was struck by Herbert Shipley.

> The time has come when we can no longer escape the issue. We
> have to be honest with ourselves until it hurts . . . the time for
> talk is pretty nearly over. We who stand for the Kingdom of God
> and His righteousness must begin as we may to live it. In so far as
> this idea of a New Beginning really takes hold on us—first as
> individuals, then as groups, as churches, as communities, as
> colonies—in so far as we are compelled to grow up into new ways
> of life by the spirit of love; to live consciously as members of one
> another; so far shall we be on the way to the realisation of a new
> social order—the only one that will have within itself the final
> answer to the problems of poverty and war.[3]

As an outcome of this conference, a provisional service committee was constituted to serve the community movement in
whatever way was practicable. Its members included several
who had experience of community problems and all shared a
sense of the immanence of community development. As they
affirmed in their first unofficial report 'all believe that a new
social order based on co-operation, not competition must result
from any real and widespread effort to interpret the spirit and
teaching of Christ in everyday living; all agreed that the time
for action is likely to be brief; that any step towards a more
conscious ordering and co-ordination of the communities' interests should be taken now'. This Community Service Committee
operated from 'Chancton', Dartnell Park, West Byfleet, Surrey,
with no funds and no 'organization' in any sense of the word.

[1] *Community in Britain* (1938), 125.
Another supporter of the Llano experiment was Aldous Huxley who, in *Adonis
and the Alphabet* (1956), has given a sympathetic picture of it.
[2] ibid., 128.
[3] ibid., 156.

By March 1939 the British Llano Circle felt themselves strong enough to issue a journal called *Community Life*. This gave details of small experiments like the Elmsett Community, established by Edmund Cocksedge at Nova Scotia Farm, Ipswich; Tylthrop House Agricultural Establishment at Kingsey in Oxfordshire (formed by Jewish Refugees in September 1939); and the Southend Community at 34 Retreat Road in Westcliffe-on-Sea and later at Oakwood, Brook Hill, Wickford.

Both Bairstow and St. John died in the first year of the war and *Community Life* did not long survive them. St. John's novel *Why Not Now?* (1939) envisaged Great Britain ruled by a prime minister who believed in the principles of 'Voluntary Socialism'.[1]

(10)

The community movement had obtained a fresh infusion of strength from the establishment of the Cotswold Bruderhof at Ashton Keynes, Wiltshire, on 19 March 1936. Eberhard Arnold, its founder, embodied forces that had been bringing communities into being for the previous century. A great grandson of Johannes Ramsauer (one of Pestalozzi's collaborators), a grandson of Franklin L. Arnold (an American missionary), and the son of a professor of Church History at Breslau, he had been educated at Halle and received his Ph.D., for a thesis on 'Primitive Christian and Anti-Christian Elements in the Development of Nietzsche's Thought'. He married the daughter of a professor of law and in 1914 became secretary of the Student Christian Movement in Germany.

Steeped in the writings of St. Francis, Peter Waldus, Eckhart, John of the Cross, Jacob Boehme, Fichte, Jean de Labadie, Count Zinzendorf, Pestalozzi and Tolstoy, Arnold was the veteran of a community originally founded at Sannerg in Hesse-Nassau, which had moved in 1926 to the Rhoen Bruderhof, where it had 158 members. Two years later Arnold united with the Hutterites. The Nazis forced a number of the

---

[1] A short biography of St. John is included as a preface to *Why Not Now?* (1939). Bairstow was a member of a community at Riverside, Melton Mowbray, in the First World War, which devoted itself to caring for mentally defective children. *Community Life* also gave an account of the Homer Lane experiment in June–July 1940. For the Elmsett Community see *Community in a Changing World* (West Byfleet, 1942), 84–89 and 171–3.

Rhoen Bruderhof community to emigrate to Liechtenstein in 1933, and finally on 14 April 1937 to abandon it altogether. Three of its members were imprisoned, and the rest were left with only a small bundle of clothing. They came to England and established the Cotswold Bruderhof. Here both the Liechtenstein and Rhoen Bruderhof exiles rallied and in two years 250 men, women and children were living in community, sustained by 70 shorthorn cattle, 120 Shropshire sheep, 1,000 poultry, 30 beehives and a 10-acre garden. Characteristically graceful buildings rose on the site and soon they were issuing a journal, *The Plough, Towards the Coming Order*, and a steady stream of pamphlets.[1]

Ashton Keynes was so successful that a second Bruderhof at Oaksey, five miles away, was founded in March 1938 and a third was projected near Birmingham. But the Second World War made this impossible. Most of the members were Germans and the Home Office could not guarantee their freedom. They sold their communities and used the money to emigrate to Paraguay. It looked as if they would leave England without trace, for 350 of them migrated at the height of the Battle of the Atlantic, in ten groups. The first of these, after living at Fernheim (the colony of the American Mennonites in Paraguay) for six weeks, migrated to eastern Paraguay, where they purchased the Primavera Estancia of 20,000 acres, situated thirty miles from the small river port of Rosario. Only three members were left behind to complete the sale of the Cotswold Bruderhof. These three by Christmas 1941 had gathered around them nineteen more and began to consider re-establishing a new Bruderhof in England. After consultation with Paraguay they decided to search for a farm, going out in twos and threes to scour the Midlands and Wales. Within three months they discovered a farm of 182 acres, at Lower Bromdon, near Ludlow. They also established contact with a small community at Bromsash, near Ross-on-Wye, three of whose members joined them.

They moved to Lower Bromdon in March 1942. Though a fine site, 1,000 ft. high on the ridge between the Clee Hills, with wide views over the Welsh hills to the west and the industrial

[1] See *Illustrated* for May 1939 together with *The Individual and World Needs* (1938), *God and Anti-God* (1939), *The Early Christians after the Death of the Apostles* (1939), and *The Hutterites* (1940).

Midlands to the east, the farm was mostly old neglected pasture land, officially graded as class 'C' and known locally as 'dog and stick' farm. Only six acres were arable, the rest was bracken or else soured by constant grazing and lack of cultivation. The twenty who moved in had no experience and equipment. The younger women had to gather firewood, garden and care for the the sheep and cows. With the help of friends and of the people with whom they did business in the neighbouring towns, they got by. At first the farmhouse was large enough to house most of the community. The single men slept in the granary on straw. The dining-table was a piece of boarding on an iron stand surrounded by boxes.

Two members of the Paraguayan community, Sydney and Marjorie Hindley, returned in the autumn to live in an attic. Their reports of the first months of settling at Primavera encouraged members to think of the re-establishment of an English branch once more and so the name 'Wheathill Bruderhof' was ceremonially adopted. To mark the occasion eleven new members were received at the end of December, so that by the end of 1942, the community numbered thirty-three, thirteen more than at the beginning. They also made contact with other communal groups. One was at Adam's Cot, which joined them.[1]

A range of loose boxes was converted to provide two cottages for others returning from Paraguay: the Masons and Paul families with six children. An army hut, formerly a dining-room, was converted into living accommodation and meetings had to be held in part of the barn. A wooden dining-room was built for the first marriage at the Wheathill Bruderhof in October 1943. By the end of 1943, it numbered eleven families with twenty-two children; sixty-nine in all. A small school was established. A householder or steward, house mother, storekeeper and work distributor showed that an organization was taking shape.

Their great shortage was water which had to be carried from a spring several hundred yards distant and when this ran dry,

[1] Adam's Cot attracted in 1942 George Ineson, previously a member of a small community influenced by D. H. Lawrence in Cornwall. He established, on leaving Adam's Cot in 1942, a community in the Forest of Dean, on Taena Farm. This lasted till 1951, when, having become a Roman Catholic, he established a Catholic community at Whitley Court, near Prinknash Abbey. For the story see George Ineson, *Community Journey* (1956).

from a neighbouring farm. The stock suffered, so in April 1944 they took over the adjoining farm (Upper Bromdon, of 165 acres) and work began on a 100-ft. deep bore hole. This brought ample water to both farms. The extra rooms in the new farm-house provided living accommodation and the additional fields greatly helped the farm work. Since the original buildings of Lower Bromdon lay down a long drive and those of the new Upper Bromdon lay on the roadside, the centre of the farm work was moved to Upper Bromdon. But accommodation and land made it necessary to buy in the autumn, a third farm. This was Cleeton Court, lying conveniently along the southern boundary of Upper and Lower Bromdon and stretching to the foot of Titterstone Clee Hill, on which it carried the rights of free hill grazing.

Taken in the spring of 1945, Cleeton Court's first occupants were two of the three couples who were married at a triple wedding in the spring. This wedding symbolized the diverse religious backgrounds of the new recruits: Roman Catholic and Jew, Agnostic and Baptist, Evangelical and Anglican. With such a large household to be maintained, intensive mechaniza-tion was necessary.[1] The community extended its scope still further and at the time of writing is considering the establish-ment of another branch near London.

By 1960 there were communities in Connecticut, New York, the Pennsylvania mountains, Germany and Paraguay all flourishing.[2]

(11)

Perhaps the best known of the community experiments made since 1945 are those associated with Group Captain Leonard Cheshire, V.C., a British observer when one of the atom bombs was dropped on Japan. Launched at a public meeting presided over by Lionel Curtis, the community took shape near Market Harborough at Gumley. This was a country house with forty-five bedrooms which was loaned rent-free to the community, which numbered, at its peak, some fifty members. But difficulties arose over the industrial activities of the group (at one time

[1] *Ten Years of Community Living: The Wheathill Bruderhof* (Bromdon, 1952).
[2] Jane Tyson Clement, 'Brotherhood is a way of Life', *Smith College Alumnae Quarterly*, LII (1961), 71–73.

they were making felt balls). But a second community, at Le Court, Liss, in Hampshire, struck out on different lines, developing into a centre for the incurably sick.

From this sprang numerous others. The R.A.F. Stations at Predannack, Bromley (in Kent), East Preston (in Sussex), Ampthill (in Bedfordshire), and Staunton Harold (in Leicestershire), were next in a chain of homes that, under a trust, was to spread over the world. By 1960 committees in various parts of the globe were active in raising funds to found similar homes.[1]

[1] Leonard Cheshire, V.C., *The Face of Victory* (1961).

10

$\diamond$

The New Towns

$\diamond$

(1)

'WELWYN is so scandalously unique', wrote Clough Williams-Ellis in 1928, 'that few even of those who have heard of it really grasp what it is, what it has done, and what it stands for.'[1] Those who grasped what it could stand for were the industrialists, who realized that amenities which their forebears like Robert Owen or Titus Salt had to provide, were here provided for them. For industrialists were now preferring a place where amenities were being either dealt with as part of a major problem affecting an area already industrialized, or were being voluntarily taken over by responsible bodies directly interested in the settlement of industry in a new area and undertaking the consequent responsibilities.[2] From the opening of the Shredded Wheat factory in 1926 Welwyn developed rapidly, becoming a trading estate as well as a garden city. The trading estate and the housing suburb were the two characteristic social growths of the mid-war years: and both owed much to the motor car. Welwyn built factories which firms might rent, and twenty-five acres were so developed. Firms became anxious to lease land for their own factories; about seventy were built, employing some

---

[1] Clough Williams-Ellis, *England and the Octopus* (London, 1928), 145.
[2] *Royal Commission on the Distribution of the Industrial Population* (*Barlow Report, 1940*), *Minutes of Evidence*, 648.

3,500 persons. By 1934 the Marley Report was recommending the building of satellite towns on the model of Welwyn.

Trading estates offered a visible palliative to unemployment. The Government recognizing this, appointed commissioners under the Minister of Labour and the Secretary of State for Scotland respectively, to foster them. Four special areas, Glamorgan, Tyneside, West Cumberland and the middle industrial belt of Scotland, were placed under a Commissioner, Sir Malcolm Stewart. He recommended that financial assistance be given, and the Special Areas Reconstruction Association Limited was, therefore, set up by the Treasury.[1] Three major trading estates took shape at Treforest (Glamorgan), Team Valley (Durham and Tyneside) and Hillington (Glasgow): established at costs of £1,400,000, £800,000 and £400,000 respectively.[2]

In addition, 3,000 families were to be settled on smallholdings and co-operative farms. The Land Settlement Association, the Welsh Land Settlement Society and certain county councils undertook the allocation, whilst the Commissioner for Special Areas provided the capital for buying the land, developing the estate, equipping the holdings and the central farm and helping to cover the working costs. A training period of eighteen months was organized by the Unemployment Assistance Board. When finished, the settlers were given a tenancy. The total cost of resettlement was to involve expenditure of over £3 million. By 30 September 1937, land had been acquired for 1,757 families, 797 men were working with their families and 252 had begun training.[3]

Other lessons of Welwyn were applied in Manchester. There E. D. Simon, chairman of the housing committee of the city council, gazed to the south where, in the wooded reaches of Cheshire, lay an estate uncontaminated by the smoke of Manchester and the fumes of Stockport. He called in Patrick Abercrombie, who urged the council to buy it, and they did. Two thousand acres of land were obtained and a special committee was set up to deal with it. For one reason and another, it took a

[1] Report of Sir George Gillett (Cmd. 5595); Report of Sir D. A. Hoy (Cmd. 5604), *Minutes of Evidence.*
[2] *Barlow Report, Minutes of Evidence,* 264.
[3] *Barlow Report,* 265.

considerable time (up to 1930) to acquire full rights over the 5,500 acres required for a suburb planned by Barry Parker of Letchworth and Hampstead. It was known as Wythenshawe, and so much did Simon think of it that he took, when ennobled by the king, the title of Lord Simon of Wythenshawe.

In two years from its beginning in 1932, 4,000 houses were built. The plan envisaged shops and factories, public buildings, and a generous reservation was made for parks, an agricultural belt, parkways and spinneys. By 1935 Wythenshawe already had a larger population than either Letchworth or Welwyn. E. D. (later Lord) Simon, looking back in 1933 on developments, remarked: 'If great cities are not only allowed, but encouraged to extend their borders and to purchase land, more Wythenshawes will grow up, and the twentieth century will be marked by the development of a series of satellite garden towns which will be one of its chief glories.'[1] It still, however, lacks the planned town centre.

(2)

The danger of these new estates and suburbs becoming soulless concentration camps, Siberian establishments without a community spirit, animated the formation of the New Estates Community Committee in 1928. This tapped and channelled the regenerative idealism already manifested in the settlement movement founded by Canon Barnett and strengthened by their federation in 1920 as the British Association of Residential Settlements. Two new post-war bodies founded in the previous year, the Evacuational Settlements Association and the National Council of Social Service, joined together with the British Association of Residential Settlements to found the New Estates Committee in 1928. Thanks to the Housing Act of 1936 it was able to obtain funds from the rates, and thanks to the Carnegie Trust it was able to provide ninety-two community centres and draw up plans for eighty-two more. After the Second World War, in 1945, the National Federation of Community Associations was established.[2]

[1] E. D. Simon and J. Inman, *The Rebuilding of Manchester* (1935), 53; Stanley Gale, *Modern Housing Estates* (1949), 190–270.
[2] L. E. White, *Community or Chaos* (1950); F. G. Stephenson, *Community Centres: a Survey. Twenty Years a-Growing, 1928–1952.*

(3)

The idea of a neighbourhood unit, stemming from M. P. Follett's *The New State* (1918) was powerfully if inauspiciously extended in 1926, in a small house in Queen's Road, Peckham, when each of 100 families agreed to pay 1s. a week as a fee for periodical health overhauls.[1] Their participation in a community increased till in May 1935 a Health Centre of concrete and glass was opened with a gymnasium, theatre and nursery. On the top floor were consulting rooms, changing rooms and biochemical laboratories. On the first floor there was a cafeteria.

The Peckham Health Centre was the first of its kind in the world. It cost £7,000 a year to run and when the Second World War broke out 875 families (3,000 members) were in continuous membership. During the war the building was used as a factory. When it ended the Halley Stewart Trust gave it a three-year grant to reopen. Five hundred and fifty families (2,000 individuals) presented themselves as members but the National Health Service rendered its main function obsolete.[2] But that did not prevent K. E. Barlow taking the lead in trying to rebuild a community of homes as well as a health centre at Coventry, near which he bought a farm for that purpose.[3] Similar projects were mooted at Dronfield, near Sheffield, but came to nothing.

(4)

Echoes of a strident voice, heard before and after the First World War, now reverberated in England. A call for *A Hundred New Towns for Britain* had been made in 1933 by ex-serviceman 347485, advocating the creation of seventy-six new towns in England, fifteen in Scotland and nine in Wales. Each town was to cover four square miles and house 50,000 people. The total cost, £100 million, was to be met by the Treasury and the

[1] Clarence Perry, *The Neighbourhood Unit: a Scheme of Life for the Family-Life Community* (1929).

[2] Innes H. Pearse, 'Pioneering in London'. (Paper to Community Service Society, N.Y., 1948.)

John Comerford, *Health the Unknown. The Story of the Peckham Experiment* (1947).

G. Scott Williamson and I. H. Pearse, *Biologists in Search of Material* (1938.)

I. H. Pearse and G. Scott Williamson, *The Case of Action. A Survey of Everyday Life under Modern Industrial Conditions* (London, 1931).

[3] *Freedom*, 28 June 1947.

scheme was to be effected in ten years. The pseudonym thinly disguised the author A. Trystan Edwards who had, since before the First World War, been building up an armoury of argument to prove that intelligently planned terrace housing offered a far sounder and more satisfying answer to the problems of urban overcrowding than the 'monotonous diffuseness' of the Garden City.[1]

Edwards' idea caught on. His pamphlet ran to three editions and an association was formed to push the scheme. Lord Semphill, Canon H. R. L. Shepherd, Sir Edwin Lutyens, Professor S. D. Adshead and Sir Robert Hadfield rallied to support him. A letter published in *The Times* and signed by twelve prominent public figures commended the scheme to a wider public. Within two years the association had some effect, as in 1935 the Marley Committee reported on Garden Cities and Satellite Towns. Moving their premises in 1936 to 23 Grosvenor Place, the Hundred New Towns Association now conducted a vigorous campaign against the tendency to 'build upwards' and 'centralize' housing. It promoted an exhibition on 22 October 1936 to draw attention to the 'forbidden' houses that were 'designed for gentlemen of the slums'. As the *Journal of the Royal Institute of British Architects* remarked: 'If we dare not do what the Hundred New Towns Association suggests, or if we have followed their arguments sympathetically and disagree with their conclusions, other proposals must be made which are at least capable of realization by an intelligently directed community as those put forward by the Hundred New Towns.'[2] Trystan Edwards himself, in letters to the *Journal*, drew attention to the density of new housing and its effect on inhabitants. Finally, when a Royal Commission was appointed in 1937 to consider the redistribution of the industrial population (the Barlow Commission) the case for the Hundred New Towns Association, was put by Trystan Edwards himself on 9 May 1938. It was, said the commission, the 'boldest plan submitted'.[3] To E. D. (later Lord) Simon, writing in the heat of war-time recon-

[1] *Town Planning Review*, IV (1913), 155, 316–17.
[2] *Journal of the Royal Institute of British Architects*, 7 December 1935, 6 June 1936, 7 November 1936, 9 January 1937. See also *Modern Terrace Houses. Researches on High Density Development* (London, 1946).
[3] *Barlow Report*, 593.

struction, Edwards' proposals were 'imaginative and stimulating'.[1]

In elaboration, they were also persuasive. His case for high-density terrace houses of forty per acre (instead of the garden city semi-detached cottages of twelve to the acre), involved putting yards on the flat roofs. He asked for wedges into, instead of green belts circling, the new towns. The only architectural answers to the problem of sociability were, to Edwards, continuous streets. Thirty-five of his new towns were to be by the sea, but all would act as scavengers for the existing rabbit-hutches strung along the arterial roads.

Circumstances sharpened the need for new towns, and put the flesh of practicability, indeed of necessity, about his skeletal suggestions. Large industrial centres were a liability by 1939 and the case for breaking them up was by no means as Utopian as it had seemed twenty years before.[2] The motor car had already destroyed the boundaries of the city, and now the aeroplane destroyed its appeal. Electricity made available by the Grid (itself a construction of the inter-war years) had emancipated industry, given the proper encouragement, from the coalfields. New towns were, in fact, practical problems. The Utopian was coming into his own.

(5)

Shadows of moral criticism as well as of military expediency now hung over the towns of Britain. 'The diffusion of an urban psychology', wrote J. V. L. Casserley, 'far beyond the borders of the towns is a matter of the utmost gravity. The urban mentality has triumphed in the national system as a whole.'[3] It was time for those shadows to lift, and one person at least was determined that they should not fall across the new towns he was dedicating himself to promote. This man was F. J. Osborn of Welwyn.

He orchestrated, and played with vigour, the score of the Barlow Report. From its cold analytical structure he compounded stirring appeals to the hearts and intellects of the

[1] E. D. Simon, *Rebuilding Britain: A Twenty Year Plan* (1945), 183.

[2] cf. W. Craven-Ellis who proposed, in *The Rebuilding of Britain* (1935), the demolition of over four and a half million houses, the creation of agricultural belts round all towns, and urged the Government 'to organize land settlement and communal cultivation on a large scale'.

[3] M. B. Reckitt and J. V. L. Casserley, *The Vocation of England* (1941), 40.

thinking public by convening the three most significant, if not the most important, conferences of the century on this subject. A hundred and eighty-one delegates attended the first, at Oxford in March 1941. They included Lord Samuel, whose Utopian novel *An Unknown Land* depicted a state where towns of 40,000 were the rule; Patrick Abercrombie, whose *Preservation of Rural England* (1926) had been followed up on the Council for the Preservation of Rural England; and members of the Barlow Commission.[1]

At the second at Cambridge, in the spring of 1942, Osborn was in his best form. Flaying the 'policy of town canning' (as he aptly described the compressed cities of the day), he urged the formation of associations, which, under a central authority, would establish 'daughter towns', separated by stretches of open country from existing cities. For full measure, he argued for the rights of county councils and private groups to sponsor such associations through a central planning authority. These new towns were to be of a planned maximum of 35,000 people, living on some 2,000 acres, with another 6,000 acres zoned for permanent agricultural use. Osborn envisaged the appropriation of from 250,000 to 300,000 acres in the ensuing twenty-five years, accommodating from 5–6 million people.[2]

At the third conference, held in London in 1943, ways and means of rebuilding were discussed, and Osborn spoke of the compulsive magnitude of the task of 'unscrambling the entire unsavoury omelet cooked in the past two generations by indecent standards of housing'. He sounded a tocsin for

'the building of fifty new towns, coupled with extensions of analogous magnitude to existing country towns'. This he argued 'would greatly ease the financial and planning problems of central rebuilding . . . it really does mean, over a large field, a New England after the war, ideal living and working conditions for millions of people in a few years, and a practical plan of amelioration of our existing cities'.[3]

[1] F. E. Towndrow, ed., *Replanning Britain, being a summarized report of the Oxford Conference of the Town and Country Planning Association, Spring 1941* (1941).

[2] H. Bryant Newbold, ed., *Industry and Rural Life, being a summarized report of the Cambridge Conference of the Town and Country Planning Association* (1942).

[3] Donald Tyerman, ed., *Ways and Means of Rebuilding* (1944), 54.

F. J. Osborn also seized the occasion to issue the first two editions of a *Planning and Reconstruction Year Book* (1942), which showed that the Town and Country Planning Association was on its toes. It had need to be, as in 1943 a Ministry of Town and Country Planning was created. That it was created at all, we should thank the Barlow Commission's recommendation that it should be; a recommendation supported by two other official reports issued during the war: one on Land Utilization in Rural Areas (the *Scott Report* of 1942)[1] and the other on compensation (the *Uthwatt Report* of 1942).[2]

(6)

As the German bombers pounded the older towns to ruins, planning new towns was particularly urgent. Patrick Abercrombie's *Greater London Plan* (of 1944) proposed the establishment of from seven to ten new satellite towns. In the same year provision was made for compulsory acquisition of land involved in such reconstruction.

Professor S. D. Adshead, in *A New England* (1941) had suggested that alternate terraces in old towns should be pulled down and their sites converted to gardens. He appealed for the establishment of fifty new towns, much larger than Osborn's, of from 40,000 to 200,000 people: some satellites to London, others arranged in constellations on their own.[3] Sir Ernest Simon in *Rebuilding Britain: A Twenty Year Plan* (1945) was so anxious to live up to his desire 'not to paint a Utopia', that he advocated only half a dozen new towns. But he urged that they should be founded 'immediately after the war, either as satellite garden towns or as separate garden cities'. He also supported the idea of neighbourhood units of 10,000 persons.[4]

C. B. Purdom in *How Should we Rebuild London* (1945) went even further. He proposed that 'at least fifty (new) towns in the Home Counties would be necessary in post-war Britain'.

(7)

'Green fields can forge as strong a social bond as any com-

---

[1] *Report of the Committee on Land Utilisation in Rural Areas.*
[2] *Uthwatt Report* (*Scott Report*, Cmd. 6378, 1942) (Cmd. 6386, 1942).
[3] S. D. Adshead, *A New England* (1941). On page 174 he gives a map showing the distribution of his proposed new towns.
[4] E. D. Simon, *Rebuilding Britain: A Twenty Year Plan* (1945), 187 and 225.

munity centre of brick and stone.' So the Reith Committee reported in 1946 to the Minister of Town and Country Planning on the guiding principles on which new towns should be established and developed 'as self-contained and balanced communities for work and living'. These guiding principles were duly framed. 'Our responsibility', it went on, ' . . . is to conduct an essay in civilisation, by seizing an opportunity to design, solve and carry into execution for the benefit of coming generations the means for a happy and gracious way of life.'[1]

'The three dimensional vision of a New Jerusalem', which Lloyd Rodwin[2] saw inspiring some members of the Labour Government, led to the passage of the New Towns Act in August 1946 and the establishment of public corporations to bring them into existence. The Town and Country Planning Act in 1947, called for the preparation, by 145 counties and county borough authorities, of comprehensive development plans by 1951, with provision for revision at intervals. New factories of over 5,000 sq. ft. had to be licensed by the Board of Trade to secure conformity with planning policy. Compensation was to be secured from a fund of £300 million.

In four years the Minister, Mr. Lewis Silkin, was responsible for starting fourteen new towns, at a total cost of over £100 million. In the subsequent five years only one more was started —near Glasgow—and no more will be erected without parliamentary approval. Eight of these new towns are near London: Stevenage (2 November 1946); Crawley (9 January 1947); Hemel Hempstead (4 February 1947); Harlow (25 March 1947); Welwyn Garden City (20 May 1948); Hatfield (20 May 1948); Basildon (4 January 1949) and Bracknell (17 June 1949). Two are near Glasgow: East Kilbride (6 May 1947) and Cumbernauld (9 December 1955). Two are attempts to weld mining villages into towns: Peterlee (10 March 1948) and Glenrothes (30 June 1948). One is a trading estate: Newton Aycliffe (19 April 1947). Two are steel towns: Corby (1 April 1950) and Cwmbran (2 November 1949). The average area covered by these new towns is 4,633 acres and ranges from 880 acres (Newton Aycliffe) to 10,250 acres (East Kilbride).

[1] (Cmd. 6759), p. 4.
[2] Lloyd Rodwin, *The British New Towns Policy* (Cambridge, Mass., 1956), 21.

The total acreage of all these new towns equals that of the cities of Manchester and Sheffield, and the ultimate population —some 668,000 people—is equal to half the population of Manchester and Sheffield. Of this population 337,961 was settled by 31 March 1957.[1]

Paradoxically, decentralization was difficult to foster. In three cases (Stevenage, Hemel Hempstead and Crawley) law suits were initiated against the Minister of Town and Country Planning, and in four others (Harlow, Crawley, Bracknell and Corby) local objections secured drastic modifications of the original plan. In one case, Stevenage was actually christened Silkingrad by some who felt strongly about the overriding of local views.

The principles evolved in these new towns have proved so successful that one of their designers, Gibberd of Harlow, has been employed to design a private enterprise new town at All Hallows near the Isle of Grain.[2] Now, as these 'prairie towns' are taking shape under the great earth scrapers, one inevitably wonders into what pattern the $3\frac{1}{2}$ million houses that will be built in the next forty years will fall.

As this survey draws to a completion in a living-room at East Kilbride in the County of Lanark, the author has been talking to a professional sociologist employed by the Corporation and reflecting on the protean changes of the community principle that have been nourished in this county since Robert Owen set to work. That sociologist was later, incidentally, to be the only Labour candidate to gain a seat in Scotland in the 1959 general election. The story of social experiment is episodic, fitful and intermittent. Yet the pieces all hang together and the products need no longer to be relegated to the interstices and margins of history. The American publishers of Harold Orlans' study of Stevenage recognized this when they entitled it *Utopia Ltd.*

These new towns are the social laboratories of today. In them patterns of post-second millennial living may well take shape. Already Stevenage (in true Geddesian fashion) has put up suggestions for its own university, and others are deploying the architectural virtues of their schools as multi-purpose social institutions.

---

[1] V. G. J. Sheddick, 'New Towns as Socio-Scientific Experiments', *Planning Outlook*, IV (1958), 5–21.

[2] W. E. Adams, 'A private enterprise new town', *Town Planning Review*, XXVIII (1957), 181.

11

◇◆

Epilogue

◇◆

(1)

ENGLISH History has become so Mandevilled (or Namierized) by questions as to whose hand is in the till, or whose interest is to be served, that the story of those who tried to save society behind its collective back has been ignored. The very term 'Utopian' is now associated with eccentricity and futility. Marx and Engels began the process (as they began so much else) by describing the 'promoters of duodecimo editions of the new Jerusalem,'[1] as 'fanatical', 'superstitious' and 'pedantic'. Sidney Webb accused them of having too little faith in human nature, and of 'throwing up the sponge in despair'.[2] To Bernard Shaw they were just funny :–

> When they were managed by men who had made fortunes, like Robert Owen, in private commerce, they made a hopeless mess of communism. And when the managers were all amateurs they split at once into the few born bosses who could manage, and the ideal-

---

[1] 'The Communist Manifesto', in Karl Marx' and Frederick Engels' *Selected Works* (Moscow, 1951), i 59–60. *Socialism: Utopian and Scientific*, op. cit., ii. 117–18. Written in 1877 it was published in England in 1892.

[2] *Socialism True and False*, 20. See also *Fabian Essays in Socialism* (1889), 30. 'Parodies of the domestic debates of an imaginary Phalanstery, and homilies on the failure of Brook Farm and Icaria, may be passed over as belated and irrelevant now that Socialists are only advocating the conscious adoption of a principle of social organization which the world has already found to be the inevitable outcome of Democracy and the Industrial Revolution.'

430

ists who thought they were going to have a happy paradise, and take it very easy. The capable ones soon found out that they could make their fortunes in the private labour market and could do nothing with the idle idealists; so they cleared out and went into business on their own account, whereupon, the linch pin being taken out of the cart, it upset; and the experiment came to an end.[1]

Philip Snowden saw them as 'the very negation of socialism'.[2] Historians have noticed them with reserve. Dr. Arthur Shadwell, though he confessed that 'their history is highly illuminating and deserving of more study than it has received', was yet constrained to agree with the socialists of his day who regarded them as irrelevant.[3] The utmost that Arnold Toynbee would allow them was that 'they aspire to arrest a downward movement'. Toynbee saw them operating only in the context of broken-down, disintegrating societies. But then, broken-down, disintegrating societies were Toynbee's business, and his civilizations were breaking down from the beginning.[4]

P. C. Gordon Walker, a Labour Party leader of the 1950s is particularly hard on those who attempt to translate the millennium into reality. 'It leads', he wrote, 'to inhumanity: for imperfect men have to be governed as if they were perfect.'[5] Even more recently Christopher Hill has described the idea of an egalitarian rural community as 'an unconscionable time dying', and explained this by 'the traditions of Anglo-Saxon freedom, of lost rights and lost property which it was still hoped to recapture and to those dying institutions which it was still hoped to revivify'.[6]

Sociologists (who tend to be Utopists of the chair rather than the field) have found them equally irrelevant even though the very existence of sociology owes so much to them. Thus F. Stuart Chapin described the community founders as 'trying to

---

[1] S. Winsten, *Henry Salt and His Circle* (1951), 124.

[2] P. Snowden, *Socialism and Syndicalism* (1913), 60

[3] Arthur Shadwell, *The Socialist Movement 1824–1924* (1925), 11.

[4] A. J. Toynbee, *A Study of History*, iii (1939), 88–111, vii (1954), 360. For Toynbee's own eschatology see H. R. Trevor-Roper, 'Arnold Toynbee's Millennium', *Encounter*, viii. (June 1957), 14–28.

[5] P. Gordon Walker, *Restatement of Liberty* (1951), 22. He adds 'The consequences in practice of setting up heaven on earth are therefore extremism, contempt for peace, preference for violence, contempt for humans as they are and have been, coercion, and confusion between ends and means.'

[6] Christopher Hill, *Puritanism and Revolution* (1958), 108.

conduct a chemical experiment in a bowl of molasses',[1] and he could see little relevance in their resurrection. Ten years later, in 1957 William H. Whyte in his *exposé* of the 'organization man' of the mid-twentieth century sought, by alluding to the affinities of the organization man's philosophy with that of 'the Utopian communities of the 1840s', to strengthen his case still further. This philosophy he defined as a belief in the group as a source of creativity, belongingness as the ultimate end of the individual, and the application of science to achieve belongingness.[2]

By Whyte's time philosophers and theologians had also taken up arms against the community founders. 'Utopias in the real', wrote Bertrand de Jouvenal, 'are beyond question abominable.' As 'perfect societies whose mission it is to remould the larger society in their own image' he castigated them for 'reducing to moral slavery those whose views differ from their own'.[3] To Richard Ullmann, a Quaker, they have 'ignored the continued imperfections in all temporal perfection, and denigrated time and history by envisaging that the Kingdom had been already realised'.[4] A distinguished English novelist also derived, and gave others, much amusement by her story of a modern community peopled by 'a kind of sick people whose desire for God makes them unsatisfactory citizens of an ordinary life, but whose strength or temperament fails them to surrender to the world completely'.[5]

(2)

Yet something can be said in favour of these duodecimo editions of New Jerusalem. In a detonatingly cogent brief against the large-scale Utopian experiment, K. R. Popper endorses the piecemeal approach. 'Here', he writes, 'we may learn—or rather, we ought to learn—and change our views while we act.' He approves of them if 'bridled by reason, by a

[1] F. Stuart Chapin, *Experimental Designs in Sociological Research* (1947), 14.
[2] William H. Whyte, *The Organization Man* (London, 1957), 7.
[3] Bertrand de Jouvenal, *Sovereignty: An Inquiry into the Political Good* (Cambridge, 1957), 270 ff.
[4] R. K. Ullmann, *Between God and History* (London, 1959), 30 ff.
[5] Iris Murdoch, *The Bell* (1958), 82. The abbess of a neighbouring religious house puts it even more clearly. 'There are many people who can live neither in the world or out of it. Disturbed and haunted by God they find a work made simple and significant by its dedicated setting.'

feeling of responsibility, and by a humanitarian urge to help.' 'Otherwise', he rightly says, 'it is a dangerous enthusiasm, liable to develop into a form of neurosis or hysteria.'[1] Then again, these experiments can be seen as protests against permanent bureaucratic and hierarchical structures, against routine, inertia, and atrophy. Their leaders from Winstanley down to Murry have had charismatic qualities. Manic and millenarian, knowing only inner determination and inner restraint, they conformed to Weber's definition of 'charismatic domination' as 'the very opposite of bureaucratic domination'.[2]

In making claims on the future, the charismatics of the foregoing pages endowed English Socialism with a heart, which the contemporary intellectual surgery of the Fabians has almost fatally dissected. For the intellectual detachment of Fabian élites are poor substitutes for that sense of the beyond which was at one time the motive power of socialism.[3] To be scientific, socialism must change its name and nature for it is a creed with an overdraft on the future. 'It is something that *ought* to be', wrote Bernstein, 'or a movement toward something that ought to be.'[4] These intellectual surgeons love the Frankenstein-like impersonal, management-controlled public corporations, which have intoxicated Ernest Bevin, Attlee and Gaitskell in turn. This fateful surrender to the 'public corporation' idea took place in 1919, and from then on the British Labour Party was, as The Times remarked, 'so intent on extending the authority of the State that it has overlooked the purpose of its existence'.[5] So if the pioneer community founders can be accused of being victims of apocalyptic delusions, then Bevin, Attlee and Gaitskell, by encouraging the working class to believe that the social changes planned and proceeding under the banner of

[1] K. R. Popper, *The Open Society and its Enemies* (3rd edition, London, 1957), i. 164–5.

[2] H. H. Gerth and C. Wright Mills, *From Max Weber: Essays in Sociology* (1948), 247.

[3] 'Posthumously, the Webbs have won their battle . . . now the time has come for a reaction. Total abstinence and a good filing system are not the right signposts to the Socialist Utopia; or at least, if they are, some of us will fall by the wayside.' C. A. R. Crosland, *The Future of Socialism* (1957), 534.

[4] Peter Gay, *The Dilemma of Democratic Socialism, Eduard Bernstein's Challenge to Marx* (New York, 1952), 19. See also Stuart Hampshire in *Encounter*, V (1955), 36–41.

[5] *The Times*, 15 May 1951.

nationalization would eventually bring power to them, were likewise self-deceived.

The histology, as well as the history, of socialism in Britain has to a great extent depended on the community pioneers. Dan Irving, the Burnley stalwart of the Social Democratic Federation, was an old member of the Starnthwaite community, which he joined after losing a leg on the railway. Frank Smith, founder of the Labour Army, was a former veteran of the Salvation Army. Tom Mann and Harry Snell were active in Kapper's Newcastle colony. J. Bruce Wallace and Fred Muggeridge were props at Purleigh. James Ramsay MacDonald was the secretary of the Fellowship of the New Life.

Ramsay MacDonald in fact maintained that British Socialism derived its momentum from what he called 'man's creative, utopia-building, aspiring faculty'. 'It compels man', he wrote in 1913, 'to decline to live in a purely economic order. It will not tolerate a society in which it has a subordinate place.'[1] 'The associative impulse', as G. D. H. Cole called it, was 'not to be imagining a Utopia in the clouds', but 'giving form and direction to certain quite definite tendencies which are at work in society'. 'In a community', he wrote in 1920, 'permeated by the associative impulse . . . even artists, the least organisable of men, would respond to the associative impulses around them, and readily form co-operative groups, less stable no doubt, but still more vital by reason of their instability.'[2]

The community ideal has also attracted converts to the Labour Party like Lord Buxton, who gave as his reason for leaving the Liberals :–

> All human goodness must be social goodness. Man is fundamentally gregarious and his morality consists in being a good member of his community . . . The highest type of goodness is that which puts freely at the service of the community all that a man is and can be . . . the Kingdom of God is still a collective conception, involving the whole social life of man. It is not a matter of saving human atoms but of saving the social organism. It is not a matter of getting individuals to heaven, but of transforming the life on earth into the harmony of heaven.[3]

[1] J. R. MacDonald, *The Social Unrest* (1913), 13.
[2] G. D. H. Cole, *Guild Socialism Restated* (1919), 11 and 115.
[3] Mosa Anderson, *Noel Buxton* (1952), 115. See also E. J. Hobsbawm, *Primitive Rebels* (Manchester, 1959), 128.

It animated A. J. Penty to write in 1930 :–

A belief in the possibility of social catastrophe is as essential to the integrity of sociology as a belief in the reality of Hell in some form or other is necessary to the integrity of theology. Deny the possibility of catastrophe as social evolutionists do or did, and morality and integrity are completely undermined, while history itself becomes meaningless, for with catastrophe history abounds.[1]

It led Miles Walker to suggest, at a meeting of the British Association for the Advancement of Science in 1932, that the British Government should found a self-supporting colony of 100,000 persons to be run as an experiment by engineers, scientists and economists, to discover how it was possible for such a community to be self-supporting.

Even those who were not socialists have been affected by it. Lord Beveridge began his public life as sub-warden in Toynbee Hall as a 'protest against the sin of taking things for granted', where he associated with his future brother-in-law, R. H. Tawney. He helped the Salvation Army Colonies at Hadleigh and Osea Island. He worked for the Charity Organization Society to further the work of Octavia Hill. He was an editor of *St. George* (founded at Bourneville by the Ruskinian J. H. Whitehouse, and to which J. C. Kenworthy contributed). He was in touch with the garden city movement. Out of all these formative influences emerged the report bearing his name. For, as he himself told a group of students in the Hall of University College on 11 November 1939: 'The choice is no longer between Utopia and the pleasant ordered world that our fathers knew. The choice is between Utopia and Hell.'[2]

When socialism moved away from Utopian idealism, it lost radicalism and hopefulness and had nothing to say. Fabianism and historical materialism destroyed its red cells, for Fabianism and historical materialism are far closer to the conservative doctrine of organic necessity in society. As one recent writer lamented: 'We know too much to fall into even the slightest utopianism and without that grain of baseless optimism no genuine political theory can be constructed.'[3] Or, as another

---

[1] A. J. Penty, *Industry in a Revived Christendom* (1930), quoted, significantly enough, by M. B. Reckitt, in *A Christian Sociology for Today* (1934), 266.

[2] Lord Beveridge, *Power and Influence* (London, 1953), 355.

[3] Judith N. Shklar, *After Utopia* (1957), 271.

put it: 'Current psychoanalysis has no Utopia; current neo-orthodox Protestantism has no eschatology. This defect cripples them both as allies of the life instinct in that war against the death instinct which is human history.'[1]

The anti-bureaucratic, anarchic element in the tradition has kept alive the spirit of democratic socialism. Herbert Read, for instance, in 1940 was pleading for the 'anarchist principle . . . at every stage and in every act'. He went on,

> We shall avoid creating an independent bureaucracy, for that is another form of tyranny, and the individual has no chance of living according to natural laws under such a tyranny. We shall avoid the creation of industrial towns which separate men from the fields and the calm environment of nature. We shall control the machine, so that it serves our natural needs without endangering our natural powers. Thus in a thousand ways the principle of anarchism will determine our practical policy, leading the human race gradually away from the state and its instruments of oppression towards an epoch of wisdom and joy.[2]

Thirteen years later K. E. Boulding was even more explicit, confessing: 'I regard the lessening of coercion as one of the most fundamental long-run objectives of human organisation and one of the most profound moral tests by which any social movement is to be judged.'[3]

(3)

Motorized metropoli with their asphalt deserts still continue to throw up new messiahs of community. Perhaps the latest is Aldous Huxley, a disciple of Jacob Boehme, who in 1959 advocated the revival of 'the small country community', and the desertion of the metropolis, where 'overpopulation and over organisation' have made 'a fully human life of multiple relationships . . . almost impossible'. Huxley's alternative remedy was to 'humanise the metropolis by creating within its network of mechanical organisations the urban equivalents of small country communities.'[4]

[1] N. O. Brown, *Life Against Death: The Psycho-analytical Meaning of History* (1959), 233.
[2] Herbert Read, *Annals of Innocence and Experience* (1940), 136–8.
[3] K. E. Boulding, *The Organizational Revolution* (1953), 251.
[4] Aldous Huxley, *Brave New World Revisited* (1959), 159.

The regenerative value of these communities, so stressed by their vegetarian, back-to-the-land promoters, is receiving supplementary endorsement from those who are preoccupied with the ever increasing problem of mental health. The highly therapeutic atmosphere which prevails in such communities today, and their high level of psychological adjustment has won the approval of psychologists and psychiatrists.[1] Indeed, two of them are anxious to rehabilitate the communitarian tradition. One, B. F. Skinner, has given us in *Walden Two* (1948) a prescription for a self-sustaining autonomous community. Another, Erich Fromm, has endorsed communities as 'executed by men with a shrewd intelligence and an immensely practical sense'. Fromm holds that they are

> by no means the dreamers our so-called realists believe them to be; on the contrary they are mostly more realistic and imaginative than our conventional business leaders appear to be. Undoubtedly there have been many shortcomings in the principles and practice of these experiments, which must be recognised in order to be avoided . . . But the glib condescension implying futility and lack of realism of all these experiments is not any more reasonable than was the first popular reaction to the possibilities of railroad and later of aeroplane travel. It is essentially a symptom of the laziness of the mind and the inherent conviction that what has not been, cannot be and will not be.[2]

The relevance of their beliefs is today obtaining strange confirmation from medicine. Long before the statistical scares about carcinoma, thrombosis and ulcers, these enthusiasts stressed control of that most primeval of human frailties— over-eating. Their wholesome (or wholemeal) influence, from the vegetable diet of John Robens and Dr. Cheyne, through Charles Lane, the Ham Concordists and the Tolstoyans, sprang from the need to heighten awareness by abstaining from animal food. Tom Mann and Stafford Cripps were in the tradition in a

---

[1] J. W. Eaton and R. J. Weil, 'The Mental Health of the Hutterites', in A. M. Rose, *Mental Health and Mental Disorder* (1956), 223–39; Joshua Bierer, 'The Therapeutic Community Hostel', *The International Journal of Social Psychiatry*, VII (1960–1), 5–10.

[2] Erich Fromm, *The Sane Society* (1956), 320–1.

See also A. E. Morgan, *The Small Community, Foundation of Democratic Life* (1942), and G. Duncan Mitchell, *The Relevance of Group Dynamics to Rural Planning Problems* (Le Play House, Ledbury, Herts, 1951).

wider sense than they could foresee. Even Bernard Shaw, much as he disliked Utopians, ate the farinaceous foods they so zealously advocated.

Faith in the redemptive potential of the country community strikes another note in a long historical theme. The Rochdale pioneers resolved in 1844 'to establish a self-supporting home colony of united interests and to assist other societies in establishing such colonies'. Though they soon abandoned this resolution, an American visitor to England some fifty years later observed that 'no subject was so certain to command the interested attention of British co-operators as that of village communities'. He predicted that experiments in that direction 'would multiply in the near future'.[1]

Demarest's prediction has been fulfilled not so much in home colonies as in variants of the idea: the Peckham experiment, the county colleges pioneered by Henry Morris in Cambridgeshire in the 1920s, the community centres and myriad small groups meeting together for particular purposes.[2]

The real by-products of nearly all the English communities have been new departments of and new departures in education. The Quakers and Moravians have left an indelible legacy of experiment and tolerance. Lee was an instigator of charity schools; Owen a pioneer of infant schools; Greaves and Minter Morgan explorers of the school as a centre of socialization; whilst Davidson's outline of what the study of education should be in the universities is still far from realized. The Drummond chair of Political Economy was founded by a charismatic of that name. The Cowper-Temple clause in the 1870 Education Act was the work of another. Indeed the school base, the comprehensive school and the county college have roots far more English than the refracted ideas of John Dewey. These roots can be traced back to J. Howard Whitehouse, to Ruskin, and earlier. Utopian interests in education were satirized by Bernard Mandeville in an appendix to *The Fable of the Bees*, and Mandeville was the one thinker whom William Law, Minter Morgan and F. D. Maurice wished to refute.

[1] H. D. Lloyd, *Co-partnership* (1893), 97.
[2] For example Farmerservice, begun in 1943, is a printing co-partnership, described in *Christian Principles in Industry. A Review of an Experiment and a vision for its future* (1949), and The Scott Bader Commonwealth, established in 1951, described in *Scope*, August 1956.

As enzymes which kept dissent alive, these communities have persisted and reformed in spite of every discouragement, because their promoters had what David Riesman calls 'the nerve of failure'; the ability to face the possibility of defeat without being morally crushed.[1] This 'nerve of failure' is sustained by a fervour we can savour in *The Pilgrim's Progress*, *The Vicar of Wakefield*, *The Isle of Innisfree* or the luminous prose of Blake, Coleridge, Ruskin and Lawrence. All exhale the breath of hope.

(4)

Sociology has not developed in Britain as it has in Germany and America. This has been partly due to the persistence of piecemeal Utopianism (better named empiric experimentation). For in Germany, where the subject became academic, one of its more profound exponents, Karl Mannheim lamented, that 'just at the highest stage of awareness, when history is ceasing to be blind fate, and is becoming more and more man's own creation, with the relinquishment of utopias, man would lose his will to shape history and therewith his ability to understand it'.[2] With this, one of the most distinguished American sociologists, David Riesman, agreed when he wrote that 'A revival of the tradition of Utopian thinking seems to me one of the important intellectual tasks of today.'[3] Another American sociologist also exhibits in his recent writing an overtly millenarian nostalgia. C. Wright Mills in *The Sociological Imagination* sees dawning a 'fourth epoch' with limitless opportunities for making history, a new world for the sociologist to enter, swept bare of its old 'major orientations, liberalism or socialism' which have 'virtually collapsed as adequate explanations of the world and ourselves'. This Utopian spirit is so tantalizing to capture that Pitirim Sorokin has established at Harvard a Research Centre in Social Altruism. In the same country the need to speculate on future action, rather than acting on speculation about the future,

[1] David Riesman, *Yale Law Journal*, LVII (1947), 136–8.

[2] Karl Mannheim, *Ideology and Utopia* (London, 1936), 236. Though written in 1929 in Germany, it had a vogue in England in the ferment of the Second World War.

[3] Riesman, loc. cit., see also Dennis Gabor, 'Inventing the Future', *Encounter* XIV (1960), 15. 'It is a sad thought indeed that our civilization has not produced a *new vision* which could guide us on to the new "Golden Age" which has now become physically possible.'

has led Margaret Mead to suggest that universities should establish Chairs of the Future.[1] Such professors might then consider what man might be, as well as what he has been or is. If her suggestion were to find favour, the occupant of a Chair of the Future might well, in an off-moment, reflect on how blinding is the vision, how compulsive the effect, and how infinitely indestructible is a Utopia. He or she might even rewrite this book, or persuade a professor of theology to do it.

Community experiments, according to A. E. Morgan, are 'among the most important and universal ways in which societies the world over have maintained their vitality and advanced in type'.[2] And with this the English philosopher H. J. Blackham agrees. He sees them as making 'gallant and striking special contributions' to a free society where they can combine vitality and humanity, with freedom and amenity.[3] For transcending the value of the small community is the experimentation it exemplifies.

It is to be hoped that the tradition will continue, for as Aldous Huxley sagely observed in 1956:

> For anyone who is interested in human beings and their so largely unrealised potentialities, even the silliest experiment has value if only as demonstrating what ought not to be done.[4]

[1] *Science*, CXXVI (1957), 957–961.
[2] *The Future of Community and the Community of the Future* (Yellow Springs, Ohio, 1957), 140
[3] H. J. Blackham, *Political Discipline in a Free Society* (1961), 175.
[4] A. Huxley, *Adonis and the Alphabet* (1956), 100.

Index